State of the Peoples

A Global Human Rights Report on Societies in Danger

This book is dedicated to the thousands of
cultures that have disappeared over the past
five centuries, victims of blindness and greed.

Marc S. Miller, Project Director

With the staff of Cultural Survival

State of the Peoples

A Global Human Rights Report on Societies in Danger

Beacon Press   Boston

Beacon Press
25 Beacon Street
Boston, Massachusetts 02108-2892

Beacon Press books
are published under the auspices of
the Unitarian Universalist Association of
Congregations.

Grateful acknowledgment is made for
permission to use the following material:
"Ethiopia's Uncertain Future," reprinted from
Crawford Young, ed., *The Rising Tide of Cultural
Pluralism*, © University of Wisconsin Press;
"War of the Rices," © Winona LaDuke

99 98 97 96 95 94 93   8 7 6 5 4 3 2 1

Text design by Karen Wong

Library of Congress Cataloging-in-Publication Data
State of the peoples: a global human rights report on societies
   in danger/Cultural Survival; edited by Marc S. Miller.
       p.   cm.
   Includes bibliographical references and index.
   ISBN 0-8070-0220-8 (cloth). —ISBN 0-8070-0221-6 (paper)
   1. Indigenous peoples—Legal status, laws, etc.
   I. Miller, Marc S.   II. Cultural Survival, Inc.
K3242.S73   1993
342'.0873—dc20
[342.2873]   93-24013
                           CIP

TABLE OF CONTENTS

PREFACE

BY ROBERT F. KENNEDY, JR.

As an environmental lawyer engaged in protecting threatened ecosystems throughout North and South America, I have witnessed the destruction of rivers, lakes, seas, and forests, along with the ancient societies that occupy these precious environments.

Last spring I hosted a meeting on the subject at my home in Mount Kisco, New York. At the table sat the Pewenche *cacique* (headman) José Antolín, leader in the fight against the Bío Bío River dams in southern Chile. The proposed dams will drown ancestral Pewenche lands. Across the table sat Grand Chief Matthew Coon Come, who for 10 years has led Northern Quebec's Cree in their battle to block a giant dam project that will inundate an area the size of Lake Erie and alter the ecology of the Cree's homeland, eastern North America's largest wilderness. Together with environmental and human-rights activists from both continents, we spent the afternoon discussing strategies for protecting tribal lands and the cultural and ecological values they support.

The Pewenche and Cree experiences fit a pattern that I see repeated around the globe. Energy companies, logging and mining interests, and publicly owned utilities, driven by booming populations and accelerating demands for energy and virgin materials, are invading the planet's most remote areas. They build dams that inundate these lands with water or roads that flood them with colonists. Sometimes they leave behind toxic materials that poison both land and water.

In almost every case, human-rights violations precede these invasions. People already live on these lands—usually aboriginal people who have retreated to wildernesses that were once too remote or inhospitable to support Western commerce or agriculture. As development forces these people to relinquish their culture and economies and their claims to their homelands, efforts to avert environmental destruction merge with the struggle for human rights.

For indigenous cultures, this is most often a struggle for the recognition of group rights—the rights of a particular people to maintain its culture, religion, traditional lands, and collective control of natural resources. Because the assertion of group rights is the most potent barrier to wilderness invasions, group rights are usually the developers' first target. Corporations shun negotiations with organized tribal confederations and instead justify invasions of tribal lands by finding and compensating individuals with a colorable claim to the desired parcels. Often, those individuals have never lived by any notion of property ownership and may be ill prepared to assess the market value of land or the long-term burden its sale would impose upon children, family, or tribe. I have seen U.S. oil companies obtain million-dollar properties in Ecuador in exchange for an outboard motor and the price of a few coffee beans.

Governments—whether under economic pressure to mine natural resources or acting in the name of "slum clearance," economic growth, or national security—often encourage such charades to disenfranchise Indians. Thus Ecuador has made it illegal to pay petroleum royalties to tribal confederations. Instead it encourages oil companies to "divide and conquer" by making small settlements with individual "landowners." Elsewhere, homesteading policies and tax subsidies encourage outsiders to take over Indian lands. Some governments promise Indians per capita distribution of royalties, thereby bypassing group decision

vii

making. Others blatantly ignore indigenous land claims. Ecuador, like most Latin American countries, officially classifies large tracts of Indian lands as "unoccupied," leaving them open to homesteaders and speculators. Indians who have occupied these lands for hundreds of years lack the resources to hire attorneys and assemble proofs to obtain land titles.

Other policies encourage aboriginals to privatize and sell communal homelands piecemeal. According to Chief Antolín, the principal threat to Pewenche culture is a Chilean initiative to undermine communal control of Pewenche homelands and instead distribute land titles among individual Pewenche. This would make it easier for developers to obtain the land through distress sales or by eminent domain. The U.S. government initiated a similar strategy under the notorious 1899 Dawes Act, which allowed speculators to obtain control of millions of acres of Indian land—and the underlying mineral resources.

The Currency of Power

Three observations about aboriginal rights are particularly relevant to environmentalists. First, traditional cultures are as valuable to humanity as the environments they steward. Second, efforts to plan the uses of wilderness lands outside the context of a partnership with their indigenous occupants offend the notion of justice. Third, speaking pragmatically, the world's remaining large tracts of wilderness cannot be saved without the cooperation and help of their indigenous stewards. In other words, to save the globe's remaining wilderness, we must proceed under the banner of human rights, particularly group rights.

These observations suggest that environmentalists must embrace the objective of ensuring the right of indigenous peoples to control their lands, including the right to exclude activities that could destroy their cultures and livelihoods. To obtain and safeguard these rights means committing ourselves to the empowerment of aboriginal groups. And if such a commitment is to go beyond lip service, we must, among other things, help those groups to rebuild or obtain sustainable economic systems for both domestic production and for open market trade if desired.

For aboriginal peoples, the most obvious and reliable way to obtain money is through economic control and sustainable exploitation of the resources on their own lands. Environmentalists should therefore assist wilderness peoples in their battles to obtain full title to their lands, as well as to the resources above and below those lands.

Environmentalists may find three aspects of this troubling. Yet the recognition of group rights mitigates each of these real concerns.

First, Western culture and money are often toxic to indigenous culture. There are frequent examples, from the Alaskan oil royalty disbursements to Brazil, where per-capita distribution of tribal wealth and land has caused tribal disruption and individual injury. Strong group rights, however, reduce divisive pressures by maintaining the integrity of tribal lands and reinforcing traditional mechanisms for sharing and distributing group resources.

Second, environmentalists worry that the exploitation of ecosystems under group control will be no less destructive than those under individual ownership. This is a possibility; in practice, however, group-controlled ecosystems have fared much better, probably because collective decisions about resource use involve thorough and thoughtful deliberation. Impulsive and poorly informed decisions are less likely, as is the potential for distressed or greedy individuals to alienate traditional group properties. Pine Ridge Reservation Sioux, for example, the poorest people in the United States, have rejected a series of lucrative offers by private companies to construct environmentally questionable facilities on tribal lands. In this and many other cases, the group dynamic tends to emphasize cultural and religious attachments to the land. It should not surprise us that the groups that best protect these lands are the same groups that have been their successful stewards for thousands of years; after all, they have the strongest links to the land they occupy.

Third, some environmentalists question whether indigenous cultures can retain their "special" rights after being "contaminated" by Western money and material goods. Quebec's giant dam-building utility, Hydro Quebec, raised this very question in its defense against a 1978 Cree lawsuit. Hydro Quebec argued that since the Cree used snowmobiles and high-powered rifles, ate hamburgers, and wore down jackets, they could no longer claim to be a distinct culture with special group rights to tribal lands. In response, skillful Cree lawyers called native trappers and storytellers, hunters and fishers, mothers and fathers to testify, in their own language, about their lives, beliefs, and traditions. This extraordinary transcript proved beyond doubt that the Cree retain a rich culture interwoven with their heritage, driven by hunting and fishing, and intricately connected to the land. The Court agreed.

The Next Millennium

All cultures are dynamic. Human beings have flourished because they can take advantage of new technologies, from the horse to the bow to the wheel. Indigenous peoples are not zoo animals to be frozen against their will in time. The injustice of rejecting this principle is evidenced in the absurd and humiliating fate of the Chachi Indians, who under Ecuadorian law only retain their land rights so long as they retain their traditional mud headdresses so pleasing to tourists. If South American Indians want rubber boots to

protect themselves from snakes or Western clothes to shield their skin from insects or inoculations for their children, we have no right to deny them these. Their use of these things should not compromise or affect their legal rights over their traditional homelands. Those rights must be continuously reaffirmed, for the sake of humanity and for the sake of these last wilderness areas.

The link between endangered societies and ecosystems underlies *State of the Peoples*. Emphasizing pluralism and group rights, this long-needed book presents innovative solutions to the challenges confronting wilderness cultures—environmental degradation, ethnic conflict, cultural disintegration, and poverty and economic development. The book's approach to group rights combines respect for individuals with an appreciation of the concerns facing distinct cultures within plural societies.

As you read *State of the Peoples*, entire societies are disappearing in the face of war, disease, poverty, and unwise and indiscriminate development. Yet their fate and ours are not settled. In the last decade of the twentieth century, control over land and resources is both an urgent necessity for indigenous peoples and the best hope for invaluable rain forests and other endangered ecosystems. Like a canary in a coal mine, the life or death of these peoples may indicate how well we will all fare in the next millennium.

ACKNOWLEDGMENTS

Preparing *State of the Peoples* combined a labor of love with just plain labor. Fortunately, the love prevailed because of the hundreds of people who labored so hard, almost all without pay, to make this book appear during the UN Year of the World's Indigenous People.

At the top of my personal debt list is Jason Clay, the founder of Cultural Survival Enterprises and *Cultural Survival Quarterly*. Second is Pam Solo. As the executive director of Cultural Survival when this project began, she gave me the mandate to turn an idea that had long floated in the air of possibility into reality. Pam and Jason stand as the intellectual, political, and inspirational godparents of *State of the Peoples*.

No one worked harder on *State of the Peoples* than Jennifer Rathaus, who coordinated the Resources for Action section. Working alongside Jenny and myself were a team of invaluable researchers, led by Kristen Guida, Genevieve Lecko, Lucy de Meijer, Oona Paredes, Nicholas Ribis, Kristen Ruckstuhl, Dee Siegel, and Rebecca Sholes.

All the staff of Cultural Survival contributed. Linda Belamarich, Mac Chapin, Celina Chelala, Jonathan Dawson, Sofia Flynn, Amy Grunder, Nickie Irvine, Rob Leavitt, Ted Macdonald, Jr., Maria Mulkeen, Mary Moore, and Bill Threlkeld made special contributions, earning special thanks.

The regional coordinators—Mac Chapin, Dan Connell, Michael Fisher, Gail Fondahl, Michael Herzfeld, Robert Hitchcock, Lamont Lindstrom, Ted Macdonald, Jr., John Mohawk, Toby Volkman, Geoff White—took on a large, exacting task; most went further than asked. I give you all a great thanks, as I do to the 150 contributors, who responded with (almost) uniform understanding and skill to deadlines ranging from two months down to one day.

Leslie Baker, Karen Wong, Anne Read, Meg Wilcox, the staff of Cultural Survival Canada, Jordana Friedman of Cultural Survival United Kingdom, Christine Volante, and Melanie Tang all played critical roles at one time or another, from researching obscure facts to translating illegible faxes from overseas.

A generous grant of hardware and software from Apple Computer arrived just in time—and was absolutely necessary to this project. Likewise, many thanks to my colleagues who showed patience when this book took over more than its fair share of Cultural Survival's computer and other resources.

Finally, my personal gratitude to the team at Beacon Press runs deep, especially to Deanne Urmy. Thank you for your strong vote of confidence in *State of the Peoples* when it was just an idea and a proposal. Thank you for believing Cultural Survival could meet its own impossible deadline. And thank you for helping me get through this long, arduous, and personally rewarding effort.

Marc S. Miller
Jamaica Plain, MA

FROM THIS DAY FORWARD

BY RIGOBERTA MENCHÚ TUM

For a decade, Rigoberta Menchú Tum, a K'iche' Maya woman, has lived in Mexico, one of thousands of Guatemalan refugees from the counterinsurgency terror engulfing her homeland. In 1992, her efforts to advance human rights in Guatemala gained international recognition when she was awarded the Nobel Peace Price.

On February 17, 1993, Menchú addressed the UN Commission on Human Rights in Geneva about its work during the UN International Year of the World's Indigenous People and about its role in preparing the Declaration on the Rights of Indigenous Peoples. This text is adapted from that speech.

It is gladdening that the United Nations has declared 1993 as the International Year of the World's Indigenous People. This year should promote learning about the often grave situation of indigenous peoples and encourage our participation at all levels. So, too, will *State of the Peoples* promote understanding and exchanges among the diverse cultures of our world.

We must not lose this historic opportunity to change the relationships among different cultures. There are still inequalities in how the problems of indigenous people are approached. Indigenous people continue to be marginalized from the fundamental decisions that affect their destiny.

There are immediate claims that merit effective responses and that must lead to concrete actions in this International Year of the World's Indigenous People.

The United Nations, through the Declaration on the Rights of Indigenous Peoples, should guarantee that the individual and collective rights of indigenous people are not violated. It should encourage its member states to permit and promote the participation of indigenous people in actively defending their own rights at the national, regional, and continental levels.

It is also necessary to grant indigenous organizations a more central place in UN forums. The United Nations should implement programs in favor of indigenous peoples and consult us about the priorities of our claims. We want UN agencies, in all their work, to provide opportunities for the contributions and participation of our people.

We want the United Nations and the international community to realize, from here onward, the facts of diversity and plurality. The United Nations should lead and we all must work toward eliminating discriminatory and racist practices, such as apartheid in South Africa, "ethnic cleansing," the upsurge of xenophobia, and the closing of borders.

The present situation in my country, Guatemala, is a case of grave and systematic violations of human rights, meriting the use of all possible mechanisms, including new ones, for procuring full respect for human rights. From this day forward, the adequate treatment of human rights in Guatemala is a debt the international community owes to the victims. Above all, it is a debt to indigenous peoples.

I am convinced that peace is more than a symbol. It is at the heart of the entire society. And I insist, once again, that symbolic acts are not sufficient for indigenous peoples. Our civil, political, economic, social, and cultural rights cannot wait any longer.

Societies in Danger

1 **ANISHINABE** *(see page 40)*

The Anishinabe, who inhabit a region often called "the wild rice bowl," face two threats to their cultural and economical relationship with wild rice. The first is the degradation by industrial society of the balanced ecosystem of marshes, lakes, and streams that has supported their culture for centuries. Pollution is reducing yields and destroying natural rice beds.

The second is the theft of Anishinabe "intellectual property." Conventionally farmed "wild" rice now dominates the market and has pushed the price of real wild rice so low that many lakes go unharvested, severely eroding the Anishinabe economic base.

2 **TAWAHKA** *(see page 54)*

In Honduras, an advancing colonization front—driven by expanding population and declining resources in nearby regions—threatens the ability of the 1,000 remaining Tawahka Sumu to maintain their identity as a distinct society. The Tawahka, living in lush rain forests along the Patuca River, have played a key role in conserving Central America's forests. Given legal backing, they can keep outsiders out of one of the most biologically diverse areas in Honduras.

The Tawahka have propsed the creation of a biosphere reserve and are vocal advocates for protecting their forests. However, Tawahka land rights even in a reserve bearing their name are far from assured, especially since Honduras has no clearly defined indigenous policy.

3 **BUSHMEN** *(see page 33)*

In Namibia, only 2,000 out of some 35,000 Bushmen still possess some of their ancestral territory. Gaining secure land tenure for these former foraging peoples is literally a matter of life and death.

Except for the Ju/'hoan, who are well organized to defend their rights, the few Bushmen who can find jobs are unpaid pastoral serfs or poorly paid agricultural laborers. Most Bushman peoples live as squatters around towns or on farms belonging to both black and white communal and commercial farmers.

4 BURMA *(see page 7)*

In a flimsy boat, a 13-year-old Rohingya girl flees with her family from western Burma to storm-swept Bangladesh. Her family makes the journey, because they fear that soldiers of Burma's military regime will rape her.

A young woman of Mon-Karen parentage leaves Burma to seek refuge in Thailand and ends up in a Thai jail. A brothel called the "Peace 1 Hotel" bails her out and forces her, at gunpoint, into prostitution.

Two Karen grandmothers run away from an army camp where they had been kept as slaves.

Such reports of abuse strongly indicate that ethnic minority women are the targeted victims of systematic repression in Burma.

5 BOSNIA *(see page 15)*

A people are at risk in Bosnia-Herzegovina. Out of a population of 4.3 million, some 170,000 people have died, 1.7 million have been displaced or have become refugees, and perhaps 20,000 women have been raped. Religious, cultural, and civic sites have been ravaged. The violence, systematically directed against a people as a group, amounts to genocide.

The nationality under siege, which might be called Bosnian, consists mainly of Muslims but includes Serbs, Croats, and others who reject ethnic exclusion. The consciousness that the chauvinist regimes of Serbia and Croatia must destroy, for political as well as territorial reasons, is "Bosnian-ness," an ethos of coexistence and a living contradiction to claims that the people of the Balkans can't live together.

6 PENAN *(see page 23)*

The sago and rattan, the palms, lianas, and fruit trees lie crushed on forest floors throughout the state of Sarawak in Malaysia. As the trees fall in the forest, a unique way of life, pursued for centuries, is collapsing in a single generation. Of an estimated 100,000 indigenous people who roamed the forests of Sarawak at the turn of this century, only the nomadic Penan remain.

The Penan of northeast Sarawak number about 7,600 in all, of whom 25 percent are settled. The remainder are semi-settled or nomadic and depend on the rain forest for most of their needs. If the government of Sarawak continues to have its way, Penan land will be laid waste within a year and the people will be forced from the land.

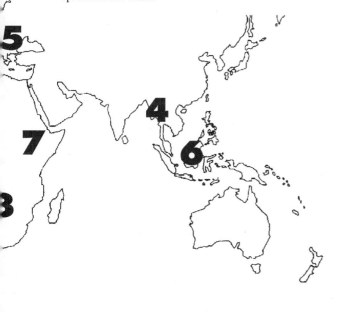

7 ETHIOPIA *(see page 46)*

After many years of war and turmoil, Ethiopians are unlikely to accept the sort of system they had before—being ordered around by outsiders, denied their honor and their rights, and shortchanged on services and opportunities. They want peace, stability, and a chance to rebuild, and they are also aware of the rewards for staying together. Yet they will require evidence that their needs will be dealt with fairly.

As dozens of organizations representing different ethnic groups seek to reconstruct Ethiopia, attempts to downplay ethnic distinctiveness and grievances are not based on the realities of life. Ethiopia's ethnic politics differ little from those elsewhere in the world.

AN INTERNATIONAL AGENDA

BY JULIAN BURGER

In June 1993, over 200 indigenous people traveled to Vienna on the occasion of the second World Conference on Human Rights. They had come to ask the United Nations to make a real commitment to their rights and development. At Vienna, as in other international forums, indigenous peoples are demanding self-determination, a major UN-wide initiative to improve their social and economic situations, and full and equitable participation in international gatherings that raise matters of concern to them.

These far-reaching objectives aren't pipe dreams; they are realizable in the near future. However, positive changes can't come too soon. Indigenous people are the single most disadvantaged and discriminated-against group in every society. In rich countries and poor, they suffer appalling neglect and marginalization as victims of two colonialisms, one historical and one contemporary.

The historical record is familiar. No one doubts the fateful impact on the indigenous peoples of the Americas of what UNESCO ingenuously calls the "encounter of two cultures." It was a human disaster. The story of the Americas is duplicated in other regions subjected to the scourge of European colonialism: Australia, New Zealand, the Pacific, Africa, and Asia, including the vast area in the East and North of the former Soviet Union.

The legacy of that history in the day-to-day life of indigenous peoples cannot be ignored. Consider official government statistics. In New Zealand, indigenous peoples are 7 times more likely to be unemployed than the average person; 50 percent of prisoners are Maaori although Maaori make up only 9 percent of the population.

In Australia, Aboriginal people have a life expectancy 20 years less than the average and are 14 times more likely to go to prison. Indigenous people make up over 60 percent of Guatemala's population but only 150 out of the 25,000 students who are in higher education. In Canada, infant mortality among indigenous people is over twice the national average.

These consequences of colonialism are one reason why so many indigenous people want the international community to take action. But there is another reason, perhaps even more critical. Indigenous peoples are victims of a modern-day colonialism, driven by humanity's determination to know all, explore all, exploit all. The insistent impulse to turn the planet into an interlinked whole, with global production, marketing, and communications, has brought a powerful, impatient world to the doorsteps of indigenous peoples.

As more accessible resources are exhausted, the search for raw materials escalates in comparatively neglected regions. Indigenous peoples sit on some of the world's last remaining natural resources, and both the rich countries of the North and the elites of the developing nations of the South want to exploit these stores, perhaps for legitimate development but just as likely for the profit of distant shareholders. At the same time, as the world population soars well past 5 billion people, pressure rises to open up potential living spaces.

Contemporary colonialism is devastating the everyday lives of indigenous peoples. In the quest for resources and land, the great wildernesses have become El Dorados and escape valves. Few of the 50 million indigenous inhabitants of the world's rain forests—who depend on it for food, medicine, shelter, and income—have escaped the assault of loggers, settlers, miners, and dam-builders. In Amazonia and several Asian countries, poor farmers, squeezed off their own lands by agro-industry, have migrated in massive numbers onto indigenous peoples' territory. Today, the indigenous people of Amazonia are outnumbered 16 to 1. By early in the next century, Indonesia plans to move up to 10 million people from Java to indigenous lands on the outer islands.

Mining and large-scale hydroelectric schemes threaten to displace, or have already displaced, hundreds of thousands of indigenous and tribal people. For example, a series of dams on India's Sardar Sarovar River imperils nearly 100,000 people, most of whom are tribals. Under the government's plans, many people will be removed and receive virtually no land or monetary compensation, and will probably end up swelling the already vast unemployed and marginalized slum-dwelling population in towns. And India's dam project is but one of many that are changing the lives of indigenous people throughout the world.

Toward a Declaration of Rights

Often denied recognition of their concerns in the countries where they live, indigenous peoples are asking the international community to extend and guarantee their rights. Once neglected and excluded from international forums, indigenous people are pursuing a number of possibilities for political action in this domain. Indigenous criticism of the only international instrument protecting their rights—the International Labor Organization's Convention No. 107—as assimilationist and paternalistic contributed to its review and subsequent revision. Since 1989, ILO Convention No. 169 has recognized the distinct cultures and right to self-development of indigenous peoples.

Similarly, pressure by indigenous peoples, human-rights activists, and environmentalists led the World Bank to change many of its policies. And in 1992, several hundred indigenous peoples from the Americas, Asia, Africa, Europe, and Oceania were active at the United Nations Conference on Environment and Development—the 1993 "Earth Summit" in Rio de Janeiro—ensuring that Agenda 21, the action plan to implement the conference recommendations, addresses at least some of their concerns.

In the clash of interests and cultures that arises from the new colonialism, the United Nations emerges as a key player. In 1982, the United Nations created the Working Group on Indigenous Populations. This body is the only place in which the United Nations grants indigenous peoples an established right to speak as indigenous peoples, nations, and organizations.

The Working Group has two important mandates. First, it reviews developments affecting indigenous peoples, providing an opportunity for indigenous people to give first-hand testimony on their specific problems. The Working Group has generated expert meetings, critical studies, and various kinds of practical action. The proposal for an International Year of the World's Indigenous People began in the Working Group, and three expert seminars have given rise to comprehensive recommendations on racism, self-government, and environment.

Second, the Working Group elaborates standards for protecting indigenous rights. That task has accelerated in the 1990s, with a focus on preparing a comprehensive declaration on the rights of indigenous peoples (*see page 83 for the text of the draft declaration*). After a decade of effort by the Working Group, the draft declaration is almost ready to move to the Commission on Human Rights and the UN General Assembly. No international instrument has been discussed more intensely by the people it is meant to benefit.

5

When adopted by the General Assembly, the draft declaration will form the basis for a new relationship of indigenous peoples with states and with the United Nations. Perhaps most important, it states that "Indigenous peoples have the right to autonomy and self-government in matters relating to their internal and local affairs. " The document affirms the right of indigenous peoples to self-determination and to control their lands and resources. It emphasizes the right of indigenous peoples to determine membership in their societies, establish their own institutions according to their own practices, and retain and develop their own customs, laws, and legal systems. And it asserts the right of indigenous peoples to maintain their differences and determine their future collectively.

The draft declaration specifically recognizes the right of indigenous peoples to protection against cultural genocide, defined as any form of forced assimilation or deprivation of their distinct cultural characteristics. Paralleling this right, the draft declaration includes the right to the protection of sacred sites, the restitution of cultural property, and the repatriation of human remains.

The draft declaration also incorporates principles of greater access to and control over public services. Broadly speaking, there are two reasons indigenous people fare far worse than any other group according to every socioeconomic indicator: a lack of access to services (sometimes as a result of discrimination) and the delivery of services that are inappropriate, alien, or culturally unacceptable. The draft declaration amplifies what some countries have made official policy: a system of services that indigenous people themselves plan and implement.

Indeed, times have changed dramatically since the United Nations held the first World Conference on Human Rights in 1968. At that time, the term "indigenous people" wasn't even part of the language; indigenous people were considered a remnant of the past, destined to an inexorable assimilation into mainstream societies. In 1993, by contrast, the second World Conference on Human Rights asked the General Assembly to proclaim a decade for indigenous peoples. Just as this International Year of the World's Indigenous People has generated public support for the rights of indigenous peoples, a decade of commitment to their rights and well-being would provide a framework for the next chapter of progress for indigenous peoples.

Julian Burger is responsible for the indigenous peoples program at the United Nations Center for Human Rights. He is the author of *Gaia Atlas of First Peoples: A Future for the Indigenous World* (Anchor Books, 1990) and *Report from the Frontier: The State of the World's Indigenous Peoples* (Zed Books, 1987). The views in this article do not necessarily reflect those of the United Nations.

EDITH MIRANTE

BY EDITH T. MIRANTE

Burma's Ethnic Minority Women: From Abuse to Resistance

A 13-year-old Rohingya girl flees western Burma to storm-swept Bangladesh. Her family makes the journey, in a flimsy boat, because they are afraid that soldiers of Burma's SLORC (State Law and Order Restoration Council) regime intend to rape her.

A young woman of Mon-Karen parentage leaves Burma to seek refuge in Thailand and ends up in a Thai jail. She is bailed out by a brothel called the "Peace 1 Hotel" and is forced, at gunpoint, into prostitution.

Two Karen grandmothers run away from a SLORC army camp where they had been kept as slaves. In the forest, they announce to the bears, tigers, and evil spirits that they would rather die than go back to the labor camp.

These stories, and countless like them, have been told by women and girls of Burma's ethnic minorities to me and others—both individuals and

7

"Most of the women were gang-raped, one after another, all night long. Even my sister, six months pregnant, was not left alone."

organizations—who investigate human rights in Burma. The patterns of abuse strongly indicate that ethnic minority women are the targeted victims of systematic repression in Burma. At the same time, these women are at the forefront of efforts to end such violations of basic rights. The dual roles of victim and resister have emerged during decades of military dictatorship and ethnic strife.

Burma, the largest country of mainland Southeast Asia, has a multi-ethnic population of about 43 million people. (The SLORC changed its name to Myanmar, but pro-democracy Burmese and other ethnic minorities reject the change.) Traditionally, the status of women in most of Burma's ethnic groups has been high. Although Buddhism, the majority religion, considers women a somewhat inferior incarnation to men, in everyday life they are perceived as equal. Women's rights in marriage, divorce, inheritance, and employment have been guaranteed under law since Burma gained its independence from Britain in 1948. Decades of military rule, however, have undermined women's status, especially in the ethnic minority frontier regions.

Burma's current conditions stem from ancient ethnic clashes, which intensified during World War II. Over the centuries, peoples from the north and west, including the Burmese (also known as Burmans), Mons, Arakanese, and Shans, migrated along great river valleys and established civilizations. As these monarchies clashed, rising and falling in turn, other peoples settled in the frontier mountains in tribal political structures: the Kachins, Karens, Chins, and many subgroups. Some of Burma's peoples are of the Mon-Khmer language group, others of the Tibeto-Burman, Sino-Tai, or Bengali ethnicities.

Syndromes of civil warfare, economic exploitation of weaker groups, and authority decentralized in frontier principalities were in evidence when the British Raj colonized Burma in the nineteenth century. The colonists appeared to favor frontier ethnic groups like the Karen, granting them considerable autonomy. The largest ethnic group, the Burmese of the central plains, felt ill compensated for their rice growing and other skills.

When the Japanese Imperial Army invaded in 1942, many Burmese welcomed it as a way to drive out the British, while frontier ethnic groups provided fighters for the Allies. When the war ended, the Japanese, Americans, and British left, but the indigenous conflicts were never resolved. Rebel armies immediately formed to fight the predominantly Burmese central government for more regional autonomy. In 1962, citing the need to preserve national unity, General Ne Win usurped power from a democratically elected government; he and his officers have remained in charge ever since.

The SLORC, a junta of Ne Win's favorite minions, has administered Burma since brutally suppressing a massive prodemocracy uprising in 1988. It has built up its army, the Tatmadaw, with expensive weapons from China and Yugoslavia, to continue attempts to subdue rebellious ethnic minorities. Sworn to enforce national unity at all costs, the Tatmadaw wages a counter-insurgency war by attacking ethnic minority civilians.

In the frontier war zone, women are frequently captured and used as "human shields" in front of the Tatmadaw so rebel forces will hold their fire. A 52-year-old Karen woman told me of her front-line experience:

Before they reached the fighting place, the soldiers made the four women go in front. The Burmese soldiers were behind us. . . . They tied us. Behind our backs. To go in front so that the Karen soldiers, if they saw us, they wouldn't shoot us because we are Karen.

Logging on the Burma-Thailand border

Tatmadaw units force women to walk ahead of them, sweeping the paths with branches to detonate any anti-personnel land mines planted by rebels. Very recent reports indicate that women are now being commanded to bring along two of their children when on mine-sweeping duty so their own children would be vulnerable to the mines. Village women suspected of being wives or relatives of rebel soldiers or dissidents are often held hostage by the Tatmadaw, tortured for information, and, in many cases, executed.

A pervasive Tatmadaw practice is to take "porters" to carry heavy supplies in the war zone. These civilians—prisoners and ordinary ethnic minority villagers—aren't paid for their labor and get sparse rations during captivity. Those who fall ill or are considered uncooperative are often beaten and left to die in the jungle or are executed. There are accounts of the babies of female porters being killed if they make noise, or as a way of terrifying the captives into submission. Men and boys, women and girls are seized for porter duty, and the females are routinely raped.

This account by Khin Khine Soe, a 20-year-old Arakanese woman, is typical:

Some SLORC soldiers came to the house and said my sister and I would have to go with them. We refused, but they forced us at gunpoint. On the way to Byu Ha military camp they raped both of us. When we arrived at the camp they put us together with a group of porters. . . . The soldiers would never let us rest, and we never got any water when we went over mountains. . . . All we ever got to eat was a little bit of rotten rice, but we often went hungry for more than a day. . . .
At night we tried to sleep all together, but the women had to go sleep wherever the soldiers dragged us. One officer the soldiers all addressed as "Bo Gyi" came and took away the same young Indian girl every night. Because of my youth I was terrified every night, so I always tried to hide among the elderly women. But even so, my turn usually came not long after the Indian girl. Most of the women were gang-raped, one after another, all night long. Even my sister, six months pregnant, was not left alone. Then every morning we had to haul our loads again. My sister got very weak and sick. After ten days, one time I came back to the group after a brief absence and she was gone. The soldiers wouldn't tell me what happened to her, and I still don't know.

Khin Khine Soe managed to escape to a rebel-held area, where she was interviewed by Kevin Heppner, a Canadian relief worker. "I'm sad and afraid because I think of all the women who haven't escaped," she told Heppner. "I think that even women who somehow survive being porters will still have to suffer by finding out they're pregnant afterwards."

Burma's military regime has consistently used rape as a tactic against ethnic minority civilians. Distinct from sporadic instances of rape, which

9

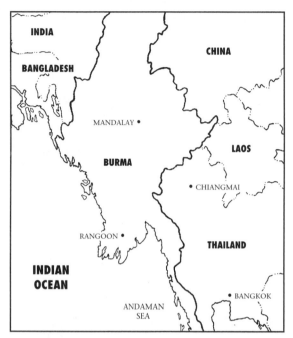

Refugee women and children from Burma are often forced into prostitution, particularly in Thailand and Southern China.

occur in many war zones, this is an element of military strategy. The Tatmadaw uses rape to encourage ethnic minority villagers to emigrate to nearby countries en masse, leaving depopulated security zones along the borders. Rape is also directed against women who are suspected subversives. Reports of gang-rape by low-ranking soldiers are common, as are reports of selective rape by officers. Rape with objects like guns or bamboo poles, which often kill the victim, has been reported from all ethnic minority areas, as has torture of pregnant women, including execution by disembowelment.

In 1992, some 300,000 refugees of the Rohingya ethnic group, Muslims from Burma's Arakan State, ended up in squalid encampments in Bangladesh. Along with other civilian abuses, including the burning of mosques and a gulag of forced labor camps, the refugees described a systematic campaign of terror-rape by the Tatmadaw.

A military buildup in the area had apparently been accompanied by one of the largest-scale uses of tactical rape in Asia since Japan's 1937 occupation of Nanking, China. It is worth noting that present-day Burma is ruled by a general trained under that same Japanese fascist military.

A 1992 Asia Watch report, "Burma: Rape, Forced Labor and Religious Persecution in Northern Arakan," included many accounts of the sexual violation of Muslim women in that state by the Tatmadaw, including these two reports from women who had escaped to Bangladesh:

One afternoon in early December 1991, soldiers announced that all Muslims must leave. Aisha and her husband made no preparations to do so because they had no place to go. That night, while her husband and children were sleeping under their blankets, five soldiers kicked down the door of their house. They said they were collecting laborers. Aisha told them her husband was not there. "Then we'll take you," she said they told her. Then they carried her outside, tore off her clothes, blindfolded her with a rag, and while two or three held her, each of the five took a turn raping her. They tore her pierced earrings out. At some point during the violence, she was aware of her husband emerging from the house to defend her. . . . Using a long-bladed work knife, the soldiers then hacked him to death, leaving his body in front of Aisha. She herself lay on the ground injured and bleeding, and the soldiers said they would return for her. When she had recovered enough to travel, she gathered her five children and father, and left on foot. They caught a boat to Bangladesh at Parampur Crossing.

A widow, Rohima said that soldiers from the Charmael Camp, Lontin Battalion, regularly forced Muslim men and youths of Shigdarpara to do hard labor. They were picked up, house by house, whenever soldiers needed workers. But in recent months, girls between the ages of 12 and 16 were being collected in the same way, from house to house. Survivors of these abductions had always been raped, and Rohima was worried about her own daughter. She also had three sons, aged 14 to 6. One day in December 1991, a letter from the military post four miles away was delivered to Rohima's house: it said to send her daughter to the camp. Rohima did not respond. Soon thereafter, four or five soldiers burst into the house where Rohima and her four children had finished their evening meal. All they said was, "We're taking your daughter sightseeing." They picked her up and carried her out screaming, clubbing her brother of 16 as he tried to protect her from them. Rohima waited six weeks for news of her daughter from the camp. She decided then to leave Burma for Bangladesh.

Tatmadaw "strategic hamlet" campaigns, in which ethnic minority villages are relocated to walled camps under army surveillance to deprive rebels of indigenous support, have intensified and expanded. Now hundreds of thousands of civilians are marched from place to place and put to work as army slaves in construction, agriculture, logging, and mining projects to provide supplies and income for the SLORC. Such slave labor is used to build railways or to clear roads for logging concerns and oil or gas pipelines in concession areas used by multinational corporations. The new "Death Railway" under construction, which will link Loikaw with Aung Ban in northeastern Burma, is one such forced labor scheme. In October 1992, a Reuters reporter asked Lt. Col. Than Han, of the SLORC's Border Areas Development Committee, which has received UN funding, about deaths of laborers. He replied: "Every day people are dying. It's a normal thing. . . . They sweat a lot, they lose weight, and they have some health problems." A Karenni woman, Naw Lah Gay, who escaped from the Deemawso labor camp, described "normal" events on the project:

> *I was taken from Deemawso camp to work on the railway in April. Many women had to go. I was the only person from my family who went that time. I walked to Pay Ko as part of a group of five people. At the railway we had to work from 7 a.m. to 4 p.m. In the morning I had to cook, then all the rest of the day I had to carry rocks. . . . I saw one man beaten by a SLORC officer because he was sick. The officer didn't even ask anything, just started kicking him with his army boots.*

Such abuse of ethnic minority people has sent an exodus of refugees to neighboring countries, including an estimated 3,000 to India, 30,000 to China, 70,000 to 200,000 to Thailand, and the 300,000 in Bangladesh. These refugees lead a precarious existence in those countries, rarely recognized as anything but illegal aliens. They are hunted and persecuted by security forces and subject to involuntary repatriation to Burma. Their labor is exploited in agriculture, fishing fleets, and manufacturing.

Refugee women and girls from Burma are often forced into prostitution, particularly in Thailand and southern China. Both Thailand and China's Yunnan Province have high infection rates, espe-

11

Women and girls from Burma's frontiers are sold to Thai brothels with the connivance of Burmese and Thai military and police. They are advertised as "AIDS free," but they don't remain AIDS free for long.

Women serve in combat in some rebel armies. The presence of tough young women in uniform has broken down foreign stereotypes of Asian femininity as well as local standards of demure behavior.

cially among prostitutes. Women and girls from Burma's frontiers are sold to Thai brothels with the connivance of Burmese and Thai military and police. They are advertised as "AIDS free" because they come from a country with little foreign contact, but they don't remain AIDS free for long. There have been reports of abuse (and possibly execution) of prostitutes who are found to be H.I.V.-positive and have been repatriated to Burma from Thailand.

Ethnic minority women from Burma when in Thai immigration custody are routinely raped and sold out of the jails to Thai brothel-keepers. Mistreatment of ethnic minority women from Burma seeking refuge in Thailand has included the "beauty contest" auctioning of tribal women to be "minor wives" for Thai officials in the border areas and the freak-show tourism promotion of "exotic" women from Burma's indigenous tribes. Women of the Padaung tribe, a matriarchy whose members traditionally use metal coils to elongate their necks, are particularly vulnerable to this form of exploitation. Advertised as "the giraffe women," Padaung refugee women are held captive on the Thai side of the border and made to pose at fairs and tourist traps for Thais and foreigners.

Decades of nonstop military human rights abuse in the frontier areas of Burma have destabilized traditional societies, as long-standing villages are uprooted and large segments of the population disappear, only to become porters, refugees, and even massacre victims. In addition, the forests of many indigenous peoples are vanishing fast. The SLORC has sold logging concessions to firms from neighboring countries (mainly Thailand and China) which then clear-cut the

frontiers in their search for teak and other valuable hardwoods. Withstanding these kinds of pressure, rebel forces that represent ethnic hopes for autonomy have often served to strengthen cultural identity. This has been the case with the national movements of the Mons, Karens, Kachins, and some others, including the Karennis, Pa-Os, Palaungs, and Chins.

Within these militarized frontier societies, which are distinguished by a sense of cultural and physical danger, women are increasingly examining their own roles. The Shan ethnic resistance movement was founded in the mid-1950s by the Maha Devi of Yaunghwe, a woman who had been a member of Burma's first parliament. For the most part, however, women's participation has taken on a high profile only in recent years. Organizations that started out as "ladies' auxiliaries" have grown in influence. The Kawthoolei Women's Organization of the Karen indigenous people administers settlements of displaced people on both sides of the Burma-Thailand border and oversees development projects and vocational training in such traditional women's skills as weaving. In Burma's remote north, the Kachin Women's Association carries on significant work in health education, rehabilitating war-wounded people, and economic empowerment for women.

Burma's highest-profile activist is Aung San Suu Kyi, an ethnic Burmese woman. Her National League for Democracy won over 80 percent of the votes in a 1990 national election, even though she has been under house arrest, incommunicado, since July 1989. She received the 1991 Nobel Peace Prize in honor of her firm, articulate commitment to nonviolent change, but the SLORC did not allow her party to take office and continued to hold her prisoner. Suu Kyi's sympathy for the ethnic minorities, which echoes that of her father, Aung San, a leader who was assassinated at the time of Burma's independence, has earned her great admiration in the frontier areas. A popular picture shows her in ceremonial Kachin dress: the embroidered sarongs she favors, which have become a democracy symbol on city streets, are Kachin in origin.

Despite Burma's obvious willingness to vote for female leadership, women have been underrepresented on the political scene, although some feminist groups existed briefly before the SLORC suppressed the 1990 election results. Women are absent in the upper echelons of the Tatmadaw, although General Ne Win's daughter, Sanda Win, an army officer, does wield some power behind the scenes.

The rebel parties and alliances have few women in high posts, but this seems about to change. The Karen rebels named the first five women to their central committee in 1991. Mra Raza Lin, a young woman who had organized general strikes in Arakan during the 1988 uprising, now leads an important nonviolent resistance group among the Buddhist Rakhine people.

Women of Burma's frontier ethnic groups have long been prominent in health care, dating back to mission hospital training and World War II. Dr. Cynthia Maung, a 35-year-old Karen, is particularly noteworthy. Leaving central Burma for the Thai border at the time of the 1988 uprising, Dr. Cynthia set up a clinic for refugees in an old barn. She treated endemic diseases—malaria, typhoid, hepatitis, dysentery—as well as wounds from gunfire, shelling, and land mines. Eventually she created a string of clinics and established medical training programs and mobile medic teams that provide care deep in the war zone. She has also brought women's health pro-

Akha tribespeople

grams and AIDS education to extremely isolated areas. Dr. Cynthia is active on several medical and political committees, taking part in the alliance of ethnic rebel groups with Burmese dissidents against SLORC rule.

In the late 1980s, when Mon women were allowed to join the New Mon State Party, they demanded the chance to serve in the Mon rebel army as well. They fought as regular combat troops, perhaps inspired by Chama Devi, queen of an ancient Mon empire. Women also serve in combat in the Kachin tribe's formidable guerrilla force and in some other rebel armies. More often, they are on the front lines as medics, doctors, or nurses, helping civilians and soldiers alike. The presence of tough young women in uniform has broken down foreign stereotypes of Asian femininity as well as local standards of demure behavior.

Sometimes traditional beliefs relate to such militarization in interesting ways. For example, the Shans think that a bullet shot by a woman soldier can overcome an enemy soldier's magical anti-penetration tattoos to wound or kill him. Since many of Burma's peoples believe that women possess strong resources of mystical power, few fron-

13

tiersmen are as powerful as a woman with a gun—and her own antipenetration tattoos.

In the nonviolent part of the struggle for democracy, ethnic minority women in exile have worked tirelessly to make people in other countries aware of Burma's plight. Shan, Karen, Kachin, Pa-O, and other female activists have organized demonstrations around the world, lobbied governments and international organizations for refugee aid, and publicized issues like the destruction of Burma's rain forests and the threats of AIDS and forced prostitution.

These are revolutionary times in Burma. The Burmese majority underground has joined forces with frontier rebels of all ethnicities to oppose the SLORC. This political and military movement is increasingly conducive to a social rebellion in which women seek to seize their human rights. Civilians, especially women, continue to be the primary victims in Burma's frontier war, but

Kachin hospital in northern Burma

resistance is now as much women's role as is victimization.

Edith T. Mirante, the author of *Burmese Looking Glass: A Human Rights Adventure?* (Grove Press, 1993), directs Project Maje, an agency that monitors and reports on the situation in Burma.

How You Can Help

Write the chairman of the SLORC. Demand that the junta hand over power to Aung San Suu Kyi's elected National League for Democracy, the best chance for peace and fair treatment of all ethnic groups: Gen. Than Shwe, State Law and Order Restoration Council, Ministry of Defense, Signal Pagoda Rd., Yangon, Burma.

Write the foreign ministers of Thailand and China and demand they stop supporting the SLORC, begin treating refugees from Burma humanely, and keep their hands off Burma's forests: Mr. Prasong Soonsiri, Foreign

Minister, Foreign Ministry, Government House, Nakorn Pathom Rd., Bangkok 10300, Thailand; Mr. Qian Qichen, Foreign Minister, Foreign Ministry, 225 Chaoyangmennei Daijie, Beijing, People's Republic of China.

Two major U.S. oil companies are in joint exploration ventures with the SLORC despite an abusive military presence in their concession areas. Write their chief executives and tell them to terminate their relationship with the SLORC: H. Laurence Fuller, Amoco Corp., 200 East Randolph Dr., Chicago

IL 60601; Earl R. Johnson, Texaco Exploration, Inc., 2000 Westchester Ave., White Plains, NY 10604.

The other major U.S. company in Burma is PepsiCo, owner of Pepsi-Cola, Pizza Hut, Kentucky Fried Chicken, Taco Bell, and Frito-Lay. Burmese students and human rights groups have called for a boycott of PepsiCo products. Write and tell PepsiCo to stop doing business under the SLORC: Wayne Calloway, Chairman of the Board, PepsiCo, Purchase, NY 10577.

The War in Bosnia: Seeds of Wars to Come

BY ANTHONY BORDEN

A people are at risk in Bosnia-Herzegovina, the former central republic of Yugoslavia. Out of a population of 4.3 million, some estimates indicate that more than 170,000 people have died, approximately 1.7 million have been displaced or made refugees (40 percent of the population), and up to 20,000 women have been raped. Religious, cultural, and civic sites have been ravaged—especially the beautiful ancient towns of Sarajevo and Mostar. As the nationalist programs behind the war, as well as countless testimonials and other evidence, make clear, the violence is systematically directed against a people as a group and therefore amounts to genocide.

If the war has been waged to destroy a people because of their identity, it also serves to impose that identity. In a cruel irony, Bosnians now suffer for being something they never were—firmly identified ethnic groups—and the prospect of a nation-based state for Bosnia's majority ethnic group arises at the very moment that people, and their potential nation-state, are close to extinction.

The fact is the identity of the population most at risk in Bosnia—generally considered to be Muslims—defies precise definition. Much confusion has resulted (and much violence has been fueled) because vicious propaganda from both

15

aggressor states (Serbia and Croatia) claims at one moment that Muslims are Serbs or Croats who happen to have converted to Islam, and at another moment that they are fundamentalist *Mujahedin*, a terrifying "other."

These claims resonate throughout international public and governmental opinion. In particular, the official peace process under the auspices of the United Nations and the European Community is deeply infected with the idea that the conflict concerns three ethnic "sides" with ancient animosities. The war is generally conceived of as an ethnic one, a battle among ancient tribes, with Serbs led by ex-psychiatrist Radovan Karadzic, Muslims led by Bosnian president Aliji Izetbegovic, and Croats led by a changing array of political leaders backed by Gen. Mate Boban. The relationship between the Serb and Croat forces and their respective "motherlands" has appeared sometimes direct, sometimes divorced, adding to confusion over whether this is a war of aggression or a civil war. Whichever view has appeared prevalent at a given moment, the main driving force of conflict has been understood to be hatred itself. This view of the war as chaotic and incomprehensible has fed the paralysis in the international community and offers a free hand to warlords on the ground.

There are indeed vexing historical questions of how the Muslim population of 1.9 million came into being in Bosnia, but the main obstacle to defining the population at risk in Bosnia-Herzegovina is that for so long it resisted defining itself. The people in Bosnia—at a crossroads of three religions and surrounded by often predatory, chauvinistic states—developed a unique regional identity stronger than their cultural, predominantly religious differences.

The real nationality under siege might properly be called Bosnian—consisting mainly of Muslims but including Serbs (Orthodox), Croats (Catholic), Yugoslavs (nonreligious or of mixed ethnic/religious parentage), and others who reject ethnic exclusion. The consciousness that the chauvinist regimes of Serbia and Croatia must destroy, for political as well as territorial reasons, is "Bosnian-ness," an ethos of coexistence strongly Muslim-influenced but drawing from the whole population.

Bosnian-ness is a living contradiction to the claims that the people of the Balkans can't live together. As such, the tragedy of Bosnia's demise is compounded by a regional political crisis for which international institutions and Western governments bear substantial responsibility. The destruction of Bosnia means the destruction of one of the region's most pluralistic, progressive forces, and it almost certainly would fuel further war throughout the Balkans.

Fragile for Centuries

Bosnia has long been a fragile and ethnically mixed area. The Bosnian principality emerged in the 1300s, with the seizing of territory later known as Herzegovina. Bosnian rulers dominated the neighboring states for a time, reinforcing a Bosnian regional consciousness even in Croat- and Serb-populated regions. Bosnia was also the center of the Bogomil heresy. A little-understood religious sect that may have led to the Bosnian Church, it reasserted Bosnian individuality from other Slavs on a religious level.

The Turkish conquest of Bosnia in 1463 initiated a wave of conversions, and by the end of the seventeenth century three-fourths of the Bosnian population was Muslim. Most Bosnians, especially the landed gentry, saw the economic and political advantages of associating with the occupying power, and the region became an Ottoman stronghold, with some autonomy within the empire. Whereas Christian Slavs may have viewed Bosnian Muslims as "Turks," Bosnian Muslims carefully distinguished themselves—speaking "Bosnian" rather

Bosnian-ness is a living contradiction to the claims that the people of the Balkans can't live together.

than Turkish, for example. Islam provided yet another means to forge a regional sensibility. In any case, national identities were weak at best in medieval Bosnia. Conversions occurred in all directions: the number of Muslims increased and the numbers of Catholics and Orthodox alternately fell and rose. Families split across religions, for spiritual, political, or financial reasons.

The concept of a Bosnian, later Muslim, nationality developed for many of the same self-protective reasons that caused a Bosnian regional consciousness to take root. With the decline of the Ottoman Empire and later the Congress of Berlin in 1878, Bosnia-Herzegovina fell under Austro-Hungarian control and assumed the borders it would have until 1918. The new imperial power was keenly aware of the dangers of nationalist and religious separatism among Serbs and Croats. At the same time, it wanted to assuage Muslims, some of whom had fled to Istanbul while others set up small resistance efforts. The Austro-Hungarian response was to encourage the ideal of a multi-religious Bosnian nationality, a concept that had historical resonance, particularly among Croats and Muslims. With Serb-Croat tensions rising, however, this ideal gained hold only among Muslims. In a region of competing religions under threat from predatory neighbors, Muslims had to chart a careful middle course.

These pressures became most severe as the concept of nationalist identity, distinct from and deeper than religious identity, grew stronger. Muslims, equated with the dreaded "Turks," could hardly align with Serbs. Croats flattered Muslims as the "flower of the Croat nation," but an alliance with them could be no more natural and would inflame tensions among the rival

camps. Some Muslims, especially the elite with interests at stake, declared themselves as one or the other nationality. Some people changed ethnic identification for the sake of convenience. But the large majority, especially peasants, rejected both national affiliations. Bosnian Muslims have supported large unified state structures, as opposed to ethnically defined territories, to avoid the obvious risk of any carve-up by outside forces.

The relatively tolerant attitudes of Islam—unlike Christianity's view of Islam, Islam doesn't consider Christianity a heresy—have meant that Bosnian or Muslim identity wouldn't be as aggressive as neighboring national movements. Bosnian liberalism has also been a way to sidestep the impossible national question. Clearly, Muslims couldn't claim the long national development of the main Slav tribes of Serbs, Croats, and Bulgars. And unlike more recent national groups—Slovenes, Montenegrins, and Macedonians—their main identifying feature is not language or location but religion.

Whatever its definition, the Bosnian/Muslim national identity was bound to be "weaker"—a commendable trait that would have tragic consequences.

Two Yugoslavias

In the years before World War I, alliances shifted among all three groups in Bosnia, but Muslim-Serb tension dominated at the war's end, from Serb grievances over Muslim landholdings to Muslim anger over the assassination of Archduke Ferdinand. At the war's end, Alexander Karadjordjevic, descendant of a Serb warrior, declared the Kingdom of Serbs, Croats, and Slovenes, with Bosnia-Herzegovina essentially a Serbian province.

17

This first Yugoslavia did little to ease the Serb-Croat nationalist vice that was squeezing Muslims, but for pragmatic reasons Muslims supported the unified state. The Yugoslav Muslim Organization, or JMO, founded in 1919, sought to chart a course between Serb and Croat pressure on Muslims to declare a nationality. JMO leaders were defensive about

KEVIN WEAVER

Bosnian Muslim troops

heading a religious-based party but also rejected the notion of a distinct Muslim nationality. Instead, the JMO blamed its political organizing on those (i.e., Serbs) who had persecuted them because of their religion.

Neither a name change to the Kingdom of Yugoslavia in 1929 nor the declaration of a royal dictatorship in 1931 resolved the kingdom's national and political tensions. During World War II, the Axis powers installed the fascist government of Ante Pavelic in Croatia, which included all of Bosnia-Herzegovina. Although various estimates suggest that Croats killed at least 300,000 Serbs (some Serb estimates are as high as 700,000), around 100,000 Muslims also were killed, the highest percentage of deaths in relation to total population of all the groups.

The end of the war brought the second Yugoslavia of Marshal Josip Broz Tito, whose partisan forces were explicitly multiethnic. Seeking to soothe nationalist tensions, Tito created six

republics. The establishment of a distinct Bosnian republic was essential if the federation were to balance the strengths of the Serbian and Croatian republics and guarantee a space for the nationally undecided Muslims.

The federation's policy on its diverse nationalities began with the aim of unifying people under the ideal of a Yugoslav nationalism. Bosnia-Herzegovina—with its diversity and, perhaps not incidentally, as the country's military and industrial base—would serve as the fount of this Yugoslavism. The republic was sometimes called Little Yugoslavia, and the tolerant Bosnian Muslims were expected to lead the way.

In the early 1960s, however, state nationalities policy shifted to a less grand concept: a community of coexisting nations. This change, reflecting and encouraging distinct group consciousnesses, was marked by a revision in the 1961 census that now allowed people to register as "Muslims in the ethnic sense." The shift culminated in 1971 with the inclusion of Muslims (not just in Bosnia) as a nationality. By 1991, 44 percent of Bosnia's population had registered as Muslim, 31 percent as Serb, 17 percent as Croat, and 7 percent as Yugoslav.

The debate over the 1971 census foreshadowed many of the interconnected problems now facing the region. Leading figures from Serbia, including Dobrica Cosic, now federal president of the new rump Yugoslavia, declared that it was senseless to consider Muslims as a nationality. Croatian writers essentially argued that Muslims were actually Croats. The Communist Party newspaper in Macedonia decried "Muslim hegemonism" and argued that "Muslims who speak Macedonian are Macedonian." Having achieved national status, some Muslims argued that Muslims were the "only real Bosnians" and pressed for separate Muslim institutions to oppose Serb and Croat institutions. They also unsuccessfully sought to alter the constitution to make Bosnia a "republic of Muslims," just as Serbia and Macedonia were republics of their nations.

At the height of the census debate, a longtime Muslim activist wrote a 50-page treatise that would resonate through the mid-1980s and eventually become one of the most controversial texts of the war. "The Islamic Declaration," written by Alija Izetbegovic, now the president of Bosnia, has been taken as proof of intentions to establish an ethnically pure Islamic republic. It led to the 1983 trial of Izetbegovic and 12 other Muslims on charges of "hostile and counter-revolutionary acts." Izetbegovic and three other defendants were sentenced to 14 years in prison. Today, the Belgrade and Zagreb regimes use the text as proof of a jihad in Bosnia, from which they must protect their respective national populations there.

Izetbegovic is deeply religious and, albeit a bumbling politician, a humane and essentially liberal person. His declaration does little more than summarize Islamic ideas, with a focus on reasserting values common to many Third World reformists at the time. The text does call for an Islamic order, which the document argues can't recognize the principle of a secular state or coexist with non-Islamic institutions. But, Izetbegovic responded at his trial, the declaration explicitly rejects the idea of such a state in a country without a strong Muslim majority.

Two decades later, Izetbegovic does deserve much blame for the war, but scratching through faded texts for hard-line religious leanings is a distraction. The question is not whether Bosnian Muslims are or may become fundamentalist, an absurd notion. The proper question is whether, after centuries of weaving around the explosive national issue that Serbs and Croats were anxious to impose, Izetbegovic's championing of nation-based politics in the fragile republic could have led to anything but a nightmare.

Nationalism and War

Bosnia is a paradox: it is a land of harmony and hatred, of convergence and conflict. At one glance, love has held it together. In Mostar in 1913, a dying Muslim *hodja* (a religious figure) gave up his son for adoption to his best friend, the Serb Orthodox priest. The *hodja*'s grandson, married to a woman of Serb and Croatian descent, is now deputy editor of the Sarajevo daily *Oslobodjenje*. In another view, cohesion came from a "balance of fear" in which no group dared push the national question too hard.

Many Bosnians simply saw no difference among ethnic groups; the only real distinguishing feature of Muslims was their names, if that. Indeed, only 17 percent of the respondents to a 1985 poll in Bosnia declared themselves religious believers, well below the rates in Kosovo, Croatia, and Slovenia. One-quarter of the population came from ethnically mixed marriages, which would seem to make it impossible to declare an affiliation with any single nation. People's sense of their own identity—as opposed to a box they might check on a census form—was as likely to be Bosnian, Sarajevan, or Yugoslav as any ethnic group; even more likely it may have been doctor, taxi driver, laborer.

To highlight the similarities among Bosnians is not to deny differences. Bosnia wouldn't have represented an achievement of coexistence if there were not an array of cultural and other distinctions to mesh. Sarajevo's breathtaking beauty lay precisely in its skyline: a mosque nestled by a cathedral near a church (or even a synagogue). Even now, Sarajevans gather for a year-end festival in which religious figures of many faiths address a mixed congregation.

Differences have, of course, been most apparent in religious practice. Even if many Muslims didn't fast for the whole of Ramadan (or even for any of it), didn't have several wives (basically only a mat-

19

ter for jesting), or didn't abstain from alcohol (the plum brandy is too good), these religious practices still formed part of distinct social textures. Especially in the countryside, many cultural distinctions remain. For Muslims, these differences may be apparent in religious-based features such as eating baklava at the end of the annual fast; in more cultural ones such as wearing a fez; or in decorative ones such as slight differences of detail on various local ceremonial clothes.

Islam's most substantial impact has been in the realm of values, not ritual. Hospitality, honesty, and cleanliness have pervaded the lives of Muslims, practicing or not. This coda of relationships helps explain the Bosnian mindset, in which a neighbor's differences are a simple fact of life, not a threat.

The mixture of tolerance and necessity that had ensured coexistence in Bosnia was not matched by political organizing after the collapse of the communist system. The blame for this lies with the ruling parties in Belgrade and Zagreb, who set up affiliated nationalist parties in Bosnia, with designs on dividing up the country. The blame also lies heavily on Izetbegovic, who set up the Muslim Party for Democratic Action shortly after being released from prison in 1988. (Some extremists in the party did hope for a Muslim-dominated state, pushing a more liberal wing to split off into a secular party.) And Bosnians themselves share responsibility for voting in the first free elections in 1990 predominantly along national lines.

A central explanation for the nationalist political polarization throughout Yugoslavia in the early 1990s lies in the huge ideological, economic, and social chasm left by the collapse of communism. The liberating demise of communism shattered most of the ways in which people had organized and identified themselves. In particular, the collapse of an entire economic system spread fear into everyday lives.

Two new organizing principles presented themselves. The first was a liberal democracy with an uncertain open market and a complex notion of citizenship. This option, dependent on an active, well-informed civil society, was fatally handicapped by the country's lack of democratic experience and seriously weakened in its lack of easy answers.

In this distorted and explosive vacuum, the second option, a nationalist politics, provided a new sense of identity. Unfortunately, it also provided a platform for dangerous populist chauvinist politicians. With an ugly tendency to polarize opposing groups, nationalism spread easily among peoples accustomed to accepting state authority. In Belgrade and Zagreb in particular, hate-filled propaganda infected the major media, playing up nationalist conflicts and creating widespread fear. (In Bosnia, the parties, especially the Serbian Democratic Party, sought to splinter the existing media organizations along ethnic lines. Several media resisted, and a multiethnic staff still produces Sarajevo's *Oslobodjenje*.)

Historically, Bosnia had held together by resisting strict definitions of its people and by delicately balancing itself between Croatia and Serbia. These fine lines could no longer be walked. At a notorious summit in 1991, Serbian president Slobodan Milosevic and Croatian president Franjo Tudjman negotiated a detailed plan for dividing up the country, leaving "just a little bit of Bosnia," as Tudjman put it, for the Muslims.

20

It is the international community, particularly the European Community, that bears responsibility for finally sparking the nightmare.

Inside Bosnia, the parties established a power-sharing government based on a collective presidency, with Izetbegovic, leader of the largest party, as president.

Crushed into Cantons

Given Bosnia's ethnic commingling, the prospect of a Bosnian war was horrifying to contemplate. In early 1992, as if oblivious to the risks, the United Nations even placed the headquarters of its ex-Yugoslav operations in the neutral zone of Sarajevo, only to see it fall a few months later, like the rest of the city, under heavy shelling.

Yet it is the international community, particularly the European Community, that bears responsibility for finally sparking the nightmare. Led by Germany, the selective recognition of Croatia by other countries—well before Serb minority rights were secured or any idea of a comprehensive regional settlement had been raised—tossed away the most important political mediation lever. It also compelled Bosnia, which couldn't remain in a new Yugoslavia made up of Serbia and Montenegro, to hold an independence referendum in February 1992. Given the polarization at the time, the result was predictable: Muslims and Croats voted for independence from Yugoslavia, and a Serb boycott destroyed the power-sharing government.

Determined to preserve the boundaries of Bosnia-Herzegovina, Western governments extracted an agreement from Belgrade and Zagreb to leave the borders untouched in return for the right to define spheres of influence in the republic. Thus, in February 1992, the European Community gave official birth to the project of cantonization. More than a year of war later, this idea, renewed as the Vance-Owen plan to divide Bosnia into 10 ethnically determined provinces, remains at the top of the international agenda—and impossible to impose.

The plan is a form of apartheid. In a country with no ethnically homogeneous territories of any great size, it would relegate about 40 percent of the population (by prewar demographics) to minority status. Such a proposal could only lead to the mass relocation of populations. The measures known as "ethnic cleansing"—from detention camps and murders to mass rapes and the shelling of Sarajevo—are the explicit aim, not the consequence, of the war. This extraordinary violence has been essential to instill widespread hatred and fear and destroy any ideal of living together as Bosnians. Rather than "cleansing," the war has strengthened homogenization—scarring the variegated prewar map of Bosnia with the deep stains of chauvinistic ethnicity, poorly approximated by the Vance-Owen maps.

In spring 1993, the conflict hurtled toward some kind of crescendo. Most Sarajevans survived the harsh winter, but about 11,000 died from shelling or from the cold, nearly every structure in the city was ravaged, and the siege continued. In eastern Bosnia, Serb forces maintained a stranglehold on the last Bosnian-held towns that might block a land corridor from their stronghold in the east to Serbia proper. In the west, the border between Croatia and the strongly Croatian areas of Herzegovina all but melted away as Mostar, the major city in the area, was devastated in Muslim-Croat battles. The peace process gained signatures here and there on artfully crafted con-

Split, Croatia

KEVIN WEAVER

21

stitutional and cease-fire documents, but at every turn its efforts on the ground—from airdrops to no-fly zones to aid convoys—faltered in contradictions and controversies.

As Bosnia disintegrated, the international debate was stuck in a rut. Are the cantons the right size and shape? What about lifting the one-sided arms embargo on the Bosnians? Should the world "intervene"?

All along, these have been the wrong questions. Even with the displacement of up to 40 percent of the population, the most creative cartographers couldn't devise maps acceptable to both the Bosnian government and the Serb forces. The sterile yes/no debate on intervention only fed paralysis, as the new U.S. administration fell in with the view of other Western governments that nothing could be done.

In fact, much had already been done. Nearly every diplomatic step had encouraged ethnic homogenization. Most scandalously, the arms embargo had been imposed as part of an ostensibly forceful mediation process, but there had never been any faith or forcefulness in the process. In other words, outside governments had denied Bosnians the right to self-defense while offering nothing in return. In short, they became directly complicit in the genocide. Without doubt, the region's complexities and the fascist-like regimes in Belgrade and Zagreb make mediation extraordinarily difficult. But Western governments failed to achieve a peaceful, just solution because they never sought one.

Why this is so is certainly a troubling and complex question, but the history of Bosnia and the day-to-day reality prior to the war make it clear that a positive resolution requires putting a priority on civil and democratic measures rather than on maps or signatures. It would mean comprehending extreme ethnic politics not as an inevitable result of historic animosities and the

post-communist transformation but as the deliberate manufacture of vicious populist leaders. It would mean spending as much time and political capital locating and nurturing forces for progressive civil politics as have been expended identifying primary individual culprits.

A constructive Balkan policy would have made an international transitional authority or trusteeship the starting point of negotiations. It then would have sought demilitarization, negotiated constitutional provisions, and debated regional decentralization. It would have demanded, and compelled, the opening of besieged cities, especially Sarajevo, as an historical example of multicultural coexistence and a living proof of any effort's political aims. It would have supported independent media—essential to reducing fear and reorganizing progressive forces.

Simplest of all, the policy would have abandoned the rhetoric of "ethnic sides." In the worst self-fulfilling prophecy, the failure to recognize the diversity and complexity of Bosnia has ensured its people's devastation and degradation, seeding the region with ethnic chauvinism and resentment for conflicts to come.

Anthony Borden directs the Institute for War & Peace Reporting, a non-profit organization seeking to inform international debate through alternative news and analysis from regions at war. He is editor of "WarReport," IWPR's bulletin on the crisis in the Balkans. This article draws heavily on conversations with Zoran Pajic of Sarajevo University.

Bosnia Resources:
Ivo Banac, *The National Question in Yugoslavia*, Cornell University Press, 1984.
Breakdown: *War and Construction in Yugoslavia*, Institute for War and Peace Reporting, 1993.
High Poulton, *The Balkans: Minorities and States in Conflict*, Minority Rights Group, 1991.
Sabrina P. Ramet, *Nationalism and Federalism in Yugoslavia, 1962–1991*, Indiana University Press, 1992.
Cornelia Sorabji, "Ethnic War in Bosnia?" *Radical Philosophy*, Spring 1993.

BY WADE DAVIS

Death of a People: Logging in the Penan Homeland

WADE DAVIS

It is just after dawn and the sound of gibbons runs through the forest canopy. The smoke of cooking fires mingles with the mist. A hunting party returns, and the movement of the men reveals that they have killed a wild pig. One dart and the people eat for a week.

This mountaintop, where generations of Penan have come to pray, looks out over a pristine rain forest, past the clear headwaters of one of Sarawak's ancient rivers to distant mountains that rise toward the heart of Borneo. There on the horizon, coming over the mountains from seven directions and descending into the valley, are the scars of advancing logging roads. The nearest is six miles from this encampment of nomadic Penan. When the wind is right, you can hear the sound of chain saws, even at night.

Sarawak

Virtually no place in Penan territory is free of the sound of machinery. If the Sarawak government continues to have its way, this valley will be laid waste within a year, and the people will be forced from the land.

Straddling the equator and stretching 800 miles east to west and 600 miles north to south, Borneo is the third-largest island on earth. Six major rivers and hundreds of smaller streams drain the isolated center of the island, where the mountains rise to over 13,000 feet. Eighty percent of Borneo is blanketed by extraordinarily rich tropical rain forest. Three countries claim parts of the island, with Indonesian Kalimantan encompassing the southern two-thirds; to the north the oil-rich sultanate

of Brunei is flanked by the Malaysian states of Sarawak and Sabah.

Malaysia is the world's leading exporter of tin, palm oil, rubber, and pepper—and tropical timber. Sarawak encompasses roughly 38 percent of Malaysian territory. Among some 27 distinct ethnic groups in the state, the Melanau and Malay comprise one-fifth of the population of 1.2 million; another 30 percent of the people are Chinese or recent immigrants from Southeast Asia.

Close to half the population is Dayak, a term that refers to more than a dozen indigenous peoples, including the Iban, Bidayuh, Kenyah, Kayan, Kedayan, Murut, Punan, Bisayah, Kelabit, and Penan. The Penan, in northeastern Sarawak, number about 7,600, of whom 25 percent are settled. The remainder are semi-settled or nomadic and depend on the rain forest for most of their needs. Of an estimated 100,000 indigenous people who roamed the forests of Sarawak at the turn of this century, only the nomadic Penan remain.

"From the Forest, We Get Our Life"

Related in spirit to the Mbuti pygmies of Zaire and the wandering Maku of the Amazon, the Penan long depended on the forest for food. As hunters and gatherers, they moved through the immense wooded uplands that give rise to the myriad affluents of the Baram River in Sarawak's Fourth Division. Isolated groups of Penan ranged east into Indonesian Kalimantan and north into Brunei.

Due in part to a remarkable variety of soil types, complex geology, dramatic topography, and a broad range of climates, the forests of the Penan are among the richest, most diverse on earth. They may, in fact, represent one of the oldest living terrestrial ecosystems. Moreover, Borneo has remained remarkably stable: its forests have been essentially undisturbed for millennia. Until this century, human impact was slight.

Within the traditional Penan homeland are all the major forest types to be found inland from the coast in Borneo. These forests harbor a great many endemic species. No fewer than 59 genera and 34 percent of all plant species in the world are found only on Borneo. The fauna includes 30 unique birds and 39 endemic mammals, including such rare and endangered animals as the Sumatran rhino and the orangutan. One survey of 22 acres identified over 700 species of trees, more than have been reported for all North America.

For the Penan, this forest is alive, responsive in a thousand ways to their physical and spiritual needs. Its products include roots that cleanse, leaves that cure, edible fruits and seeds, and magical plants that empower hunting dogs and dispel the forces of darkness. There are plants that yield glue to trap birds, toxic latex for poison darts, rare resins and gums for trade, twine for baskets, leaves for shelter and sandpaper, and wood to make blowpipes, boats, tools, and musical instruments. All these plants are sacred, possessed of souls and born of the same earth that gave birth to the people. "From the forest," they say, "we get our life."

The Penan view the forest as an intricate, living network. Imposed from their imagination and experience is a geography of the spirit that delineates time-honored territories and ancient routes that resonate with the place names of rivers and mountains, caves, boulders, and trees. As much as myth or memory, the landscape links past, present, and future generations.

Stewardship permeates Penan culture, dictating the manner in which Penan use and share the environment. This notion is encapsulated in *molong*, a concept that defines both a conservation ethic and a notion of ownership. To *molong* a sago palm is to harvest the trunk with care. *Molong* is climbing a tree to gather fruit rather than cutting it down, harvesting only the largest fronds of the rattan, leaving the smaller shoots so they may reach proper size in another year. Whenever the Penan *molong* a fruit tree, they place an identifying sign on it, a wooden marker or a cut of a machete. The mark signifies effective ownership and publicly states that the product is to be preserved for harvesting later. In this way, the Penan acknowledge specific resources—a clump of sago, fruit trees, dart-poison trees, rattan stands, fishing sites, medicinal plants—as familial rights that pass down through the generations.

Identifying psychologically and cosmologically with the rain forest and depending on it for their diet and technology, the Penan are skilled naturalists, with sophisticated interpretations of biological relationships. A recent and cursory examination of their plant lore suggests that the Penan recognize over 100 fruit trees, 50 medicinal plants, 8 dart poisons, and 10 plant toxins used to kill fish. These numbers probably represent but a fraction of their botanical knowledge.

Logging Is "Good for the Forest"

Today the Penan and their Dayak neighbors occupy the front lines of perhaps the most significant environmental struggle of our era—the effort to protect the integrity of the world's forests. The rate of deforestation in Malaysia is the highest in the world. In 1983, Malaysia accounted for 58 percent of the total global export of tropical logs,

25

The Penan and their Dayak neighbors occupy the front lines of perhaps the most significant environmental struggle of our era—the effort to protect the integrity of the world's forests.

with over 90 percent of the wood going to Japan, Taiwan, and South Korea. By 1985, three acres of forest were being cut every minute of every working day.

With primary forests in peninsular Malaysia becoming rapidly depleted, the industry increasingly has turned to Sarawak. Between 1963 and l985, 30 percent of the forested land of Sarawak was logged. In 1985, 670,000 acres were logged, providing 39 percent of Malaysian production and generating $1.7 billion in foreign exchange.

Logging is destroying the Penan's homeland.

Another 14.3 million acres—60 percent of Sarawak's forested land—are held in logging concessions.

The banks of the Baram River in Sarawak's Fourth Division are lined for miles with stacked logs awaiting export. Although petroleum accounts for a far larger percentage of Sarawak's export earnings than timber, revenues from the oil fields flow almost entirely to the federal government. By contrast, the Sarawak government controls the forestry sector in the state. As of

1985, licensed logging concessions in Sarawak totaled 14.2 million acres; 23 percent had been exploited and the rest was scheduled for logging.

On paper, Sarawak has one of the world's most experienced and well-funded forestry departments, and its forest policy is impressive. In practice, forest management serves the interests of the ruling elite, which uses its control of the licensing of logging concessions as a source of personal wealth and a means of retaining economic and political power. The authority to grant or deny logging concessions lies strictly with the minister of forestry. Between 1970 and 1981, and since 1985, the highly coveted forestry portfolio has been retained by the chief minister.

That the Ministry of Forestry is used for political and personal financial gain became evident in April 1987. During an election campaign, Chief Minister Datuk Patinggi Hagi Abdul Taib Mahmud announced he was freezing 25 timber concessions totaling 3 million acres, all belonging to relatives and friends of former Chief Minister Tun Abdul Rahman Yakub. Estimates of the value of these holdings ranged from $9 billion to $22 billion. In retaliation, Tun Abdul Rahman Yakub revealed the names of politicians, friends, relatives, and associates connected to Datuk Patinggi Hagi Abdul Taib Mahmud, who together controlled 4 million acres. Between them, these two factions controlled a third of Sarawak's forested land. Ironically, the two antagonists are themselves related.

The granting of logging concessions has been, in effect, a means of creating a class of instant millionaires, and nearly every member of the state assembly has become one. With a resource worth billions of dollars, the stakes are high. In a

In just a few years, the indigenous peoples of Sarawak have seen their clear streams choked with sediment and debris.

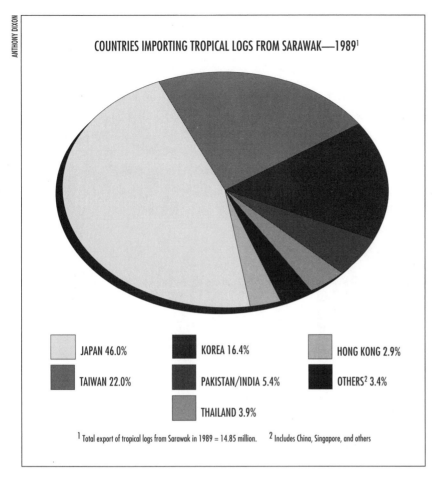

ANTHONY DIXON

COUNTRIES IMPORTING TROPICAL LOGS FROM SARAWAK—1989[1]

JAPAN 46.0%　　KOREA 16.4%　　HONG KONG 2.9%

TAIWAN 22.0%　　PAKISTAN/INDIA 5.4%　　OTHERS[2] 3.4%

THAILAND 3.9%

[1] Total export of tropical logs from Sarawak in 1989 = 14.85 million.　　[2] Includes China, Singapore, and others

extract the logs. Japan provides the insurance and financing for the Japanese ships that clog the South China Sea. Once sawn in Japan, most of the wood produced by the oldest and perhaps richest tropical rain forest on earth goes into throwaway packing crates and disposable construction forms for pouring concrete.

Studies by the World Wildlife Fund suggest that selective logging as practiced in the hill forests of Sarawak removes about 34 percent of the natural cover. Yet industry advocates maintain that selective cutting doesn't hurt the forest in the long term. Minister of the Environment and Tourism James Wong has even stated that logging is "good for the forest." When presented with scientific information suggesting otherwise, Wong replied, "I will not bow to experts. I am the expert. I was here before the experts were born."

In theory, selective logging has far less environmental impact than the clear-cutting typical of temperate rain forests. In contrast to the desolation throughout the Pacific Northwest of North America, logged areas of Sarawak remain green, rapidly flushing out with secondary vegetation that creates an illusion of paradise. But this masks the difficulty of extracting, in an environmentally sound manner, a few select trees from a given area of tropical rain forest. In practice, most logging in Sarawak occurs with little planning and

recent election, political parties spent over $24 million competing for a mere 625,000 votes. The only car factory in Sarawak produces BMWs.

Ultimate responsibility for exploiting the rain forest lies with powerful Japanese trading houses. Japan depends on Malaysia for 85 to 90 percent of its tropical wood imports; half of Sarawak's production goes north to Tokyo. In a 1984 speech, quoted in Evelyn Hong's *Natives of Sarawak,* then Malaysian federal minister Leo Moggie acknowledged that "Sarawak timber companies are dependent on these [Japanese] trading houses for their intricate line of credit." Japanese banks provide start-up loans to local logging companies. Japanese companies and Japanese aid finance the purchase of bulldozers and heavy equipment to no technical supervision. Decisions on how the trees will be cut and how they will reach the specified landing areas lie strictly with the "faller" and the operator of the bulldozer or skidder. Working on a contract basis with their income dependent on their production, these men, often poor, uneducated, and far from home, fighting off hunger with a chain saw, place little importance on the environmental implications of their actions.

Skid trails and landings have laid bare over 40% of the forest floor.

Arriving at a setting, the bulldozer operator establishes a landing and then follows the faller from log to log, skidding them one at a time, expanding his trail as the faller works deeper into the cutting block. The faller drops the trees in the direction most convenient to him. To reach them, the bulldozer must carve long, winding, and even circular tracks into the forest floor. With time at a premium, the bulldozer is constantly on the move. Every activity—turning or lifting the logs to attach the cables, pushing smaller logs together, maneuvering the bulldozer into place to begin the haul—further damages the forest.

In many parts of Sabah, skid trails and landings have laid bare over 40 percent of the forest floor. As logging removes the forest canopy, exposing the soil to rain, the compaction of the ground by the extractive process reduces the soil's

capacity to retain water. This dramatically increases erosion, which is further exacerbated by road-building techniques that pay little attention to drainage or grade.

In just a few years, the indigenous peoples of Sarawak have seen their clear streams choked with sediment and debris. The federal government's own five-year plan states that "soil erosion and siltation have become Sarawak's main water-pollution problem." In many parts of the state, rivers are permanently turbid; the impact on fish is disastrous.

"We Will Fight Back"

In 1987, Dayak anger over logging exploded. After seven years of appealing in vain to the government to end the destruction of their homelands, the Penan, on February 13, 1987, issued a firm and eloquent declaration:

We, the Penan people of the Tutoh, Limbang, and Patah rivers regions, declare: Stop destroying the forest or we will be forced to protect it. The forest is our livelihood. We have lived here before any of you outsiders came. We fished in clean rivers and hunted in the jungle. We made our sago meat and ate the fruit of trees. Our life was not easy but we lived it contentedly. Now the logging companies turn rivers to muddy streams and the jungle into devastation. Fish cannot survive in dirty rivers and wild animals will not live in devastated forest. You took advantage of our trusting nature and cheated us into unfair deals. By your doings you take away our livelihood and threaten our very lives. You make our people discontent. We want our ancestral land, the land we live off, back. We can use it in a wiser way. When you come to us, come as guests with respect. . . .

If you decide not to heed our request, we will protect our livelihood. We are a peace-loving people, but when our very lives are in danger, we will fight back. This is our message.

Like the scores of letters, appeals, and petitions sent by Dayak peoples to state and regional authorities, this proclamation was ignored, so the Penan took direct action. On March 31, 1987, armed with blowpipes, they blocked a logging road in the Tutoh River basin. In April, Kayan at Uma Bawang blockaded a road that pierced their territory.

In every instance, the barriers were flimsy, a few forest saplings bound with rattan. Their strength lay in the people behind them. These human barricades—made up of men, women, and children, the old and the young—which began as a quixotic gesture, an embarrassment to the government, grew into a potent symbol of resolve. Within eight weeks, operations in 16 logging camps had been brought to a halt. By October, Penan, Kayan, and Kelabit communities had shut down roads at 23 sites. In all, some 2,500 Penan from 26 settlements took part. For eight months, despite hunger, heat exhaustion, and harassment, the indigenous peoples maintained defiant, yet peaceful, blockades, disrupting the logging industry and frustrating authorities.

The dramatic action electrified environmentalists in Malaysia and abroad. Press coverage in Australia, Europe, and the United States stimulated concern that grew steadily into a sustained international protest. The Malaysian and Sarawak governments responded defensively, imposing severe restrictions on the media. Military and security forces were brought into play, and police joined the logging companies in dismantling the blockades.

In October 1987, Prime Minister Mahlathir Mohamad invoked the Internal Security Act to incarcerate 91 critics of his regime. Among those detained was Harrison Ngau of Sahabat Alam (Friends of the Earth) Malaysia, a Kayan environmentalist and the most vocal supporter of Dayak resistance. At the same time, 42 Kayan of Uma Bawang were arrested. They were accused of obstructing the police, wrongful restraint, and unlawfully occupying state lands. The last charge, in particular, was received bitterly. After all, the people of Uma Bawang had established a blockade on their own land to protect their legally recognized rights.

Although the dramatic police action temporarily ended the blockades, it also precipitated a battle that exposed the essential illegality of the logging. According to the Sarawak land code, native customary rights are inviolable. Since the state had granted logging concessions without a clear demarcation of customary lands, the rights of thousands of Dayak had, by definition, been compromised. On July 26, 1987, a Kayan, charged with obstructing a public thoroughfare, was acquitted: the magistrate concluded that he had blocked a road on customary land and had acted in a legitimate defense of his rights.

To protect the logging industry, the state government took legislative action. In November 1987, it added Amendment S90B to the Forest Ordinance, making it an offense for any person to obstruct the flow of traffic along any logging road. Penalties for violating Amendment S90B include two years imprisonment and a fine of over $2,000.

29

The injustice of Amendment S90B was obvious. Lolee Mirai, Penan headman of Long Leng, spoke of the purpose of the amendment: "We, who have rights to the land, were, instead, arrested, and not the timber companies who have caused damages to our land and properties. The law protects only the companies and causes us to suffer more. The law is not good. It unjustly allows outsiders and the logging companies to come and damage our land."

The government believed that blockades would never again disrupt the flow of timber. They were wrong. In May 1988 blockades went up near Long Napir, halting the logging operations of Minister Wong. Two more blockades sprang up in the Upper Baram in September, and four more

blockades were quickly dismantled. Then, in September, indigenous peoples in 19 communities in the Upper Limbang and Baram erected 12 new barricades. By the end of the fall, 4,000 Dayaks had shut down logging in nearly half of Sarawak.

By early 1990, however, the logging industry, supported by all the power of the Malaysian government, had recovered. To this day the blockades in Sarawak continue.

In a Single Generation

After years of futile lobbying and peaceful protest, the Penan look to the outside world for support. Just before the September 1989 blockades, 80 indigenous leaders signed a joint statement: "We ask for help from people all over the world. We are people with a proud culture and way of life that is built on our forest and land. Don't take our forest and culture and dignity away. We thank everyone who thinks of us and helps us, even though you are so far away. It is knowing this that keeps us alive."

Without international pressure, Sarawak is unlikely to recognize the rights of the Penan or protect their forest homeland. Authorities have indicated that they intend to maintain the forests of Sarawak as the exclusive preserve of the state and the domain of the political elite. These same authorities have made it clear that they will tolerate no opposition. Encounters with the police grow more brutal with every new blockade.

in October. Between November 1988 and January 1989, blockades occurred at seven sites, and the Sarawak Forestry Department arrested 128 Dayaks, mostly Penan.

By mid-1989, the legislation, repeated arrests, and long and expensive trials appeared to have broken the Dayak resistance. Sporadic

WADE DAVIS

"We are people with a proud culture and way of life that is built on our forest and land. Don't take our forest and culture and dignity away."

It is imperative that the global community respond to this situation. If the Penan are to have the opportunity to choose their own destiny, their forest homeland must be protected. Moreover, the interests of the Penan as well as those of neighboring Dayak peoples must be balanced with the need to protect the biological integrity of the land, now delineated by Gulung Mulu National Park, which lies at the heart of Penan territory.

The creation of a biosphere reserve is an obvious and appropriate solution. A biosphere reserve combines forest preservation with the subsistence needs of surrounding communities. Typically, a reserve consists of a series of concentric zones, with a core of permanently protected forest at the center. Moving outward is a series of increasingly intensive utilization zones. In the first zone, indigenous people can hunt, collect medicinal plants, and harvest natural products. In the next zone, people may farm and gather wood. Settlement occurs in a third zone, which acts as a buffer from encroaching development.

Local initiative and the direct involvement of national and regional authorities are critical to establishing and maintaining a biosphere reserve. Fortunately, Sarawak can meet both conditions. In 1987, an intra-governmental report of the State Task Force on Penan Affairs called for establishing two biosphere reserves for the nomadic Penan. In 1990, the Penan Association endorsed the concept, substantially increasing the proposed boundaries to surround Gunung Mulu National Park and to include a large portion of the northeastern section of the Fourth Division.

To date, however, the Sarawak government has neither implemented the task force's recommendations nor endorsed the biosphere-reserve concept. Instead, government representatives often suggest that environmentalists and anthropologists want to sequester indigenous peoples in living zoos. "No one," Wong stated, "has the ethical right to deprive the Penan of their right to socioeconomic development and assimilation into the mainstream of Malaysian society."

Wong's statement is true, but so is its corollary. Penan surely have the right to determine the degree to which they enter Malaysian society, even as they respect their obligation to protect the integrity of Penan civilization. That many Penan still desire to pursue their traditional subsistence activities is evident in the Penan Association's numerous public statements.

The issue, then, hangs in the balance. The creation of a biosphere reserve, the meaningful recognition of Dayak rights, and the adoption of sustainable forestry practices all will depend on the actions of each and every one of us who cares about the fate of the Penan, other Dayak peoples, and their forest homelands. Ultimately, we are all responsible.

Today, throughout Sarawak, the sago and rattan, the palms, lianas, and fruit trees lie crushed on the forest floor. The hornbill has fled with the pheasants, and as the trees fall in the forest, a unique way of life, morally inspired, inherently right, and effortlessly pursued for centuries, is collapsing in a single generation.

Wade Davis is executive director of the Endangered People's Project. His books include *The Serpent and the Rainbow* (Simon and Schuster, 1985), *Passage of Darkness* (UNC Press, 1988), and *Shadows in the Sun* (Lone Pine Press, 1992). This essay is adapted from *Penan: Voice for the Borneo Rainforest* (Pomegranate Press, 1993).

31

Penan Resources

Peter Brosius, *The Axiological Presence of Death: Penan Geng Death Names,* University of Michigan doctorai dissertation, 1992.

Marcus Colchester, *Pirates, Squatters, and Poachers: The Political Ecology of Dispossession of the Native Peoples of Sarawak,* New series of Survival International Documents No. 7, 1989.

Wade Davis and Thom Henley, *Penan: Voice for the Borneo Rainforest,* Pomegranate Press, 1993.

Evelyn Hong, *Native Of Sarawak: Survival in Borneo's Vanishing Forests,* Institut Masyarakat, 1987.

World Rainforest Movement, 8 Chapel Row, Chadlington, OX 7 3NA, England.

Sahabat Alam (Friends of the Earth) Malaysia, 43 Salween Rd., 10050 Penang, Malaysia.

Endangered Peoples Project, P.O. Box 1516, Station A, Vancouver, BC Canada, V6C 2M7.

Rainforest Action Network, 450 Sansome St., Suite 700, San Francisco, CA 94111.

How You Can Help:

In *Earth in the Balance*, Vice President Al Gore describes the Penan as "resistance fighters" and refers to their struggle with the logging interests of Sarawak as the "front lines of the war against nature now raging throughout the world."

WADE DAVIS

As a senator, Vice President Gore twice received Penan delegations on Capitol Hill. On April 2, 1992, he introduced a resolution into the Senate urging the United States "to call upon the Government of Malaysia to act immediately in defense of the environment of Sarawak by ending the uncontrolled exploitation of the rain forests of Sarawak, by reducing the annual rate of timber cutting by at least two-thirds, and by formally recognizing and upholding the customary land rights and the internationally established human rights of all indigenous peoples of such Government."

The resolution also requested that "it should be the policy of the United States to call upon the Government of Japan to investigate the activities of certain private companies of Japan in contributing to the destruction of the Sarawak rain forest, and therefore to the destruction of the culture of the indigenous peoples of Sarawak."

Vice President Gore is now in a position to encourage the governments of both the United States and Malaysia to act. The best hope for the Penan and other indigenous nations of Sarawak is the eloquence and good will of the Vice President. Write to him and urge that he continue his support for their cause by complementing his powerful rhetoric with concrete diplomatic initiatives.

The Ju/'hoan Bushmen: Indigenous Rights in a New Country

BY MEGAN BIESELE

L ong before Namibia became an independent country, the leaders of the liberation movement in South African-run South West Africa knew they would inherit a difficult legacy in minority rights from the previous apartheid government. Kaire Mbuende, now Namibia's Deputy Minister of Agriculture, wrote in a preindependence position paper that the region's Bushman peoples were particularly disadvantaged because of the violence with which apartheid had transformed them into landless wards of an uncaring state. What sets Bushman societies apart, he wrote, "is not that their tradiational way of life has survived but the cruelty through which it was transformed."

Mbuende identified two successive processes of domination responsible for the transformation. The first is South Africa's homelands

(Bantustan) policy. In 1970, the government's Odendaal Commission, which limited ethnic groups to "homelands" (incidentally greatly expanding the land under white commercial control), greatly reduced the land area on which Bushmen had traditionally made a decent living through skilled hunting and gathering. The second process of domination was the government's internal settlement schemes. Under South African rule, immigrant settlers, both black and white, dispossessed the great majority of Bushman groups, and the preindependence Directorate of Nature Conservation deprived them of many of their traditional foraging grounds. Many Bushman groups, such as the Khoe of West Caprivi, were peremptorily resettled out of game reserve areas into places where they knew little about local wild foods and had no access to land on which to earn a living. Both processes—the Bantustans and resettlement—were excuses for dispossessing Africans of their territories and for increasing white ownership of the most valuable commercial land.

Since the South West African Peoples Organization (SWAPO) came to power in March 1990, President Sam Nujoma and his government have pursued vigorous affirmative action policies toward Bushman peoples to redress some of the offenses committed when South Africa controlled the country. Practical considerations, however, including the fragmentation and dispersal of most Bushman communities under apartheid, have made affirmative action difficult to put into practice. In Namibia, only 2,000 out of some 35,000 Bushmen still possess a portion of their ancestral territory; in Botswana over two-thirds of the 47,000 Bushmen have lost all their land.

The exception to the general rule of dispossession are the 2,000 Ju/'hoan Bushmen of Namibia, who live in a region known until 1990 as Eastern Bushmanland. Today the Ju/'hoansi retain a small but significant part of their ancestral land and live in intact communities. At one point, Nyae Nyae, their traditional name for the area, encompassed 27,000 square miles, although it covers less than one-tenth of that area now.

By their own efforts, the Ju/'hoansi are ennobling the very word *Bushman*, long a pejorative

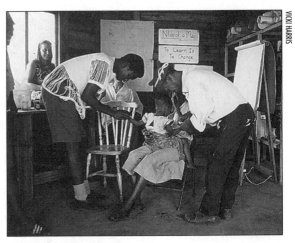

Village health worker

term. (Government officials, development and aid organizations, and scholars often call these people San, but that word too has had negative connotations.) Aware of their historical privileges, which derive from geographical isolation and other factors, the Ju/'hoansi have taken an exemplary role in regard to other Bushmen in Namibia and, indeed, in southern Africa.

In fact, many of the positive human-rights statements to be made about Bushmen in Namibia apply only to the Ju/'hoansi. In the rare cases when other Bushmen can find jobs, they are unpaid pastoral serfs or poorly paid agricultural laborers. Most Bushman peoples live as squatters around towns or on farms belonging to both black and white communal and commercial farmers.

Moreover, although Bushmen receive special attention from the government, their land rights remain precarious. Although secure land tenure for these former foraging peoples is literally a matter of life and death, that goal seems unattainable unless they gain a more central role in national and international politics. Many interests, from land-hungry pastoralists to the government's need to find a place to settle people returning from exile, threaten Bushman lands and livelihoods. Dangers to Bushman survival are thus profound, involving their social and economic situation as well as their status as a minority.

Systematic surveys would be a necessary first step in knowing how to ameliorate the Bushmen's human-rights situation, but few studies have documented the conditions of life among the many dispossessed Bushmen living in rural or urban slums. In addition, communities and even families are fragmented, which limits the opportunities for Bushman peoples to organize themselves to press for better conditions. Beyond that, it is difficult to generalize about the many Bushman groups, who speak at least a half dozen languages. And even this fails to consider the many Bushman peoples dispersed in small groups on other peoples' farms all over Namibia, and in neighboring Botswana, Angola, and Zambia as well.

By contrast, the well-documented situation of the Nyae Nyae Ju/'hoansi, living in their original communities around the administrative center at Tjum!kui, provides a core of information—and a programmatic model—for advancing the territorial, political, economic, and cultural rights of Namibia's Bushman minority. Since 1986, these indigenous people of Nyae Nyae have forged a powerful grassroots political organization, the Nyae Nyae Farmers' Cooperative (NNFC), which is even beginning to reach out to the other, more fragmented communities.

Land Rights and Survival

For Bushman people, with virtually no resources except those in the natural landscape, the question of land rights is one literally of survival. For many decades, as we have seen, the land-tenure situation for Bushman peoples in Namibia has been precarious.

The Ju/'hoansi of Nyae Nyae were an exception to this rule. In the 1980s, the Ju/'hoansi used local organizing to preserve a fraction of their traditional land. In 1987, the NNFC defeated a nature-conservation plan to create a game reserve for tourists in Nyae Nyae.

Up until the National Conference on Land Reform and the Land Question held in Windhoek, Namibia, in 1991, the NNFC's priority was to secure Ju/'hoan tenure in Eastern Bushmanland. At this meeting, an official and groundbreaking event for the new country, the NNFC worked to inform the government about the Ju/'hoansi's traditional system of land use, hoping that its long-term viability could act as a model for rational land allocation for communal land occupied by Bushman peoples. The system regulates the numbers of people who have access to limited resources such as bush foods and water and makes community sharing of mobile game possible. It also fosters, through agreement, close cooperation among kin-based groups.

The prospects for secure land tenure in Nyae Nyae took a significant step forward at the 1991 land conference. One resolution that was adopted promised special protection for the land rights of Bushman communities. Then-Minister of Lands, Resettlement, and Rehabilitation Marco Hausiku also informally assured the NNFC that the system

35

> Many interests, from land-hungry pastoralists to the government's need to find a place to settle people returning from exile, threaten Bushman lands and livelihoods.

Slim assurances of land rights, dependent on a sympathetic land minister and in the absence of definitive legislation, represents a shadow of the security Ju/'hoan Bushmen need.

would provide the basis for land allocations in Nyae Nyae in the future. He added that other Bushman areas, which might have different systems, would also receive attention to traditional land-use patterns.

After the conference, NNFC delegates posed several questions for Hausiku, President Nujoma, and SWAPO leader Moses Garoeb about implementing its resolutions. These questions remain central to ensuring Bushman land rights:

• How will the government assure that "economic expediency" not take precedence over the special protections guaranteed for Bushman land rights? In other words, legislation is crucial; communal land rights must be as secure as those for any individual landholdings in Namibia.

• What concrete protection will the government give to communities in the event of encroachments on their land, for instance, by people who have more cattle?

• How will the government ensure that local people are represented adequately on any land boards that might be established to allocate rights to agricultural land, water, and grazing areas.

The Ju/'hoansi have received no definite answers to these questions. The Ministry of Lands has set up a "technical committee" to investigate putting the conference resolutions into practice, but it has not dealt with communal lands. Thus the legal status of Nyae Nyae lands, like that of all communal lands, remains ambiguous throughout Namibia.

One important precedent regarding illegal settlement on communal lands has been set. During an August 1991 visit to Nyae Nyae, President Nujoma declared that anyone wishing to settle on communal land must receive the permission not only of the Ministry of Lands but also of the area's traditional leaders. The NNFC soon had the opportunity to test whether the government would back up this promise when settlers from nearby Hereroland came without permission to three Ju/'hoan communities and began to water their cattle from community boreholes. After consulting with the illegal settlers, co-op members, backed by a promise of support from local police and the regional commissioner, escorted them peacefully back to the Hereroland border. Minister Hausiku affirmed in *The Namibian* newspaper that the Ju/'hoansi's action was legal and gave it his endorsement.

Unfortunately, this slim assurance of Nyae Nyae land rights, dependent on having a sympathetic Land Minister and in the absence of any definitive legislation, represents but a shadow of the security the Ju/'hoan Bushmen need. In 1992, Hausiku transferred to another ministry, and it is unclear whether his successor, or the Ministry of Lands in general, will honor the spirit of the 1991 conference as they prepare legislative packages for the National Assembly. And, of course, more fragmented Bushman communities, representing far more people, have far less assurance that they will have access to the land they need to survive.

Political Rights: Lessons to Learn

In 1989, when UN advisors arrived in Namibia to facilitate the transition to independence, Bushman peoples were among the beneficiaries of the UN's information campaign leading to Namibia's first free election. However, the dispersal of too few advisors, on top of generally low school attendance and literacy rates, made it hard for Bushmen to learn about their political rights. Moreover, some farmers in isolated areas have preferred to keep their Bushman laborers in ignorance so that they won't agitate for better wages or other benefits.

As with land rights, sharing information about political rights has been more effective in the Nyae Nyae area due to efforts of the NNFC. But even in Nyae Nyae disinformation campaigns by the opposing political parties are common, as they were before the first election. Such actions severely undermine the possibility of creating an informed electorate.

Dealing a further blow to Nyae Nyae political rights, in 1993 Namibia's Delimitation Commission announced that Tjum!kui, one of nine main regional groups, would be lumped together with much of Hereroland in a new Otjozondjupa Region. Though the few people living in the Nyae Nyae area couldn't have expected the full regional autonomy that might ensure the viability of the *n!ore* system, very different land-use and leadership patterns are now included within the one region. This situation will doubtless lead to problems. In particular, it is hard to imagine how the Ju/'hoansi, who are egalitarian, traditionally leaderless former foragers, will compete successfully in local governments with hierarchically organized Herero pastoralists who have vowed publicly to take over Bushman lands. Numbers are also an issue here: the Herero outnumber Ju/'hoansi by a factor of more than three in the new region.

Bushman groups incorporated into other new regions will experience similar difficulties in establishing effective local political voices. In such cases, there are not only very low population numbers to contend with but also language differences and salient differences in cultural style concerning representative leadership.

Nevertheless, Namibian Bushman peoples are undergoing a politicization process. Again, this awakening is led to some extent by the example of the Nyae Nyae Farmers' Cooperative, which has gained a voice in local and national forums and has informed itself about securing government services. By July 1992, this grassroots group had established enough strength to convene an

MELISSA HECKLER

Nyae Nyae preschool

environmental planning conference on its own turf that drew the participation of ministers and other government officers.

The 1992 meeting established firm guidelines for local control of natural resources, a process in line with the realization by the world's indigenous minorities that they can and must vocally demand their political and environmental rights. Seen this way, the 1991 National Land Conference was the first in a series of national and international venues

37

The families of Bushman workers on farms and cattle posts often must work for the owner, usually without pay.

prominently to include Namibian Bushman peoples and their concerns. By 1992 Bushmen were chairing the conferences themselves.

Economic Rights: Depending on the Tolerance of Others

In their employment on farms and cattle posts, Namibia's Bushmen face continuing discrimination. Wage levels are very low, and employers tend to pay them only irregularly. Most Bushman herders receive few, if any, work benefits such as health care or vacations. The families of workers on farms and cattle posts often must work for the owner, usually without pay. Some Bushman herders, echoing the conditions of marginal workers everywhere, say they are the last people hired and the first fired, with no recourse.

All too often, a general cultural prejudice against Bushmen as "lazy and shiftless" prevails in farm labor systems. Rural people in general in Namibia haven't been able to press with any success for better treatment by the livestock industry, in which employers vehemently resist any efforts to improve wages and working conditions. On the Gobabis Farms to the south—to which many Ju/'hoansi were taken, far away from their families in Nyae Nyae, during the 1950s in the process known as "blackbirding"—workers are treated extremely poorly. Few have any chance for economic advancement. In some other cases, of course, Bushman workers receive a decent wage, but this and other benefits depend on the personalities and whims of farm employers, just as land rights now depend on having sympathetic individuals in high government offices.

Well over 70 percent of Namibian Bushmen are unemployed. This would not be as serious as

it sounds if they still had access to land on which to hunt and gather or to farm for a living. But because the great majority of Bushmen are also landless, they must rely on the tolerance of others. As a result, their economic rights will be severely threatened for a long time to come.

Wage discrimination must be one of the first abuses to end as Bushmen negotiate their new political identity. A commitment on the part of Namibia to creating parity in wage scales for farm workers might help. Wage discrimination against Bushman workers in Botswana and some other neighboring countries could come to an end, too, if Namibia embarrassed these countries by forging better labor policies of its own.

Honoring Diversity

Against this dismal background, cultural continuity and language rights provide Namibia's Bushman peoples with a ray of hope. Under its Basic Education Reform Program, the Ministry of Education and Culture has made a substantial commitment to minority-language education for the first three years of school. This commitment echoes sound educational policy: in the developing world, it has become clear that the best route to literacy lies in gaining proficiency first in the mother tongue, then generalizing this skill to English or another national language. Basic Education Reform includes reinforcing the Ju/'hoan language as a pilot project; future educational efforts will extend this example in other Bushman communities and for other languages.

Government policies also aim to address, rapidly and substantially, the question of Bushman school attendance rates, which are the worst of any ethnic group in Namibia. The hiring of a few Bushman teachers, under affirmative-action policies, has increased greatly the attractiveness of formal education to Bushman students and their parents. The Namibian Ministry of Education and Culture is establishing literacy classes in Bushman communities as part of a nationwide attempt to raise literacy rates, and people of all ages are enrolling.

Again, a meeting has been key to advancing Bushman rights. A 1992 regional conference in Windhoek on Bushmen and development provided much impetus for these indigenous peoples to trust that the new government will respect their cultures and languages. Breathtaking in scope, the resolutions that emerged—on topics ranging from education and culture, to land rights and social welfare, to employment and water resources—chart an ambitious path toward social equality and dignity for Bushman peoples, as well as toward a sustainable future for them as citizens of new African states. Foremost among the resolutions are those seeking to ensure Bushman people secure land on which to pursue self-determination and resolutions meant to establish for them a voice in their countries, a voice both genuinely heard and genuinely their own.

This and other conferences held in Namibia mark the start of a creative dialogue both among Bushman peoples themselves and with their national and international friends. This dialogue partakes of an agenda appearing among indigenous minorities everywhere and represents a chance to prove that strength in building a new country can come from honoring cultural diversity.

Nevertheless, ideas, whether aired in national or international settings, can take a very long time to translate into reality at the grassroots level. This is particularly true for a highly visible minority such as the Bushman peoples, who, throughout history, have been alternately mythologized as noble savages and pushed aside by more aggressive economic interests and social systems. It will be important for Namibia's record on minority rights that the progressive stance generally taken by the SWAPO-led government continue and grow. It is just as important that officials and the general population prove that they take minority rights seriously at the community level.

The single most vulnerable area for Bushmen remains the lack of land-rights legislation, along with the closely related question of representation in local governments. Because African countries have tended to let commitments on these issues slide for minorities after the initial enthusiasm and publicity surrounding independence, other countries must continue to focus attention on Namibia and help it sustain, in practice and in detail, its present good intentions. Even in an enlightened political climate, the continuing threat to the survival of the Bushmen can't be overestimated.

Megan Biesele, a social anthropologist, works for the Ju/'hoan Bushmen as a translator and is documenting their events and meetings for their grassroots organization, the Nyae Nyae Farmers' Cooperative.

39

How You Can Help

Contributions and information exchanges may be facilitated through the following organizations:

Nyae Nyae Development Foundation of Namibia, P.O. Box 9026, Windhoek, Namibia (264)61-36327; fax: (264)61-225997.

Kalahari Peoples Fund, c/o James Ebert, 3100 Ninth, NW, Albuquerque, NM 87107 (505)344-9676; fax: (505)344-2444.

Kalahari Support Group, c/o Keizersgracht 682, 1017 ET Amsterdam, Netherlands (31)2208-96524.

BY WINONA LADUKE

WAR OF THE RICES

It's a misty morning on Big Chippewa Lake. An Anishinabe couple drags a canoe to the water's edge. The woman boards in front and sits on her haunches. The man pushes the canoe off and jumps in behind her. As they pole toward the wild rice beds, they can feel the September dampness. The man rises, head just above the tall stalks of rice. The woman pulls the rice over her lap with a stick and gently raps it with another. This is the wild rice harvest on White Earth Reservation. The Chippewa, Anishinabeg as we refer to ourselves, call the rice *manomin*—"gift from the creator." The August-to-September time of rice ripening and harvest is *manomine-ike-gisis*, "the rice-making moon."

There are many wild rice lakes on our 1,300-square-mile reservation in Minnesota. Big Chippewa Lake, about 50 miles east of Moorhead, is a favorite harvesting location for many families and a prime feeding ground for ducks and Canada geese. Big Rice Lake, the largest lake on the reservation, can yield 200,000 pounds of rice. In a good year, more than 100 canoes might be on Big Rice Lake. Names like Bonga, Big Bear, Ponsford, and Rice Lake Landing all denote traditional harvest areas for families and villages on the reservation.

The Anishinabe live in five U.S. states—Montana, North Dakota, Minnesota, Wisconsin, and Michigan—and three Canadian provinces—Saskatchewan, Manitoba, and Ontario. The area, often referred to as "the wild rice bowl," contains a balanced ecosystem of marshes, lakes, and streams that has supported Anishinabe culture for centuries. We still maintain this land and preserve it under treaties and agreements with the British, Canadian, and U.S. governments. Five Anishinabe reservations in Wisconsin and Minnesota contain 40 percent of the world's natural wild rice beds, and these governments have reserved many of the region's lakes for the traditional harvest of wild rice.

Although *Zizania aquatica* is called "wild," Anishinabeg play an active role in maintaining and growing this rice. We use dams to keep the beds from becoming too deep in the spring, which prevents the rice sprouts from reaching the surface, or too shallow during the dry season. We also hand-seed rice beds and sometimes tie the rice heads in bundles to prevent the early ripening grains from dropping off before harvest. We're bound to the crop culturally and spiritually. "We've done it for so long it just comes naturally," says Brian Wichern, a ricer from Big Bear Landing on Big Rice Lake.

Two things threaten our cultural and economical relationship with wild rice. The first is the degradation of the wild rice ecosystem by industrial society. Pollution is reducing yields and destroying natural rice beds.

The second is the theft of our "intellectual property." Conventionally farmed, paddy-grown "wild" rice now dominates the market and has pushed the price of real wild rice so low that many lakes go unharvested, severely eroding the economic base that lake rice provided for Anishinabeg. Of about 12 to 15 million pounds of wild

COURTESY OF MANITOK WILD RICE CO.

rice produced each year, only about 300,000 pounds are hand harvested in Minnesota. Paddy producers there and in California grow about 4 million pounds and 6 million pounds, respectively. Canadian lake-harvested rice accounts for 3 million pounds. "Wild" rice is now even being produced in Eastern Europe.

The contributions of Anishinabeg—and other indigenous people—to Western agriculture, medicine, and the arts have yet to be recognized, much less paid for. Because the "market" does not value or compensate us for our knowledge—our resource—we cannot make a living in traditional ways. When a native arrow poison shows up in a pharmaceutical giant's "discovery," or when university-trained scientists cultivate wild rice strains we developed over centuries, these uses raise the question of rights. Western law protects the intellectual property rights of researchers, corporations, universities, government agencies. Indigenous people deserve the same rights.

41

"We are doing something that our ancestors did, and we are doing it the same way. How do you quantify the loss of that?"

Endangered Resource

For native peoples, ricing season traditionally started well before the rice-making moon. They prepared harvesting tools—ricing pole, ricing sticks, winnowing baskets—from wood and birch bark. Each lake had a ricing boss who monitored the water levels and the crop's progress and determined when to prepare the rice beds for harvest.

Each White Earth family had a designated ricing area. In the weeks before the harvest, families would prepare the campsites, secure their equipment, and carefully tie off the rice. Because rice ripens at different rates, many families would harvest on more than one lake. Each lake produces rice with slightly different characteristics. The length and shape of the grain varies, as does color, which ranges from gold to various shades of green, red, or brown.

Pairs of ricers started early and worked until midday, letting the rice "rest" for the afternoon. The afternoons were reserved for drying, parching, and "jigging," activities in which both young and old would participate. The rice was set out to dry on large pieces of birch bark borrowed from the sides of houses. The dried rice then was parched in a cauldron, giving it a distinctive flavor and a more uniform, darker color.

Next the parched rice was placed in a shallow pit lined with birch bark and deerskin. Children wearing new moccasins would "jig" the rice, dancing on the grains to separate the hulls from the kernels. The jigged rice was winnowed in a large birch bark basket, and the process was repeated until all the rice was cleaned.

The main tools of the rice harvest are still canoes, poles, and threshing sticks, but much of the harvest is now machine processed, as in the Mahkoonce Corner plant on the White Earth Reservation. But whatever the processing method, the first rice is used for a Megwetch Manomin Feast to celebrate the harvest and to give thanks.

Industrial and agricultural pollution and altered water levels from damming rivers and draining wetlands for development have taken a toll on rice production. In northern Minnesota, for instance, the Army Corps of Engineers has maneuvered water levels for downstream cities and the tourist industry. In Wisconsin, industrialized cranberry production has caused a seepage of chemicals into some wild rice beds.

The rice beds also face competition from proliferating weeds that have choked off many natural rice beds. "Exotics such as Eurasian mil foil have completely taken over many Northern lakes," says Dave Reinke, business manager of Manitok Wild Rice, a company that markets native hand-harvested rice. "Sport fishermen using exotics such as carp and rusty crayfish for bait have introduced those species to isolated lakes. The carp reduce rice stands by eating the seed rice that falls into the water. Also, because they are bottom feeders, they sometimes make the water so turbid that the rice seedlings are unable to get enough light to sprout." In Wisconsin, rusty crayfish have wiped out so many natural wild rice beds that the state has declared natural wild rice a scarce resource.

Paddy Rice vs. Wild Rice

Even more threatening to the Anishinabe way of life is domesticated wild rice—"tame" rice to Indians.

In the mid-1960s, Uncle Ben's and other large food processors started to add wild rice to some products, creating a huge market for wild rice and spurring efforts to mass-produce it. At first, Minnesota farmers made rice paddies by flooding cropland and transplanting seedlings from nearby lakes. The yields were mediocre until University of Minnesota researchers developed a wild rice strain that thrived in artificial conditions and could be harvested easily by machine.

This paddy rice differs from traditional wild rice in two important ways. First, as food historian Raymond Sokolov points out in *Natural History Magazine*, "Its seeds do not shatter at maturity and fall on the ground, and all the seeds mature at the same time." That makes it feasible to harvest the rice mechanically. Second, says Sokolov, "Wild wild rice shatters—that's what made the Indian method possible—the threshing stick gives the seeds the last nudge they need and sends them shattering into the canoe. . . . [This] leaves the plants intact so that the immature seeds can continue to ripen for later harvesting."

In the mid-1970s, some Minnesota paddy growers and marketers took a chance and began to move wild rice production to California's commercial rice fields. Because wild rice won't sprout unless it is exposed to the cold, the growers placed the seed in cold storage before planting in the Sacramento Valley.

The gamble paid off. Yields tripled those in Minnesota. The drier climate eliminated some diseases, and the advanced technology in place for California's white-rice industry lowered production costs. In addition, many white-rice growers were receiving federal "set-aside" payments to withhold land from production and trim crop surpluses. Because wild rice technically is a grass, farmers could plant it, sell it, and keep the set-

aside money to boot. Paddy wild rice production boomed.

By 1977, paddy rice represented more than three-fourths of the "wild rice" crop. In 1986, California produced more than 11 million pounds, exceeding the U.S. demand. Federal officials closed the set-aside loophole, and the bottom fell out of the wild rice market. The industry was swamped with producers and a surplus crop.

On the White Earth Reservation, the surplus wreaked havoc. The price for green rice at the lakeside dropped from a dollar a pound in 1986 to between 35 and 45 cents a pound by 1989. Even so, native ricers were hard-pressed to find a buyer. "People used to count on rice harvests to buy school clothes for their kids, chain saws for winter, fix their cars, and take care of basics," says Frank Bibeau, president of the Minnesota Hand Harvested Wild Rice Association. "That money went into those Northern rural communities and boosted everybody's income, Indian and non-Indian alike." The loss of rice income on reservations, where 75 percent unemployment is common and where families had depended on ricing for 40 percent of their incomes, was keenly felt.

Ten years ago, the Minnesota Department of Natural Resources sold 17,000 ricing permits a year. In 1988, it issued fewer than 2,000. The number of state-certified rice buyers dropped from 80 to 19. "The paddy growers ruined everything," says Daniel Isham, a traditional hand-harvester from Orr, Minnesota. "You can't even sell hand-finished rice anymore. I can't make a minimum wage today."

The native community has lost more than wages. Many defining cultural events are closely tied to the harvest. Traditional family reunions

Industrial pollution and altered water levels from damming rivers and draining wetlands for development have taken a toll on rice production.

and community rituals have been endangered. "It is not just food for the belly, but food for the head," says Chuck Beaulieu, a Leech Lake ricer. "We are doing something that our ancestors did,

COURTESY OF MANITOK WILD RICE CO.

and we are doing it in the same way. How do you quantify the loss of that?"

"Besides that," says Bibeau, "it was something that cut through all the racism that exists in the North and that an Indian and a white guy could do side by side on the lake. Now there is nothing to cut through that."

Jim Rickert, a wild rice grower and president of the California Wild Rice Growers Association, admits that paddy production has hurt many Native Americans and their traditional culture. In his opinion, "Native Americans are not going to be able to compete unless they adopt modern production methods."

"The Way We Do It"

Turning their lakes into paddies isn't what traditional harvesters have in mind. Wild rice is inconsistent because it is wild; that's what makes it unique.

To compete with paddy producers many native ricers have organized buying and market-

ing co-ops. For example, Saskatchewan Indian Agricultural Products, owned and operated by 72 Cree bands in Canada, markets lake-grown wild rice. Because there is no indigenous wild rice crop in northern Saskatchewan, the Cree introduced it by seeding several isolated lakes. They had no traditional harvesting conventions to guide them, so they have developed their own. One is the use of airboats, similar to those found in the Florida Everglades, to gather the rice. The boats are fitted with a bar across the bow that acts much like the traditional ricing stick; as the boat races through the rice, the bar knocks the grain into the boat.

On shore, the rice is bagged and sent to a processing plant in LaRonge, Saskatchewan. From there it is shipped to Grey Owl Foods, the company's U.S. division in Grand Rapids, Minnesota, for packaging and distribution. Jeff Borg, U.S. distribution manager for Grey Owl, says the company's marketing focuses on the difference between paddy rice and lake rice. "Most consumers are just not aware of the differences. We feel lake-harvested wild rice is a unique natural product, organically grown, with a distinct quality. It should command a premium price."

Ikwe, a small wild rice harvester and distributor in Osage, Minnesota, buys and sells wild rice from about 100 harvesters on White Earth Reservation. Ikwe offers hand-harvested rice "since that is the way we do it down here," says Margaret Smith, a 70-year-old Ikwe founder. She and other craftswomen and wild rice harvesters founded Ikwe—the word means "woman" in Anishinabe—to keep the income from their products on the reservation. According to Smith, "Half the Indians on the reservation rice, and people deserve a good price for their work." Through Ikwe's efforts, the price of rice on White Earth Reservation has increased considerably. In 1992, the price for its green rice was more than a dollar per pound.

"If this crop had been a traditional mainstay of white people, you can be sure we'd have a tough truth-in-packaging law."

Fighting for Property Rights

Unfortunately, many consumers still believe that all wild rice is hand harvested, and no national law requires that labels clearly distinguish paddy rice from lake rice. In their efforts to receive a premium price for real wild rice, traditional harvesters were encouraged in 1977 when Minnesota designated it as the state grain and passed the Wild Rice Labeling Law. The statute proclaims that "all wild rice which is planted or cultivated and which is offered for wholesale or retail sale in this state shall be plainly and conspicuously labeled as 'paddy grown.'"

This law, combined with state and federal statutes that forbid the marketing of conventional products as Native American, should have made lake-harvested rice competitive. Unfortunately, the Minnesota Department of Agriculture has never enforced the law, and paddy rice continues to sport brand names and art that suggest it is lake harvested. In a 1988 letter to Agriculture Department inspectors, one official wrote, "We have been trying to get this wild rice labeling law enforced for a number of years, without much success."

Although the department appears unable to protect the native wild rice industry, it has no problem supporting paddy producers. "Minnesota allocated more than $15 million in the past 20 years to the development of paddy rice," says Bibeau. "Not a cent went to the Indians. Plus, the very labels that said 'state grain' weren't made available to Indians or natural rice wholesalers, only to the paddy rice industry."

Ron Dicklich, a state senator, believes that Minnesota has consciously ignored labeling violations and still favors the paddy industry. "It is hypocritical," Dicklich says. "If this crop had been a traditional mainstay of white people, you can be sure we'd have a tough truth-in-packaging law." And, Bibeau notes, "Native Americans just don't have the political constituency or financial resources to get this done on a national level."

Likewise, U.S. law allows individuals and companies to patent and copyright the products of research, and people are rightly outraged when the fruits of their mental labor are stolen. But when such labor results from hundreds of years' worth of care and experimentation by indigenous people, property claims seem to go out the window. For centuries, Anishinabeg have used wild rice for specific purposes and for specific attributes. If we had not served as guardians of this resource, it might have disappeared long ago.

The question is, Who owns the idea of "wild rice"? In other words, who owns the many natural genetic materials now in demand by the Western world? Ownership and wealth go hand in hand: if you own something, you can generate income.

Granted, scientists, corporations, and states can incur considerable costs in bringing products like cultivated wild rice onto the market. To date, however, indigenous people's rights to either the basic raw materials or the knowledge that can unlock their use has been consistently denied. This imbalance must change.

"Native American hand-harvested rice is the origin of the whole industry," Mary Sullivan, who heads the wild rice division of the Leech Lake Reservation, says. "If that tradition fails, natural wild rice will be only a memory. We feel it is a tradition worth preserving."

Winona LaDuke directs the White Earth Land Recovery Project.

45

Ethiopia's Uncertain Future: The Potential of Ethnic Politics

BY HERBERT S. LEWIS

In June 1991, Mengistu Haile Mariam's "Dergue," the apparatus that had controlled Ethiopia since 1974, fell. While the leaders of the Eritrean Peoples Liberation Front (EPLF) made it clear that the Ethiopian state of Eritrea would become independent, an unprecedented conference convened in Addis Ababa on July 1, 1991, to reorganize the rest of the country. Twenty-seven organizations, nineteen explicitly based on ethnic (or "national") groups, emerged from exile or from the countryside to reconstruct Ethiopia.

With no dissent, the delegates declared their belief in the human and democratic rights of individuals. With only slight argument, they affirmed "the right of nations, nationalities, and peoples" to preserve their identities, administer their own affairs, and declare their independence when these rights are "denied, abridged, or abrogated."

Ethnic opposition groups in Ethiopia had long claimed they were dominated primarily by one group, the Amhara; now the delegates declared that era to be at an end. The various ethnic groups that had begun rebelling in the 1960s had finally triumphed.

The reaction of many members of the elite in Addis Ababa and abroad was not so positive. Fears were expressed about the potential disintegration of Ethiopia, and several lines of argument claimed that this would not only be a disaster but was unjustified as well. It was said that so much intermixture and intermarriage had taken place that it was difficult to say who is what or where one's ethnic homeland might be.

Another line of argument denies that the Amhara dominated all other peoples, claiming instead that the ruling group was actually a mixed population, including Amhara, Tigre, Oromo, Eritreans, and others. Some contend that the extent of ethnic inequality has been exaggerated and emphasize instead class-based inequality under which Amhara and Tigre peasants suffered equally. Above all, many Ethiopians and foreign observers believe that the Ethiopian state has established a powerful discourse of nationhood over the past half century.

Attempts to downplay ethnic distinctiveness and grievances in Ethiopia are not based on the realities of life in that empire. They represent the partial view of an influential elite. Although this view may be supported by reason, personal experiences in elite institutions, and the conventional wisdom of our time, it is severely limited. It is focused on the North and the "modern" sector of Addis Ababa and other major cities, and shows no awareness of the history, conditions, and attitudes of the great majority of the people of Ethiopia in the rest of the country.

A much broader view—one not based on the centers of power—helps clarify events in Ethiopia today. In fact, Ethiopia's ethnic politics differ little from those elsewhere in the world in the last decade of the twentieth century. Many Ethiopian groups retain their identity as distinct peoples, even if some of them have received their modern names and definition only recently. These identities, when combined with a sense of having been dominated and wronged by other groups, may be powerful motivators for change.

The idea of self-determination is in the air, and with today's global communications no place or people will be ignorant of it for long. Whether they approve or not, those concerned about the future of Ethiopia and its peoples must understand these realities.

Origins of the Modern Empire

Although Ethiopia has a history of monarchy stretching back more than two millennia, its kingdoms were restricted primarily to the Northwest until the nineteenth century. At various times during the past 1,000 years, Northern influence and control extended farther south and east. The modern Ethiopian empire was created only during the last century or so as a result of the military expansion of the Amhara rulers of Shoa.

Following the breakup of the old Ethiopian empire late in the 1700s, many pretenders to the throne fought for supremacy during "the era of the princes." These rivals came from three main groups: the *Amhara* and *Tigre* representing the Ethiopian Christian tradition and the northernmost *Oromo* groups, the Azebu, Raya, Yeju, and those of Wollo and northern Shoa. Most Oromo retained their own language and identity, although some became Christian or Muslim.

In 1889, Menelik II, the Amhara king of Shoa, assumed the title of emperor and established supremacy over other Northern groups. Between

47

The Ethiopian empire formed during the same period as British and French African empires and via many of the same means: through conquests, some of them quite brutal.

1875 and 1898 he expanded his empire to four or five times its original size, almost to Ethiopia's current borders. The victorious forces included Tigre and Oromo soldiers and commanders, as well as others, but the ultimate control, glory, and prevailing influence belonged to the Shoan Amhara.

The Ethiopian empire was formed during the same period as British and French African empires and via many of the same means: through conquests, some of them quite brutal. If a people submitted without a fight, it might be allowed to keep its own leaders and some measure of autonomy. If it resisted, the result might be massacres, expropriation, and dislocation. Although they kept Ethiopia free of European domination, Yohannis IV, Tewodros II, Menelik II, and Haile Selassie I all subjugated many other peoples.

The Northern conquerors established control over peoples who had a wide range of social structures and practices, which were usually ignored or destroyed. Some, such as the people of Kafa, Janjero, Male, and six Oromo regions, had their own kings and queens. Others had no states but ran their affairs through a variety of arrangements, including political systems based on elections, large assemblies, and various associations. Thus, while monarchies existed among some conquered peoples, others maintained a high degree of egalitarianism.

Language is the single most important marker of ethnicity, and the peoples added to the empire spoke about 70 different languages among them. Some languages were spoken by only a few thousand people, others had hundreds of thousands of speakers. At least 15 million speak Oromo today.

There has been no proper census in Ethiopia, and recent population estimates in the range of 50 million are only guesses. Still, one fact stands out: the Amhara and their allies became masters of many peoples who greatly outnumbered them, perhaps by three to one. These once independent peoples—speaking their own languages, following their own customs, political systems, and religions, and pursuing their own ecological and economic regimes—were to become subject peoples by about 1900.

Ethiopian Rule

There seems to be no debate about the harshness of Ethiopian colonial rule: it was basic, crude, and exploitive. The Amhara didn't hide behind a cloak of a "civilizing mission." From the beginning, local administration was in the hands of the victorious soldiers, or *neft'enya* (riflemen or armed retainers), as they are known and execrated. Their only qualifications were their guns and their foresight at having signed up for the campaigns.

The conquerors established a series of fortified towns (*ketema*) and garrisoned troops in and around them. For their support, the new rulers and the troops were apportioned to local farmers (*gebbar*—"tribute giver"), who were forced to deliver wealth and provide a wide range of labor services. Usually the emperor also rewarded some indigenous leaders with grants of land and authority. These leaders, or *balabbat*, served as further instruments of rule for the emperor and the alien elite. As with chiefs appointed to such positions by European colonial rulers, the *balabbat* organized labor and resources for the central government and for the *neft'enya*, assessed and collected taxes, and helped keep order.

From the late 1950s on, the central government sent more salaried administrators to govern these areas. Because these administrators were overwhelmingly either Amhara or from some other Northern groups, anyone who expected to succeed in a government position had to conform to Amhara models and speak Amharic. Whether these administrators and the *neft'enya* were actually Amhara—or only half Amhara, or came from Gondar instead of Shoa, or were Tigre or Oromo who had adopted Amhara lifestyles—they were outsiders. Precise origins would not have mattered to a Southern *gebbar*; it was the Amhara who ruled.

At least until the 1974 revolution that installed the Dergue, the administration's primary aim was to keep order and extract wealth for the emperor and the state, while each landowner and government functionary tried to profit as best he or she could. Except for the development of schools in larger towns, the government provided virtually no services, and until the 1960s the schools were attended mostly by children of the *neft'enya*. For the many millions who lived outside the towns, even these amenities were lacking. Missionaries supplied almost all modern health care outside Addis Ababa, yet these scarce medical centers and small hospitals were located only near larger population centers.

To a large extent, towns were alien enclaves within the conquered areas. Amharic became their primary language, even if the people on their fringes couldn't speak it. Educated Oromo describe how they were mocked or punished for speaking Oromo, despite their language's predominance in their area. The same story could be told by speakers of any of the other 70-odd languages.

The courts offer another example of the indignities suffered by those who weren't Amhara. In larger towns, the government established courts in which Amharic was the only language. A person who didn't speak Amharic had to hire an interpreter as well as a lawyer, while a stranger with no knowledge of that person's culture, expectations, traditions, or values made the decisions. According to University of Manchester anthropologist Paul Baxter, "Even a case between two Oromo before an Oromo-speaking magistrate had to be heard in Amharic." No wonder people avoided these courts.

In the 1960s, the government organized parliamentary elections, but elected officials could do

Tent city: Ethiopian refugee camp, mid-1980s

little to aid their people, even if they had wanted to. A telling account by Baxter indicates the extent to which local people were excluded. In the 1969 election, the Arussi Oromo in one district elected two Arussi to Parliament. "The Governor however regarded the result as subversion of the proper political order and had one of the candidates disallowed (the other was thought to be protected by Swedish Aid patrons) and ordered a fresh poll. During the second poll, Arussi voters were threatened, some imprisoned, and the majority prevented from voting so that a Christian Northerner was declared elected."

This discussion of schools, courts, and elections gives a false impression of modernity. In fact, these institutions barely touched the great mass of the people except those living in or near major towns. In 1965 and 1966, I worked in a farming community about 70 miles west of Addis Ababa, just off a good road and about 10 miles from a substantial town. Only a handful of the community's young students could speak Amharic, and the closest school and modern medical service were in town. People came in contact with the government mainly if they got into trouble with the police, and perhaps when they were ordered to pay taxes. They rarely turned to the local *balabbat* or the courts but had their own system of conflict resolution.

In short, these country people hardly participated in an Ethiopian national culture. They recognized that Haile Selassie I was powerful; many

49

even thought his power was supernatural. If this was the extent of national consciousness a short distance from the capital, imagine what it was like for the vast majority of peoples of the South, East, and West.

Most people in the conquered areas then had little practical, sentimental, or ideological reason to accept a discourse of Ethiopian nationhood. At best, they would have been ignorant of it or indifferent; at worst, they would have been alienated and at least potential rebels. And although the "socialist" Dergue may have made schools and other services more available, it also increased extractions and interfered more in the lives of all of them.

The Growth of Modern Politics

Haile Selassie's efforts to transform Ethiopia into a modern state stimulated political activity, despite his strenuous efforts to contain this development. After a failed coup attempt in 1960, university and secondary school students became more politically conscious and obstreperous. Among these were non-Amhara who by then were entering schools in increasing numbers. In the main, their causes weren't those of their ethnic groups, but were the same as those stirring Ethiopian students of all backgrounds.

During the late 1960s, these activists preached student rights, freedom, and, above all, land reform. "Land to the Tiller" was their slogan. Oromo and other non-Amhara students could readily identify and participate in these movements. Many young Oromo became Marxist, as with that whole generation of Ethiopian students, and they were among the most avid early supporters of the revolutionary regime, the Dergue. In addition, after 1969 the student movement embraced the ideals of equality for all nationalities and respect for the languages and cultures of others. Added to the goals of modernization and democratization, these ideals, too, inspired many non-Amhara.

In 1967, an episode occurred that became a portent for some educated Oromo. The government banned the Mech'a-Tulama association, an Oromo self-help organization, and arrested its leaders, including General Tadesa Biru. Tadesa had had a successful career in the police, was a Shoan Christian, and had seemed "assimilated" until his disillusioning experience in high office led him to organize his Oromo brethren. The fate of Tadesa and the movement influenced many Oromo. According to Bereket Habte Selassie, now a professor of law and government at Harvard University, some went underground and began to lay the groundwork for the Oromo Liberation Front (OLF) by organizing among Oromo farmers and urban dwellers.

More commonly, it was only in the late 1970s that educated Oromo began to believe that the new regime, despite its rhetoric and initial land-reform program, didn't represent a new deal or equality. Some had helped plan and implement land reform until, like Tadesa Biru, their proximity to power led them to conclude that the old patterns of domination were continuing under the "new *neft'enya*," as they called them. According to Bereket, the Oromo had hoped that farmers would be permitted to elect representatives to the newly formed peasants' associations, but the Dergue meant to use these as instruments for increasing its own control. When Oromo in Jimma and Harar demanded in 1978 that the Oromo language be used for teaching in the early grades, their demonstrations, Bereket reports, "were suppressed violently, with some 250 students killed." Young Oromo began to defect abroad or to join the OLF.

A common pattern, then, was for a young person first to become a Marxist and support the revolution, and later, disaffected, to turn to the aspirations of his or her own group. Although this argument focuses on the Oromo, it applies to many of the national liberation movements that formed before and after the revolution, the most prominent being those of the Eritreans, the Somalis on the eastern borders, the Oromo, and the Tigre. The new regime was no more willing than the old to permit any ethnic organization or activity that it didn't sponsor and control.

The Growth of Oromo Nationalism

The Oromo, by far Ethiopia's largest ethnic group, stretch from the far North of the country as far south as the Tana River in Kenya and from the borders of Somalia to those of Sudan. The many far-flung and quite different Oromo groups had no overall integration in the centuries before the Shoan conquest, and various Oromo groups fought each other in the past. But Amhara overlords made all Oromo groups (except those in Kenya) subordinate to one power.

Rarely was all quiet on the Oromo front. There were revolts by the Azebu and Raya in the North in 1928–1930, in Wellega in 1936, and in Bale Province in the 1960s. Each of these was localized, but news of a 1964 rebellion in Bale against the government and its tax collectors spread and increased Oromo political awareness. That rebellion, Paul Baxter reports, "demonstrated that determined Oromo could wage effective guerrilla warfare against the Addis Ababa authorities." At the same time, contacts in the "modern sector" made Oromo aware of "just how numerous, extensive and similar the Oromo peoples were."

The Dergue accelerated this process by organizing and politicizing everything. Haile Selassie's government had done little but extract wealth and try to keep order, but the Dergue penetrated all corners of society. Government-controlled organizations, increasing demands on people's time and resources, and interference with farmers,

traders, and students all raised political awareness. Most egregiously, the Dergue carried out a program of forced resettlement: Northerners who spoke different languages and had different religions and cultures were settled on Oromo land. The Dergue then forced Oromo and other Southern farmers and herders into compact villages, driving people used to living in dispersed homesteads to cluster in settlements that were inappropriate and even disastrous economically, ecologically, and socially.

Over the years, a number of Oromo political movements emerged. The largest is the OLF. Its major rival is the Oromo People's Democratic Organization (OPDO), which developed under the aegis of the Ethiopian Peoples Revolutionary Democratic Front (EPRDF). The OLF, in particular, has assumed the rhetoric, symbols, and activities common to similar movements all over the world. Apart from pursuing military action, for example, they campaigned to introduce literacy in the Oromo language. In speeches and publications, they reject Amharic names for Oromo places and insist on the original Oromo ones. The Oromo *gada* system, a republican organization of assemblies, elections, and rotating officers, is central in the ideology of Oromo nationalism.

Immediately after the fall of the Dergue in 1991, Oromo from all over the country, many of whom had never had contact before, came together for political action. Not only had they had little opportunity to meet prior to then, but they had been forbidden to hold public gatherings. Oromo groups held two great meetings in July, one an effort to settle a major dispute between the OLF and the OPDO and the other a feast to celebrate Oromo unity. Growing feelings of power, pride, and political potential characterized these deeply emotional meetings.

The history of Oromo consciousness has followed a common pattern in the rise of ethnic

51

nationalism among colonized peoples. In the first stage, superior force overcame initial resistance to the empire, and the Oromo settled into lives of quiet desperation, disliking the outsiders but finding themselves forced to tolerate them. In the second stage, as the young became educated and learned about politics, many initially identified with the larger unit, in this case the Ethiopian empire. Discovering that the needs of their own people were not to be met, however, they grew disenchanted. Finding their ethnic fellows still among the insulted and injured, they turned to ethnopolitics. These ethnic parties are now in a position to decide the future of Ethiopia.

The Prospects for Ethiopia

During the 1970s and '80s, Ethiopian politics was notable for its many factions and ideologies, including numerous variations on Marxist-Leninist themes. But the regime was brought down by the very "narrow nationalists" the Dergue feared, and it is they who are now trying to work out a future for Ethiopia.

At the July 1991 conference, after affirming their support for the Universal Declaration of Human Rights and its emphasis on individual rights, the delegates turned to the rights of the nationalities. Under the direction of Meles Zenawi, leader of the Tigre Peoples Liberation Front, a section of the EPRDF, the assembly agreed to form an ethnically balanced government and to decentralize the state. A proclamation issued after the conference affirmed "the right of nations, nationalities, and peoples" to:

a) Preserve its identity and have it respected, promote its culture and history, and use and develop its language;

b) Administer its own affairs within its own defined territory and effectively participate in the central government on the basis of freedom, and fair and proper representation;

c) Exercise its right to self-determination of independence, when the concerned nation/nationality and people is convinced that the above rights are denied, abridged or abrogated.

The successful implementation of these principles is far from certain. What does seem sure is that there are two deeply divided views in Ethiopia. The Amhara, not all of them elite, see only disaster in this formula and blame the TPLF and OLF for pushing the ethnic/national issue. The representatives of many of the ethnic movements, on the other hand, would probably present a similar picture to the one I have, but more forcefully. Any middle ground is difficult to find. Beyond everyone's grievances against the Amhara, each group may have claims against its neighbors, just as occurred in the breakup of the Soviet Union and Yugoslavia. Negotiation will be very difficult and the outcomes are unpredictable.

It will do no good to try to argue that a particular group has no grounds to set itself apart—in terms of recognition, autonomy, or even independence. The anthropologist Fredrik Barth pointed out in 1969 that it is not cultural content that marks boundaries between ethnic groups; such boundaries exist despite "objective" similarities or differences. The leaders of the Eritrean independence movement are arguably as close culturally, linguistically, and historically to the Tigre, and almost as close to the Amhara, as any people can be. Yet Eritreans chose to fight a terrible war for

The Dergue forced Southern farmers and herders into compact villages, driving people to cluster in settlements that were disastrous economically, ecologically, and socially.

The Ethiopian "discourse of nationhood" stands little chance unless the perceived needs of its many nations are met.

independence for 30 years. And the "similarity argument" has done little to keep Yugoslavia or Czechoslovakia together.

Similarly, the Eritrean case should caution those who feel they can talk others out of a movement with a "more objective" view of history. Eritrea became an Italian colony in 1889, but after Italy lost its colonies as a result of World War II, the UN General Assembly decreed in 1950 that it should be "federated" with Ethiopia as an autonomous unit. (The United Nations called for independence for Libya and Somalia, Italy's other African colonies.) In 1962, Haile Selassie's government abolished the federation and began to rule Eritrea directly. It seems like a simple case, but Eritrean nationalists and Ethiopians who believe that Eritrea must be part of Ethiopia can argue endlessly over the "facts" and the interpretation of them. Once the issue has been joined, few of those who have grievances are convinced by the arguments of "the enemy," no matter how scholarly the case.

The world today is awash in ethnopolitics, and it is the nature and definition of nation-states that is coming into question. Over the past 20 years, we have witnessed a great new diffusion of the idea of self-determination. The Ethiopian "discourse of nationhood" stands little chance against this new set of ideas and sentiments unless the perceived needs of its many nations are met. Meeting these needs will take a great deal more openness than opponents of ethnic self-assertion now evidence.

After many years of war and political turmoil, people in Ethiopia want peace, stability, and a chance to rebuild. People are very aware of the great costs of separation and they don't take the prospect of fighting for independence lightly.

They are also aware of the rewards for staying together as a united Ethiopia. But they are unlikely to accept willingly the sort of system they had before—being ordered around by outsiders, denied their honor and their rights, and shortchanged on services and opportunities. They will require evidence that their needs will be dealt with fairly.

The feelings of many non-Amhara today can be represented by the words of a well-educated member of the Sidama Liberation Movement, spoken at the time of the July 1991 conference:

We want to live together, but we want to be respected as human beings, as Sidama, as a people, a culture, a language. We must have a part in this country, not as second-class citizens, not as foreigners, but as full partners. Before we didn't want to live with Addis Ababa as our capital, but there is new hope that as priorities shift we can participate as full partners and not be dominated by an elite minority.

After speaking of the Sidamo region's wealth in fertile soil, coffee, and gold, he added:

Until now we only gave and got nothing in return. No roads, no clinics, no schools. Our resources were taken for the elite, so they could send their children to school in Addis Ababa and abroad. But we no longer will accept this. We want to use these resources, to share with others and get something in return.

53

Herbert S. Lewis is a professor of anthropology at the University of Wisconsin-Madison and a member of the African Studies Program. He conducted extended field research in Ethiopia in 1958–1960 and 1965–66 and has spent shorter periods of time there as recently as 1991. His publications include *A Galla Monarchy: Jimma Abba Jifar, Ethiopia, 1830–1932,* (University of Wisconsin Press, 1965) and *After the Eagles Landed: The Yemenites of Israel,* (Westview Press, 1989).

Securing a Homeland: The Tawahka Sumu of Mosquitia's Rain Forest

BY PETER H. HERLIHY

In Central America, as in many places around the globe, the issues of conserving forested lands and territorial autonomy for indigenous peoples often intertwine. Native groups inhabit remote wilderness regions on which valuable forests still stand. Increasingly, the advance of agricultural colonists threatens these ethnic territories, which contain much of the region's surviving natural resources.

Central American governments have established 240 "protected areas," including national parks and biosphere reserves, that aim at conserving natural resources and forested lands but pay little attention to the rights or roles of the resident indigenous forest peoples. Only a small number of these are "indigenous

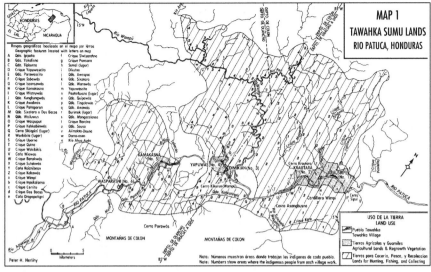

MAP 1
TAWAHKA SUMU LANDS
RIO PATUCA, HONDURAS

USO DE LA TIERRA
LAND USE

Peter H. Herlihy

lagoons and swamps, is home to the Miskito Indians. The lesser-known western hilly uplands, covered by pristine tropical rain forests, are home to one of the region's smaller indigenous groups, the Sumu Indians. Their population, which is composed of three main linguistic divisions, occupies the rain-forested Mosquitia interiors of Nicaragua reaching north and crossing into Honduras. While most of the 10,000 Sumu have been terrorized by the 10-year contra-Sandinista war in Nicaragua, a small Honduran group of under 1,000 Tawahka Sumu escaped most of the impacts of the conflict.

The Tawahka live in the lush rain forests along the Patuca River at the center of an ecological corridor spanning from the Caribbean Sea deep into Nicaragua. These indigenous peoples have played a key role in conserving the rich biological heritage of the region. They use rainforest habitats without destroying the tall canopy cover. According to Louisiana State University geographer William Davidson and Fernando Cruz, an anthropologist at the National Autonomous University of Honduras, the Tawahka have been the dominant culture in the area for at least four centuries. But now, an advancing colonization front, driven by expanding population and declining resources in nearby regions, threatens the ability of the Tawahka, whose territories lack any official protection, to maintain their identity as a distinct society.

When aggressive colonists began invading their lands in the mid-1980s, the Tawahka

reserves," in part because Panama, Costa Rica, and Belize are the only Central American countries with legal indigenous territories. Nevertheless, a strong correlation exists between the location of protected areas and the distribution of native societies, mainly because indigenous people have been the stewards of Central America's natural heritage over the centuries. As a mapping project jointly sponsored by Cultural Survival and National Geographic Society graphically illustrates, most of Central America's standing forests are also home to the region's original inhabitants. While indigenous cultures occupy or draw upon roughly 30 percent of Central America's protected parks, these "cultural parks" account for about 85 percent of the total protected land area. Indigenous peoples depend on the resources in these parks for their livelihood. Conversely, the conservation of these areas depends on how the resources are exploited.

Most of the tropical forests and indigenous territories in one of Central America's most important ethnic wildlands, the Mosquitia region of eastern Honduras and Nicaragua, are not under protected status. The popularized "Mosquito Coast," an area of pine-covered savannas laced with a network of

55

If the Tawahka lose their rights to their forested homelands, it will mean the end of the forests for everyone.

responded by forming their first political federation, the Indigenous Tawahka Federation of Honduras (FITH). Since then, working with government and private organizations and lobbying state and international authorities, this small and endangered indigenous population has struggled to secure control over its ancestral territory.

The Tawahka have organized to place their proposal for a Tawahka biosphere reserve, an internationally recognized concept for protecting endangered habitats, on the Honduran agenda. They have become vocal advocates for protecting their forests and natural resources. With the help of conservation and development organizations, from Honduras and around the world, the Tawahka can develop the mechanisms to combine traditional and Western land-management techniques for such a reserve. Given legal backing, they can keep outsiders off their lands, thus halting the destructive advance of the colonization front into the Mosquitia and safeguarding the most remote and biologically diverse area in Honduras.

Yet the battle is far from over. Although the Tawahka's economy is adapted to a life that uses the forest without destroying it, they must carry on their struggle for territorial autonomy within the Honduran political system. But the Honduran government has no clearly defined indigenous policy, nor has it had an exemplary environmental or human-rights record. In particular, Honduras has no clear policy or mechanism for establishing Indian reserves or territorial status. If the Tawahka lose their rights to their forested homelands, it will mean the destruction of the ecological corridor and the end of the forests for everyone.

Organizing for Survival

Indigenous peoples increasingly see protected areas as a way to promote their territorial autonomy; the Honduran state sees the areas as a way to conserve valuable natural resources. This confluence of interests is evident in the Mosquitia, which since prehistoric times has been an important indigenous homeland for the Tawahka and other groups. Because these lands stayed isolated through the colonial era, and were outside the main political and economic arenas, their natural and cultural heritage remains largely intact. A strip extending from the Caribbean Sea southward through Honduras and across the Río Coco into Nicaragua represents the largest, least-exploited expanse of rain forest in Central America.

Honduras contains most of this rainforested corridor, including diverse natural habitats from the Miskito Coast and Plátano River headwaters to the ranges of the Montañas de Patuca and the Cordillera Entre Ríos. The south-central part of the corridor is Tawahka Sumu territory, and the western and central parts are the domain of the Pech. To the north, Miskito Indians have lived on the coast since the eighteenth century, joined by Garífuna in the nineteenth century.

It is the Honduran portion of the corridor that faces the greatest immediate threat from colonists. Primarily over the past 20 years, settlers have entered the corridor along lumber roads. They have cleared pristine rain forest, planted pasture grasses, and introduced cattle. They have already displaced Tawahka and other indigenous populations from their lands as the colonization frontier penetrates Indian territories.

Recognizing the ecological and cultural importance of the Mosquitia region, the Honduran government established a biosphere reserve around the Plátano River watershed in 1980, the first such reserve in Central America. Although this has offered some security for Miskito, Pech, and Garífuna communities in the north, the Tawahka live outside the bounded park but exploit lands within its southern limits.

Tawahka efforts to control their homelands began in earnest in 1985 when MOPAWI (an acronym based on the Miskito phrase *Mosquitia*

Tawahka villagers and FITH leaders discuss the "biosphere" concept.

Pawisa—Development of the Mosquitia) began a program to help the Tawahka organize for economic and political development. In 1987, MOPAWI collaborated with the Honduran Council for the Development of Native Cultures (CAHDEA) and the Internationale Gesellschaft fur Menshenrechte, a German development group, to help launch the Tawahka federation FITH. The federation's charter calls for control of the Tawahka's historic lands and natural resources.

At the same time, MOPAWI initiated plans to enable Mosquitia's indigenous communities to secure legal recognition for their communal land-tenure system. The Land Legalization Program emerged in response to what had happened elsewhere in Honduras when indigenous people had lost their land to invading colonists. In 1988, FITH and the other indigenous groups of the Mosquitia signed their own declaration calling for

the Honduran government to legalize their lands. The document calls for the recognition that indigenous land use includes areas of forest not cut or put under agricultural production.

However, only after an armed and aggressive group of *ladinos* (non-Indians) moved onto Tawahka lands in 1989 did a grassroots impetus to reclaim territory develop. FITH denounced the invasion to the National Agrarian Institute (Institución Nacional Agraria—INA), asking the government agency to declare formally the boundaries of Tawahka territory. INA did, in fact, spell out that military force would be used against outsiders who invaded indigenous territories, making special reference to the Tawahka case. This first group of *ladinos* retreated.

Just as important, INA, together with indigenous and local government officials, signed a landmark agreement concerning indigenous land tenure in Mosquitia. The agreement proposed a regional process to issue provisional guarantees to "community lands," thereby breaking with a de facto government policy that awarded plots only to individual landholders. The agreement called on indigenous people to protect and conserve natural resources and to respect the laws of the state. At the same time, INA would initiate steps to grant legal property rights to the indigenous communities.

To implement this agreement, each native community would define and map its own borders, with the Tawahka going first. The villagers from Krausirpe, the largest Tawahka community on the Patuca River with about 58 households and 390 inhabitants, responded quickly, mapping their lands. Without any professional training, the map was crudely constructed. In November 1989, INA issued a provisional guarantee to a Krausirpe community territory, covering 29 square miles, based on the villagers' delimitation.

57

The Regional Approach

INA's "community-based" approach was far from adequate for fulfilling the needs of the Tawahka. Other Tawahka communities are located just upriver from Krausirpe around the juncture of the Patuca with the Wampú River. A land-use study by this author showed six Tawahka villages there containing a total of about 650 people in 1990 (*see map 1*). The land use of the Krausirpe villagers overlapped with that of the other villages. Combined, the six Tawahka villages exploited about 300 square miles of forest. The villagers cultivated only about 5 percent of this area, and used the other 95 percent for hunting, fishing, and extracting construction materials. Krausirpe villagers thus depended on a much larger resource area than their provisional guarantee allocated. Nor could their lands be separated from those of other Tawahka villagers, who shared the same forest.

Further problems emerged due to the Tawahka's lack of training in modern mapping techniques. Because INA technicians, unfamiliar with the Patuca River, misinterpreted the crude map drawn by the villagers, the provisional grant ended up being smaller than the delimitation made by the Indians. Moreover, the community-based approach to land titling would leave small islands of forested indigenous lands surrounded by a sea of invading colonists, thereby breaking up traditional Tawahka subsistence territories into a checkerboard of forest and pasture.

In 1990, such drawbacks led INA to initiate a broader regional approach toward indigenous land rights. Indigenous Tawahka and Miskito leaders, MOPAWI Land Legalization Program director Andrew Leake, anthropologist Fernando Cruz, and I met with INA director Juan Ramón Martínez, and we agreed on a proposal to create a reserve around the Tawahka land-use area that would connect the Plátano River Biosphere Reserve to the north with the Nicaragua border to the south (*see map below*). It was thought this "protected corridor" would block the eastward advance of colonization. The reserve would function as both a biological reserve for forests and a cultural sanctuary for the Tawahka. Based on this proposal, FITH asked INA legally to recognize a 900-square-mile "Tawahka Forest Reserve" centering on the main Tawahka land-use area.

58

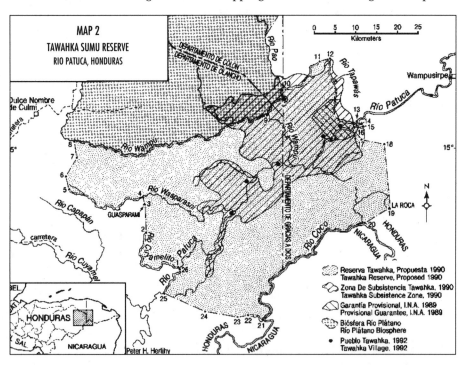

MAP 2
TAWAHKA SUMU RESERVE
RIO PATUCA, HONDURAS

Reserva Tawahka, Propuesta 1990
Tawahka Reserve, Proposed 1990
Zona De Subsistencia Tawahka, 1990
Tawahka Subsistence Zone, 1990
Garantía Provisional, I.N.A. 1989
Provisional Guarantee, I.N.A. 1989
Biósfera Río Plátano
Río Plátano Biosphere
Pueblo Tawahka, 1992
Tawahka Village, 1992

Peter H. Herlihy

To create a Tawahka Forest Reserve, however, has not proved easy, even though INA inventories show no private land titles in the area. No one seriously questions Tawahka claim to these lands, but Honduran law does not include the concept of an indigenous reserve. A few indigenous communities have land titles dating from the seventeenth and eighteenth centuries, and twenty-one Tol (Xicaque) and two Pech (Paya) communities gained titles during the 1860s. However, these awards, which included only small areas around villages, don't reflect indigenous resource-use patterns. The most recent indigenous land title, awarded to the Tol in 1929 and covering a scant 11 square miles, is the largest legally defined indigenous area in Honduras.

Although INA acknowledged the legitimacy of the Tawahka desire to legalize their homeland, it lacked the power to award reserve status to such a large area; apparently only a congressional or presidential decree could do that. This impasse generated a flurry of activity including a search for legal precedents for such a decree. The Forestry Law, in combination with parts of the Honduran Constitution and the Agrarian Reform Law, seemed to offer some basis for establishing a Tawahka Forest Reserve. Director Porfirio Lobo Sosa of the Honduran forestry agency COHDEFOR verbally supported the idea, despite some doubts about setting aside so much land for fewer than 1,000 people. In general, the administration of President Rafael Callejas seemed interested in conserving these forest resources and the cultures in them, but apparently the only way the reserve could be approved was by congressional action.

Besides official sympathy, the Tawahka's fight for a reserve received widespread support from abroad. For example, Cultural Survival has provided financial and technical support for MOPAWI's land-legalization efforts, as well as for the development of the fledgling Tawahka federation. The United Nations Program for the Natural Environment, the International Union for the Conservation of Nature, the World Wildlife Fund, and the Nature Conservancy all favor the reserve and recognize the Tawahka as key players in protecting the Honduran-Nicaraguan borderlands.

A Tawahka Biosphere

The emerging consensus focused discussions on the idea of a biosphere—an internationally recognized concept—and how it might fulfill the Tawahka's requirements. In 1991, a German consultant agency working for COHDEFOR proposed an enlargement of the Plátano River Biosphere Reserve southward to the Patuca River, covering about half of the proposed Tawahka reserve. Later proposals added the remainder of the Tawahka proposal plus the forests of the Cordillera Entre Ríos and the Montañas del Warunta into one mega-biosphere.

At a special meeting of FITH in January 1992, Tawahka leaders discussed the necessity for their reserve to function as a both biological and cultural reserve. MOPAWI representative Andrew Leake and I explained that the biosphere reserve was the only concept that appeared to serve this dual function. Because the Plátano River Biosphere Reserve already existed, the category seemed to have legal standing within Honduras. After prolonged discussion of related manage-

59

The most recent indigenous land title in Honduras was awarded to the Tol in 1929. Covering a scant 11 square miles, it is the country's largest legally defined indigenous area.

VINCENTE MURPHY

The subsistence way of life of the Tawahka is based on the rational use of forest resources.

ment, zoning, and land-tenure issues, Tawahka leaders endorsed the idea that the Tawahka community, through its own federation, would manage the "Tawahka Biosphere Reserve" in coordination with the government. FITH would seek technical and financial support from Honduran and international agencies to prepare a management plan. Once the reserve was established, the Ministry of Natural Resources would solicit international status for it under the United Nations Man and the Biosphere Program.

Since the January 1992 meeting, the Tawahka reserve has gained support as the central "bridge" in the binational ecological corridor linking the Plátano Biosphere with Nicaragua's BOSAWAS Natural Resource Reserve covering the rain forests and Sumu villages across the Río Coco to the south. Conservation and indigenous-rights organizations, at both the national and international level, are lobbying for its establishment. And the Callejas administration has responded to concerns to protect this important part of Honduras. Under pressure from Honduran conservation and indigenous organizations, foresters, and concerned citizens to change its forestry policy, the administration has recently turned down requests for lum-

ber concessions in Mosquitia. Such was the case when COHDEFOR was pressured to sever negotiations with Chicago-based Stone Container Corp. for a 40-year lease to cut timber in the region.

In fact, a regional "environmental politics" seems to be emerging. At a 1992 meeting, the Central American presidents signed a biodiversity agreement recognizing the Honduran/Nicaraguan borderlands as a priority for conservation. Callejas and Nicaraguan President Violeta Chamorro further agreed to establish a binational system of protected areas called *La Solidaridad* that would include the Plátano River and Tawahka areas connected to the BOSAWAS reserve extending from the Caribbean Sea deep into Nicaragua.

Callejas has since signed a decree calling for studies to establish the boundaries of the Tawahka Biosphere Reserve and the re-delimitation of the Plátano Biosphere within one year. The government has established an inter-agency committee to delimit a reserve system called *PLAPAWANS* (an acronym of initials from the Plàtano, Patuca, and Wanks/Coco rivers), which will cover the Honduran portion of *La Solidaridad*. Heading the group are the Ministry of Defense and the Honduran National Commission on the Environment (CONAMA)—an almost unprecedented and certainly powerful combination—that probably reflects the state's interests in conservation and indigenous issues as much as security concerns over the once conflictive border area.

A significant event in promoting the biosphere proposal and the active role of the Tawahka in it came with the First Congress on Indigenous Lands of the Mosquitia. This 1992 meeting culminated a three-month participatory process through which indigenous people learned to complete questionnaires and conduct mapping exercises and community-led land-use assessments. The project mapped the land-use patterns of Mosquitia's indigenous communities for presentation at the congress. Conducted by Cultural Survival's Mac Chapin, MOPAWI's Andrew Leake, and myself, the effort enabled the native Mosquitia peoples to document with conventional maps their use of the region's land. It made the indigenous groups more aware of the crucial conservation and development issues affecting their communities. And they learned to produce reliable data, in a form acceptable by government agencies, to document their problems and conditions.

The congress also provided a critical forum in which high-ranking government authorities on resource use and conservation could listen to indigenous people. During the event, the *PLAPAWANS* committee solicited indigenous recommendations on the proposed borders of the reserve system and accepted suggestions for delimiting the Tawahka reserve and the enlarged Plátano Biosphere.

As now conceived by the governmental committee, the *PLAPAWANS* reserve system will center on two national parks, three surrounding indigenous reserves, and a wide buffer zone that will separate colonists from parks and reserves. One park covers the Plátano River headwaters, the other includes the Cordillera Entre Ríos. The Tawahka area will be one of the so-called "indigenous reserves." Another covers the northern sector of the *PLAPAWANS* system and includes twenty-one Miskito, one Garífuna, and four Pech, settlements, while the remaining reserve along the eastern boundary contains ten Miskito villages on the Patuca River. Many other indigenous communities are found around the periphery. The entire system will include about 6,000 square miles.

Great Expectations

Undeniably, there is real concern on the part of the Honduran government, international conservationists, and human-rights advocates to con-

serve the Tawahka's natural and cultural heritage. The Tawahka and the Honduran government need a reserve that functions as both an environmental park and an indigenous homeland. All parties involved apparently hope that the Tawahka and other indigenous groups will receive legal title to their lands.

Nevertheless, many issues still threaten the Honduran government's acceptance of the Tawahka Biosphere proposal. It is even possible

This Tawahka Sumu hunter shows off a pavon he shot four hours by foot away from his village.

that Honduras could create a Tawahka reserve without guaranteeing the Tawahka any legal rights to use the land within it, such as was done initially in the Plátano Biosphere case.

The *PLAPAWANS* committee continues with its work, apparently aiming at providing a basis for establishing all the protected areas in the reserve system under one congressional act. But while the *PLAPAWANS* committee sometimes uses the "indigenous" or "anthropological" labels to designate ethnic divisions, the concept of an indigenous reserve still must find some articulation in Honduran law. Indeed, there remains a lack of clarity concerning the state's role with regard to managing and conserving forests occupied by indigenous people.

Tawahka lands can't be legally titled to outsiders while the reserve proposal is pending, but *ladinos* are settling lands and harvesting timber there anyway.

As approval of the Tawahka reserve—under whatever label—awaits congressional action, the colonization front continues to threaten Tawahka lands and outside commercial interests petition access to the resources of the Mosquitia. The blocking of recent lumber concessions demonstrates that there exists strong support for conserving the natural and cultural heritage of the region. But although the Tawahka lands can't legally be titled to colonists or other outsiders while the reserve proposal is pending, *ladinos* have recently settled lands and harvested timber there anyway. The government has done little to stop these advances.

Despite the lack of clear policies for establishing indigenous territories, the Tawahka seek a protected area that will meet their need for territorial autonomy without sacrificing the country's needs for conservation and economic development. And regardless of whether the Tawahka secure their territory, they have raised outside awareness concerning their land rights while strengthening their own political organizations and efforts to determine and control their own lives.

While politicians fiddle and forests burn, a small and vulnerable culture could disappear. The fledgling indigenous organization FITH brings little political and economic clout to the struggle. The Tawahka need support from all concerned parties to continue their roles as stewards of the rainforested nucleus of *La Solidaridad*. The final verdict on the Tawahka reserve proposal will likely determine the success of conservation efforts in the Mosquitia, as well as influence how other Central American states will view the place of indigenous peoples in natural and cultural conservation initiatives in the region.

Peter H. Herlihy, a cultural geographer at the University of Kansas, has lived in the Mosquitia for extended periods over the past four years. For more than a decade, with support from Fulbright, the Organization of American States, and the International Union for the Conservation of Nature, he has worked on indigenous land and conservation issues in Central America, especially in Panama and Honduras.

How You Can Help

International environmental groups must recognize the importance of protecting the human rights of indigenous peoples. Encourage environmental groups of which you are a member to recognize the land claims of the Tawahka and other indigenous societies.

Write to Honduran President Rafael Callejas and ask him to support a Tawahka reserve with full land rights for the Tawahka people according to a proposal supported by the Tawahka themselves: President Rafael Callejas, Casa Presidencial, Tegucigalpa, Honduras.

To support the Tawahka financially, contributions can be sent to Cultural Survival, 215 First St., Cambridge, MA 02142. Please make checks payable to Cultural Survival and include a note specifying that your contribution is to be used for the Tawahka project.

Resources for Action

LOOKING BACK TO GO FORWARD: PREDICTING AND PREVENTING HUMAN RIGHTS VIOLATIONS

BY JASON W. CLAY

Although many may lament the demise of indigenous cultures, few comprehend either the global magnitude or the implications of this loss. Yet if we do not look back to connect the symptoms of human-rights violations with root causes, we will never be able go forward and predict and prevent such inhumanity.

The study of the destruction of indigenous cultures reveals that in almost every case, the interests of states and of the nations of indigenous peoples living within them have been in direct conflict. There is no better time than the present to accept that premise, both because the world's remaining indigenous peoples face unprecedented dangers and because the very concept of the state is itself coming into question. The Berlin Wall, the Soviet Union, and Yugoslavia are not all that have crumbled. Basic assumptions about states and their relationship to nations—to

indigenous peoples, if you will—are under attack as well, in Europe and throughout the world. The rise of nationalism—the implication that group identity is as important as citizenship within a state—and calls for democracy and autonomy demonstrate that highly centralized, top-down authority can vanish overnight.

Indigenous peoples are taking the lead in challenging the notion that states are a foundation for either peace or environmental security. At stake is not the existence or even the legitimacy of states but rather the survival of peoples, an issue that involves such diverse issues as cultural and religious freedom, language rights, and political autonomy. However, no single issue affects the survival of indigenous peoples as much as the state appropriation of the resources, in particular land, that indigenous peoples require if they are to survive as recognizable societies. It is the global

Notes on the chart:

This chart extrapolates language information contained in *Ethnologue: Languages of the World* (Barbara F. Grimes, editor, Summer Institute of Linguistics, 1992) to suggest the size and number of indigenous groups in the world. The chart uses information about first-language speakers.

When *Ethnologue* provides the number of speakers of a language out of what it calls an "entire ethnic group," the statistic for the entire group is used. *Ethnologue* describes ethnic group as a socio-political unit, and membership does not always agree on a one-to-one basis with speakers of languages. But for the purposes of this chart it is the size of an indigenous group that is most important here.

As with *Ethnologue*, this chart includes language groups rather than dialects when this distinction is possible. However, some dialects are spoken only by groups that consider themselves as

indigenous peoples. In other cases, such as the Hutu and Tutsi of East Africa, different groups speak the same language.

Land rights, particularly group homelands, are a primary factor in distinguishing indigenous groups from ethnic groups, which are not included in this chart. But this distinction, too, is problematic. For example, *Ethnologue* contains good data on all languages spoken in a country only when such data is of interest to the book's contributors.

When population estimates vary, the chart reflects the lowest figures. In some cases, no population estimates are available and that group falls in the "unknown" category. This chart assumes that such groups are small, but that assumption can't be verified.

The chart is based on the most recent data available, but that is the 1960s in a few cases.

appetite for resources that fuels the threats to indigenous peoples.

States and Nations

Recent history is characterized by dramatic and opposing changes in the statistics about states and nations. In fact, there is no such entity as a "nation-state" if that term means that a nation and the state represent the same people. Every state contains more than one nation, try as many states might to eliminate or assimilate ("melt") them all. Every state is multinational; put another way, every state is an empire. And states rule like empires—from the top down.

There are now more than 190 states in the world, up from only 50 before World War II and 170 as recently as 1989. More than 200 states will exist by the year 2000. Thus even though it may seem that states have existed forever, most are brand new. It seems naive to expect today's chaotic state system to stabilize at all.

By contrast, the world's 6,000 or so indigenous groups have been around for centuries, even millennia. Indigenous peoples are defined primarily

---

In the few instances when a group is divided between two or more countries and no other basis is available for estimating separate populations, the chart divides the total population equally.

The abbreviation "n.a." (not available) signifies that the numbers are unknown for a population within a country; a zero means there is evidence that a country contains no groups of that size.

"Cross Borders" refers to the number of groups within that country whose populations cross international borders.

In conclusion, most of these figures are tentative. The data is presented in the expectation that its publication for review and evaluation will yield better information. Send comments to Populations, Rights and Resources, 1101 Highland St., Room 411, Arlington, VA 22201.

Languages and Peoples

	1–5,000	5,001–50,000	50,001–250,000	250,001–1 million	Over 1 million	Unknown	Cross Borders
AFRICA							
Algeria	1	2	2	3	2	5	7
Angola	6	12	6	4	3	10	22
Benin	2	18	17	5	1	6	23
Botswana	8	3	1	1	n.a.	13	9
British Indian Ocean Territories	1	0	0	0	0	0	1
Burkina Faso	16	27	20	3	2	6	30
Burundi	1	0	0	1	1	0	2
Cameroon	68	106	29	5	2	63	73
Cape Verde Islands	1	0	1	0	0	0	2
Central African Republic	15	23	9	4	n.a.	40	44
Chad	21	53	13	1	1.	28	43
Comoros Islands	n.a.	n.a.	n.a.	1	n.a.	1	1
Congo	16	16	5	1	1	19	36
Côte d'Ivoire	11	27	11	7	2	4	17
Djibouti	0	0	1	1	0	0	2
Egypt	n.a.	1	1	1	3	1	4
Equatorial Guinea	3	2	0	1	0	0	4
Ethiopia	34	31	13	6	8	18	19
Gabon	17	16	2	n.a.	n.a.	4	21
Gambia	4	3	4	1	n.a.	4	11
Ghana	11	30	17	6	3	1	26
Guinea	3	14	6	3	2	1	18
Guinea Bissau	6	6	4	1	n.a.	3	16
Kenya	7	13	18	7	7	1	14
Lesotho	n.a.	n.a.	n.a.	n.a.	1	1	2
Liberia	2	15	9	2	3	3	11
Libya	2	2	n.a.	n.a.	2	5	5
Madagascar	1	0	0	0	1	0	1
Malawi	n.a.	2	3	4	1	1	9
Mali	3	9	6	9	1	1	23
Mauritania	2	2	1	0	2	0	5
Mauritius	0	0	0	1	0	0	0
Mayotte	n.a.	n.a.	n.a.	n.a.	n.a.	1	1
Morocco	n.a.	n.a.	n.a.	n.a.	4	2	4
Mozambique	1	6	6	9	4	3	16
Namibia	7	7	3	n.a.	n.a.	2	15
Niger	2	7	1	5	2	2	17
Nigeria	107	141	50	18	11	101	48
Reunion	0	0	0	0	0	0	0
Rwanda	0	0	0	0	1	0	1
Sao Tomé e Principe	0	0	0	0	0	0	0
Senegal	9	15	6	6	1	1	26
Seychelles	0	0	1	0	0	0	1
Sierra Leone	1	6	7	2	2	1	11
Somalia	2	3	2	1	1	0	2
South Africa	2	n.a.	4	3	6	9	14
St. Helena	0	0	0	0	0	0	0
Sudan	35	62	17	7	1	16	39
Swaziland	0	0	0	1	0	0	1
Tanzania	5	34	45	22	5	11	21
Togo	9	14	11	3	n.a.	2	27
Tunisia	n.a.	n.a.	n.a.	n.a.	1	6	n.a.
Uganda	6	4	12	9	6	2	19
Zaire	34	59	36	16	8	58	51
Zambia	3	8	17	5	1	3	26
Zimbabwe	1	4	5	4	1	0	13
Subtotal	**486**	**803**	**422**	**190**	**104**	**459**	**854**

65

No single issue affects the survival of indigenous peoples as much as the state appropriation of the resources, in particular land, that indigenous peoples require if they are to survive as recognizable societies.

by a unique language, by a long-term relationship to a homeland, and by the one-time exercise of political control over their destinies. Simply, indigenous people lived in their homeland before the arrival of more recent migrants. States mean little—or little that is constructive—to most indigenous peoples.

Why should indigenous peoples identify with the states that claim to govern them but give them no voice? The past century of "progress" and "civilization" provides good evidence that more indigenous cultures have disappeared than during any previous 100 years. Although more laws, treaties, and conventions protect human rights and outlaw genocide than ever before, it is arguable that the most violations occur today as well. Brazil has "lost" an average of one nation per year since the turn of the century—a loss amounting to one-third of its cultures existing in 1900—as government officials and planners have done their best to appropriate Indian rights to the Amazon.

At the heart of the matter is the state-building, nation-destroying process, a process founded on the belief that indigenous peoples and states can't coexist. One way states get rid of peoples is to ban their languages or at the very least denigrate them or prohibit their teaching in public schools. It's impossible to know how many self-identified peoples have disappeared—many were unknown to outsiders—but language provides the best available data. Although it is not a perfect reflection of a people's identity, language is an important win-

dow on the world's cultural diversity. More than half the world's 15,000 known languages have disappeared already; only 5 to 10 percent of the remaining 6,000 to 7,000 are likely to survive another 50 years.

States also attack cultural practices, local religions, and community-centered governments. States can't exploit resources—land, trees, minerals, water—without denying the rights of the inhabitants, indigenous peoples, who have lived on and maintained this base and who often hold parts or all of it sacred. To look at this process another way, states are destroying indigenous peoples even faster than the often fragile resources these groups have used and maintained for centuries.

These states are rarely, if ever, created by those who are governed by them. For the past century, white men thousands of miles distant have created the boundaries of most new states. And they do so because self-governed entities are cheaper than colonial occupation. Make no mistake: Europeans and North Americans are essentially seeking trading partners who can ensure politically stable economic systems and the free flow of goods.

These so-called "nation-states" reflect the image and interests of, at best, a few of the indigenous groups in each state. Dictatorships and one-party states are the norm, and the elites dominating these new Third World states control foreign investment and foreign assistance—military and developmental—both of which reinforce their power. Such elites typically fix local commodity prices and control exports. Together, these economic activities account for two-thirds of state revenues. The final third is derived from taxes, often disproportionately levied on disenfranchised indigenous peoples.

Those who control states make and interpret the laws, usually in their own image and interests. They say who owns which resources. These elites determine the legality of specific religions, languages, cultural traditions, and holidays. Because these practices are integral to the survival of indigenous peoples, such policies often trigger violent confrontations.

Against this background, the rise of nationalism is no surprise. Many indigenous peoples are examining the costs and benefits of being incorporated into states. They did not create the states that govern them, and these governing structures have little reason for being other than to expropriate the very resources that indigenous people require for the survival of future generations.

Indigenous Rights and Natural Resources

Despite this history of cultural destruction, at least 600 million indigenous people retain both a strong identity as part of an indigenous society and an attachment to a specific territory. These indigenous peoples are distinguished from ethnic groups who may have immigrated to lands that hold no sacred meaning for them. Also, ethnic groups usually make a tacit accommodation with the state system, trading away political autonomy for the ability to retain and practice other cultural beliefs.

Still, except for a few isolated indigenous societies, the dividing line between what is indigenous and what is an immigrant ethnic population is neither clear cut nor stable. Calls for autonomy in former socialist states show that even groups thought to be ethnic can desire local control and

Languages and Peoples

	1–5,000	5,001–50,000	50,001–250,000	250,001–1 million	Over 1 million	Unknown	Cross Borders
NORTH AMERICA							
Canada	54	12	n.a.	n.a.	n.a.	3	27
Greenland	0	1	0	0	0	0	0
Mexico	112	97	14	5	n.a.	12	7
St. Pierre and Miquelon	0	0	0	0	0	0	0
U.S.A.	137	23	3	n.a.	n.a.	8	33
Subtotal	**303**	**133**	**17**	**5**	**0**	**23**	**67**
CENTRAL AMERICA AND THE CARIBBEAN							
Anguilla	0	0	0	0	0	0	0
Antigua	0	0	0	0	0	0	0
Bahamas	0	0	0	0	0	0	0
Barbados	0	0	0	0	0	0	0
Belize	0	2	0	0	0	0	2
Bermuda	0	0	0	0	0	0	0
British Virgin Islands	0	0	0	0	0	0	0
British West Indies	0	0	0	0	0	0	0
Costa Rica	5	n.a.	n.a.	n.a.	n.a.	1	1
Cuba	0	0	0	0	0	0	0
Dominica	n.a.	n.a.	n.a.	n.a.	n.a.	1	n.a.
Dominican Republic	0	0	0	0	0	0	0
El Salvador	1	2	0	0	0	0	3
Grenada	0	0	0	0	0	0	0
Guadeloupe	0	0	0	0	0	0	0
Guatemala	4	32	12	2	n.a.	1	10
Haiti	0	0	0	0	0	0	0
Honduras	3	2	0	0	0	0	3
Jamaica	0	0	0	0	0	0	0
Martinique	0	0	0	0	0	0	0
Netherlands Antilles	0	0	0	0	0	0	0
Nicaragua	2	3	1	0	0	0	2
Panama	5	2	1	0	0	0	7
Puerto Rico	0	0	0	0	0	0	0
St. Kitts-Nevis	0	0	0	0	0	0	0
St. Lucia	0	0	0	0	0	0	0
St. Vincent/Grenadines	n.a.	n.a.	n.a.	n.a.	n.a.	1	n.a.
Trinidad and Tobago	0	0	0	0	0	0	0
U.S. Virgin Islands	0	0	0	0	0	0	0
Subtotal	**20**	**43**	**14**	**2**	**0**	**4**	**28**
SOUTH AMERICA							
Argentina	14	4	1	2	n.a.	3	13
Bolivia	30	3	1	n.a.	2	6	11
Brazil	201	8	n.a.	n.a.	n.a.	27	51
Chile	4	1	1	1	n.a.	4	4
Colombia	59	9	1	n.a.	n.a.	23	40
Ecuador	12	4	1	1	1	1	7
Falkland Islands	0	0	0	0	0	0	0
French Guiana	6	1	0	0	0	0	6
Guyana	6	0	0	0	0	0	3
Paraguay	13	5	n.a.	n.a.	1	1	9
Peru	55	26	6	n.a.	2	10	21
Surinam	8	2	1	0	0	0	6
Uruguay	0	0	0	0	0	0	0
Venezuela	34	4	n.a.	n.a.	n.a.	2	30
Subtotal	**442**	**67**	**12**	**4**	**6**	**77**	**201**
ASIA							
Afghanistan	21	6	3	2	5	9	23
Bahrain	n.a.	n.a.	n.a.	1	n.a.	1	2
Bangladesh	12	8	6	5	2	2	28
Bhutan	1	1	2	3	n.a.	2	6
Brunei	5	3	1	n.a.	n.a.	1	8
Cambodia	9	5	1	1	1	0	7
China	28	24	29	19	27	29	70

even put forth claims for autonomy or independence. Whether groups stay within existing state political systems, attempt to set up new ones, or seek some degree of autonomy over specific regions depends to a great extent on whether they have long-standing claims to specific homelands. Indigenous peoples become ethnic groups, overtly incorporated into states, largely when they lose their land rights.

Few, if any, indigenous groups willingly relinquish these rights. Many have been forced out by governments, individuals, or corporations; others have "abandoned" their lands as a result of widespread disease brought by contact with outsiders. Some indigenous people have lost land rights as a result of not-so-subtle constitutional manipulation. For example, the United States and many other countries have, at one time or another, discussed or even implemented legislation eliminating the right of groups to collectively control their land. And legal hair-splitting allows states to separate land rights from rights to the timber, minerals, water, or genetic matter on it.

Nevertheless, even after centuries of displacement and expropriation, indigenous peoples account for some 10 to 15 percent of the world's population. And although many groups have disappeared, the population of the remaining groups may equal or even surpass that of all indigenous peoples prior to contact with outsiders. After being decimated through European colonization from 1500 to 1945, the populations of many of the world's indigenous cultures have surged since 1900, especially since World War II. Ironically, this is precisely the

period during which most of the world's states appeared. Thus most states emerged exactly when many nations felt that their increasing numbers made it possible to seek more autonomy and to regain the political independence that colonialism had denied them.

At the same time, indigenous peoples have traditional claims over some 25 to 30 percent of the earth's land area and resources. Since World War II, many states, and corporations as well, have realized that of the various "inputs" to production, land and natural resources are the most limited and the hardest to replace. This has led to the invasion of remote areas and the appropriation of the resources found there. Because indigenous peoples occupy—in justice, own—most of these areas, this appropriation can only proceed after denying the rights of the inhabitants. Indian nations throughout the Americas have lost their lands to state-sponsored colonists. Pastoralists throughout Africa have lost land to the more numerous agriculturalists in control of states. Oil has been taken from the Kurds in Iraq, as it has from other nations, without compensation because such groups lack subsoil rights. Profits from the sale of natural resources accrue to those who run the state.

In short, the appropriation of the resources of indigenous peoples causes conflict. That leads to weapons purchases, which leads to debt, which leads, in turn, to the need to appropriate more resources. It is a spiraling and deadly escalation. Indigenous peoples that attempt to survive—that is, continue to speak their language, practice their religion, and retain rights to the resources that

Those in charge of states see the controlling of indigenous peoples as essential, yet it is the very same state policies that fuel the hostility of indigenous peoples and make control imperative.

future generations will require—are perceived to be enemies of the state's authority. Such groups are destroyed. It doesn't take sophisticated weaponry to destroy indigenous peoples, although Iraq employed poison gas to eliminate the Kurds. The military has wielded rifles and fence posts in Guatemala to destroy Mayan villages. Measles-infected blankets have effectively destroyed Brazilian Indians when decrees have failed. The Tutsi in Burundi used *pangas* (machetes) and simple firearms to put down a Hutu rebellion (85 percent of the population), killing 30,000 people and forcing another 50,000 to flee as refugees.

Those in charge of states see the control of indigenous peoples as essential, yet it is the very same state policies that fuel the hostility of indigenous peoples and make control imperative. State-sponsored programs, from relocation and colonization to resettlement, are attempts to dominate indigenous peoples and their lands and resources. Food and famine are weapons in these conflicts. Displacement, malnutrition, environmental degradation, refugees, and genocide are commonplace.

Nor does any state ideology seem better than the others at protecting indigenous peoples—or at promoting pluralism, which is another way of accomplishing the same goal. States on both the left and the right, as well as religious and sectarian states, repress indigenous rights—Ethiopia and Guatemala, Indonesia and Azerbaijan, Malaysia and Israel, Sudan and South Africa, Bosnia and Burma.

Industrialized countries are not passive or unwitting observers in these dramas; they actively promote and support highly centralized, top-down governments around the world. Investments, political interference, and manipulation help maintain the power of ruling groups. Foreign and military assistance support the dictatorships and single-party states that maintain the flow of

Languages and Peoples

	1–5,000	5,001–50,000	50,001–250,000	250,001–1 million	Over 1 million	Unknown	Cross Borders
Hong Kong	1	0	0	0	0	0	0
India	92	122	56	25	39	71	81
Indonesia, Irian Jaya	193	30	3	n.a.	n.a.	20	16
Indonesia, Javaand Bali	1	n.a.	n.a.	2	4	2	2
Indonesia, Kalimantan	31	36	10	1	1	1	16
Indonesia, Maluku	87	36	3	n.a.	n.a.	5	n.a.
Indonesia, Nusa Tenggara	15	22	10	6	1	7	n.a.
Indonesia, Sulawesi	38	44	23	3	2	5	4
Indonesia, Sumatra	2	13	13	15	7	1	n.a.
Iran	1	6	4	8	6	22	20
Iraq	n.a.	1	2	1	5	6	11
Israel and Palestine	6	1	3	n.a.	2	2	5
Japan	n.a.	1	n.a.	1	1	10	2
Jordan	n.a.	n.a.	n.a.	n.a.	2	1	3
Kazakhstan	1	1	1	0	1	0	3
Korea, North	0	0	0	0	1	0	1
Korea, South	0	0	0	0	1	0	1
Kuwait	1	n.a.	1	n.a.	1	1	4
Kyrghyzstan	0	1	0	0	1	0	2
Laos	40	21	8	1	1	18	46
Lebanon	n.a.	1	n.a.	n.a.	1	1	3
Macau	0	1	0	1	0	0	2
Malaysia, Peninsula	17	4	n.a.	1	n.a.	2	2
Malaysia, Sabah	25	21	3	n.a.	2	4	18
Malaysia, Sarawak	33	9	1	1	n.a.	2	13
Maldives	0	0	1	0	0	0	1
Myanmar	18	36	16	7	4	21	57
Nepal	29	26	6	6	3	27	28
Oman	n.a.	n.a.	1	1	n.a.	2	3
Pakistan	18	11	12	4	12	7	26
Philippines	44	63	26	8	9	15	7
Qatar	0	0	1	0	0	0	1
Russia, Asia	23	12	2	3	1	2	8
Saudi Arabia	n.a.	n.a.	n.a.	n.a.	2	4	2
Singapore	0	1	0	0	0	0	2
Sri Lanka	1	n.a.	n.a.	n.a.	2	1	2
Syria	1	1	n.a.	1	3	1	7
Taiwan	8	6	2	n.a.	2	10	n.a.
Tajikistan	5	2	0	0	1	0	6
Thailand	26	19	4	1	7	14	40
Turkey	3	5	5	3	2	2	12
Turkmenistan	n.a.	1	n.a.	n.a.	1	1	2
United Arab Emirates	1	0	0	1	0	0	1
Uzbekistan	n.a.	1	n.a.	2	1	1	4
Vietnam	33	26	10	8	1	9	47
Yemen	1	n.a.	n.a.	n.a.	1	1	2
Subtotal	871	628	269	142	164	343	657
EUROPE							
Albania	n.a.	1	1	1	2	2	5
Andorra	1	2	0	0	0	0	3
Armenia	n.a.	n.a.	n.a.	n.a.	1	1	2
Austria	1	3	n.a.	2	1	1	8
Azerbaijan	4	2	1	0	1	0	4
Belarus	0	0	0	0	1	0	1
Belgium	0	1	1	0	2	0	4
Bulgaria	2	2	1	1	1	3	10
Croatia	n.a.	n.a.	n.a.	n.a.	1	1	1
Cyprus	2	0	1	1	0	0	3
Czechoslovakia	1	1	4	1	2	4	12
Denmark	0	2	0	0	1	0	3
Estonia	1	0	1	0	1	0	3
Finland	3	1	n.a.	1	1	1	6
France	n.a.	1	3	3	2	6	9

69

resources needed by multinational corporations to feed the so-called developed world's voracious appetites for consumer goods.

Predicting and Preventing Human-Rights Violations

This is the context in which indigenous rights are eroded. Indeed, it is the context that already has eliminated most of the world's indigenous groups. It is time to go beyond documenting human-rights abuses and start preventing them. This means doing more than extinguishing the human-rights fires that spring up throughout the world; it requires addressing the specific conditions that lead states to violate indigenous rights.

Toward this end, I direct an effort to assemble a computer database of information on the languages of the world. The idea is to use language information as the core for a database on indigenous peoples. This project now includes information on numbers of people, the languages and dialects they speak, various names for each group, areas where each lives, and whether members of the group live in more than one state (*see chart*).

Driven by the states/nations analysis, the next step will be to add information that will reveal conditions that would enhance or threaten the survival of a specific people. In other words, to determine or predict what makes indigenous peoples vulnerable to abuses by states. What types of information do activists and scholars need to gather about the world's more than 6,000 indigenous societies in order to begin to identify and predict—and *prevent*—ethnocide and genocide?

In building this database, the questions that follow are critical to learning which indigenous groups are most threatened and under which circumstances. Using the answers as initial guidelines, it is apparent that few of the world's indigenous cultures have a strong chance of surviving even another 50 years.

Size: Does the group have enough members to reproduce itself? Is it large enough to withstand epidemics? What evidence is available on this topic? For example, if the scientific consensus is that groups of 5,000 or fewer are at severe risk, then over 3,000 nations are now at risk, including three-fourths of all the indigenous peoples in the Brazilian Amazon.

Resources: What resources are on lands owned or occupied by the group in question? Are these resources scarce locally? In particular, what resources might those wielding power covet? What resources—such as timber, precious or strategic minerals, oil, water, arable land, or genetic or chemical material—are in demand internationally? Are the values of these materials on local, national, and world markets changing? What legal rights does a group have to the resources on its land? Which resource rights are ambiguous or not defined in law? Are the resource rights sufficient for the group to continue its way of life? For example, does a hunter-gatherer group own the trees and water as well as the land? Can minerals be exploited without a group's consent?

Language: Does the state allow the group to use its own language? Is the language written? Can the language be taught in local schools? Do textbooks exist in the language? The uniqueness of each culture is reflected in its language. Most cultures have concepts, ideas, and specific words that do not translate well, if at all. As languages disappear, cultures die.

Cultural Practices: Does the state protect or deny any of the group's cultural and religious practices? Are the group's cultural practices tolerated? Are its members forced to participate in the cultural practices of those who dominate the state? Does the state constitution protect the group's religion? What religious-based conflicts have occurred between the group and others? Does the state have an official religion? Are or have peoples been forced to convert to it?

Divided Groups: Is the group divided between two or more states? Can the group continue its cultural, religious, and resource-use practices across the borders? Have the states respected or sought to dismantle indigenous political structures? Has this made it difficult to maintain cultural identities across borders? Are groups that straddle borders seen as threats to either state, special security risks, or potential allies with neighboring states?

Conflicts and Alliances: Does the group have a history of conflicts with other peoples or with the state? Do other groups have the power within the state to impose their will? Has the group ever aligned with another group or another state in ways that might jeopardize its future relationship to another group or state?

Refugees and Displaced People: Have members of the group ever fled across state boundaries as refugees? Has the group ever been displaced or relocated? Do the groups or states responsible still have power?

The Oromo, a nation of some 20 million people in Ethiopia, have a saying: You can't wake a person who's pretending to sleep. It is time to realize that states do not see indigenous rights as being in their best interest. States were not created by or for local people. But if states are to be effective at preserving the world's cultural diversity and the resources necessary to sustain life on earth, they must be democracies built from the bottom up, not empires imposed from the top down.

Jason Clay is the founder of Cultural Survival Enterprises and founding editor of *Cultural Survival Quarterly.* He is currently co-director of Rights and Resources, a nonprofit organization based in Washington, DC. Jennifer Rathaus provided the information for the tables.

Languages and Peoples

	1–5,000	5,001–50,000	50,001–250,000	250,001–1 million	Over 1 million	Unknown	Cross Borders
Georgia	1	1	1	2	1	0	3
Germany	1	3	2	n.a.	n.a.	10	8
Gibraltar	0	0	0	0	1	0	1
Greece	1	2	2	n.a.	2	1	5
Hungary	2	1	2	0	1	0	5
Iceland	0	0	1	0	0	0	0
Ireland	1	0	1	0	1	0	3
Italy	n.a.	2	6	1	8	5	7
Latvia	2	0	0	0	1	0	2
Liechtenstein	0	1	0	0	0	0	1
Lithuania	1	0	0	0	1	0	2
Luxembourg	0	0	0	1	2	0	3
Malta	0	0	0	1	1	0	2
Moldova	0	0	2	1	0	0	3
Monaco	1	2	0	0	0	0	3
Netherlands	0	0	0	1	1	0	2
Norway	1	2	n.a.	n.a.	1	3	5
Poland	0	0	2	0	3	0	3
Portugal	n.a.	n.a.	n.a.	n.a.	1	1	1
Romania	n.a.	1	2	n.a.	2	4	9
Russia, Europe	14	11	12	11	2	4	18
San Marino	0	1	0	0	0	0	1
Slovenia	0	0	0	0	1	0	1
Spain	1	1	1	1	3	5	4
Sweden	1	1	n.a.	1	1	3	7
Switzerland	0	0	1	1	3	0	4
Ukraine	n.a.	2	2	n.a.	2	2	8
United Kingdom	1	n.a.	1	1	1	5	1
Yugoslavia	n.a.	1	3	2	4	2	9
Subtotal	**43**	**47**	**54**	**34**	**61**	**64**	**195**
PACIFIC							
American Samoa	0	1	0	0	0	0	1
Australia	227	2	n.a.	n.a.	n.a.	30	1
Belau	6	1	0	0	0	0	1
Cook Islands	3	1	0	0	0	0	1
Fiji	1	3	n.a.	1	n.a.	2	1
French Polynesia	4	2	1	0	0	0	1
Guam	0	2	1	0	0	0	2
Kiribati	0	0	1	0	0	0	1
Marshall Islands	0	1	0	0	0	0	1
Micronesia	14	4	0	0	0	0	2
Midway Islands	0	0	0	0	0	0	0
Nauru	1	1	0	0	0	0	0
New Caledonia	30	3	n.a.	n.a.	n.a.	2	n.a.
New Zealand	0	0	0	1	0	0	0
Niue	1	0	0	0	0	0	1
Norfolk Island	1	0	0	0	0	0	1
Northern Mariana Island	0	1	0	0	0	0	1
Papua New Guinea	685	129	6	n.a.	n.a.	37	16
Pitcairn	1	0	0	0	0	0	1
Samoa	0	0	1	0	0	0	1
Solomon Islands	51	13	n.a.	n.a.	n.a.	2	n.a.
Tokelau	1	0	0	0	0	0	1
Tonga	3	n.a.	n.a.	n.a.	n.a.	2	1
Tuvalu	1	0	0	0	0	0	0
Vanuatu	100	4	n.a.	n.a.	n.a.	2	1
Wake Island	0	0	0	0	0	0	0
Wallisand Futuna	1	1	0	0	0	0	2
Subtotal	**1,131**	**169**	**10**	**2**	**0**	**77**	**38**
TOTAL	**3,296**	**1,890**	**798**	**379**	**335**	**1,047**	**2,040**

71

Indigenous Peoples and the State: Rights and Reality

**LAND
RIGHTS**

Australia

The 1992 *Mabo vs. Queensland* decision acknowledged the existence of native land titles. However, it left unresolved the definition of native title rights and the questions of which lands are subject to native titles and which indigenous people are the legitimate holders of native title rights. No compensation is payable for native titles lost prior to the decision, and titles to remaining lands can be extinguished in various ways.[1]

Brazil

The period established by Brazil's Constitution for demarcating all indigenous lands in Brazil ends in October 1993. Demarcation that should have taken place in 1992 was not carried out due to a lack of financial resources. Congress approved only 4.8 percent of the funding requested by FUNAI, the government Indian agency. In 1993, FUNAI asked for $16,781,000 for its work; the government budget request sent to Congress was for $1,654,000.[2]

Papua New Guinea

On June 26, 1992, the government approved the April-Salumei Timber Rights Purchase, one of Papua New Guinea's largest industrial forest operations, one day before parliament passed a strict new forest act. Thus, the operation will fall under an older, less restrictive act, with fewer requirements for local control. Some landowners agreed to the deal under threat of legal action and without receiving full information about what it meant. Villagers, many of whom are illiterate, were told they would be taken to court if they didn't agree. The logging could displace up to 1,300 Bitara and Bahinemo peoples from eight villages and destroy a million acres of rain forest.[3]

Venezuela

On August 1, 1991, President Carlos Andres Perez signed a decree setting aside over 30,000 square miles as a "biosphere reserve" to protect the environment and the indigenous people of the upper Orinoco and Casiquiare rivers. The decree guarantees the right of indigenous people to use the land, woods, and waters in their traditional territories, and it forbids colonization. However, the decree implies no legal land titles for indigenous inhabitants. These lands are considered to be the property of the state, leaving Indians the right to use them but not own them.[4]

**RELIGIOUS
RIGHTS**

Indonesia

Indonesia does not recognize the ancestor worship of the Sumba islanders and the Weyewa as a religion. State ideology calls upon its citizens to demonstrate national unity by believing in one god, excluding ancestor worship. The government is pressuring the Weyewa to end their ritual practices and convert to Islam, Buddhism, or Christianity. A child must have a birth certificate endorsed by Christian officials to enroll in school.[5]

[1.] *Regional Councillor*, January 1993.
[2.] Amnesty International, "Information Packet," Indigenous Peoples of the Americas Campaign.
[3.] *See* "Oceania" in the Global Rights Summary in this volume.
[4.] *Cultural Survival Quarterly*, Winter 1992
[5.] *Cultural Survival Quarterly*, Spring 1992.

Malaysia

Malaysia's Department of Aboriginal Affairs aims to absorb the Orang Asli into the Malay population by converting them to Islam and inducing them to adopt the Malay way of life. The Orang Asli do not want to become Malays, and the low quality of education they have received and their lack of economic resources have prepared them only for integration on the bottom rung of Malaysian society.[6]

North America

The 1978 American Indian Religious Freedom Act lacks any mechanisms for enforcement. Court decisions have further weakened the act by failing to protect Native American sacred sites. Native American leaders and environmental, human-rights, and religious groups are drafting amendments that would provide concrete mechanisms for enforcement, protect Native Americans' access to sacred objects, defend their right to use substances vital to their ceremonies, support the right of prisoners to practice Native American religion, and protect sacred sites.[7]

WAR

Burma

Burma's junta has perpetuated decades of ethnic conflict by brutalizing minorities. The ruling officers are mostly Burmese. Civilians from other ethnic groups (including Mons, Shans, and the indigenous Karens, Kachins, and Chins) are routinely subjected to rape, torture, and interrogation. Forced relocations are common. Attacks on actual rebels have lessened while the army concentrates on frontier civilians. Vast tracts are being deforested and depopulated, leaving "free-fire" zones where Karens once lived.[8]

Bougainville

A 1988 dispute over the revenue from and environmental effect of the Panguna Copper Mine escalated into an independence war involving the whole island, as well as Buka Island. The Bougainville Republican Army forced Papua New Guinea government troops to withdraw in 1990, but Papua New Guinea reestablished control over much of the island with a blockade of medical and other supplies that has left thousands dead. Several mini-wars have arisen between pro- and anti-rebel factions. Summary executions of suspected rebel sympathizers have been alleged, and 50,000 people have been displaced into government "care centers."[9]

Guatemala

Over the past three decades, government forces have killed 100,000 civilians (mostly Mayan Indians) and "disappeared" tens of thousands more. The army's systematic "scorched-earth" policy in rural areas has focused on the highland provinces of El Quiché, San Marcos, Huehuetenango, and Alta Verapaz. At least 43,000 refugees fled to Mexico, but a few thousand began to return in 1993, despite continuing repression by the Guatemalan military.[10]

Tajikistan

Resurgent communist armies, seeking to suppress Islamic political power, have driven tens of thousands of Tajik Muslims from their land. More than 25,000 people have been killed and 500,000 displaced since 1991.[11]

73

6. See "Southeast Asia" in the Global Rights Summary in this volume.
7. "Action for Cultural Survival," March 26, 1993.
8. "Action for Cultural Survival," March 26, 1993.
9. See "Oceania" in the Global Rights Summary in this volume.
10. New York Times, February 7, 1993; Daniel Faber, Environment Under Fire, Monthly Review Press, 1993.
11. New York Times, February 7, 1993.

Notes on Ethnocide

Region or People	Historical Impact on Indigenous Peoples
Tasmania[1]	About 5,000 indigenous people in 1642 About 6 in 1842
Australia[2]	300,000 indigenous people in 1700s 60,000 by 1900
Nicaragua[3]	825,000 indigenous people in 1492 61,106 in 1675
Latin America[4]	50,000,000 indigenous people in 1492 3,500,000 by mid-1600s
Central America[5]	5,625,000 indigenous people ca. 1492 540,000 by 1650
Hispaniola[6]	1,000,000 indigenous people in 1492 15,000 in 1518
Hawaii[7]	300,000–800,000 indigenous people in 1778 48,000–70,000 by 1900
North America[8]	3,790,000 indigenous people in 1492 250,000–350,000 by 1900
Caribbean[9]	3,000,000 indigenous people ca. 1492 Declared extinct within a generation
Peru[10]	9,000,000 indigenous people in 1520 670,000 in 1620
California[11]	300,000 indigenous people in 1800 20,000 in 1890 10,000 by 1950
Chamorro (Oceania)[12]	80,000 indigenous people in 1668 Fewer than 5,000 in 1741 1,500 by 1783
Bushmen (Southern Africa)[13]	200,000 indigenous people at contact 55,000 in 1921

1. "Ten Thousand Years of Solitude: The Bizarre Story of People Cut off from the World," *Discover*, March 1993.
2. Julian Burger, *Aborigines Today: Land and Justice*, Anti-Slavery Society, 1988.
3. William M. Denevan, ed., *The Native Population of the Americas in 1492*, 2nd ed., University of Wisconsin Press, 1992.
4. W. George Lovell and Christopher H. Lutz, "The Population History of Spanish Central America," in Robert McCaa, ed., *The Peopling of Latin America: Sources, Interpretations, and Commentary*, forthcoming; Darcy Ribeiro, *The Americas and Civilization*, Allen and Unwin, 1971.
5. William Denevan, *Native Population*; Daniel Faber, *Environment Under Fire: Imperialism and the Ecological Crisis in Central America*, Monthly Review Press, 1993.
6. Denevan, *Native Population*.
7. David Maybury-Lewis, *Millennium*, Viking, 1992; "Declaration from Independent Hawai'i," *Earth Island Journal*, Winter 1993; J.D. Bisignani, *Hawaii Handbook*, Moon Publications, 1989.
8. Denevan, *Native Population*; "Re-Viewing the Map," *Cultural Survival Quarterly*, Fall 1992.
9. Denevan, *Native Population*.
10. William M. Denevan, "The Pristine Myth: The Landscape of the Americas in 1492," *Annals of the Association of American Geographers*, 1992.
11. *Covert Action*, Spring 1992; "North American Census, 1492," *Pacific Discovery*, Winter 1992.
12. David Stanley, *Micronesia Handbook*, Moon Publications, 1989.
13. Carmel Schire and Robert Gordon, eds., *Future of Former Foragers: Australia and Southern Africa*, Cultural Survival Occasional Paper 18, 1985.

Nuclear War: Uranium Mining and Nuclear Tests on Indigenous Lands

UNITED STATES

Yakima, Colville, Nez Perce, Coeur d'Alene, Spokane, Kalispell, Umatilla, Klickitat

Hanford Nuclear Reservation in Washington state has caused dramatic increases in cancer rates among indigenous peoples. Radioactive gases and fluids released between 1944 and 1977 directly affected fish and wildlife. Eight out of nine reactors at the facility were water-cooled from the Columbia River, affecting the fish that provide Indians with food and economic subsistence. In 1957, Dawn Mining Co. began operating the Midnight Mine only a few miles from the Spokane Reservation in Washington state. The mine was closed in 1981. The leftover uranium mining pits hold contaminated water. One pit has 450 million gallons of contaminated water; another holds 150 million gallons of less contaminated water. A major concern is the contaminated water seeping into Lake Roosevelt.[1]

Navajo, Hopi

Uranium mining and above-ground nuclear-weapons tests have occurred for about 50 years on and around these reservations. Since 1942, the reservation lands and the surrounding areas of the Navajo and Hopi have been mined for uranium. From 1946 to 1968, 13 million tons of uranium were mined on the Navajo Reservation. The largest underground uranium mine on Navajo and Hopi lands operated from 1979 to 1990. The worst nuclear accident happened at Uranium Mill, which is south of the Navajo Reservation. More than 1,000 open-pit and underground uranium mines on the reservation are abandoned, unreclaimed, and highly radioactive. Some 600 dwellings on Navajo tribal lands are contaminated with radiation. Former uranium mining and milling districts of the Navajo Reservation suffer from cancer and leukemia clusters and birth defects.[2]

Western Shoshone, South Paiute

The Nevada Test Site is in the traditional land-use area of the Western Shoshone and South Paiute. The U.S. government appropriated the land in 1951 for exploding nuclear weapons. The Western Shoshone are the most bombed nation on the earth: 814 nuclear tests have been done on their land since 1951. Substantial radioactive fallout has contributed to a high concentration of cancer and leukemia on the reservation.[3]

Mescalero Apache, Prairie Island Mdewakanton, Minnesota Sioux, Skull Valley Goshutes, Lower Brule, two Alaskan native communities, Chickasaw, Sac and Fox, Eastern Shawnee, Quassarie, Ponca

These tribes have all applied to be sites for Monitored Retrievable Storage (MRS), a temporary solution to the problem of storing vast amounts of high-level nuclear waste. Such waste now sits at 110 nuclear power plants. The MRS sites would keep the waste for 40–50 years. The safety of these plants is still under question.[4]

CANADA

Inuit, Chipewyan, Metis, Anishinabe

A German company wants to establish the Baker Lake Mine in the Northwest Territories, 40 miles from an Inuit settlement. The 50 percent unemployment rate in this community gives the company leverage in opening the mine. The project includes one uranium mill, two open pits, and tailings covering 20 square miles.[5]

Cree, Chipewyan, Metis

Saskatchewan Province has been called the "Saudi Arabia of Uranium Mining." Four uranium deposits are being mined, the largest of which is

75

1. Ester Krumbholz and Frank Kressing, *Uranium Mining, Atomic Weapons Testing, Nuclear Waste Storage: A Global Survey*, World Uranium Hearing, 1992; *New York Times*, October 3, 29, and 30, 1990; Kimberly Craven, "Information Compiled for the World Uranium Hearing Briefing Book," Southwest Research and Information Center, 1992.

2. John Redhouse, "Overview of Uranium and Nuclear Development on Indian Lands in the Southwest," Redhouse/Wright Productions, 1992.

3. Krumbholz and Kressing, *Uranium Mining; High Country News*, December 1990; Worldwatch Institute, State of the World, Norton, 1991; Harvey Wasserman and Norman Solomon, *Killing Our Own: The Disaster of America's Experience with Atomic Radiation*, Delacorte Press, 1982.

4. "Minority Trends Newsletter," Summer 1992; Native Nevadan, June 1992; *Third Force*, March/April 1993; Craven, "World Uranium Hearing."

5. Krumbholz and Kressing, *Uranium Mining*.

Cigar Lake, with estimates it could supply 14,000 tons of uranium annually. Construction is planned to begin in 1994. The other mines in this area are Cluff Lake (now shut), Key Lake (which produces 12 percent of the world's uranium), Beaverlodge, and Rabbit Lake. From 1975 to 1977, a half million gallons of untreated waste went into Wallaston Lake. Radioactive contaminates still leak into the lake through groundwater channels.[6]

OCEANIA

Kokatha, Arabana

The Roxby Downs Mine/Olympic Dam has one of the world's largest deposits of uranium, producing 1.5 million tons of tailings a year. This affects an area of "mound spring," where artesian water naturally rises to the surface, that has a profound significance to local aborigines. The miners refuse to grant compensation to the aboriginal caretakers of the land for the sacred sites that have been destroyed by mine development. Olympic Dam operates under considerable secrecy and prohibits the Kokatha access to sacred sites without an escort of company personnel.[7]

Martujarra

The CRA Company has discovered one of Australia's largest uranium deposits inside Rudall National Park on indigenous lands. The mining would affect a women's sacred dreaming site at Mount Cotten, and mining would be done directly on Martujarra lands. The Martujarra have been unable to stop the mining because they have no property rights to their land.[8]

Aborigines (various)

From 1952 to 1963, the United Kingdom exploded nine aboveground nuclear bombs in Emu, Monte Bello, and Maralinga, affecting 11 aboriginal tribes. Radioactive contamination was widespread, and entry into large contaminated areas is still prohibited.[9]

Yami

In May 1982, Taiwan started to dump low-level radioactive waste on Lanyu, which is populated by 2,900 Yami. The first dump site is two miles from their villages. Strong opposition has mounted among the Yami against the establishment of a second nuclear dump. Ironically, Taiwan plans to establish its fifth national park in the vicinity of the dumps.[10]

Micronesians

In the 1940s and 1950s, the United States used Bikini, Enewetak, and Johnson atolls and Christmas Island for testing nuclear weapons. Among the short-term effects on the indigenous people were nausea, vomiting, and hair loss. Four weeks after tests, the white-blood-cell counts of many islanders were down 70 percent. The long-term health effects include high rates of cancers, miscarriages, birth defects, leukemia, and thyroid tumors. Four decades later, the people of Bikini Atoll are unable to return home, despite U.S. government promises that their homeland would be inhabitable again; the level of radioactive contamination is still too high.[11]

AFRICA

Tamacheq

From 1960 to 1965, France conducted above-ground nuclear-weapons tests in the Sahara desert, but it has released no information on contamination or on the people affected. There are also large deposits of uranium in the Hoggar Mountains that if mined are potentially harmful to the Tamacheq and other indigenous peoples.[12]

Tamacheq, Ful

Uranium is the major export of Niger, amounting to 90 percent of the country's 1980s exports. Niger's infrastructure is centered around uranium

6. Krumbholz and Kressing, *Uranium Mining*; Roger Moody, *The Indigenous Voice: Visions and Realities*, Vol. 1, Zed Books, 1988, Uranium Institute, 15th International Symposium, 1991.
7. Krumbholz and Kressing, *Uranium Mining*.
8. Julian Burger, *Gaia Atlas of First People*, Anchor Books, 1990; *Future for the Indigenous World*, Gaia Books, 1990; Moody, *Plunder!*; Partizans/Cafca, 1991; Judith L. Boice, "Searching for Uranium in Western Australia," Campaign for Indigenous Peoples Worldwide, 1993; Krumbholz and Kressing, *Uranium Mining*.
9. Arjun Makhijani, *Radioactive Heaven and Earth,* International Commission to Investigate the Health and Environmental Effects of Nuclear Weapons Production and the Institute for Energy and Environmental Research, 1991.
10. Krumbholz and Kressing, *Uranium Mining; Japan-Asia Quarterly Review,* Vol. 20, Nos. 1 and 2; *New York Times,* March 23, 1988.
11. Makhijani, *Radioactive Heaven and Earth.*
12. Krumbholz and Kressing, *Uranium Mining;* Makhijani, *Radioactive Heaven and Earth.*

mining. The mining occurs mostly in the desert region, which not only causes ecological damage to the land, but also affects nomadic tribes.[13]

Ovambo

The world's second-largest open-pit uranium mine is in Namibia, owned by the Rossing Co. Most of the mining is done by hundreds of Ovambo laborers who live in neo-colonial housing villages and work under an apartheid management system. They are exposed to high levels of radiation from radon gases. There are concerns that water-borne radiation from tailings left from mining operations could contaminate the Khar River.[14]

Khoikhoi, Bantu-speaking groups

South Africa has conducted one known nuclear-weapons test, on September 22, 1979. South Africa has three principal uranium deposits: Palaborwa, Witwatersrand, and Karoo Basin (Cape Province). The Bantu-speaking peoples are exposed to the hazards of mining and radioactive emissions from tailings because they work in these mines or have settlements nearby. South Africa is one of the world's largest producers of uranium and platinum-group metals. The mining industry is relatively unregulated, which results in many environmental problems, especially for black communities where mining smelters spew sulfur dioxide and toxic air pollutants. The traditional territory of the Khoikhoi in Northern Cape Province is slated to be a dump for radioactive materials.[15]

FORMER SOVIET UNION

Kazakh, Khanty, Mamsi, Evenk, Yakut, Chukchi, Eskimosy

The former Soviet Union conducted at least 713 nuclear-bomb tests above and below ground at many sites, affecting many indigenous peoples. The two main testing and nuclear sites are located at Semiplantinsk in Kazakhstan and Antic Island of Novaya Zemlya in Siberia. Although the government conducted no known health-effects research, it can be assumed that radioactive fallout affected local indigenous peoples. The Chukchee suffer from tuberculosis, 90 percent have chronic diseases of the lung, and the average life expectancy is 45 years.[16]

INDIA

Ho, Santal, and Mundu

Jadugara Mine produces 200 tons of yellow cake annually and affects the Ho, Santal, and Mundu. Many workers in the mine are tribal people who are illiterate and are forced to do the dirtiest jobs. They are exposed to high levels of radiation and don't have the proper protective gear. Many indigenous miners suffer from a high incidence of lung disease.[17]

Rajasthani and Bhil

The one confirmed nuclear underground test in 1974 in India caused the Rajasthani and Bhil tribes to move from their traditional lands.[18]

CHINA

Uigur, Kazakh, Kirgiz, Xibo, Tajik, Uzbek, Tatar, Western Mongols, Tibetan

All these peoples are affected in one way or another by uranium mining, bomb testing, and nuclear waste disposal. Uranium mines are scattered all over China. An "atomic factory" planned in the Gobi desert will affect such minorities as Mongols, Muslim Dugans, and Hui Chinese. Some of the world's richest uranium sources are located in Tibet, but the area is generally unsuitable for large-scale uranium mining. One hot spot for uranium mining in Tibet is the Riwoche Hill, a sacred site to Tibetans.[19]

13. Krumbholz and Kressing, *Uranium Mining*; OECD Nuclear Energy Agency and the International Atomic Energy Agency, "Statistical Update 1990: Uranium. Resources, Production and Demand."

14. Greg Dropkin and Davis Clark, 1992, "Past Exposure. Revealing Health and Environmental Risks of Rossing Uranium," Namibia Support Committee/PARTIZANS; Moody, *Plunder!*.

15. "Food First Action Alert," Fall 1992; Krumbholz and Kressing, *Uranium Mining*.

16. Krumbholz and Kressing, *Uranium Mining*; Makhijani, *Radioactive Heaven and Earth*.

17. Makhijani, *Radioactive Heaven and Earth*; Krumbholz and Kressing, *Uranium Mining*.

18. Krumbholz and Kressing, *Uranium Mining*; Makhijani, *Radioactive Heaven and Earth*.

19. Krumbholz and Kressing, *Uranium Mining*.

Stealing Lives: Exploiting Strategic Minerals

Australia
In 1957, Comalco, Ltd., a subsidiary of Kaiser Corp. and Rio Tinto Zinc, received government permission to mine bauxite on 5,000 square miles of aboriginal reserve land at less than 1 percent of the prevailing mining rental rates. The company also received timber, cattle-grazing, water, and farming rights and an exemption from the Clean Water Act. Comalco forced everyone in Weipa off their traditional land and confined them on a 308-acre, government-controlled compound. People now depend on hand-outs. Comalco has plans to open bauxite mines on the Aurukun Reserve, south of Weipa. The Aurukun had stopped the project, but the government canceled the reserve status of Aurukun and Mornington land.[1]

Colombia
The Makuna are hunters, fishers, gatherers, and agriculturalists. Gold mining disturbs their livelihood and religious practices by indiscriminately cutting forests and polluting rivers.[2]

Nauru
In 1906, open-pit phosphate mining began on the island of Nauru. The mine will probably run dry in 1996 and leave four-fifths of the island uninhabitable. Already Nauruans must import all supplies, including water. The import-based diet and forced sedentary lifestyle have reduced the life span of Nauruans, who now have one of the highest rates of diabetes in the world. The destruction of the subsistence economy has also damaged the economic and social independence of Nauruan women. Nauru became independent in 1968 and bought the mine for $21 million. It is seeking reparations from the former BPC nations.[3]

New Caledonia
New Caledonia has 40 percent of the world's nickel deposits, an industry important to France's military and nuclear-energy programs. Employment benefits for the indigenous Kanak are negligible. Nickel is a carcinogen with no identified safe level of exposure. New Caledonian ore also contains asbestos, which causes pleural cancer. Low-income housing has been built down-wind from a smelter, and people grow food on toxic tailing dumps. New Caledonia has high rates of lung cancer and childhood leukemia and the world's record for asthma-related deaths. Kanak life expectancy is low, especially among women.[4]

Philippines
In 1974, Bontoc women set up barricades against the gold mining by Benquet Consolidated Mining Corp. The next year, eight companies, headed by Benquet, petitioned President Ferdinand Marcos to prohibit all indigenous gold panning. He complied, depriving thousands of families of their key source of income. In 1986, Benquet denied Comote gold panners traditional mining rights and sent armed guards to drive them out. That same year, President Corazon Aquino appointed the former head of Benquet as minister of finance.[5]

United States
The livelihoods of the Gros Ventre and Assiniboine in Montana are threatened by a proposed expansion of the Zortman-Landusky gold mine, which could release more than a billion gallons of cyanide solution into the local watershed. Water samples taken on the reservation just below the mine already show elevated levels of lead, arsenic, cadmium, selenium, manganese, and nitrates. Mining will also severely damage the traditional religious and medical function of the Little Rocky Mountains.[6]

1. Julian Burger, *Report from the Frontier: The State of the World's Indigenous People,* Zed Books, 1987; Roger Moody, *Plunder!* Partizans/Cafca, 1991; Roger Moody, ed., *The Indigenous Voice: Visions and Realities,* Vol. I, Zed Books, 1988.
2. *Cultural Survival Quarterly,* Spring 1992.
3. *See* "Oceania" in the Global Rights Summary in this volume; Worldwatch Institute, *State of the World, 1992,* Norton, 1993; *Tok Blong SPPF,* No. 42, February 1993.
4. Burger, *Report from the Frontier; Tok Blong SPPF,* No. 42.
5. Moody, *The Indigenous Voice.*
6. *See* "United States and Canada" in the Global Rights Summary in this volume.

Stealing Lives: Exploiting Energy Resources

Canada
Since the early 1970s, development in the massive James Bay hydroelectric project has affected the traditional hunting and fishing areas of Cree Indians and the Inuit. The Cree were forced to sign a settlement in 1975 without public hearings or an environmental impact study. The lives of 9,000 Cree have been severely disrupted by the project's first phase, which wiped out Cree hunting and trapping grounds and displaced the Chisabi Cree community. Plans for more megaprojects were launched in the late 1980s.[1]

Ecuador and Colombia
Once numbering in the thousands, fewer than 700 Cofan survive after 20 years of oil development by Texaco. Airstrips, helicopters, roads, and dynamite have destroyed traditional livelihoods, leaving the remaining Cofan dependent on oil-camp food supplies.[2]

Nigeria
After 30 years of oil exploitation in their territory, the 500,000 Ogoni can no longer fish, farm, or hunt because the rivers are polluted and the farmlands have been rendered unproductive. Since 1958, Shell and Chevron have extracted $30 billion in oil from Ogoni land, yet Ogoni communities lack telecommunications, hospitals, electricity, roads, pipe-borne water, industry, and well-equipped schools. Unemployment is as high as 85 percent. Innumerable oil spills from outdated equipment have driven fish offshore, where the Ogoni are not equipped to fish.[3]

Peru
The Aguaruna and Huambisa oppose the invasion of their lands in the Upper Maranon River basin by Edward Callan Interests and Halliburton Geophysical Services, both based in Houston, Texas. Peruvian troops are protecting the prospecting activities of these oil companies.[4]

Philippines
Although Mount Apo is a national park and an ancestral home for the Bagobo and eight other indigenous peoples, the Philippine National Oil Company (PNOC) began exploratory drilling in 1985 at its base to test the potential for geothermal energy. The government denied the project an exploration permit in 1988, but PNOC went ahead anyway; by 1989 two test wells had been built. PNOC intends to build more roads and to dig as many as 40 geothermal wells. In 1989, the nine tribes signed a compact to defend their area. For expressing concern for their forests, indigenous leaders are called communists and detained and harassed by paramilitary forces. The military has bombed ancestral domains.[5]

Russia
In Siberia, Marathon Oil, Global Natural Resources, Gulf Canada, Mitsui, and others threaten vulnerable arctic ecosystems and the traditional subsistence economies of Chukotka, Evenk, Eskimosy, Yakut, and many other indigenous peoples.[6]

United States
The United States is developing geothermal energy in Hawaii's sacred Wao Kele O Puna rain forest. In 1985, the area was approved for development even though in 1898 the land had been dedicated to the use of Hawaiian people in perpetuity. Geothermal development denies native Hawaiians their right to worship and to gather medicinal plants. Geothermal wells produce toxic hydrogen sulfide gas, sulfuric acid, arsenic, lead, mercury, manganese, cadmium, and other heavy metals and toxic chemicals.[7]

1. *Cultural Survival Quarterly*, Winter 1992; *Cultural Survival Quarterly*, Spring 1992; Aboriginal Rights Coalition (Project North), "Amazon North: The Assault on Aboriginal Lands in Canada," 1992; Cultural Survival Canada Fact Sheet, "Quebec," 1992.
2. Burger, *Report from the Frontier: The State of the World's Indigenous People*, Zed Books, 1987.
3. *Cultural Survival Quarterly*, Summer 1993.
4. *World Rainforest Report*, Vol. IX, No. 1, 1993.
5. Robin Broad with John Cavanagh, *Plundering Paradise: The Struggle for the Environment in the Philippines*, University of California Press, 1993; *see* "Southeast Asia" in the Global Rights Summary in this volume.
6. Burger, *Report from the Frontier; see* "North Asia" in the Global Rights Summary in this volume; *Cultural Survival Quarterly*, Fall 1992.
7. *Earth Island Journal*, Winter 1993; *Cultural Survival Quarterly*, 14(4) 1990.

Stealing Lives: Exploiting the Forests

Canada
In the late 1980s, the Alberta government issued 20-year cutting permits, covering no less than a third of the province, to a dozen companies. One lease, to Daishowa, a Japanese pulp and paper company, comprises all the traditional lands of the Lubicon Cree. In addition to clear-cutting, four new pulp and paper mills will use the highly toxic bleached-kraft method. Daishowa started clear-cutting Lubicon land in 1990, ignoring the many attempts of the Lubicon to stop the logging.[1]

Chile
The araucaria tree—perhaps earth's oldest living tree species—is at the center of Pewenche religion and spiritual and physical sustenance. Since a white cattle rancher claimed legal rights to the Quinquen Valley in southern Chile in the early 1900s, the Pewenche have resisted logging. In 1976, Chile gave the araucaria "natural monument" status, which should have ended all logging. Illicit cutting and burning continued, however, due to a loophole: once a section of forest was burned, the dead but often useful remains of the araucaria could be legally logged. A 1987 decree removed all legal protection for the araucaria, and logging is accelerating.[2]

Indonesia
In West Papua, exploitation by the Korean firm Intimpura threatens the last remaining Moi rain forest. Earlier logging disrupted the Moi's livelihood, sources of medicine, and access to sacred places. The fish the Moi once caught have disappeared. The Moi have met with Intimpura representatives, the Indonesian forest service, and local government officials, and have undertaken direct action. The company and government officials reject the Moi's claim to their *adat* (ancestral domain).[3]

Indonesia
In the 1970s, the Indonesian military, police, and civilian officials used threats, intimidation, and force to make the Asmat log their own trees—which are central to their culture—for logging companies. The pay was well below the minimal government-set wage, and no compensation was provided for the loss of trees. The cost of tools supplied to villagers was deducted from their wages. People who refuse to work were labeled subversives, and harsh military actions answered protests.[4]

Sri Lanka
The nomadic hunter-gatherer Veddha have been pushed away and barred from ancestral hunting grounds and forests by officials serving illegal logging interests and commercial hunters. Several years ago, many Veddha were talked into accepting relocation in two large colonies in the Nahaweli hydro-electric and irrigation project, but part of the community now plans to return to the forest to try to sustain a traditional livelihood. There are concerns about starvation if the government doesn't allow them to hunt and gather food in their former domain.[5]

Thailand
Karen have become illegal squatters in forestry reserves created for logging. They are denied access to the forest and its products and sometimes removed with force. Traditional cultivation of swidden plots has become impossible. A road network built in the 1960s opened the highlands to Thai and foreign mining and logging companies, leading to watershed pollution and soil erosion. The Karen's economic deterioration threatens to extinguish them as a people. Poverty and malnutrition are forcing young Karen into low-paying jobs and prostitution.[6]

1. Aboriginal Rights Coalition, "Amazon North: The Assault on Aboriginal Lands in Canada," 1992; Cultural Survival Canada Fact Sheet, "Alberta," 1992.
2. *Cultural Survival Quarterly,* 14(4) 1990.
3. *Cultural Survival Quarterly,* Winter 1992.
4. Elaine Brière and Susan Gage, "The Indonesia Kit," East Timor Action Network, 1991; see "Southeast Asia" in the Global Rights Summary in this volume; *Cultural Survival Quarterly,* Fall 1991; *Cultural Survival Quarterly,* 14(4) 1990.
5. *Cultural Survival Quarterly,* Spring 1992.
6. Burger, *Report from the Frontier: The State of the World's Indigenous People,* Zed Books, 1987.

The Trade in Timber

Top 10 Exporters of Tropical Timber, 1990 (cubic meters)*

Country	Volume	Selected Affected Peoples
Malaysia	26,501,000	Penan, Orang Asli, Melabit, Kayan, Iban, Bidayah, Kenyah, Kelabit, Murat, Punan
Indonesia	8,845,000	Yamdena, Asmat, Batak, Amungme, Mentawa, Moi, Bitara, Bahinemo, Mae-Enga, Kapaku, Dayak, Dani, Chimbo, Asmat, Yaifer, Tiert, Amberon
Cameroon	1,180,000	Baaka Pygmy, Bakola Pygmy, Efe Pygmy
Côte d'Ivoire	1,090,000	
Gabon	1,090,000	
Papua New Guinea	1,088,000	Bitara, Bahinemo, Auyu
Liberia	809,000	
Brazil	746,000	Kayapó, Arara, Parakana, Araweté, Uru-Eu-Wau-Wau, Tupari, Ashaninka, Zoró, Nambiquara, Hahaintesu, Cinta Larga, Paiter, Macurapi, Canoê, Aikana
Congo	455,000	Baaka Pygmy
Ghana	419,000	
Philippines	351,000	Lumad, Bontoc, Hanunoo, Ifugao, Ibaloy, Kalinga

Top 10 Importers of Tropical Timber, 1990 (cubic meters)*

Country	Volume
Japan	15,623,000
Republic of Korea	4,696,000
Thailand	3,358,000
France	1,700,000
India	1,324,000
United States	1,313,000
Italy	1,310,000
United Kingdom	1,107,000
Netherlands	1,070,000
Germany (West)	1,018,000

* includes log, sawn wood, veneer, and plywood production
Source: International Tropical Timber Council, "Annual Review and Assessment of the World Tropical Timber Situation, 1990-1991."

81

Top 10 Exporters of Tropical and Temperate Timber, 1990**

Country	Exports
Canada	$11,592,461,000
United States	$10,091,658,000
Sweden	$4,025,528,000
Malaysia	$3,249,514,000
Indonesia	$3,149,089,000
Finland	$2,891,461,000
Germany (West)	$2,288,406,000
Austria	$2,130,451,000
France	$1,809,629,000
Belgium-Luxembourg	$1,411,147,000

Top 10 Importers of Tropical and Temperate Timber, 1990**

Country	Exports
Japan	$12,083,076,000
United States	$7,662,969,000
Germany (West)	$6,488,442,000
United Kingdom	$5,242,344,000
Italy	$4,601,045,000
France	$3,286,130,000
Republic of Korea	$2,627,450,000
Netherlands	$2,484,962,000
Belgium-Luxembourg	$1,569,509,000
Spain	$1,533,771,000

** includes pulpwood and wastepaper, wood-shaped sleepers, other wood rough (squared), pulpwood, chips, wood waste, fuelwood, charcoal, wood sheets, veneer sheets, reconstituted wood, improved reconstituted wood
Source: United Nations, *International Trade Statistics Yearbook*, 1990.

In Search of Homes

This table identifies the countries with the most people displaced within their homelands as a result of human conflict or forced relocation. Although internally displaced civilians share many characteristics with refugees who cross state borders, they are generally ineligible for international refugee assistance. This chart is based on reported official estimates. Actual figures are much higher. For example, tens of millions of peoples displaced by the Soviet Union are not included.

Internally Displaced Civilians, December 31, 1992

Sudan	5,000,000
South Africa	4,100,000
Mozambique	3,500,000
Somalia	2,000,000
Philippines	1,000,000
Angola	900,000
Bosnia and Herzegovina	740,000
Ethiopia and Eritrea	600,000
Liberia	600,000
Sri Lanka	600,000
Afghanistan	530,000
Burma	500,000–1,000,000
Peru	500,000
Iraq	400,000
Lebanon	400,000

This table identifies countries that have generated the most refugees. Counts may understate the total from a given country because asylum states don't always specify countries of refugees' origin. This table excludes people in refugee-like circumstances who aren't recognized by governments as refugees or asylum seekers. It also excludes refugees who have been offered permanent resettlement in another country. In 1992, for example, 44,336 Vietnamese resettled in the United States and 125,355 members of religious minorities left the former Soviet Union for Israel and the United States. This chart is based on official estimates; other estimates are much higher.

* indicates widely varying reports
Source: U.S. Committee for
   Refugees, "World Refugee
   Survey, 1993."

Sources of the World's Refugees and Asylum Seekers, December 31, 1992

* Afghanistan	4,286,000
Palestinians	2,658,000
* Mozambique	1,725,000
* Former Yugoslavia	1,697,800
Bosnia and Herzegovina	940,000
Croatia	350,000
Serbia and Montenegro	75,000
Other and Unspecified	332,800
* Somalia	864,800
Ethiopia and Eritrea	834,800
* Liberia	599,200
Angola	404,200
* Azerbaijan	350,000
* Burma	333,700
Sudan	263,000
* Armenia	202,000
* Rwanda	201,500
* Sierra Leone	200,000
Burundi	184,000

Draft Declaration on the Rights of Indigenous Peoples

For the past decade, indigenous peoples, through the Working Group on Indigenous Populations, which is affiliated with the UN Human Rights Commission, have been preparing the Declaration on the Rights of Indigenous Peoples. When completed and ratified, it will be the first document recognized under international law that both deals specifically with indigenous peoples and emerged on the basis of significant indigenous leadership. The draft, which could reach the UN General Assembly for approval during 1993, incorporates a number of provisions from other international treaties, guidelines, and conventions, especially Convention 169 of the International Labor Organization. Although it is far-reaching, the ILO convention comprises more a set of recommendations, and it incorporated indigenous input only after much criticism of an early version; moreover the convention has yet to be ratified by the United States and many other countries.

Preambular Paragraphs

Affirming that all indigenous peoples are equal in dignity and rights to all peoples in accordance with international standards, while recognizing the right of all individuals and peoples to be different, to consider themselves different, and to be respected as such,

Considering that all peoples contribute to the diversity and richness of civilizations and cultures, which constitutes the common heritage of humankind,

Reaffirming that all doctrines, policies and practices based on racism and racial, religious, ethnic or cultural superiority are scientifically false, legally invalid, morally condemnable and socially unjust,

Reaffirming also that indigenous peoples, in the exercise of their rights, should be free from discrimination of any kind,

Concerned that indigenous peoples have been deprived of their human rights and fundamental freedoms, resulting, inter alia, in the dispossession of their lands, territories and resources, as well as in their poverty and misery,

Recognizing the urgent need to respect and promote the inherent rights and characteristics of indigenous peoples, especially their rights to their lands, territories and resources, which derive from their cultures, spiritual traditions, histories and philosophies, as well as from their political, economic and social structures,

Welcoming the fact that indigenous peoples are organizing themselves in order to bring an end to all forms of discrimination and oppression wherever they occur,

Convinced that increasing the their control of indigenous peoples over development affecting them and their lands, territories and resources will enable them to continue to strengthen their Institutions, cultures, and traditions, as well as to promote their development in accordance with their aspirations and needs,

Recognizing also that respect for indigenous knowledge and practices contributes to sustainable development and management of the environment,

Emphasizing the need for demilitarization of the lands and territories of indigenous peoples, which will contribute to peace, economic and social progress and development, understanding and friendly relations among nations and peoples of the world,

Reaffirming the importance of giving special attention to the rights and needs of indigenous elders, women, youth, children, and disabled,

Recognizing in particular that it is in the best interest of indigenous children for their families and communities to retain shared responsibility for their upbringing, training and education,

Believing that indigenous peoples have the right freely to determine their relationships with States in a spirit of coexistence,

Considering that treaties, agreements and other constructive arrangements between States and indigenous peoples continue to be matters of international concern and responsibility,

Noting that the International Covenant on Economic, Social and Cultural Rights and the International Covenant on Civil and Political Rights affirm the fundamental importance of the right of self-determination of all peoples, by virtue of which they freely determine their political status and freely pursue their economic, social and cultural development,

Bearing in mind that nothing in this Declaration may be used as an excuse to deny any people their right of self-determination,

Encouraging States to comply with and effectively implement all international instruments as they apply to indigenous peoples, in consultation and cooperation with the peoples concerned,

Believing that this Declaration is a first step in the recognition, promotion and protection of the rights and freedoms of indigenous peoples in the development of relevent activties of the United Nations system in this field;

Solemnly proclaims the following Declaration on the Rights of Indigenous Peoples:

Operative Paragraphs
PART I

Indigenous peoples have the right to the full and effective enjoyment of all of the human rights and fundamental freedoms which are recognized in the Charter of the United Nations and in international human rights law;

Indigenous peoples are free and equal to all other human beings and peoples in dignity and rights, and have the right to be free from discrimination of any kind based on their indigenous origin or identity;

Indigenous peoples have the right of self-determination, in accordance with international law subject to the same criteria and limitations as apply to other peoples in accordance with the Charter of the United Nations. By virtue of this, they have the right, *interalia*, to negotiate and agree upon their role in the conduct of public affairs, their distinct responsibilities and the means by which they manage their own interests.

An integral part of this is the right to autonomy and self-government;

Indigenous peoples have the right to participate fully in the political, economic, social and cultural life of the State while maintaining their distinct cultural, economic, social and cultural characteristics;

PART II

Indigenous peoples have the collective right to exist in peace and security as distinct peoples and to be protected against any type of genocide.

Consequently, they have the individual rights to life, physical and mental integrity, liberty and security of person;

Indigenous peoples have the collective and individual right to be protected against ethnocide and cultural genocide, including the prevention of and redress for:

(a) Removal of indigenous children from their families and communities under any pretext;

(b) Any act which has the aim or effect of depriving them of their integrity as distinct societies, or of their cultural or ethnic characteristics or identities;

(c) Any form of forced assimilation or integration by imposition of other cultures or ways of life;

(d) Dispossession of their lands, territories or resources;

(e) Any propaganda directed against them;

Indigenous peoples have the collective and individual right to maintain and develop their distinctive characteristics and identities, including the right to identify themselves as indigenous;

The right of an indigenous person to belong to an indigenous nation or community is a matter of his or her individual choice and no disadvantage of any kind may arise from the exercise of such as choice;

Indigenous peoples shall not be forcibly removed from their lands or territories. Where relocation occurs it shall be with the free and informed consent of the indigenous peoples concerned and after the agreement on a fair and just compensation and, where possible, the option of return;

Indigenous peoples have the right to special protection and security in periods of armed conflict. States shall observe international standards for the protection of civilian populations in circumstances of emergency and armed conflict, and shall not:

(a) Recruit indigenous people against their will into the armed forces and, in particular, for use against other indigenous peoples;

(b) Recruit indigenous children into the armed forces under any circumstances;

(c) Force indigenous people to abandon their lands and territories and means of subsistence and relocate them in special centers for military purposes;

PART III

Indigenous peoples have the right to revitalize and practice their cultural traditions. This includes the right to maintain, protect and develop the past, present and future manifestations of their cultures, such as archeological and historical sites and structures, artifacts, designs, ceremonies, technologies and visual and performing arts and literatures, as well as the right to the restitution of cultural, religious and spiritual property taken from them without their free and informed consent or in violation of their laws. Scared places and cemeteries of indigenous peoples should be preserved and respected;

Indigenous peoples have the right to manifest, practice and teach their spiritual and religious traditions, customs and ceremonies; the right to maintain, protect, and have access in privacy to religious and cultural sites; the right to the use and control of ceremonial objects; and the right to the repatriation of human remains;

Indigenous peoples have the right to revitalize, use, develop, and transmit to future generations their languages, oral traditions, writing systems and literatures, and to designate and maintain their own names for communities, places and persons. States shall take effective measures to ensure that indigenous peoples can understand and be understood in political, legal and administrative proceedings, where necessary through the provision of interpretation or by other appropriate means;

PART IV

Indigenous peoples have the right to all levels and forms of education, including access to education in their own languages, and the right to establish and control their own educational systems and institutions;

Indigenous peoples have the right to have the dignity and diversity of their cultures, traditions, histories and aspirations reflected in all forms of education and public information. States shall take effective measures, in consultation with indigenous peoples, to eliminate prejudice and to promote tolerance, understanding and good relations;

Indigenous peoples have the right to the use of and access to all forms of media in their own languages;

PART V

Indigenous peoples have the right to participate fully at all levels of decision-making in matters which may affect their rights, lives and destinies through representatives chosen by themselves in accordance with their own procedures

Indigenous peoples have the right to participate fully, through procedures

> "Human rights involve group rights, not just individual rights. Many people are coming to realize that the rights we value most, the values we cherish most, are realized only as part of a community."
>
> *Tim Coulter, Potawatomi, Director, Indian Law Resource Center*

85

determined in consultation with them, in devising legislative and administrative measures that may affect them. States shall obtain the free and informed consent of the peoples concerned before implementing such measures;

Indigenous peoples have the right to maintain and develop their economic and cultural systems, to be secure in the enjoyment of their own means of subsistence, and to engage freely in their traditional and other economic activities, including hunting, fishing, herding, gathering, forestry and cultivation. Indigenous peoples who have been deprived of their means of subsistence are entitled to just and fair compensation;

Indigenous peoples have the right to special measures for the immediate, effective and continuing improvement of their economic and social conditions, including in the areas of employment, vocational training and retraining, housing, health and social security;

Attention shall be paid to the special needs of indigenous elders, women, youth, children and disabled;

Indigenous peoples have the right to determine and develop priorities and strategies for their development. In particular, indigenous peoples have the right to determine and develop all health, housing and other economic and social programs affecting them and, as far as possible, to administer such programs through their own institutions;

Indigenous peoples have the right to their traditional medicines and health practices, including the right to the protection of vital medicinal plants, animals, and minerals;

PART VI

Indigenous peoples have the right to recognition of their distinctive and profound relationship with their lands and territories. The use of the term "lands and territories" in this Declaration means the total environment of the lands, air, water, sea, sea-ice, flora and fauna and other resources which indigenous peoples have traditionally owned or otherwise occupied or used;

Indigenous peoples have the collective and individual right to own, control and use their lands and territories. This includes the right to the full recognition of their laws and customs, land-tenure systems and institutions for the management of resources, and the right to effective measures by States to prevent any interference with or encroachment upon these rights;

Indigenous peoples have the right to the restitution of lands and territories which have been confiscated, occupied, used or damaged without their free and informed consent, and where this is not possible, to just and fair compensation. Unless otherwise freely agreed upon by the peoples concerned, compensation shall preferably take the form of lands and territories at least equal in quality, quantity and legal status;

Indigenous peoples have the right to the recreation and protection of the total environment and the productive capacity of their lands and territories, as well as to assistance for this purpose from States and through international cooperation. Military activities and the storage or disposal of hazardous materials shall not take place in their lands and territories, unless otherwise freely agreed upon by the peoples concerned;

Indigenous peoples have the right to special measures to protect, as intellectual property, their sciences, technologies and cultural manifestations, including genetic resources, seeds, medicines, knowledge of the properties of fauna and flora, oral traditions, literatures, designs and visual and performing arts;

Indigenous peoples have the right to require that States obtain their free

Resolution 169 of the International Labor Organization has been ratified by only four of the 33 Latin American and Caribbean nations. It includes 80 percent of the rights that Indians are fighting for and covers the rights to land, education, culture and development.

Interpress Service, January 27, 1993

and informed consent prior to the commencement of any projects on their lands and territories, particularly in connection with natural resource development projects or exploitation of mineral and other subsurface resources. Pursuant to agreement with the indigenous peoples concerned, just and fair compensation shall be provided for any such activities and measures taken to mitigate adverse environmental, economic, social, cultural or spiritual impact;

PART VII

Indigenous peoples have the right to autonomy and self-government in matters relating to their internal and local affairs, including culture, religion, education, information, media, health, housing, employment, social welfare, economic activities, land and resources management, environment and entry by non-members, as well as internal taxation for financing these autonomous functions;

Indigenous peoples have the right to determine the structures and to select the membership of their autonomous institutions in accordance with their own procedures;

Indigenous peoples have the right to retain and develop their customs, laws and legal systems, in a manner not incompatible with universally recognized human rights and fundamental freedoms, and to have these recognized in the legal systems and political institutions of the States;

Indigenous peoples have the right to determine the responsibilities of individuals to their own community in a manner not incompatible with universally recognized human rights and fundamental freedoms;

Indigenous peoples have the right to maintain and develop contacts, relations and cooperation, including activities for spiritual, cultural, political, economic and social purposes, with other indigenous peoples across borders;

Indigenous peoples have the right to the observance and enforcement of treaties, agreements and other constructive arrangements concluded with States or their successors, according to their original intent. Upon the request of the indigenous peoples concerned, States shall provide for the submission of disputes which cannot otherwise be settled to competent international bodies;

PART VIII

States take effective and appropriate measures, in consultation with the indigenous peoples concerned, to give full effect to the provisions of this Declaration. The rights contained herein shall be adopted and included in national legislation in such a manner that indigenous peoples can avail themselves of such rights in practice;

87

Indigenous peoples have the right to adequate financial and technical assistance, from States and through international cooperation, to pursue freely their political, economic, social, cultural and spiritual development, and for the enjoyment of the rights contained in this Declaration;

Indigenous peoples have the right to have access to and prompt decision by mutually acceptable and fair procedures for the resolution of conflicts and disputes with States, as well as to effective remedies for all infringements of their individual and collective rights;

The organs and specialized agencies of the United Nations system shall contribute to the full realization of the provisions of this Declaration through the mobilization, *inter alia,* of financial and technical cooperation;

The United Nations shall monitor the implementation of this Declaration through a body at the highest level with special competence in this field and with the direct participation of indigenous peoples. United Nations human rights bodies shall promote respect for the provisions of this Declaration;

PART IX

The rights contained herein constitute the minimum standards for the survival and well-being of the indigenous peoples of the world;

Nothing in this Declaration may be interpreted as diminishing or extinguishing existing or future rights indigenous peoples may have or acquire;

Nothing in this Declaration may be interpreted as implying for any State, group or person any right to engage in any activity or to perform any act contrary to the Charter of the United Nations or to the Declaration on Principles of International Law concerning Friendly Relations and Cooperation among States in accordance with the Charter of the United Nations.

Statement of the International Alliance of the Indigenous-Tribal Peoples of the Tropical Forests (Excerpts)

Penang, Malaysia, February 15, 1992

We, the indigenous-tribal peoples of the tropical forests, present this charter as a response to hundreds of years of continual encroachment and colonization of our territories and the undermining of our lives, livelihoods and cultures caused by the destruction of the forests that our survival depends on.

We declare that we are the original peoples, the rightful owners and the cultures that defend the tropical forests of the World.

Our territories and forests are to us more than an economic resource. For us, they are life itself and have an integral and spiritual value for our communities. They are fundamental to our social, cultural, spiritual, economic, and political survival as distinct peoples.

The unity of people and territory is vital and must be recognized.

All policies towards the forests must be based on a respect for cultural diversity, for a promotion of indigenous models of living, and an understanding that our peoples have developed ways of life closely attuned to our environment.

Therefore we declare the following principles, goals and demands:

Respect for Our Rights

Respect for our human, political, social, economic and cultural rights, respect for our right to self-determination, and to pursue our own ways of life.

Respect for our autonomous forms of self-government, as differentiated political systems at the community, regional and other levels. This includes our right to control all economic activities in our territories.

Respect for our customary laws and that they be incorporated in national and international law.

Where the peoples so demand, nation states must comply with the different treaties, agreements, covenants, awards and other forms of legal recognition that have been signed with us indigenous peoples in the past, both in the colonial period and since independence, regarding our rights.

An end to violence, slavery, debt peonage and land grabbing; the disbanding of all private armies and militias and their replacement by the rule of law and social justice; the means to use the law in our own defense, including the training of our people in the law. . . .

Territory

Secure control of our territories, by which we mean a whole living system of continuous and vital connection between man and nature; expressed as our right to the unity and continuity of our ancestral domains; including the parts that have been usurped, those being reclaimed and those that we use; the soil, subsoil, air and water required for our self reliance, cultural development and future generations. . . .

Decision-Making

Control of our territories and the resources that we depend on: all development in our areas should only go ahead with the free informed consent of the indigenous people involved or affected. . . .

Development Policy

The right to be informed, consulted and, above all, to participate in the making of decisions on legislation or policies and in the formulation, implementation or evaluation of any development project, be it at local, national or international levels, whether private or of the state, that may affect our futures directly.

All major development initiatives should be preceded by social, cultural and environmental impact assessments, after consultation with local communities and indigenous peoples. All such studies and projects should be open to public scrutiny and debate, especially by the indigenous peoples affected.

National or international agencies considering funding development projects which may affect us, must set up tripartite commissions—including the funding agency, government representatives and our own communities as represented through our representative organizations—to carry through the planning, implementation, monitoring and evaluation of the projects.

The cancellation of all mining concessions in our territories imposed without the consent of our representative organizations. Mining policies must **prioritize**, and be carried out under, our control, to guarantee rational management and a balance with the environment. In the case of the extraction of strategic minerals (oil and radioactive minerals) in our territories, we must participate in making decisions during planning and implementation. . . .

Forest Policy

Halt all new logging concessions and suspend existing ones that affect our territories. The destruction of forests must be considered a crime against humanity and a halt must be made to the various anti-social consequences, such as roads across indigenous cultivations, cemeteries and hunting zones; the destruction of areas used for medicinal plants and crafts; the erosion and compression of soil; the pollution of our environment; the corruption and enclave economy generated by the industry; the increase of invasions and settlement in our territories.

Logging concessions on lands adjacent to our territories, or which have an impact on our environment, must comply with operating conditions—ecological, social, of labor, transport, health and others—laid down by the indigenous peoples, who should participate in ensuring that these are complied with. Commercial timber extraction should be prohibited in strategic and seriously degraded forests. . . .

Biodiversity and Conservation

Programs related to biodiversity must respect the collective rights of our

89

peoples to cultural and intellectual property, genetic resources, gene banks, biotechnology and knowledge of biological diversity; this should include our participation in the management of any such project in our territories, as well as control of any benefits that derive from them.

Conservation programs must respect our rights to the use and ownership of the territories we depend on. No programs to conserve biodiversity should be promoted on our territories without our free and informed consent as expressed through our representative organizations. . . .

Intellectual Property

Since we highly value our traditional technologies and believe that our biotechnologies can make important contributions to humanity, including "developed" countries, we demand guaranteed rights to our intellectual property, and control over the development and manipulation of this knowledge. . . .

Kari-Oca Declaration

The World Conference of Indigenous Peoples on Territory, Environment and Development issued this statement several days before the convening of the 1992 "Earth Summit" in Rio de Janeiro, Brazil. Signed at Kari-Oca, Brazil, on May 30, 1992, this declaration reflects both hopes the signers held for the subsequent Earth Summit as well as anger at the peripheral role afforded to indigenous peoples in the official proceedings.

Preamble

The Indigenous Peoples of the Americas, Asia, Africa, Australia, Europe and the Pacific, united in one voice at Kari-Oca Village express our collective gratitude to the indigenous peoples of Brazil.

Inspired by this historical meeting, we celebrate the spiritual unity of the indigenous peoples with the land and ourselves.

We continue building and formulating our united commitment to save our Mother the Earth.

We, the indigenous peoples, endorse the following declaration as our collective responsibility to carry our indigenous minds and voices into the future.

Declaration

We the Indigenous Peoples, walk to the future in the footprints of our ancestors.

From the smallest to the largest living being, from the four directions, from the air, the land and the mountains, the creator has placed us, the indigenous peoples upon our Mother the Earth.

The footprints of our ancestors are permanently etched upon the land of our peoples.

We the Indigenous Peoples, maintain our inherent rights to self-determination. We have always had the right to decide our own forms of government, to use our own laws to raise and educate our children, to our own cultural identity without interference.

We continue to maintain our rights as peoples despite centuries of deprivation, assimilation and genocide.

We maintain our inalienable rights to our lands and territories, to all our resources—above and below—and to our waters. We assert our ongoing responsibility to pass these onto the future generations.

We cannot be removed from our lands. We the Indigenous Peoples, are connected by the circle of life to our land and environments.

We the Indigenous Peoples, walk to the future in the footprints of our ancestors. . . .

United Nations Conference on Environment and Development Agenda 21, Chapter 26:
Recognizing and Strengthening the Role of Indigenous People and Their Communities

Adopted on June 14, 1992, Agenda 21 is the official document growing out of the Rio de Janeiro "Earth Summit." Perhaps the major question regarding Chapter 26, as well as the entire Agenda 21, is whether the United Nations and its member countries will follow up their words with concrete actions and funding.

Basis for Action

26.1 Indigenous people and their communities have an historical relationship with their lands and are generally descendants of the original inhabitants of such lands. In the context of this chapter the term "lands" is understood to include the environment of the areas which the people concerned traditionally occupy. Indigenous people and their communities represent a significant percentage of the global population. They have developed over many generations a holistic traditional scientific knowledge of their lands, natural resources and environment. Indigenous people and their communities shall enjoy the full measure of human rights and fundamental freedoms without hindrance or discrimination. Their ability to participate fully in sustainable development practices on their lands has tended to be limited as a result of factors of an economic, social and historical nature. In view of the interrelationship between the natural environment and its sustainable development and the cultural, social, economic and physical well-being of indigenous people, national and international efforts to implement environmentally sound and sustainable development should recognize, accommodate, promote and strengthen the role of indigenous people and their communities.

26.2 Some of the goals inherent in the objectives and activities of this program area are already contained in such international legal instruments as the ILO Indigenous and Tribal Peoples Convention (No. 169) and are being incorporated into the draft Universal Declaration on Indigenous Rights, being prepared by the United Nations Working Group on Indigenous Populations. The International Year for the World's Indigenous People (1993), proclaimed by the General Assembly in its resolution 451164 of 18 December 1990, presents a timely opportunity to mobilize further international technical and financial cooperation.

Objectives

26.3 In full partnership with indigenous people and their communities, Governments and, where appropriate, intergovernmental organizations should aim at fulfilling the following objectives:

(a) Establishment of a process to empower indigenous people and their communities through measures that include:

(i) Adoption or strengthening of appropriate policies and/or legal instruments at the national level;

(ii) Recognition that the lands of indigenous people and their communities should be protected from activities that are environmentally unsound or that the indigenous people concerned consider to be socially and culturally inappropriate;

(iii) Recognition of their values, traditional knowledge and resource management practices with a view to promoting environmentally sound and sustainable development;

(iv) Recognition that traditional and direct dependence on renewable resources and ecosystems, including sustainable harvesting, continues to be essential to the cultural, economic and physical well-being of indigenous people and their communities;

(v) Development and strengthening of national dispute-resolution arrangements in relation to settlement of land and resource-management concerns;

(vi) Support for alternative environmentally sound means of production to ensure a range of choices on how to improve their quality of life so that they effectively participate in sustainable development;

(vii) Enhancement of capacity-building for indigenous communities, based on the adaptation and exchange of traditional experience, knowledge and resource-management practices, to ensure their sustainable development;

(b) Establishment, where appropriate, of arrangements to strengthen the active participation of indigenous people and their communities in the national formulation of policies, laws and programs relating to resource management and other development processes that may affect them, and their initiation of proposals for such policies and programs;

(c) Involvement of indigenous people and their communities at the national and local levels in resource management and conservation strategies and other relevant programs established to support and review sustainable development strategies, such as those suggested in other program areas of Agenda 21.

Activities

26.4 Some indigenous people and their communities may require, in accordance with national legislation, greater control over their lands, self-management of their resources, participation in development decisions affecting them, including, where appropriate, participation in the establishment or management of protected areas. The following are some of the specific measures which Governments could take:

(a) Consider the ratification and application of existing international conventions relevant to indigenous people and their communities (where not yet done) and provide support for the adoption by the General Assembly of a declaration on indigenous rights;

(b) Adopt or strengthen appropriate policies and/or legal instruments that will protect indigenous intellectual and cultural property and the right to preserve customary and administrative systems and practices.

26.5 United Nations organizations and other international development and finance organizations and Governments should, drawing on the active participation of indigenous people and their communities, as appropriate, take the following measures, inter alia, to incorporate their values, views and knowledge, including the unique contribution of indigenous women, in resource management and other policies and programs that may affect them:

(a) Appoint a special focal point within each international organization, and organize annual interorganizational coordination meetings in consultation with Governments and indigenous organizations, as appropriate, and develop a procedure within and between operational agencies for assisting Governments in ensuring the coherent and coordinated incorporation of the views of indigenous people in the design and implementation of policies and programs. Under this procedure, indigenous people and their communities should be informed and consulted and allowed to participate in national decision-making, in particular regarding regional and international cooperative efforts. In addition, these policies and programs should take fully into account strategies based on local indigenous initiatives;

(b) Provide technical and financial assistance for capacity-building programs to support the sustainable self-development of indigenous people and their communities;

(c) Strengthen research and education programs aimed at

(i) Achieving a better understanding of indigenous people's knowledge and management experience related to the environment, and applying this to contemporary development challenges;

(ii) Increasing the efficiency of indigenous people's resource management systems, for example, by promoting the adaptation and dissemination of suitable technological innovations;

(d) Contribute to the endeavors of indigenous people and their communities in resource management and conservation strategies (such as those that may be developed under appropriate projects funded through the Global Environmental Facility and Tropical Forestry Action Plan) and other program areas of Agenda 21, including programs to collect, analyze and use data and other information in support of sustainable development projects.

26.6 Governments, in full partnership with indigenous people and their communities, should, where appropriate:

(a) Develop or strengthen national arrangements to consult with indigenous people and their communities with a view to reflecting their needs and incorporating their values and traditional and other knowledge and practices in national policies and programs in the field of natural resource management and conservation and other development programs affecting them;

(b) Cooperate at the regional level, where appropriate, to address common indigenous issues with a view to recognizing and strengthening their participation in sustainable development.

Means of Implementation

(a) *Financing and cost evaluation*

26.7 The UNCED Secretariat has estimated the average total annual cost (1993–2000) of implementing the activities of this chapter to be about $3 million from the international community on grant or concessional terms. These are indicative and order of magnitude estimates only and have not been reviewed by Governments. Actual costs and financial terms, including any that are non-concessional, will depend upon, inter alia, the specific strategies and programs Governments decide upon for implementation.

(b) *Legal and administrative frameworks*

26.8 Governments should incorporate, in collaboration with the indigenous people affected, the rights and responsibilities of indigenous people and their communities in the legislation of each country, suitable to the country's specific situation. Developing countries may require technical assistance to implement these activities.

(c) *Human resource development*

26.9 International development agencies and Governments should commit financial and other resources to education and training for indigenous people and their communities to develop their capacities to achieve sustainable self-development, and to contribute to and participate in sustainable and equitable development at the national level. Particular attention should be given to strengthening the role of indigenous women.

"Today, indigenous people are among the poorest, worst housed and least paid. They usually have less access to education and welfare than other members of society."

Boutros Boutros-Ghali
Speech to the United Nations
to open the UN Year of
Indigenous People.
December, 1992

93

For many years, the World Bank, the major multilateral funder for economic development, drew anger from indigenous people, indigenous-rights advocates, and environmentalists. Critics could point to a long list of misguided bank-funded projects, such as the disastrous Polonoroeste Project in Brazil. Begun in 1982, this $1.6 billion road-building effort caused massive deforestation and destroyed indigenous economies. After widespread criticism, the bank halted payments on its loan to the Polonoroeste Project in 1985. These guidelines derive from the efforts of human-rights and environmental activists to ensure that the policies of the World Bank and other national and international agencies respect the rights of indigenous peoples and promote sustainable development.

World Bank Guidelines on Indigenous Peoples (Excerpts)

March 2, 1992

This directive describes Bank policies and processing procedures for projects that affect indigenous peoples. It sets out basic definitions, policy objectives, guidelines for the design and implementation of project provisions or components for indigenous peoples, and processing and documentation requirements.

The directive provides policy guidance to (a) ensure that indigenous people benefit from development projects, and (b) avoid or mitigate potentially adverse effects on indigenous people caused by Bank-assisted activities. Special action is required where Bank investments affect indigenous peoples, tribes, ethnic minorities, or other groups whose social and economic status restricts their capacity to assert their interests and rights in land and other productive resources. . . .

Objective and policy

The Bank's broad objective towards indigenous people, as for all the people in its member countries, is to ensure that the development process fosters full respect for their dignity, human rights and cultural uniqueness. More specifically, the objective at the center of this directive is to ensure that indigenous peoples do not suffer adverse effects during the development process, particularly from Bank-financed projects, and that they receive culturally compatible social and economic benefits.

How to approach indigenous peoples affected by development projects is a controversial issue. Debate is often phrased as a choice between two opposed positions. One pole is to insulate indigenous populations whose cultural and economic practices make it difficult for them to deal with powerful outside groups. The advantages of this approach are the special protections that are provided and the preservation of cultural distinctiveness; the costs are the benefits foregone from development programs. The other pole argues that indigenous people must be acculturated to dominant society values and economic activities so that they can participate in national development. Here the benefits can include improved social and economic opportunities, but the cost is often the gradual loss of cultural differences.

The Bank's policy is that the strategy for addressing the issues pertaining to indigenous peoples must be based on the *informed participation* of the indigenous people themselves. Thus, identifying local preferences through direct consultation, incorporation of indigenous knowledge into project approaches, and appropriate early use of experienced specialists are core activities for any project that affects indigenous peoples and their rights to natural and economic resources.

Cases will occur, especially when dealing with the most isolated groups, where adverse impacts are unavoidable and adequate mitigation plans have not been developed. In such situations, the Bank will not appraise projects until suitable plans are developed by the borrower and reviewed by the Bank. In other cases, indigenous people may wish to be and can be incorporated into the development process. In sum, a full range of positive actions by the borrower must ensure that indigenous people benefit from development investments. . . .

Global Rights Summary

Due to colonial neglect and historical isolation, the Pacific Islands, encompassing the world's most diverse range of indigenous cultures, continue to sustain many ancestral life-ways. Fewer than 6.5 million in all, the peoples of Oceania possess a vast repository of cultural traditions and ecological adaptations. Papua New Guinea (PNG) alone is home to about 780 distinct vernaculars. Oceania thus has the most to lose, culturally speaking, from the pressures of global political and economic change.

Spread across a vast expanse of ocean, Pacific Island peoples occupy an array of environments, from PNG's massive mountains to the atolls and lagoons of European fantasy to Auckland's urban jungles. Most people live in Melanesia's land-rich states (Papua New Guinea, Solomon Islands, Vanuatu), where 85 percent of the population is rural and often nearly self-sufficient. Still, well over one-fourth of the over two million Micronesians and Polynesians live in cities or circulate to metropolitan centers in Australia, New Zealand, and the United States.

Despite diversity, all Pacific societies are small and vulnerable. A typical linguistic group consists of only a few thousand people. Even moderate changes in, for example, fertility patterns can have drastic consequences for cultural survival. Indeed, many cases of "language death"—the disappearance of not only a spoken language but the cultural memory that goes with it—are on record.

Environmental forces pose a major threat to island communities. A typhoon can denude an atoll of living vegetation and ruin all sources of ground water. In Fiji and Samoa, the damage from recent major storms to villages and national infrastructure will take years to rebuild.

Demographic trends could pose an even more devastating threat. Having rebounded from sharp population declines after the invasion of European diseases and labor recruiters, many island societies now have some of the world's highest birth rates. Population growth, while fulfilling island ideals for large extended families, is rapidly outstripping the ability of the land to support subsistence lifestyles.

Politics Of Culture

If the typical indigenous society is an encapsulated minority living tenuously on the margins of a state, Oceanic peoples are anything but typical. Only in Australia, Guam, Hawaii, New Caledonia, and New Zealand are indigenous Islanders minorities in their own homelands (see also comments on Irian Jaya in the Southeast Asia region).

Except for New Caledonia, which remains a French possession, Melanesian countries won independence during the 1970s and are now governed by indigenous elites. Yet it is in this part of the Pacific that the most serious political crises have erupted. Just as "culture" and cultural survival are themes in an armed rebellion on Bougainville seeking separation from Papua New Guinea, cultural identity and integrity are invoked by the military government of Fiji to rationalize its denial of rights to Indo-Fijians.

To further complicate the picture, local traditions contain some surprising elements. For example, nineteenth-century European missionaries met initial resistance in many areas, but most Islanders long ago integrated Christianity and its practices into their daily lives. Col. Sitiveni Rabuka, who orchestrated two coups in Fiji and is now Prime Minister, seized power in part to protect and propagate Fijian Christian values along with those of chiefly custom.

Political independence has not been accompanied by economic independence. The Pacific

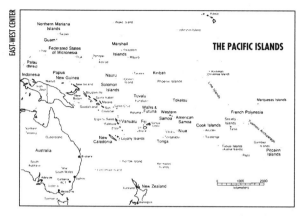

Islands are the most aid-dependent region in the world. Foreign-owned multinational companies extract timber, minerals, oil, fish, and other natural resources. Economic dependence has forced many island governments to promote large-scale development, rapidly expand tourism, and accede to the military ambitions of past and present colonial powers.

Since World War II, planners have eyed the region's wide open spaces, deep seas, and sparse population as ideal for military uses. After the United States acquired Japanese colonies in the northern Pacific, it established a major military facility in the Marshall Islands and expanded its bases in Guam and Hawaii. U.S. designs on Palau as a possible site for future military operations have stalled decolonization and produced nearly 20 years of chaos.

Some older Marshall Islanders even say that World War II never ended. Marshallese find confirmation of this in the transformation of a postwar labor camp into a nuclear-test range and, now, a missile-tracking facility. The United States tested nuclear weapons in the Marshall Islands in the 1950s and continues to use Kwajalein Atoll for missile tests. Beginning in 1993, the U.S. Strategic Target System program plans to launch four experiments a year from Hawaii to Kwajalein for ten years. For the inhabitants of Bikini, Enewetak, and Rongelap,

nuclear testing has meant a cultural catastrophe, first forcing people off their islands and then prompting law suits that have generated huge compensatory payments that have created enormous social problems.

The willingness of the residents of Bikini and Enewetak to engage in prolonged court battles to win the legal and economic resources necessary to reclaim their home islands testifies to the deep social and symbolic value of ancestral lands. For all but the most urban Islanders, land continues to be at the heart of cultural identity. But population growth, development, and militarization all threaten to alter people's relation to land and hence practices that produce and reproduce community and cultural identity. The political crisis on Bougainville bears stark testimony to the consequences of mining gone awry. A conflict that began over royalty payments and the environmental effects of a massive copper mine escalated into a full-scale civil war that has claimed more island lives than were lost in World War II, when the islands were the site of two years of fighting.

There are also grounds for optimism as official institutions come to recognize the rights of indigenous people to ancestral lands. In 1992, Australian courts recognized Aboriginal rights to land owned at the time Captain James Cook arrived 204 years ago. In New Zealand, the Waitangi Tribunal has been a forum for Maaori land claims since 1975. In Melanesia, postcolonial governments have moved to codify the rights of customary landowners and devolve the handling of land disputes to local "traditional" processes whenever possible.

Migration and Cultural Identity

Islanders whose seafaring ancestors discovered and settled remote archipelagos remain enthusiastic travelers. Migration beyond the Pacific began when Cook and other explorers took curious

Islanders to Europe. More recently, increasing numbers are settling in Pacific Rim countries. These global migrations are made necessary as the world market system integrates the economies of island states.

Some people migrate within Pacific Islands states. Competition for scarce land and educational and economic opportunities pushes Islanders to urban centers. Growing numbers of underemployed migrants trouble Pacific towns and cities. Youth gangs beset Port Moresby, capital of Papua New Guinea, where they are called "rascals."

Although some migration is circular—people eventually return to home islands—many migrants

Village children from Santa Isobel, Solomon Islands, encounter Rambo at a nightly video showing.

relocate permanently. Pacific nations now include substantial cities and towns, but most governments are hard pressed to provide basic services let alone employment opportunities to urban migrants, many of whom live in squatter settlements.

Other migrants travel further within the Pacific or beyond to Australia, the United States, and Canada. Auckland, New Zealand, has become the world's largest Polynesian city, with immigrants from Samoa, Tonga, and the Cook Islands. Guam attracts increasing numbers of people from the Federated States of Micronesia and the Northern Marianas. Migrants may spark political discord because they compete with indigenous popula-

tions for limited resources. Descendants of Melanesian migrant laborers, who have lived in Australia for a century, are in conflict with Australian Aborigines over access to government-funded assistance programs.

Some host countries have endeavored to limit immigration, yet migration remains necessary. In part, it is the way small island states must deal with rapid population growth and limited economic development. Economic remittances from migrants to their families back home provide a significant part of the gross national product of several Pacific states.

Migrations can have radical consequences. In Saipan, the population jumped fivefold from 10,000 to 50,000 in the 1980s, and the indigenous population became a minority. Adaptation to life abroad necessarily challenges island patterns of kinship and family life, although many migrant communities sustain their identity through vigorous church organizations and other less formal methods. In the rotating credit associations of Honolulu's Tongan community, people gather around the kava bowl weekly to raise money for members, often to support travel back to Tonga.

"Development" and Cultural Survival

Volcanic and coralline Pacific Islands tend to possess beauty but few economic resources. Most states rely on outside funding for their development budgets and, in some cases, operating budgets as well. However, the generosity of donors, to some degree predicated on the islands' strategic importance, may well dwindle in a post-cold war era.

Although still-vibrant subsistence economies shelter some island states, all profess an interest in sustainable development. However, the demand for income, coupled with the paucity of exploitable resources and the difficulties of small economies separated by vast stretches of ocean,

GEOFFREY WHITE

Woman of Santa Isobel carries home garden produce.

limits the options for development. Thus, economic viability, not cultural and social consequences, often drives decision-making, and urban and political elites who invite exploitation for the national good can find themselves in conflict with rural landowners.

Nickel mining continues in New Caledonia despite the effects of pollution on residential areas. Papua New Guinea encourages copper and gold mining although mine tailings pollute rivers and threaten people's health. Overseas lumber companies, many based in Asia, are buying up hardwoods stripped from rain forests throughout the Southwest Pacific. Even with the French nuclear-test moratorium, Islanders fear that Pacific Rim countries will continue to dump nuclear and other toxic wastes in their ocean. Marshall Islands entrepreneurs have entertained several dumping schemes, including the idea of

filling lagoons with polluted soil from abandoned Hawaiian gas stations.

Economic circumstance encourages island states to open themselves to another perhaps equally polluting import. Pacific states capitalize on the beauty of their islands and the diversity of their cultures to attract tourists, turning themselves and their land and seascapes into commodities.

Tourism's effects on indigenous peoples vary. Tourism can endanger the environment, provide poorly paid service jobs, and bastardize traditional arts. On the other hand, tourists can bring income and information to rural communities. Various Pacific states are working to promote informed, controlled tourism that doesn't undermine indigenous cultures or environmental balance.

Even where tourists are scarce, Islanders now encounter the world through videotape and television. In most Pacific islands, these technologies are too recent to judge their effects. Their spreading popularity, however, and the appearance of Rambo and Kung Fu on the most remote atolls and reefs, testify to the importance of concerns for the state of the indigenous peoples of Oceania.

GEOFFREY M. WHITE AND LAMONT LINDSTROM

Oceania Resources:
Center for Pacific Islands Studies, University of Hawaii, Honolulu, HI 96822.
Center for South Pacific Studies, School of Sociology, University of New South Wales, Kensington, N.S.W. 2033, Australia.
Institute of Pacific Studies, University of the South Pacific, P.O. Box 1168, Suva, Fiji.
Link magazine, Solomon Islands Development Trust, P.O. Box 147, Honiara, Solomon Islands.
Pacific Islands Development Program, East-West Center, Honolulu, HI 96848.
South Pacific Commission. Publishes "Youth Link," a quarterly newsletter. BP D5, Noumea, CEDEX, New Caledonia.
South Pacific Peoples Foundation of Canada. Publishes "Tok Blong SPFF," a quarterly newsletter. 415-620 View St., Victoria, B.C. V8W 1J6, Canada.
"Western Oceania: Caring for the Ancestral Domain," *Cultural Survival Quarterly*, Vol. 15, No. 2, 1991.

99

ABORIGINES OF AUSTRALIA

Aborigines Resources:
Aboriginal Law Center, Faculty of Law, University of New South Wales, P.O. Box 1, Kensington, N.S.W. 2033, Australia. Bimonthly updates appear in the center's journal, the *Aboriginal Law Bulletin* (subscriptions: A$26 per year).

Aborigines Action:
Strong international pressure must be brought to bear on Australian governments to act on the principles in *Mabo* and move rapidly to a meaningful settlement of Aboriginal and Torres Strait Islander claims.

For over 200 years, the legal fiction of *terra nullius*, or "empty land"— the idea that Australia was uninhabited until England colonized it—justified the invasion and appropriation of the entire continent, whose indigenous Aboriginal owner-occupiers were dispossessed without treaty or compensation. In the first major legal test of this principle, which occurred only in 1969, the court ruled that the Aboriginal claimants lacked the necessary economic and legal concepts of property.

However, the second test, begun in 1982, concluded a decade later with a momentous 1992 Australian High Court decision recognizing native title. A group of Meriam (Murray Islanders), claiming the land belonged to them from time immemorial, brought the case against the Queensland and federal governments.

Named for its principal litigant, the *Mabo* case pertains to a Torres Strait Island, but the court clearly intends its judgment to apply to all Australia. Thus, *Mabo* carries unprecedented significance for the struggles of Aboriginal and Torres Strait Islander peoples to obtain land rights.

The High Court eliminated *terra nullius* from Australian common law and affirmed land titles based on traditional Aboriginal possession. The court even raised the possibility that some aspects of a native title could survive its granting to a non-Aboriginal. Thus pastoral leases, which cover huge areas of Australia, may be subject to Aboriginal claims. In addition, some native titles might extend to nature reserves and national parks and wouldn't necessarily be extinguished by grants of the authority to prospect for minerals. In the future, the court may decide that the government owes a fiduciary duty to indigenous people, opening up the possibility of damage claims for land alienated against the wishes of title holders.

The strong positive response to *Mabo* on the part of indigenous Australians is not matched among the rest of the country's population. Although some politicians, Aboriginal leaders, and others suggest that negotiations would be preferable to costly litigation, no government—state or federal—has moved to open such discussions. Instead, there has been tacit support for mounting test cases to explore the ramifications of this landmark judgment.

At the same time, opposition is rising, particularly from conservative politicians, pastoralists, and mining companies, whose pronouncements often feature gross exaggeration and scaremongering. In the past, the mining giants in particular have orchestrated highly effective and frequently racist campaigns against Aboriginal interests. Already, some media commentators have inflamed existing anti-Aboriginal sentiments.

ROBERT AND MYRNA TONKINSON

100

BOUGAINVILLEANS OF PAPUA NEW GUINEA

The Bougainville secessionist war is entering its fifth year, with no end in sight. Geographically and culturally part of Solomon Islands, politically the North Solomons Province is part of Papua New Guinea (PNG). Bougainvilleans identify themselves as "blackskins" along with the people of western Solomons, as opposed to lighter-colored "redskins" in PNG.

Bougainvillean desires to break away from PNG were articulated first in the early 1960s and then flared up at the time of PNG independence in 1975. Secessionist talk resurfaced in 1988 in a dispute over the revenue from and environmental effect of the giant Panguna copper mine in central Bougainville. Attacks on the mine, which was critical to PNG's economy, drew a heavy-handed reaction from riot police and troops. The conflict escalated

Bougainvillean Resources:

Amnesty International, *PNG: Human Rights Violations on Bougainville,* 1989–1990.

Australian Bougainville Support Group, 34 Darvall Rd., Eastwood, Sydney, N.S.W. 2122, Australia, Phone/Fax 02-8047602.

Australian Humanitarian Aid for Bougainville, P.O. Box 222, Fitzroy, Victoria 3065, Australia, Phone/Fax 03-4177448.

and the whole island, as well as neighboring Buka Island, became mired in an independence war. The rebel Bougainville Republican Army (BRA) forced PNG government troops to withdraw in 1990. Later on that year, however, government forces gained a foothold on Buka and, by a divide-and-conquer strategy enforced by a blockade of medical supplies and other essentials, reestablished control over much of the island. Thousands have died because of the lack of medicinal provisions.

The effects of the blockade and of the rebels' ill-treatment of pro-PNG local leaders have divided Bougainvilleans. Exploited by PNG, these conflicts have touched off small-scale civil wars between pro- and anti-BRA factions, with the latter armed and supported by PNG. This phase of the fighting has led to the displacement of 50,000 people—one-third of the population—into government "care centers" (analogous to strategic hamlets). Reestablishment of PNG control has led to alleged human rights abuses in the camps, including summary executions of suspected rebel sympathizers. The government has banned journalists and human rights organizations from entering Bougainville.

Rebels controlled the provincial capital of Arawa until February 1993, and they still control the port town of Kieta and the Panguna town and mine. Fighting is sporadic in southern Bougainville, where rebel attacks mean that many care centers can only be supplied by helicopter, which leads to food shortages. Because of the lack of medical supplies in rebel areas, people have died from malaria and women have died in childbirth. Medical supplies are scarce in many government-controlled areas as well.

The PNG government's decision to abandon negotiations in favor of a military solution may render Bougainville ungovernable, no matter who is in power. Families and communities are now divided, and aggrieved parties in any dispute can count on army and police support by labeling enemies as secessionist sympathizers. But Bougainvillean nationalism won't go away. Even with a BRA defeat, a long-term military presence would drain PNG's economy and would be seen as an occupation army.

Negotiations are the only alternative to a Melanesian East Timor or Eritrea. The never-implemented 1991 Honiara peace agreement might still be the best way forward. That agreement called for the BRA to disarm and the PNG forces to withdraw, to be replaced by international peacekeepers. Elections might be held for a representative body empowered to negotiate with PNG over Bougainville's political status.

MATTHEW SPRIGGS

CHAMORROS AND CAROLINIANS OF THE NORTHERN MARIANA ISLANDS

Chamorros descend from the people who were inhabiting the Mariana Islands when Ferdinand Magellan arrived in 1521. Under Spanish rule the population dropped from an estimated 50,000 to about 1,500. Under subsequent German administration, Japanese colonization, and the U.S. administration, it rose to about 15,000. Little of the original Chamorro culture remains, however, except for a much-adapted language.

Carolinians came to the Marianas from the Central Carolinas during the Spanish era, when all Chamorros had been forcibly moved to Guam. The 3,000 remaining Carolinians on Saipan maintain much of their culture. Chamorros and Carolinians have kept their distinct identities while sharing the limited land resources.

Today, the situation of these indigenous peoples of the Northern Mariana Islands (NMI) may be unique. After 300 years of colonial domination, the

**PEOPLES OF THE NORTHERN
MARIANAS ISLANDS (1990 CENSUS)**

Filipino	14,160
Chamorro	12,555
Chinese	2,881
Korean	2,571
Carolinian	2,348
Palauan	1,620
Chuukese	1,063
Other Asian	936
Caucasian	875
Japanese	784
Pohnpeian	522
Other Pacific Isl.	197
Yapese	152
Black	24
Marshallese	92
Kosraean	17
Carolinian+	639
Chamorro+	1,639
All Other	193
TOTAL	43,345

+ = mixed

NMI voted in 1975 to become a self-governing U.S. commonwealth, the CNMI. Since 1986, its people have been U.S. citizens.

Although indigenous people control the government, they are in imminent danger of being absorbed into the U.S. mainstream. Since the mid-1980s, economic development has exploded. Imported workers outnumber the local population two to one, and four to one in the labor force. Low-paid Filipino housemaids mean that even the poorest local family can have two incomes, while children are essentially raised by a person uncommitted to local culture. The same is true in the schools, where many teachers are recruited from abroad.

Portions of the covenant that established the commonwealth, a document designed to protect the indigenous population, instead have become instruments of self-destruction. The constitution prohibits sales of land to people of non-Marianas descent. However, skyrocketing resort development land values (up to $5,000 per square yard) and 55-year leases have splintered local society, separating those with land for rent from those without. Many people have leased or sold their land to speculators of NMI descent and left for the United States. Local control of immigration has been the vehicle for importing massive numbers of workers from Asia.

The indigenous population could be unrecognizable in ten years. But before any effort can be mounted to preserve their cultures, one big question must be addressed: Do Chamorros and Carolinians want to be saved from themselves? Today, every citizen drives a car, has access to free education and adequate health care, and lives in a Western-style home. Many own second homes in the United States. On the other hand, great social changes and disruptions—drugs, rising crime, and family dislocation—are daily occurrences.

The indigenous peoples of the Marianas won't go back to grass shacks and communal property, or trade canned fish and spareribs for a diet of hard-caught fish and breadfruit. But what they must decide is what aspects of their culture they want to preserve to maintain a distinct identity.

First, the desire to preserve a cultural identity must be established. Second, a realistic inventory of traditions must be taken. And third, difficult decisions must be formulated and policies established to carry out those choices.

SAMUEL F. MCPHETRES

CHAMORUS OF GUAM

Although the Chamoru (elsewhere called Chamorro) have lived on Guam for thousands of years, the international community doesn't recognize them as a nation. The United States "freed" the island and its people in the Spanish-American War and "liberated" the islanders from Japanese occupation during World War II. After the war, the UN made the young U.S. nation the administering power over Guam.

Today, after nearly 500 years of colonization, many Chamorus are landless, illiterate, or dependent upon U.S. "generosity." Other Chamorus own land and insist on independence, but they are few in number and, due to U.S. immigration policies, face strong opposition from the non-Chamorus, who now represent most of the island's residents.

The organization Nasion Chamoru works to organize and educate people about the environment, nationhood, the right to self-determination, and Chamoru identity and spirituality. In 1992 the group won a court ruling ordering the government of Guam to implement the 18-year-old Chamoru Land Trust Act. This law provides public land for lease by Chamorus to build homes, raise crops or livestock, or establish business ventures. Nasion Chamoru also questions the U.S. military's restriction of access to certain land areas that the government of Guam claims are public.

Every year, a representative of the Organization of People for Indigenous Rights testifies at the UN, stating that the United States has failed in its obligation to provide for the exercise by the Chamorus of their right to self-determination. That group also acts as a watchdog over Guam's "Quest for Commonwealth," a decades-long effort by Guam residents to forge a new relationship with the administering power. A draft Commonwealth Act for Guam would, among many other things, recognize the Chamoru right to self-determination. However, it must be approved by the U.S. Congress and then by island voters, the majority of whom are non-Chamorus.

JAN S. N. FURUKAWA

EAST KWAIO OF THE SOLOMON ISLANDS

East Kwaio Resources:
Roger Keesing, *Custom and Confrontation: The Kwaio Struggle for Cultural Autonomy,* University of Chicago Press, 1992.
For information on the Kwaio Cultural Center, contact David Akin, 130 Lane Hall, University of Michigan, Ann Arbor, MI 48109.

The mountain Kwaio of central Malaita are the last major non-Christian group in Solomon Islands. Their religion centers on ancestral spirits, but over half of the several thousand Kwaio have become Christian and now live in large coastal villages to the western part of Malaita.

As a religious and cultural minority, the mountain Kwaio are aware of their vulnerability, and they have struggled for decades to control their affairs. Since the mid-1940s, protecting indigenous culture has been a pivotal theme in Malaitan politics, especially among the Kwaio.

The greatest dangers to Kwaio culture are Christian expansion into the mountains, the threats of land alienation and timbering, and the encroachment of foreign social and economic values. Yet few Kwaio are isolationists; most want to adopt selectively such foreign benefits as medical care, manufactured goods, and, most of all, education.

To attain these goals without compromising autonomy, the Kwaio established the Kwaio Cultural Center in 1979. Consisting of three locally run schools, an arts preservation and marketing project, a women's club, and an oral history and photographic archive, the center brought the first routine medical care to the area by coordinating visits by government doctors. The center's schools still operate, but dwindling funds threaten their continuation.

DAVID AKIN

103

EAST SEPIK WOMEN OF PAPUA NEW GUINEA

The East Sepik Council of Women (ESCOW), an indigenous women's organization, has mounted a legal challenge to logging in Papua New Guinea's Hunstein Range. This marks the first time that any organization in PNG has challenged a logging concession prior to its operation.

If the legal strategy fails, logging is likely to begin soon. Logging could displace as many as 1,300 Bitara and Bahinemo peoples from eight villages, destroy a million acres of rain forest, pollute local rivers, and greatly damage the region's biodiversity.

The concession, known as the April-Salumei Timber Rights Purchase, is one of PNG's largest industrial forest operations. In a race against regulation, the government approved the deal on June 26, 1992—one day before Parliament approved a strict new forest act. This means the operation could proceed under the older, less restrictive act, with fewer requirements for logging companies to consult with local residents.

ESCOW is contesting the concession, saying that some landowners agreed to the deal under threat of legal action and without being fully informed about what agreement. Villagers, many of whom are illiterate, were told they would be taken to court if they didn't sign.

Hunstein Range communities rely on the forest for their livelihood—a combination of subsistence farming and hunting and gathering. ESCOW has worked with the villages to develop small enterprises that utilize, but do not destroy natural resources. These initiatives include processing forest produce for sale and marketing local handicrafts and perfumes made from forest extracts.

ESCOW is also working with the PNG Department of Environment and Conservation to establish a conservation area in the region that could better meet the needs of the communities and protect the rain forest. If logging proceeds, ESCOW may not be able to complete this project.

Structural imbalances now contribute to Palauan migration to other parts of the former U.S. Trust Territory, where wages are higher. At least 29 percent of Palauans now reside off the island. To develop its own resources, Palau must retain both its educated professionals and its laborers.

JENNIFER RATHAUS

FIJIANS

Indigenous Fijians want to retain the best of their culture but at the same time involve themselves in systems that are antithetical to their traditions and values.

104

Contact with Western civilization brought harmony to the 500 islands of Fiji even as it introduced problems that continue to plague Fijian communities. Indigenous Fijians want to retain the best aspects of their cultures, but at the same time involve themselves in systems that are antithetical to their traditions and values.

Resolving this dilemma is at the heart of Fijian struggles for cultural survival. Fijians seek not only to combine the capitalist system with a mode of subsistence living that emphasizes sharing but also to blend some form of Western democracy with their tradition of consensus-building on important affairs.

Until 1970, England, which followed a policy of indirect rule, governed through Fijian chiefs and encouraged Fijians to maintain their customs. Although this protected Fijian culture, an equally important legacy of British rule has become the pressure that indigenous Fijians face to share power with others. Indians, whose ancestors the British brought here to work on sugar plantations, have outnumbered indigenous Fijians since 1946; of about 700,000 Fijians, approximately 49 percent are Indian and 47 percent Fijian.

In 1970 most indigenous Fijians embraced the new constitution—which granted equal power to Indians—only reluctantly. They were prepared to accept it because Fijians led the ruling Alliance Party. Indians, represented by the National Federation Party, were equally unhappy because the constitution didn't provide for "one person, one vote." As early as 1915, Indians had agitated for more representation in the legislature.

The issue over the constitution is economic as well as political. Indigenous Fijians lag behind economically and educationally. During the 17 years of Alliance Party rule, Fijians had hoped to improve their position. Unfortunately, affirmative action policies were often rejected as discriminatory. Many indigenous Fijians came to perceive the Alliance government as leaning toward Indian demands and eroding Fijian heritage in an effort to build a multiracial society. One result was two coups by the Fijian-dominated military in 1987.

ASESELA RAVUVU

INDO-FIJIANS OF FIJI

Indo-Fijians, most of whom are descendants of the 60,000 indentured laborers that the British rulers brought to Fiji from India between 1879 and 1916 to work on European plantations, comprise slightly less than half Fiji's population of about 700,000. Once their five-year contracts expired, most of the laborers leased land from Fijians. In time, they became the backbone of the sugar-dependent economy. Later, small numbers of free immigrants, whose descendants are now prominent in the retail sector, joined the Indo-Fijian community.

Since two military coups in 1987, several thousand skilled Indo-Fijians have left for North America, Australia, and New Zealand. This migration is likely to continue, and those who remain in Fiji face an uncertain future. Indigenous Fijians hold 83 percent of all land as an inalienable right. A good portion of the native land is leased to Indo-Fijians under the Agricultural Landlords and Tenants Ordinance, which came into effect in 1966 and will begin to expire in 1997. Will the leases be renewed at that time? Will rents rise to levels that will reduce Indo-Fijian tenants to mere sharecropper status? Will land become a tool to coerce Indo-Fijians into political subservience?

The constitution is another issue of urgency to Indo-Fijians. Promulgated in 1990, it reduces Indo-Fijians to second-class citizens. Indo-Fijians have 27 seats in the 70-seat Lower House, whereas Fijians have 37. Only four Indo-Fijians sit in the 24-seat Upper House, all appointed by the president. The present government contains no Indo-Fijian ministers.

In the awarding of scholarships, promotions, and training opportunities, Indo-Fijians are regularly bypassed, whereas Fijians occupy most senior civil-service positions. Fundamentalist Fijian Christians burn or otherwise desecrate Indo-Fijian places of worship. Half the population is non-Christian, but a Sunday Sabbath decree (now less stringently enforced than before) forbids such public activities as work or sports. Violence directed at Indo-Fijian households is common. The Taukei movement, a loose grouping of extremist Fijians who engineered the coups, has resurfaced and called for further curtailment of Indo-Fijian rights.

In 1990, the two major Indo-Fijian political parties participated in elections even though they rejected the constitution. One party backed Sitiveni Rabuka for prime minister after he promised to address matters of urgent concern, including a review of the constitution. Whether the constitution will be reviewed remains to be seen, but Rabuka stunned the nation in December 1992 with a proposal for a multiracial government of national unity.

For a multiracial country such as Fiji, winner-take-all parliamentary politics are inappropriate. Nor is any arrangement founded on ethnic chauvinism likely to succeed. Only a government that safeguards the cultural and political interests of all seems to present a viable future.

BRIJ V. LAL

105

MAAORI OF NEW ZEALAND

The Maaori number over 400,000 among New Zealand's population of 3.5 million. Traditionally a Maaori belongs to one or more of 27 major tribal groups as well as a number of smaller ones. Although Maaori land and heritage are largely rural, the people now live mainly in towns and cities. Over 3 million acres, mostly wilderness, remain in multiple Maaori ownership. Maaori lands generally support low-income sheep, cattle, and dairy industries. Forestry is an additional developing resource base.

Maaori enjoy full citizenship and also derive rights from the nineteenth-century Treaty of Waitangi. The treaty originally bound all tribes to the sovereignty of the British Crown, which in turn recognized tribal authority and guaranteed Maaori land ownership. When New Zealand became independent, the treaty was declared a nullity, and Maaoris subsequently lost land and tribal control.

In 1975, however, New Zealand established a permanent tribunal of inquiry into treaty violations. This body has heard claims on fish resources, jurisdiction over rivers and harbors, language status, and land purchases, seizures, and confiscations, among other subjects. Although the Waitangi Tribunal has only advisory powers, it has a reputation for doing thorough research.

The return of tribal assets must be separately negotiated, and progress is slow in part because at least 14 major bodies of statute recognize Maaori rights in such areas as education, health, land management, conservation, and resource management. The government has devolved responsibility for Maaori aspects of public policy to regional governments and has sought to empower tribal authorities in delivering some social services. However, the tribes remain poorly funded.

Maaori people exhibit the usual social problems associated with a post-colonial status, and government programs have made little difference. Maaori argue that tribal authorities could have more success if they were given proper funding. Thus, Maaori are pushing for the development of tribally run businesses, schools, health services, radio and TV stations, credit cooperatives, and so forth.

Language recovery is important because the proportion of Maaori speakers is dangerously low. Advocacy has led to the establishment of a Maaori Language Commission, recognition of Maaori as an official language, some funding for Maaori radio, and more access to the language through a variety of educational opportunities. Maaori themselves have started Maaori language preschools, and they are pressuring the government to offer Maaori through high school.

Poverty remains the major threat to Maaori advancement, and economic sovereignty the central issue. Many tribal groups now have business interests in forestry and fisheries; Maaori own half the New Zealand fishing industry; and the Maaori Development Corporation acts as broker for tribal enterprises. But a shortage of independent funding slows everything and has deflated enthusiasm for tribal schemes.

R.T. MAHUTA

> "The missionaries asked us to look to heaven. While we were looking up, the land was taken from beneath our feet."
>
> Maaori saying

MALVATUMAURI OF VANUATU

Vanuatu's citizens believe that the role of chiefs is essential in their culture. Established in 1977, the *Malvatumauri* (National Council of Chiefs) consists of 22 elected Ni-Vanuatu chiefs. The council protects the customs and culture of the Republic of Vanuatu.

The council has undertaken a project to build more *nakamals* (traditional chief's houses) and reclaim ancient meeting places. A national *nakamal* in the capital, Port Vila, is used for ceremonies such as weddings, custom courts, and the celebration of March 5, the national chief's day. The national *nakamal* is also used for brokering peace agreements among Vanuatu's citizens.

CHIEF WILLIE BONGMATUR MALDO

MARQUESANS

Marquesan Resource:
Motu Haka, Georges
Te`ikiehu`upoko, president,
B.P. 54, Hakahau, Ua Pou,
Iles Marquises, French
Polynesia.

In the last 150 years, Marquesans have faced the threats of French colonization, Christianization—which outlawed traditional arts as well as many ceremonies and customs—and disease outbreaks that by the mid-1920s had reduced the population to about 2,000 and life expectancy to 15.6 years for women and 16.5 years for men. Coupled with this legacy of Western contact, Marquesans have also contended with more than a century of suppression in the form of Tahitian cultural hegemony.

Nonetheless, Marquesan arts—music, dance, tattoo, sculpture—survived to shine forth in the late 1980s. Despite widespread social change, a small number of elders retain an amazing richness of traditional knowledge and form an important link between Marquesan heritage and the future. The arts, as a very visible symbol of culture, help differentiate today's 7,300 Marquesans from their neighbors, establishing a unique Marquesan identity in French Polynesia.

For Marquesans, ever wary of Tahitian domination, cultural identity becomes increasingly important as the Tahitian voice for independence grows stronger. Faced with a choice between control by France or an independent Tahiti, Marquesans overwhelmingly favor the former. Cultural survival and an overt demonstration of it are necessary to ensure that the outside world views Marquesans as a distinct people that merit a separate status and separate negotiations.

That Marquesan cultural uniqueness has economic and political significance is recognized by Motu Haka, a cultural organization that promotes Marquesan language instruction, traditional arts, and archeological projects as vital to achieving greater external recognition.

JANE FREEMAN MOULIN

MARSHALL ISLANDS

> On Majuro Atoll, government center of the new republic, and Ebeye islet of Kwajalein Atoll, a U.S. missile-tracking facility and testing range, severe overpopulation creates the conditions for dependence on outside food and wealth.

As residents of small, low-lying atolls in the central Pacific, Marshall Islanders are accustomed to life on the brink of disaster. Known for its military battles during World War II and the subsequent era of nuclear testing, the Marshall Islands still feel the impact of military concerns.

On Majuro Atoll, government center of the new republic, and Ebeye islet of Kwajalein Atoll, a U.S. missile-tracking facility and testing range, severe overpopulation creates the conditions for dependence on outside food and wealth. Overall, the population of this land-poor republic—now 45,000—is rising rapidly, erecting a barrier to an ecologically sustainable lifestyle throughout the two dozen atolls that compromise the Marshall Islands.

Production for export deteriorated during U.S. administration of the region, and, in the face of increased population pressure, Islanders have become even more dependent on outsiders. Since independence, this reliance has created disparities between rich and poor. Income is concentrated in the hands of elites at the expense of outer-Islanders and the rapidly expanding ranks of the urban poor.

The people of the northern islands—Bikini, Enewetak, Rongelap, and Utedik atolls—must face the legacy of nuclear testing through other threats to their social organization. On Bikini and Rongelap, people are negotiating repatriation settlements with the United States. Enewetak people, repatriated on a small four-islet corridor of replanted land, have found most of their atoll unusable, making them dependent on food imports. Malnutrition, diabetes, anomie, alcoholism, and increased

107

domestic and public violence are among the results. Although the causes differ, the same conditions are found throughout the Marshalls and are rampant in urban areas and on Ebeye and Majuro.

Monetary settlements of nuclear claims are a mixed blessing. Although they alleviate hardships, such payments have fueled the population increase for Bikini and Enewetak people, who have chosen to divide the products of their Nuclear Compensation Funds on a per-capita basis.

LAURENCE MARSHALL CARUCCI

MICRONESIA

U.S. NAVY

The greatest threat to the survival of Micronesians in the Federated States of Micronesia, the Marshall Islands, and the Republic of Belau is probably consumerism and the dependency it promotes. In these "nation-states" carved out of the former U.S. Trust Territory, survival is almost entirely contingent upon U.S. allotments—basically welfare transfers. The only substantive economic developments in the islands are consumer oriented.

Although U.S. authorities deny it, Micronesians had to sign away their rights to full autonomy in security treaties that were part of their "Compacts of Free Association." When these compacts expire in 2001, the security treaties will stay in effect until the United States terminates them, and the Islanders will lose their bargaining chip.

Today few Micronesians are learning how to wrest a living from the land or the sea, so they will have literally no source of subsistence when U.S. funds dry up. Micronesians will be forced to choose between starvation and abandoning their homes for life in the United States.

The most straightforward solution is simply to permit Micronesians to achieve genuine independence, with all the economic consequences this entails. They could then return to their local resources *before* forgetting how to survive on them.

GLENN PETERSEN

NAURUANS

Naruan Resources:
Nancy Viviani, *Nauru: Phosphate and Political Progress*, University of Hawaii Press, 1970.
Christopher Weeramantry, *Nauru: Environmental Damage under International Trusteeship*, Oxford University Press, 1992.

Phosphate mined on Nauru since 1906 will run out in 1996, leaving unusable, untraversable coral pinnacles in the center of the island. Nauruans never asked for the mine, and now they want their island to be repaired so they can continue living there. They want the mined area made suitable to support a population of 5,500 people who currently have to import everything they need for survival, including water.

The intrusion of mining into Nauruans' lives was negotiated without their consent by Germany and Great Britain. The British Phosphate Commissioners (BPC), consisting of Great Britain, Australia, and New Zealand, later assuming control of the venture, with Australia as the administering nation under mandates from both the League of Nations and the UN. Both mandates committed Australia and the BPC to protect the interests of the Nauruans. Nauruans sought and won independence in 1968 so that they could take over the mine—which they had to buy for $21 million—and manage their own affairs.

In a case before the International Court of Justice in the Hague, the Nauru Local Government Council is seeking reparations from the former BPC nations for loss of land and mined phosphate revenues. The council is asking the three nations to rehabilitate the portion of the island mined before 1968. The suit also charges that Nauru did not receive a fair share of the profits from mining under the BPC. According to Australian political scientist Nancy Viviani, in 1921 Nauruans received less than one percent of the amount that Australia paid BPC for the phosphate.

Nauruans are determined to stay on the island, which is their heritage and the basis of their cultural identity. They have seen what has happened to the Banabans, who were forced to give up nearby Ocean Island.

NANCY J. POLLOCK

PALAUANS

In the 1980s Palau received worldwide attention when it enacted a strong anti-nuclear constitution and continued to participate in efforts to force world powers to recognize indigenous rights to sea resources. Yet Palau's membership in international organizations has been precluded by its continuing status as the only polity still governed under the trust territory system established at the end of World War II. The other Caroline, Mariana, and Marshall islands that once comprised the U.S. Trust Territory of the Pacific Islands have become a U.S. commonwealth (CNMI) or independent nations freely associated with the United States (FSM, the Marshalls), and their citizens enjoy free entry to the United States. Guam remains a U.S. territory but is negotiating for commonwealth status.

The constraint to the passage of a compact of free association between the United States and Palau is the latter's constitutional requirement that three-quarters of the votes cast approve any waiver of the anti-nuclear clauses. The United States refuses to sign a contract that doesn't waive these clauses and allow U.S. military transit and use of land and harbors. In seven plebiscites since 1983, Palauan voters have approved the compact but not by the requisite 75 percent. In the mid-1980s, the United States and Palauan administrations put extreme economic and political pressure on Palauan citizens to ensure passage of the compact, culminating in a 1987 wave of violence. Some members of the U.S. Congress, the International Congress of Jurists, and international environmental and constitutional rights organizations lobbied against implementation of the compact through Palauan court proceedings. To date, the support offered by both pro- and anticompact interests has been overwhelming to the 20,000 Palauans.

New administrations in both the United States and Palau are expected to renegotiate the agreement, resolve the political impasse, and terminate the trusteeship. This is critical to Palau's long-term political and economic sovereignty and to its control of land and sea resources. Yet the regional economy is imbalanced by high U.S. transfers to Guam and CNMI and inflating land values spurred by Asian investment in tourism and business development in the islands. These regional imbalances contribute to Palauan migration to Guam, Saipan, and the United States, where wages are higher. At least 29 percent of Palauans now reside outside the islands. In the long run, Palau must retain its educated professionals and laborers and develop its own resources.

KAREN L. NERO

SAMOANS

From antiquity, the fragile ecosystems of the Polynesian archipelago of Samoa were safeguarded by a communal society rooted in cooperative systems of land tenure and integrated practices of resource management. Today, threats to the cultural survival of Samoans in both independent Western Samoa and American Samoa, an unincorporated territory of the United States, derive from interlocking environmental, social, and political forces.

One environmental challenge comes from rapidly intensifying population pressures, fed by both high birth rates and returning émigrés. In

American Samoa, where the growth rate is 3.7 percent per year, population increases correlate directly with the depletion of wildlife resources through deforestation, habitat degradation for construction, and the toxicity of aquatic organisms from heavy metals. Since 1986, wildlife resources in American Samoa have fallen 90 percent due to tropical storms and surges in human population. In both Samoas, population pressures have led to the degradation of coral reef biosystems and of the quality and supply of ground water.

A further challenge comes from the inadequate regulation of growth and development. In both Samoas, meaningful community involvement is lacking, and environmental impact studies are applied only erratically, if at all.

Environmental problems are exacerbated by the legacies of Western colonialism, characterized in part by a clash between Western ethics, enshrining cash and individual ownership, and indigenous ethics of group relationships and reciprocal exchanges. The resulting loss of Samoan cultural integrity has coupled with insufficient local opportunities for scientific training and employment, fostering a destructive social cycle. Unfulfilled educational and vocational aspirations foster disaffection. This translates into rising rates of substance abuse (especially alcohol) and domestic violence, including youth suicides in Western Samoa and the abuse of women and children in American Samoa.

The degradation of the condition of women and children further weakens cultural integrity and the traditionally binding relationships between genders and generations. Thus, cultural viability is undermined from within, morale erodes even further, and the cycle spirals downward.

U.S. and European agencies can assist in remedial and preventive measures by requiring that aid and development resources be allocated contingent upon the active participation of local organizations in planning and implementation. In addition, such aid should support local initiatives for scientific and applied research.

CAROLINE G. SINAVAIANA

> "The land belongs to the countless numbers who are dead, the few that are living, and the multitudes of those yet to be born. How can the government say that all untitled land belongs to itself, when there had been people using the land even before the government itself existed?"
>
> Statment from native elder

SIKAIANA

Sikaiana's synthesis of Western and indigenous customs has developed over the past 150 years. Despite many changes, its people have maintained and developed the ceremonies and practices that unite them as a community and an ethnic group.

Although geographically isolated, Sikaiana, a small atoll about 100 miles east of Malaita Island, is integrated into Solomon Islands and the world system economically and culturally. About 250 Sikaiana live on the atoll. Because the population has tripled in this century, about 500 people have moved to other parts of the Solomons, yet most migrants preserve strong ties to the atoll and consider it their home.

The atoll's isolation and small population make access the key word as the people of Sikaiana decide whether to continue or to change cultural traditions. Migrants in other parts of Solomon Islands need to maintain access to education and jobs and would benefit from better access to land. Those on the atoll need continuing access to education, tools, clothing, medical supplies, and other manufactured goods.

BILL DONNER

TAHITIANS

Tahiti Resources:

Marc Cizeron and Marianne Hienly, *Tahiti, The Other Side*, Institute of Pacific Studies of the University of the South Pacific, 1985.

Bengt Danielsson and Marie-Therese Danielsson, *Poisoned Reign, French Nuclear Colonialism in the Pacific*, Penguin, 1986.

Bengt and Marie-Therese Danielsson, "Tahiti: In Bondage to the Bomb," in David Robie, ed., *Tu Galala: Social Change in the Pacific*, Bridget Williams Books, Ltd. and Pluto Press Australia, 1992.

Pacific News Bulletin, Pacific Concerns Resource Center, P.O. Box 489, Petersham, N.S.W. 2049, Australia.

Tahiti, a 402-square-mile volcanic island in the Windward Society Islands, is the largest island in French Polynesia. The French nuclear testing program encouraged migration from the outlying islands to Tahiti. The results have been an extremely high cost of living, a lack of sewage and waste disposal facilities, inadequate health care and crowded, inadequate housing, problems that are particularly acute for those from outer islands.

Between 1956 and 1989, the population of the Windward Society Islands rose 235 percent. Today concern is whether a united Europe will bring an uncontrollable flood of Europeans to Tahiti and render Polynesians a minority in their own land.

Local officials blame a one-year suspension of French nuclear tests for the territory's $80 million debt. About 18,000 people are listed as unemployed in Tahiti, close to 13 percent of the population. Unemployment is highest among the young, uneducated, and unskilled.

Deteriorated health, poor living conditions, and unfulfilled expectations often result in Tahitians replacing Polynesian values with Western ones, including the "superiority" of Western technology and its ability to conquer nature. French is replacing Tahitian at home, and the schools teach only in French.

To a considerable extent, these conditions have grown out of 200 years of exploitation and cultural genocide—since 1767, when Europeans raised a foreign flag over Tahiti. By 1847, French military power had forced the Tahitians to cede the islands.

French exploitation of Tahiti peaked with the nuclear testing program at Moruroa, Fangataufa, and Hao. Between 1966 and 1974 France exploded 44 atomic bombs in the atmosphere. From 1975 to 1991 it exploded 131 underground nuclear bombs at the environmentally sensitive coral atolls of Moruroa and Fangataufa. Moruroa workers still report radioactive materials leaking into the ocean and waste dumped into the lagoon.

The consequences of radiation exposure to Tahitians and test-site workers have only recently begun to emerge. More Tahitians suffering from cancer are being sent to Paris and New Zealand for treatment. Leukemia, brain tumors, and other diseases associated with radiation exposure are prominent. Spontaneous abortions and babies born with physical defects or babies who die shortly after birth are increasing, particularly among the offspring of workers exposed to radiation.

During the 1970s and '80s, France's nuclear testing program generated money for Tahitians to purchase VCRs, motorbikes, and other imports, but the test moratorium and the consequent economic lag are causing people to question their dependence on a military-based economy. Open protests by antinuclear, proindependence activists have increased. Those who rely on military jobs or who run businesses dependent on sales to the military are in panic.

France is filling part of the gap by subsidizing select businesses, but it has chosen not to promote as much agriculture as some Tahitians would hope. As more Tahitians see the need to diversify the economy, the call for political change—led primarily by Oscar Temaru, mayor of Fa'a'a—gets louder and the independence movement grows larger. Some politicians have called for more French aid.

MARION KELLY

111

TOKELAUNS

Only in the past generation have the 1,600 indigenous Polynesians of Tokelau had an opportunity to launch themselves on the waves of economic and political development washing across the Pacific. Into the late 1960s Tokelau was a place of thatched houses, sailing canoes, kerosene lanterns, and a subsistence economy based on coconuts and fish. A ship came once every three months; apart from that, only Morse code messages crackled through the isolation.

"Development" changed all that. The economy is now an aid-driven one, dominated by annual budget assistance from New Zealand of over NZ$4 million. Most Tokelauns are public employees. Their houses are built out of imported materials, and outboard-powered aluminum boats have almost replaced canoes. New ideas and constraints have battered the old social order of kinship- and elder-based village polities. That old order has held, but only through radical accommodations.

The UN has guided much of the impetus for change. The atolls are, in UN jargon, a "non self-governing territory," and missions from the UN Committee on Colonialism have urged development so that people can choose realistically among independence, self-government, or complete integration with New Zealand.

For readily apparent reasons, Tokelauns are being cautious about choosing their political status. The three atolls have a combined land area of less than five square miles. Moreover, although subsistence resources are adequate, there is little to sustain an export economy.

Tokelau's greatest need is time. It needs time to develop modern political institutions on the basis of indigenous ideas rather than to be forced to succumb to pressures for a complete end to colonialism by any specified date. Tragically, it also needs time to see whether the atolls can withstand a threat from any rise in sea level accompanying global warming.

ANTONY HOOPER

TORRES STRAIT ISLANDERS

Torres Strait Resources:
Getano Lui, Jr., or Vic McGrath, Island Coordinating Council, P.O. Box 264, Thursday Island, Queensland 4875, Australia, (61-70)691-446.
Belza Lowah or Steve Mam, Torres Strait Islanders Corporation, P.O. Box 386, Brisbane, Queensland 4101, Australia, (61-7)844-2140.

North of Australia's sea border with Papua New Guinea, development projects pose significant hazards for 6,000 Torres Strait Islanders and extensive and rich marine habitats. Heavy-metal pollution in drainage from mining operations along the Fly River and transport of crude oil from the Chevron-run depot at Kutubu are major environmental threats to this geographically unique region.

The Island Coordinating Council is challenging Australia for "self-administration." It advocates local control over resources and the delivery of medical and education services; foreign policy would remain with Australia. The milestone *Mabo* land case decision in 1992 guarantees future successful land claims but avoids provision for marine tenure or local control and management by Islanders, who are still dependent upon subsistence fishing.

Furthermore, decision making on local issues critical to Islanders is conducted in Canberra, Australia's capital. There is a need for stringent compulsory pilotage for large ships passing through narrow channels of Torres Strait (such laws exist for the inland passage through Australia's Great Barrier Reef); additional Islander access to and supervision of the lucrative, nonsubsistence fisheries; and Islander-initiated, -managed and -controlled ecotourism.

JUDITH FITZPATRICK

YONGGOM OF PAPUA NEW GUINEA

Yonggom Action:

Write AMOCO, which owns 30 percent of the Ok Tedi mine. Ask the company to safeguard the ecological rights of the Fly River people. H. Laurance Fuller, Chairman and CEO, Amoco Corp., 200 East Randolph Dr., Chicago, IL 60601.

Yonggom Resource:

John Connell and Richard Howitt, *Mining and Indigenous Peoples in Australasia*, Sydney University Press in association with Oxford University Press, 1991.

In myths told by the Yonggom, people cease being human and become animals when they are denied reciprocity. Some men are rumored to possess magic that enables them to briefly assume animal form—for example, to become a crocodile to cross a river. The Yonggom universe is an animate one, with no clear boundaries between people and nature.

Three thousand Yonggom live along the Ok Tedi and Fly rivers in the interior lowland rain forest of Papua New Guinea. They plant gardens, harvest sago, hunt, and fish in their rich, tropical environment. They also raise pigs, which they exchange for cowrie shells—or nowadays cash—at regional feasts attended by hundreds of guests. Although most Yonggom prefer the pace of village life to that of urban centers, they have developed a taste for the urban amenities salt, sugar, and rice and a need for basic manufactured goods such as clothing, tools, and household supplies.

Their wish for greater participation in the cash economy initially led the Yonggom to support a large copper and gold mine, the Ok Tedi mine at Mount Fubilan, built in the mountains to their north. But serious environmental problems began almost immediately when a partially constructed tailings dam was abandoned after a landslide in 1984.

For nearly a decade all the waste generated by this huge project has been released directly into the river system. The Ok Tedi River now runs brown and cloudy and the Yonggom can no longer drink from it or swim in it. Few fish are left to catch, and in any case people are afraid to eat them. The best land, once located along the river and fertilized by rich soil washed from the mountains, is now barren. The Yonggom say that many of their sago trees no longer produce the edible starch that is their mainstay.

Mine tailings also have devastated the surrounding rain forest. The riverbed has risen in height, causing the river to overflow and inundate large areas and thus depositing tailings that have killed trees along a corridor 40 miles long and nearly two miles wide in places. Ironically, although these problems stem largely from the absence of a tailings dam, *Ok Tedi* is not only the Yonggom name for the river but also means "dam."

The Yonggom are not the only people affected. Some Ningerum and Awin villagers also live along the Ok Tedi. In the Middle Fly, the Boazi and Suki are angry about their reduced fish catch. And there is concern about the potential impact of the tailings on the swamps and lakes that provide sanctuary for fish during the Fly River's periodic severe droughts. Even downstream at the mouth of the Fly, where the Kiwai live, the increased sediment load carried by the river includes tailings from both the Ok Tedi mine and the Porgera gold mine in the Western Highlands.

Ok Tedi Mining conducts an environmental monitoring program and has established a trust fund to support village development projects. But for the people who live along the river, the mine has irrevocably changed the quality of their lives and their relationship with the environment. They are beginning to question whether any compensation would suffice without greater protection of their river system.

STUART KIRSCH

113

Throughout much of their traditional North Asian homelands, indigenous peoples are vastly outnumbered. In the autonomous areas of China, indigenous peoples make up only 44 percent of the population; in Siberia, fewer than 10 percent. Ainu in Japan constitute well under 1 percent of Hokkaido's population. The smallest officially recognized nationality groups—the Aleuts, Entsy, Negidals, Oroki, Orochi, and Tofa of Russia—number in the mere hundreds.

Colonization efforts on the part of Russia and China, the two vast empires of this area, included considerable state efforts to encourage "trustworthy" citizens to emigrate to the "frontiers." Repressive political systems furthered these demographic transfers: the peripheries of Russia, China, and Japan were favored as exile sites, spawning the inflow of prisoners, both political and criminal, onto indigenous lands.

Economic opportunities for the non-prison immigrant population have consistently exceeded those of the people already living in these regions. Han came to dominate "white-collar" posts and higher-paying jobs exploiting the natural resources of Tibet, Xinjiang, and other traditionally non-Han provinces, as did Russians in Siberia and Japanese in Hokkaido. Uigurs, Tibetans, Chukchi, Ainu, and other indigenous peoples now hold low-paying, low-prestige jobs and often suffer un- or underemployment.

Nationality policy has differed among the North Asian states and varied over time within them. In Russia, early paternalistic attempts to afford the smallest indigenous groups some protection conflicted with efforts to selectively destroy such offending cultural institutions as shamanism. But among larger groups, including the Buryats and Sakha, the Soviet state readily identified and repressed "bourgeois nationalist elements." At the same time, it recognized the territoriality of many peoples by creating an ethnically based administrative system of national region, district, and republic. Official policy increasingly encouraged Sovietization and linguistic Russification, even while feebly propounding the right of peoples to their language and cultural "peculiarities."

China's policy has fluctuated more dramatically. In the 1950s, Beijing established a number of autonomous territorial units along Russian lines, but during the Cultural Revolution it terminated all special privileges for non-Han peoples. In the early 1980s, China restored rights and the situation of indigenous peoples improved somewhat.

Such variations notwithstanding, in all North Asian countries indigenous people experience a lower standard of living, a shorter life expectancy, and greater poverty than is average for the citizenry of their encapsulating states. Indigenous regions remain among the poorest, least developed areas.

Economic systems forced upon these peoples have further undermined their well-being. Collectivization in Russia and China tore people from the land, as did the settling of nomads. Villagization programs and the amalgamation of villages, with concomitant mass relocations and the often forced abandonment of smaller settlements, further sundered peoples' ties to their lands, along with the social relations interwoven with these ties. In Russia, masculinization of traditional activities, especially reindeer herding, marginalized native women in their own milieu. Boarding schools and sedentarization policies destroyed family units and interfered with the transmission of culture from one generation to the next. China's recent economic reforms have contributed, conversely, to feminizing traditional activities among indigenous groups, as men leave for urban jobs. Here, the feminization of poverty is more pronounced.

Environmental Degradation

Policies of ethnic discrimination and neglect are not the only threats to many of North Asia's peoples. State-sponsored "development" activities have ravaged their lands, undermining traditional activities. Mining, logging, and hydroelectric development have impoverished environments, and local populations rarely have derived benefits from such exploitation. In Western Siberia, where oil drilling and transport have damaged three-

A Tofa hunter on his way to the mountains

fourths of the reindeer pasture and hunting grounds, fewer than 1 percent of the native population enjoys central heating. Karakalpaks suffer from respiratory disease, high maternal and infant mortality, and growing unemployment as the Aral Sea shrinks and pesticide-laced dusts from its bed become airborne. Water diverted from the tributaries of this shriveling sea fed cotton for a textile industry based around Moscow.

Even temporary benefits, such as employment opportunities, are rare. Resource "development" has depended largely on immigrant labor. Those arriving to make a quick ruble or yuan may feel no responsibility to the land. They poach the local fauna, including domestic animals, and carelessly set forest fires, further impairing the subsistence activities of indigenous peoples.

When challenged by local groups, the ministries developing the resources have justified their actions in terms of providing benefits for the great-

est number of citizens, if at cost to a small number. Indigenous people are often viewed not only as culturally inferior but as numerically insignificant as well. When needed, "state security" is also evoked to quell complaints. Most insidiously, China and the Soviet Union vindicated the bombing of the homelands of the Uigur, Kazakh, Sakha, and other groups in the name of state security.

Political Systems in Flux

The unraveling socialism of Russia and Mongolia offers indigenous peoples new opportunities—and poses new threats. Decentralized power, new civic and legal structures, and expressed commitments to human rights suggest a window of opportunity for indigenous people in Russia to develop legislation and institutions favorable to their cultural survival. At the same time, democratization could hurt these groups because they are minorities on their own lands. Rising Russian nationalism may block legislation protecting indigenous rights, as may the careening economy.

Foreign intervention under the guise of development aid has already threatened some groups. Shattered as its economy is, Russia will have to depend on foreign capital if it wants to develop its vast energy and mineral resources. Korean logging concerns are deforesting the traditional homelands of the Udege, while international oil and gas consortiums endanger reindeer husbandry and hunting among the Nivkhi of Sakhalin Island, and the Nentsy, Khanty, and Mansi of western Siberia.

On the other hand, appropriate international pressure may help convince foreign players that they need to proceed according to international standards on indigenous rights, rather than by weaker domestic conventions. Russia's dependency on foreign aid already has provoked action among indigenous peoples beyond its borders.

Japan's Ainu have offered a solution to the seemingly insurmountable obstacle to Japanese aid for Russia, the resolution of the Kurile Islands problem. An Ainu group has proposed this territory be established as an Ainu autonomous region.

Culture and Sustainable Development

Like many of North Asia's indigenous peoples, the Ainu are searching for new relationships with the states in which they reside as a way to secure a culturally sustainable future. These relationships include redefined legal rights over land and resources, increased autonomy in education and cultural spheres in Russia, and increased economic autonomy. Ainu propose an autonomous region. Many Siberian groups want Russia to reestablish the "national" regions and districts that were disbanded decades earlier. Some groups look toward the creation of parks to protect their rights: many Chukchi and Eskimosy support the incorporation of their homelands into the Beringian Heritage International Park. In such cases, indigenous rights must be assured, not appropriated. Too often, nature-protection schemes actually erode indigenous access to critical resources.

Tourism, especially ecotourism and ethnic tourism, suggests a potential means of capitalizing indigenous economies without necessarily compromising their environments. The survival of many of these peoples into the late twentieth century may be partly attributed to their inhabiting remote, rugged terrains. The same terrains beckon to the jaded or adventurous tourist today, while fascination with cultural "otherness" spreads.

Tourism is fraught with cultural threats, however. For far too long, the dominant peoples have attempted to "museumify" indigenous cultures, eradicating offending traits and repackaging cultures to fit stereotypes. For the Naxi, Miao, Tofa, and other North Asian groups, central and regional governments dominate the regulation of ethnic tourism. The commoditization of culture can only benefit indigenous people when they themselves control the process.

To further their struggles to control their own lives and gain more autonomy, native groups are looking beyond the border of their cultures for help. In Russia, indigenous peoples have formed pan-national groups to fight for recognition and rights: witness the Association of the Small-Numbered Peoples of the North in 1990, and the South Siberian Cultural Center.

Some groups have also reached out beyond the borders of their states to explore the possibilities of networking through international indigenous organizations. In Russia, indigenous associations have called on the state government to ratify Convention 169 of the International Labor Organization and other international conventions that protect rights of indigenous peoples. Russian Eskimosy now join with Inuit from Alaska, Canada, and Greenland in the Inuit Circumpolar Conference to formulate policies for sustainable development in the Arctic. Khanty and Mansi of western Siberia have consulted with Metis in Alberta, Canada, on how to effectively negotiate with oil developers. In 1992, Evenki in Buryatia visited Manchurian Evenki and compared experiences under the two regimes. And in China, Uigurs, Kazaks, and Kirgiz watch with great interest the evolving sovereignty of their kinfolk to the west.

GAIL A. FONDAHL

North Asia Resources:
Sacred Earth Network (Russian-English Newsletter), 267 East St., Petersham, MA 01366.
Surviving Together: A Quarterly on Cooperative Efforts to Support Civil and Sustainable Societies in Eurasia, ISAR, 1601 Connecticut Ave., NW, Washington, DC 20009 (202)387-3034.
Ian Bremmer and Ray Taras, eds., *Nation and Politics in the Soviet Successor States*, Cambridge University Press, 1993.
Charles Li and Dru C. Gladney, eds., *Minority Nationalities of China*, forthcoming.

ASIATIC ESKIMO AND CHUKCHI OF THE RUSSIAN FEDERATION

Asiatic Eskimo and Chukchi Resources:

Association of Numerically Small Peoples of Chukotka and Kolyma, c/o Tatiyana Achirgina, P.O. Box 57, Anadyr 686710, Russia.

John Tichotsky, "Use and Allocation of Natural Resources in the Chukotka Autonomous District," Institute of Social and Economic Research, University of Alaska-Anchorage, 1991.

D. Wilson, "Exploration for Oil and Gas in Eastern Siberia," in *The Development of Siberia: People and Resources*, ed. by Alan Wood and R.A. French, St. Martin's Press, 1989.

Most of Russia's 1,719 Asiatic Eskimos and 15,184 Chukchi live in the Chukchi Autonomous Republic in the northeast corner of the Russian Federation. Overall, about 10 percent of the population of Chukotka, the traditional homeland of the Chukchi and Asiatic Eskimos, is indigenous.

The Asiatic Eskimo and Chukchi peoples share not only a territory but also, in some cases, features of culture and economy. Perhaps more important, they share a history in regard to Soviet policy, and today they cooperate in organizations aimed at strengthening indigenous economies and restoring the importance of indigenous cultures.

Historically, the culture and economy of the Chukchi have fallen into two groups: sedentary coastal Chukchi, who primarily hunted seals, walrus, and whales, and nomadic tundra Chukchi, who bred reindeer. Trade, language, and even ancient family ties linked coastal and nomadic groups. The culture and economy of the Asiatic Eskimo also revolved around coastal settlements and sea-mammal hunting. Hunting mountain sheep, wild reindeer, and birds and fishing supplemented Chukchi and Eskimo diets. Chukchi and Eskimo women gathered wild plants, which were important parts of their diet. As trade with Russians, and later North Americans, developed, tea and other imports entered into indigenous diets and lifestyles.

In the early days of Soviet rule, nationalities policy was aimed at transforming Northern cultures and economies from "primitive" communal to "modern" socialist forms. This meant creating urban-industrial settlements, collectivizing indigenous communities, developing natural resources, and incorporating indigenous people into Russian society.

Collectivization entailed the liquidation of small, ethnically homogeneous villages, the involuntary relocation of inhabitants to larger multiethnic settlements, and the consolidation of small collective enterprises into large collective farms. Later, the collective farms became state farms that effectively co-opted the indigenous economy. Forced resettlement moved many people out of the tundra and away from native villages.

As rapid changes ensued throughout the Russian North, the physical and mental health of indigenous peoples was devastated. Diseases of the heart, liver, kidneys, and ear, nose, and throat and other ailments afflict native Northerners far out of proportion to their numbers. Also, the incidence of death from these conditions is higher. Infant mortality is high, and Northern peoples have an average life expectancy 16 to 18 years below that of the non-indigenous population. Moreover, Soviet education, as it implemented an assimilationist agenda, alienated children from the land and from their parents and grandparents in language, occupation, and world view. Still, it failed to integrate Northern peoples into "Soviet" society.

Economic concerns are twofold in Chukotka. One concern, based on mineral wealth, employs workers from other parts of Russia and the former Soviet Union. Important natural resources include gold, tin, tungsten, and, until recently, mercury mining. Coal deposits are exploited as well. Oil and gas exploration is underway; offshore deposits show promise despite the barriers posed by the severe Arctic environment. Indigenous people participate little in Northern industrial development and suffer from the constant influx of laborers, who compete for housing, education, health, and other services.

Indigenous branches of the economy are based on traditional subsistence practices. Reindeer breeding, the main occupation, is concentrated in state farms. Fur farming and hunting are also mainly indigenous activities and part of state farms.

117

In all economic spheres, non-indigenous people hold most of the administrative and service positions. This ethnic stratification, which segregates Russians, Ukrainians, and others from indigenous people, is maintained through unequal access to goods, services, and jobs. The status of indigenous people is further diminished by discrimination related to their language and lifestyle.

> Ethnic stratification, which segregates Russians, Ukrainians, and others from indigenous people, is maintained through unequal access to goods, services, and jobs.

Current conflicts among industry, environmentalists, and indigenous peoples center around the degradation of the environment (pastures and water resources) and subsequent harm to domestic and wild animals. Mining has used wasteful and ecologically damaging technology. The movement of heavy equipment has irreparably damaged large tracts of tundra. All-terrain vehicles also do considerable harm to the topsoil and vegetation. Ships using the northern sea route frequently dump refuse into the ocean, fouling the coast as well as the water. Inadequate sewage and refuse disposal pose serious problems for the health and safety of everyone in Chukotka. The Bilibino Nuclear Power Station rarely appears in discussions of Russia's aging nuclear power stations, yet must be included in plans to safeguard the people and environment of Chukotka.

The restoration of indigenous economies and cultures is of paramount importance. In January 1990, the Association of Numerically Small Peoples of Chukotka and Kolyma held its first meeting. The association helps villages set up local branches and has begun to organize members of various professions. An Association of Reindeer Breeders has been established, and similar associations are planned for sea-mammal hunters, native-language teachers, and health-care personnel. And increased participation in local government and in such international projects as the Beringian Heritage International Park between Alaska and Chukotka are on the agenda. Within the association, the Society of Eskimos of Chukotka addresses the effects of assimilation, alcoholism, suicide, and so forth on the cultural and biological viability of Eskimos.

The questions of who controls resources and who has priority in land use are especially critical in areas where development and ecological concerns clash with indigenous interests. Today the difficult economic situation of autonomous areas such as Chukotka, along with increasing decentralization, make it imperative that local governments search for some means of providing income for their districts. One means of doing this is through payments for land use from both industry and traditional trades; another is through promoting tourism.

Northern affairs must be administered by Northerners: this is a fundamental tenet of the native associations in Chukotka. A shift in the balance of power has to take place—from Russian to indigenous hands. At present, however, local people are ill equipped—financially, legally, or otherwise—to defend their interests.

DEBRA L. SCHINDLER

118

THE HANI OF CHINA

The 1.25 million Hani, a Tibeto-Burman people, are one of China's official minority nationalities. The many subgroups of Hani, all claiming a common ancestor, are located in Yunnan Province, many in areas closed to foreigners. The Hani have a rich ritual and oral tradition and a complex social organization and marriage system. The Hani are traditionally rice farmers. Especially along the banks of the Honghe River (Red River), one can find steep mountain terraces .

Hani Action:
Encourage China to maintain its more open policies and call on Burma and Thailand to recognize the basic rights of minority groups and provide humane living conditions for Akha. AIDS education is also important. Contact the International Institute for Hani Culture, c/o D. Tooker, Dept. of Sociology, Le Moyne College, Syracuse, NY 13214.

Some of the most serious threats to Hani culture in China came during the Religious System Reform Campaigns of 1958. Because the campaigns aimed to rid China of "local nationality chauvinism," some Hani religious and cultural practices were forbidden. At least since 1988 (and perhaps since reforms in 1979), more open government policies have allowed Hani to reestablish some traditional practices.

Another threat to Hani cultural tradition and language, both of which are learned informally in community settings, is the incorporation of younger people into national (and even international) life through education and government jobs and other non-farming work. The continued southern migration of Hani groups—such as the Akha into Burma and Thailand—seems to indicate an imbalance between land resources and population.

In the southern countries, Hani are almost refugees. The culture of these groups may be more severely threatened than the Hani in China. In Burma, fighting between the government and ethnic independence forces has left Akha living in a war zone. Especially in Thailand, poverty and the lack of citizenship and land rights force many Hani to abandon traditional practices. Many convert to Christianity, and young girls have been tempted or deceived by intermediaries searching for potential prostitutes. With prostitution, AIDS has become a problem.

DEBORAH TOOKER

KAZAKHS OF KAZAKHSTAN

In newly independent Kazakhstan, Kazakhs are the only ethnic group in the former Soviet Union that are a minority in their own country—about 40 percent out of a population of 17 million. Such issues as choice of a language and defining the country's heritage will pit the growing national aspiration of Kazakhs against the large Slavic population originally from Russia and Ukraine. The result could be violent. Defining and preserving a Kazakh identity is particularly difficult because Soviet policies of collectivization and conversion of steppe pasture into farmland almost completely disrupted the culture and economy of Kazakhs, who were originally nomadic pastoralists.

The Kazakhs have inherited two severe environmental problems that threaten their health and safety. First, as the Soviet Union's major nuclear-weapons testing ground, parts of Kazahkstan have inherited a radioactive legacy of polluted water and land. The Kazakh government is ill equipped to remedy this damage.

Second, along their country's border with the Aral Sea, Kazakhs have seen the size of the lake shrink by many miles when the Soviet Union diverted the rivers feeding it in order to support increased cotton production in Turkmenistan and Uzbekistan. This devastated Kazakh fishing along the Aral's shores. Moreover, deadly dust storms carry toxic sediments from the exposed sea bed throughout the region.

THOMAS J. BARFIELD

119

KHAKASS

Khakass Action:
Letters protesting the persecution of the national movement of Khakass people can be sent to the General Prosecutor, Russian Federation, Moscow, Russia.

For thousands of years, the 63,000 Khakass of southern Siberia have inhabited the forest steppes of the foothills of the Sayan Mountains. In the sixth century, they created a strong state and a rich culture. After a bloody war that lasted more than a century, Russians colonized Khakass lands in the mid-eighteenth century.

For almost three centuries, the Khakass have struggled for equality, freedom, and independence. Today they comprise a mere 11 percent of the population of the Republic of Khakasia, which was created in July 1991 and is part of the Russian Federation. Such demographics are one reason why fundamental political, economic, social and cultural rights aren't taken into account. Incidents of discrimination against Khakass are widespread.

In 1988, Khakasians created their own political organization, the Association of Khakass People, "Tun" (Birch), as well as an organ of self-government, the National Council of Khakass people, in 1992. However, the central and republican governments are trying to suppress both efforts.

ALEXANDER KOSTYAKOV

MIAO OF CHINA

The 7.4 million Miao, China's fourth-largest minority, are scattered over seven southwestern provinces, inhabiting mainly this region's precipitous mountainous portions. Few have benefited from the economic reforms that have widened the gaps in material circumstances throughout China. Miao families in the interior, who sometimes walk for more than an hour to carry water or to till their fields, fret about the hunger that could result from annual grain shortfalls.

More than half the Miao—those who live in rugged Guizhou Province—face additional obstacles. In most of the province, deforestation and severe population pressure on arable land have made timber, once an important source of revenue, a scarce resource. In some places, the mountains from which Miao took firewood, game, building materials, and medicines have been designated "Natural Protection Areas," addressing environmental problems at the expense of Miao living standards.

Guizhou Province's rainy, dank climate and extremely limited transportation system have also deterred tourism and joint-venture investments, double-edged processes that effect desired economic change even as they transform social and cultural relations. A few Miao counties have no significant local industries and remain classified as "impoverished."

Increasingly, Miao families have adopted an approach common among peasants all over China since the de-collectivization of agriculture: they take their children out of school at a younger age so that they can work in the household. This frees up older family members to leave home in search of temporary wage labor. Growing numbers of migrant laborers, mostly men, are flocking to Guangzhou and Shenzhen, "Special Economic Zones" on the coast.

Miao have also commodified their culture as a way to raise income, although the government tourism industry is the chief architect and beneficiary of such initiatives. Miao handicrafts are marketed widely, and in some areas cottage industries and small workshops have been established to produce crafts on a larger scale. A few young people, primarily women, have found jobs in service or entertainment based on their "colorful" traditional clothes and their skill in song and dance. Miao people do not see these trends as undesirable cultural transformations, but rather as a mode through which to heighten the group's visibility and benefit it in the long term.

The Miao Studies Association, which addresses both economic and cultural matters, recently set up a scholarship program for students who want to obtain higher educations.

LOUISA SCHEIN

NAXI OF CHINA

About 250,000 Naxi live in Lijiang Prefecture, Yunnan Province, China. In the past decade, with the de-collectivization of agriculture and the return to family farming, Naxi women have been increasingly shouldering the burden of agricultural labor. At the same time, the resurrection of local market economies has inspired some Naxi men to venture out of the villages to find work as temporary laborers or in small-scale entrepreneurial activities.

The growing trend towards the "feminization of farming" appears to be part of a broader phenomenon in rural China. It is difficult for Naxi women to resist these changes, both because the shift signals a return to an earlier labor pattern in which women did the lion's share of farming and because the Naxi associate female prestige with labor productivity. Even during China's collective era, Naxi women consistently earned more work points for labor than did Naxi men, in striking contrast to their Chinese counterparts.

While money earned outside the household has occasionally improved its standard of living, the redirection of male labor has had less of a positive impact on women's lives. Naxi girls tend to receive less schooling than their brothers, and in some cases less than their sisters educated a decade ago. Rural Naxi girls rarely attend school beyond the primary level because of the cost of schooling and the dependence on female labor in agriculture. At the age of 4 or 5, a Naxi girl rises at dawn to gather weeds for pig feed, and she frequently does farm work before and after school, unlike her brothers. Health-related problems attest to the heavy demands of women's labor as well as the physical hardship of often maintaining a family farm alone.

Some Naxi women have eloped with Chinese men to the more prosperous provinces of Zhejiang and Jiangsu, where these men claim to have residence permits allowing them to live in a town, city, or closer to an urban area. While some of these are legitimate elopements, the results can be disastrous when women, lured by prospects of urban employment, are forcibly sold by marriage brokers to poor Chinese farmers who are unable to obtain local wives or who seek minority wives not subject to the strict policy limitations on family size. The long-distance elopements of young Naxi women do not occur on a large scale but illustrate a strategy on the part of some women to respond to increased demands on female labor and to the disparity in living standards between urban and rural dwellers.

Looking for work outside the farm is a parallel strategy employed by some Naxi men who feel themselves stranded in the desolate economic terrain of the Lijiang countryside. After 1949, residence permits and grain rations effectively froze people in a geographical hierarchy, with urban residence on top and rural status determined by the productivity of the land and the proximity to towns and urban areas.

When Lijiang town opened to foreign tourism less than a decade ago, caravans of young tourists seeking exotic herbal remedies and glimpses of an "ancient China" descended. While town dwellers have begun to capitalize on tourism-related activities, beyond being cornered for photos, rural residents have had little contact with these wealthy tourists. Yet dissatisfaction grows with the awareness of the wealth that lurks as close as the nearby town. The work and marriage strategies of Naxi men and women, however flawed, are attempts to improve their lives, efforts that are rooted in the context of limited opportunities and the widening gulf in living standards between China's urban and rural residents.

EMILY CHAO

121

NENETS AND KHANTY OF THE RUSSIAN FEDERATION

ANDRE GOLOVNEV

The Yamal Peninsula of northwest Siberia has been home to humans for perhaps 4,000 years. Well above the Arctic Circle, it contains extremely large gas deposits that the Russian government is committed to extracting. However, the planned construction of a railroad and two pipelines by thousands of temporary workers will destroy much of the environment on which more than 14,000 Nenets and Khanty depend.

The earliest sedentary peoples of Yamal hunted caribou on the tundra; harpooned seals, walruses, and beluga on the waters and ice of the Kara Sea; and caught fish in thousands of tundra rivers and lakes. About a millennium ago, Nenets moved into Yamal. Eventually assimilating the older inhabitants, they followed a nomadic life based on reindeer breeding, as did a number of Khanty peoples who also settled in the region.

By the beginning of this century, a few families had amassed thousands of reindeer, but most herds ranged from several dozen to several hundred. Social institutions based on clan membership allowed people to share animals and food, to unite and divide herds, and to use all nearby resources. Religion and other cultural beliefs stressed respect for the land and its resources.

Change came to Yamal in the 1930s. The Soviet Union turned Nenets and Khanty lands over to collective farms, collectivized herds, and prosecuted rich owners. In the 1960s, the collectives became state-owned "soviet farms." Deprived of their land, subsistence rights, and reindeer, most Nenets became hired workers in reindeer-breeding state enterprises. About 1,750 indigenous nomads continued to have private herds, living on the tundra completely separate from the Soviet economic system.

Today, projected development of the Bovanenkhovskoye, Kharasaveyskoye, and other gas fields will devastate reindeer pastures, ending the remaining economic base of Nenets culture. The potential ethnocide of the Nenets and the devastation of Yamal's environment have received attention from Russian and international human-rights groups and environmentalists. Scientific teams are conducting a detailed environmental impact assessment and will soon make recommendations to the government.

The ultimate challenge is in assuring a sustainable future for Yamal's Nenets and Khanty peoples—culturally as well as environmentally. At present, the Yamal native people's association, Yamal for Future Generations, has limited experience and no legal base. The legislative status of the Yamal-Nenets Autonomous Okrug (District) is also unclear, thereby further hindering legal improvement for Yamal's indigenous people. In such circumstances, questions about gas development could be addressed without negotiations, or a few urban native elites, strongly influenced by regional bureaucrats and powerful industrial managers, could sign documents that fail to solve the problems of land, resources, and compensation in an equitable manner.

ALEXANDER PIKA AND NORMAN CHANCE

NIVKHI OF THE RUSSIAN FEDERATION

After almost 70 years of intense cultural reeducation programs under the Soviets, the roughly 4,500 Nivkhi on Sakhalin Island and in the Amur River delta are looking to the new political and economic freedoms in Russia to preserve what remains of their cultural heritage. Nivkh-language schooling for children has been revived, a Nivkh-language newspaper is being published for the first time since the 1930s, and Nivkhi have formed precarious fishing and gathering cooperatives.

Nivkhi Resources:
International Working Group
for Indigenous Affairs—
Russia, c/o Aleksandr Pika,
36 Veernaia, kor. 2, kv. 93,
Moscow 119501, Russia.
Nadezhda Aleksandrovna
Laigun, Native Affairs
Officer, 39 Kommun-
isticheskii Prospekt, Yuzhno-
Sakhalinsk 693011, Russia.

However, the co-ops signal competition for government monopolies built on the Soviet command economy, and local officials have fiercely resisted demonstrations of Nivkh entrepreneurship. For example, officials allow the Nivkh to form co-ops but deny them the right to catch more than symbolic amounts of fish.

That some Nivkhi seek to revive centuries-old traditions of fishing and gathering in concert with natural cycles testifies to the tenacity of ethnicity. Nivkhi were among the most intensely colonized of all Siberian indigenous groups in the Soviet Union. On the heels of promising reforms in the 1920s, such as the founding of hospitals and Nivkh-language schools, about one-third of all Nivkh adult men died during the Stalinist purges. By World War II, almost all Nivkh men and women worked in state-run fisheries and could only speak their native language or wear traditional dress on official holidays. In the 1960s, more than two-thirds of the Nivkhi were relocated from ancestral villages to barren state agricultural centers, initiating job and housing discrimination that leaves them subordinate to the transient Russian and Ukrainian populations.

In one respect, the predicament of Nivkh entrepreneurs is shared by people across the former Soviet Union, where optimistic government pronouncements of renaissance and reformation belie an intransigence to real privatization or any sharing of sweeping state control over resources. But the Nivkhi, like many Siberian indigenous groups, look not only to exercise their constitutional rights but their cultural autonomy as well. International attention directed to the investment-hungry governments of the area would aid these efforts.

BRUCE GRANT

OROKS OF THE RUSSIAN FEDERATION

Orok Action:
To express support for the
redrawing of pipeline routes
on Sakhalin and for the con-
tinued autonomy of Orok
herders, contact Tatiana
Roon, Sakhalin Regional
Museum, 29
Kommunisticheskii Prospekt,
Yuzhno-Sakhalinsk 693010,
Russia, or Aleksandr Pika,
International Working
Group for Indigenous
Affairs—Russia, 36 Veernaia,
kor. 2, kv. 93, Moscow
119501, Russia.

The Oroks of Sakhalin Island are among the smallest of Russia's Narody Severa—"Peoples of the North." Despite numbering only 190 in the 1989 Soviet census, their semi-nomadic lifestyle as reindeer herders has enabled them to maintain their language and traditions to a far greater degree than neighboring Siberian indigenous peoples.

Their nomadic way of life long helped Oroks maintain a certain degree of autonomy, but they were dealt a heavy blow after the 1905 Russo-Japanese war. The two countries divided Sakhalin, leaving the Oroks and their herding grounds open to equally divisive policies of colonization. In the 1920s, the Soviet government in the north became frustrated with the elusive herders, who were hard to find, hard to tax, and hard to educate in a communist setting. The Soviets attempted to settle them in 1932 into a combined herding and agricultural collective on Sakhalin's northeast shore. By obliging children to attend Russian-language schools and inducing women to remain with the children, the government tried to cleave the family unit and discourage Orok men from herding altogether.

Only one Orok herding brigade now exists, an extended family network of 10 men who follow ancestral migratory routes so familiar that the deer rarely need to be shepherded. The brigade is the nucleus for cultural revival among the Oroks, and Orok women have formed a traditional arts cooperative to take advantage of the new political freedoms in Russia to sell fur wares privately and join their husbands on the migration routes.

Today Oroks are threatened by an enormous development project that calls for obstructive oil and gas pipelines to be laid across the only remaining migratory routes for their herds. A project that doesn't account for these routes will bring the last chapter of distinctively Orok life to a close.

BRUCE GRANT

SAKHA OF THE RUSSIAN FEDERATION

The Sakha, historically called Yakut by outsiders, live in the Sakha Republic of the Russian Federation, formerly Yakutia. Siberia's Sakha are the northernmost Turkic people, intermixed with the Evenk, Even, and Yukagir.

In the 1920s, the Sakha constituted 82 percent of their republic's population, but today they number about 400,000 in a republic of slightly over 1 million. In the Sakha's own republic, the majority is Slavic, and, in Sakha eyes, this majority has inundated their vast region (four times the size of France).

Traditionally cattle and horse herders managing extended, lake-filled homesteads, many Sakha were forced into collectives in the 1930s or pushed into cities and towns through Soviet development projects and their own aspirations for education. The minerals (diamonds, gold) and energy resources (oil, natural gas) of the republic have meant an influx of temporary labor and the exploitation of its wealth at vast costs to the indigenous population, including poverty, alcoholism, and overcrowding. Permafrost-warped wooden cabins in villages rarely have plumbing, and shacks and barracks line the outskirts of boom towns. Newcomers exacerbate ethnic tensions and are blamed by the Sakha for rising crime rates.

Until the 1990s, the Sakha Republic received subsidies from Moscow, as raw materials flowed out of the republic. New agreements give Sakha leaders about 30 percent control over local resources, providing a sense of relative sovereignty but still less than the economic independence many desire. A new danger is the substitution of foreign for Soviet exploitation: fresh arrivals include Japanese and Korean lumbering firms and De Beers Diamonds.

Strip mining, wasteful lumbering, a huge hydroelectric dam, and underground nuclear testing have created literal and figurative fallout. Desertification, river pollution, and the inability of supply ships to reach major northern towns have resulted. Exploration and development bring tractors into the tundra and taiga, degrading the delicate northern environment, where some Sakha and Even have tried to maintain hunting, fishing, and reindeer breeding. Rockets launched from Kazakhstan leave a pollution trail stretching to the Arctic Sea. Ecological changes have affected families, particularly in the North, where cancer rates for children have risen and respiratory diseases are now rife. Some Viliuisk residents are moving south for their children's health, as glasnost has brought information about water and air pollution.

Sakha ecological activists have organized local protests and goaded the new, predominantly Sakha Republic legislature into action. Authorities have halted a few building projects, begun land reforms, established health centers, and introduced more rigorous monitoring of polluting industries. But they have approved a serious threat: the rail spur due to arrive in the capital, Yakutsk, in 1995.

Debate over the railroad illustrates policy tensions. Some Sakha argue for controlled development and the importance of a link to the economies of the East. Others, pleading for a more traditional way of life, say that the eco-

Sakha Resource:
Piers Vitebsky, "Yakut," in *The Nationalities Question in the Soviet Union*, ed. by G. Smith, Longman, 1990.

Sakha Action:
To inquire about helping protect the Sakha's environment, contact Nikolai Nakhodkin or Ivan Burtse at Obshchestvennyi Ecologicheskii Tsentr Iakutii, 677000 Respublika Sakha, Yakutsk, ul. Chernyshevskogo, d. 8, kv. 71, Russia.

logical and psychological costs of the railroad will be too great. Most have supported an upsurge in Sakha pride, which predated the reforms of the 1980s and intensified in the 1990s. New Sakha-language programs have been introduced in the schools, and strong cultural revival groups thrive in the cities. Over 90 percent of the Sakha speak the native language. Organized groups include Sakha Omuk (Sakha People), Sakha Keskile (Sakha Perspective), and Kut-Siur (Soul-Reason), which is oriented toward spiritual rebirth. An Association of Folk Medicine has revived practices of shamanism that had gone underground in the Soviet period.

Chances for some self-determination appear better than they have for centuries, yet Sakha perceive potential demographic, economic, ecological, and political threats. They haven't claimed territory lost when they became a Soviet "autonomous republic" because leaders fear that, once boundary disputes begin, their own republic could be carved into Slavic and non-Slavic regions. They prefer to keep the territory intact, while negotiating better deals with the Russians, who are discovering multiple facets of the Sakha and their diamonds.

MARJORIE MANDELSTAM BALZER

TIBETANS

Tibetan Resource:
International Campaign for Tibet, 1518 K St., NW, Suite 410, Washington, DC 20005. Office of Tibet, 241 East 32nd St., New York, NY 10016.

For over 40 years Tibet has been brutally occupied by the communist government of the People's Republic of China. In a systematic attempt to eliminate all physical vestiges of Tibetan culture, over one-fifth of Tibet's population has died as a result of Chinese rule, thousands more have been tortured and imprisoned, and the majority of Tibet's Buddhist monasteries destroyed. His Holiness the Dalai Lama, Tibet's spiritual and temporal leader, was forced into exile in India, where he and 120,000 Tibetans remain.

In 1965, China declared Tibet a Chinese "Autonomous Region." This designation is resolutely rejected by the Tibetan government-in-exile. China's occupation of Tibet was declared illegal by the U.S. Congress, and the United Nations has disputed China's claim to sovereignty over Tibet.

One of the greatest threats to Tibetan culture is the movement of Chinese settlers into Tibet. In the 1950s and '60s, the Chinese military constructed a series of roads throughout Tibet, bringing in soldiers to police the country and Chinese cadres to rule it. Today, ever-larger numbers of Chinese are settling in Tibet as a result of China's accelerated economic development projects in the region. The population of Lhasa, Tibet's capital, is already more than half Chinese.

This influx has led to a decline in the use of the Tibetan language, impeded access to employment for Tibetans, and increased pressure on natural resources. As China's plans to industrialize Tibet progress, the marginalization of Tibetans due to Chinese population transfer will increase.

Unfortunately, Tibetans face great risks in addressing these threats to their culture, families, and homes. Pro-independence activities often lead to imprisonment or torture. Buddhist monks and nuns have been a special target of Chinese forces.

The unique Tibetan environment has suffered, too. For example, a major hydroelectric project on Yamdrok Tso, a sacred "life-power" lake to Tibetans, was halted temporarily due to Tibetan protest over cultural and ecological repercussions from the project. However, following the death of Panchen Lama, one of the project's most outspoken opponents and a major Buddhist leader, the project has continued unimpeded.

Tibetan communities, the government-in-exile, and Western support groups have raised awareness of the human-rights situation in Tibet. Campaigns have protested religious persecution, the lack of political freedom, international funding for destructive development projects, forced abortion and sterilization of Tibetan women, and, ultimately, the ongoing occupation of the country.

CAROLE MCGRANAHAN

TOFA OF THE RUSSIAN FEDERATION

At the close of the czarist period, the Turkic-speaking Tofa of the Eastern Sayan Mountains in western Irkutsk were nomadic hunters, divided into five territorial clans and subsisting on game and wild plants. For more than a century, they had ridden reindeer into the high winter mountains to seek furs for the Russian market.

By 1932, the Soviets, disregarding clan affiliation, had gathered the Tofa into three settlements 100 roadless miles from the district center of Nizhneudinsk. The state laid claim to former clan territories and organized a collective in each settlement to direct the exploitation of the forests. Russian immigrants intermarried with Tofa and were integrated into their communities.

In the 1960s, a centralized management agency of the Irkutsk government, acting through an office in Nizhneudinsk, replaced the collectives. The agency assumed ownership of most horses and reindeer, replacing hunters' collective income with small individual salaries that were supplemented by payments for large harvests of furs and other forest products. Credit was extended against this income for hunting equipment and for renting agency horses and reindeer.

About 1,100 people, 60 percent of whom are Tofa, now live in the three settlements. Most of the rest are Russians, many of whom live much as the Tofa do. Each settlement has a primary school, with a secondary boarding school in the largest. Motorized ground travel to Nizhneudinsk is possible only when the unimproved road freezes, but regular air service reaches all the settlements.

Only Tofa elders remember their native language, but a Tofa-Russian text distributed in 1989 has led to some native-language instruction in the schools. And while clan membership is being forgotten, the Tofa still regard themselves as hunters, as natives, and as owners in common of the former clan territories, despite Russianization and long participation in the Russian market.

The agency requires men to hunt sable and squirrel for fur, Siberian elk for antlers, and musk deer for musk; to collect pine nuts, berries, and wild rhubarb; to work a number of days in village sawmills; and to cut native hay for agency livestock. Some men supplement their income by serving as guides for Soviet tourists, who, despite rustic conditions, find the Eastern Sayans attractive. Some Tofa women work as bakers, storekeepers, and office workers, but most aren't gainfully employed.

The management agency brings in outsiders by helicopter to hunt furbearing animals and gather pine nuts. To acquire hard currency, the agency has introduced foreign sport hunters to Tofa territory. Gold was discovered nearby in the 1930s, and government-sponsored mines have appeared at the fringes of traditional lands.

The Tofa see all these activities as threats to their livelihood. In 1990, the Association of Small-Numbered Peoples of Siberia was established in

Tofa Resource:
O.V. Bychkov, Etnograficheskoe Biuro, A.Ya. 5163, Irkutsk 664009, Russia.

Moscow, with Tofa affiliation. Agitation for native rights led the Irkutsk government to create a commission to study Tofa social and economic conditions; it is considering proposals to establish a Tofa native reserve as well.

Whether affirmation of native land rights would include control of subsurface resources is uncertain, because historically the state has owned those resources. And despite likely official confirmation of some Tofa land rights, other threats loom. The Tofa may find their region exploited for development in several ways, while financial benefits pass them by and a new influx of outsiders threatens the supply of wild products on which their life depends.

The Irkutsk headquarters of the management agency is being converted into a joint-stock company, with its previous Soviet directors as majority shareholders. With no apparent competition to the agency, the Tofa could find themselves debt servants to a massive private enterprise. And attempts are underway from outside Irkutsk, as well as by the agency, to establish hunting and fishing lodges for foreign visitors. Gold-mining, too, is expanding.

DON E. DUMOND

UDEGE OF THE RUSSIAN FEDERATION

In the southeast corner of Siberia, indigenous peoples are fighting against deforestation of their lands by a South Korean logging firm. Hyundai planned to clear-cut more than 650,000 cubic yards of timber annually in the upper Bikin River watershed. The Udege, numbering 1,902 in the 1989 census, have hunted and fished this area for centuries, harvesting salmon, sable, and ginseng for trade and countless other forest products for domestic use. During the Soviet period, many were torn from their traditional lands and moved into state villages. They suffer from poverty, unemployment, alcoholism, and high morbidity and mortality rates.

The Udege only learned of Hyundai's plans to log their lands after the agreements for the joint venture were in place. They fought back by appealing to the local government and blockading loggers' access. Supported by non-native locals and the Socio-Ecological Union, they appealed to a 1992 Russian law that requires the consent of indigenous peoples to any expropriation of resources from their land. The local government overturned legislation that gave Hyundai rights to cut in the area, but the regional court quickly overturned this ruling.

The fight took a positive turn in November 1992, when Udege activists and the local government appealed to the Russian prosecutor's office, which ruled against the regional court, citing both the 1992 law and the failure of Russian partners in the joint venture to complete an environmental impact assessment—the area is also home to one-sixth of the world's remaining Siberian tigers, a mere 250 animals. Meanwhile, Hyundai, which is cutting in other areas to the south, argues that it needs more forest to make its venture economically profitable and hopes to reverse the decision in its favor.

GAIL A. FONDAHL

127

UIGURS OF CHINA

One of many ethnic groups struggling for autonomy under Chinese rule, Uigurs live in poverty while China exploits their resource-rich land. Their region is officially called the Xinjiang Uigur Autonomous Province, but that name is misleading. In Chinese, Xinjiang means "new dominion," yet China first conquered the area in the third century B.C.

Recently Uigurs have watched many neighboring Turkish peoples become independent as the former Soviet Union dissolved. But China continues to

Uigur Resource:
Unrepresented Peoples and
  Nations Organization, 347
  Dolores St., Suite 206, San
  Francisco, CA 94110.

resist Uigur self-determination. Although the costs of controlling a region so far from Beijing may be high, so is the value of Xinjiang.

In the first place, Xinjiang acts as a buffer between China and Afghanistan, Pakistan, India, and the new Central Asian nations. Moreover, hidden from the world, Xinjiang has been China's nuclear testing ground, decimating many native plants and animals. Above-ground nuclear tests at Lop Nur ended only in 1983.

Larger than Alaska, Xinjiang is rich in natural resources, including 18 billion tons of oil in the Tarim basin. The profits from petroleum products--as well as those from uranium, gold, silver, iron, copper, tin, emeralds, and coal--end up in China proper. The same goes for livestock, crops, and wool.

Part of the attack on Uigurs is cultural. Several policies serve to diminish them as an ethnic group. For example, Beijing has diluted the Uigur population by importing more and more members of the Han ethnic group that led the Chinese Revolution. In 1953, when Uigurs were 75 percent of the population in Xinjiang, only 300,000 Han lived there. Today Han ranks have swollen to 6 million.

Xinjiang living standards are low for Han and Uigur alike, but schools and businesses are conducted in Chinese, a language few Uigurs speak. That gives Han an advantage in getting jobs and receiving an education, and it also gives few Han cause to learn Uigur. Government policies award bonuses for mixed marriages between Uigurs and Han.

In Xinjiang and abroad, Uigur resistance appears on the rise. Recent articles in the Chinese press decry "separatism," "anti-socialism," and "religious mania." Militant Uigurs get arms from Pakistan and Afghanistan and have organized a few bomb attacks, although China carries out most of the violence. In March 1992, Chinese troops fired on 10,000 protesters in Kashgar, killing about 100.

DAVID I. MINKOW

UTORO, ETHNIC KOREANS IN JAPAN

Early in World War II, Japanese soldiers kidnapped thousands of Koreans, forcing the men to labor in mines and factories and the women into "comfort battalions" for the Imperial Army. Since that time, the families of some of these and other Koreans have lived in Utoro in Japan. The 80 families in this village, as well as other Koreans and minorities in Japan, continue to be victimized by racial discrimination and suffer under a rigid apartheid system that denies them the rights and privileges of Japanese citizenship.

In the late 1980s, a developer, armed with eviction notices and demolition crews, arrived in Utoro and informed its residents that Nissan Shatai had sold the five-acre village. The company, part of the Nissan conglomerate that includes Nissan Motor Co., had sold the ethnic Koreans' home of 50 years without informing them.

The eviction process continues today. Nissan refuses to talk to Utoro residents, who received neither assistance after the war nor compensation for their abduction and enslavement.

ELIZABETH GARSONNIN

SOUTHEAST ASIA: A STUDY IN CONTRASTS

A few contrasts suggest the complexity of Southeast Asia: tiny Brunei, one of the world's richest nations; Vietnam, Laos, Cambodia, and Burma, among the poorest; and Singapore, Malaysia, Thailand, and Indonesia, among the fastest-growing economies.

The contrasts are not only economic. Southeast Asia hosts all the major religions in the world—including the world's largest Muslim population, in Indonesia—and countless forms of local belief and practice. Although Cambodia and some other countries are relatively homogeneous in terms of ethnicity, Indonesia and the Philippines contain an astonishing diversity of cultural identities and languages.

The ways in which ethnicity has come to be defined and activated vary enormously. As Benedict Anderson observes in *Southeast Asian Tribal Groups and Ethnic Minorities,* "Minorities came into existence in tandem with majorities—and, in Southeast Asia, very recently," born in the context of the colonial state and popular nationalism. These processes took different forms throughout a region subject over several centuries to Portuguese, Spanish, Dutch, French, British, U.S., and Japanese domination.

Not only ethnicity but also class, religion, gender, and access to political and economic elites and international power structures have shaped the lines of cleavage and struggles of local peoples in Southeast Asia. Some of these struggles are well-known, and ongoing, tragedies: the plight of Cambodians in the Pol Pot years—and the current specter of Khmer Rouge return—is one case. Another is the Indonesian invasion and subsequent annexation of East Timor in 1975-76, which resulted in the death of perhaps 200,000 people and a protracted, *intifada*-like conflict that continues today between local people and the Indonesian army.

Other struggles, particularly environmental ones, have acquired a certain popularity in the Western media: the resistance of Penan hunter-gatherers of Sarawak is perhaps the best-known example, having found its way into film and popular journalism. The rate of deforestation in Sarawak is the most rapid in the world, yet as Peter Brosius argues, more than logs are at stake—it is the "cultural density" of the Penan landscape that is in danger of being lost, literally obliterated by the opening of the forest canopy.

The Penan are not unique. The same processes that threaten them are occurring throughout Southeast Asia, as the scramble to control rich natural resources pits powerful forces against the virtually powerless: the Yamdena islanders of Maluku, the Asmat of Irian Jaya, the Orang Asli of peninsular Malaysia, and countless others whose stories are not recounted here. Desired resources go well beyond the forest: rice fields, gold and gem mines, coffee plantations, shrimp farms, coral reefs, and open seas rich in tuna continue to be sites of contention.

The extent of indigenous resistance or compliance with the demands of extractive interests varies greatly. In the Penan's case, a vast international network now watches, and affects in diverse ways, every move the participants make. In Malaysia, the Orang Asli, with other Malaysians, have founded an organization to fight for their economic and cultural rights, a move that parallels the flowering of local private organizations elsewhere in the region, especially in Indonesia, the Philippines, and Thailand. In more obscure Yamdena, however, the Indonesian military's retaliation was severe when local people attacked a logging camp. And in Irian Jaya, the Asmat seem at the mercy of brute force, corruption, and newly created "needs" for food and tobacco.

Although local elites and state authorities play significant roles, in most of these dramas an international cast of characters is also at play. Thailand presents a striking example. While taking (belated) steps to preserve the remnants of its own forests, Thailand is rapidly extracting vast amounts of timber and other resources from its poorer neighbors—Laos, Burma, Cambodia—who desperately need foreign exchange. At the same time, the Thais are engaged in a wildly lucrative gem trade on the Cambodian border, which helps to enrich (and empower) the increasingly strong Khmer Rouge. The Burmese junta uses the currency derived from selling forests (to Thailand as well as to China) to support its counterinsurgency against ethnic minority rebels, pushing hundreds of thousands of refugees to neighboring countries, where they are often unwanted and face miserable conditions.

Cultural Citizenship

Southeast Asian peoples who are losing control over their resources often are culturally disempowered as well. The convergence may be simple in the case of forest usage: hunters and gatherers, or swidden cultivators, have never been part of the settled political elite. The Malaysian government would like to persuade the Orang Asli ("original people") to adopt the "Malay way of life," including Islam. The stigma of lack of full-fledged "cultural citizenship" is similarly one of the more subtle ways the Indonesian government exerts pressure on its diverse peoples. Indonesia insists that citizens choose an officially approved religion and encourages the objectification of ethnic identities through sanctioned cultural performances, ethnic tourism, and the like. Romantic images of primitivity, authenticity, or innocence are easily deployed by governments intent on keeping peoples in their place. Thus, the Penan are seen as misbehaving children, under the influence of interfering Western environmentalists.

Economic and cultural disenfranchisement do not always go together. Even large and economically powerful communities may be defined, and discriminated against, as cultural minorities. The

PETER BROSIUS

Penan men from a nomadic group in the Tutoh River area, Sarawak

Chinese in Malaysia are a striking example. Or cleavages may be articulated in largely religious terms, as in the southern Philippines, where Muslims in this overwhelmingly Catholic country have waged a secessionist war for decades. The salience of religious identities may shift over time. In southern Thailand, for example, the Muslim minority has become more assertive in recent years in distinguishing itself from its Buddhist and Christian (Sino-Thai) compatriots.

Created ethnicities and enforced citizenship may have unintended consequences. In the Philippines, for example, a U.S. colonial grid that brought together highlanders created a novel sense of unified Igorot (highland) identity, which served

130

to mobilize diverse peoples in opposition to the building of a series of huge hydroelectric dams. In East Timor, Indonesian demands for religious affiliation have resulted in massive conversions to Catholicism, which in turn have given new strength to an oppositional church. Similarly, in an ironic recapitulation of the Indonesian nationalist struggle against the Dutch, a generation of young East Timorese, trained in Indonesian-language schools, has acquired new tools with which to criticize and resist Indonesian rule.

Porous Borders

Clearly the forces that affect the lives of millions of people in Southeast Asia go well beyond the local in the 1990s. The enormous rush on Southeast Asia's natural resources is fueled in part by the demand for plywood, scaffolding, and chopsticks in Japan. On the other hand, an international boycott of teak from Burma by those concerned with military oppression in that country may have an impact (even if very slight) on what transpires there. So too may pressure brought about by the bestowal of the 1991 Nobel Peace Prize on Aung San Suu Kyi, whose pro-democracy party won an overwhelming electoral victory but has been prevented from taking office by the ruling junta. The resurgence of the Khmer Rouge is inextricably linked to strategies of the "great" powers, as is the poverty in Vietnam. That poverty, exacerbated by the U.S. embargo on trade and aid that has been in place since 1975, prompts desperate Vietnamese to seek their livelihood in Cambodia, where they become the targets of Khmer Rouge anti-Vietnamese propaganda and, in 1993, of brutal massacres.

That such struggles are not localized, but instead cross borders in multiple and entangled ways, is suggested by the problem of AIDS. International trade in prostitution and heroin has contributed to the "wildfire" spread of AIDS throughout the remote mountains of Burma. In the northern Thai city of Chiang Mai, 70 percent of the prostitutes are said to be infected with the H.I.V. virus. Landlessness and a deteriorating subsistence economy in the hills of northern Thailand push both men and women toward prostitution and drug use, increasing their vulnerability to infection. In what may be the ultimate Cambodian irony, the UN peace settlement appears to be bringing new devastation in the form of AIDS as an influx of prostitutes in Phnom Penh (from the countryside and from Vietnam) has followed quickly upon the arrival of thousands of UN peacekeeping troops. Borders are porous, easily transgressed by the sex trade; by the trade in gems, timber, or fish; and by the movements of laborers, rebels, or peace keepers.

The porosity of borders also means, however, that ideas and information flow at astonishing speed between distant places, with unforeseen and sometimes dramatic consequences. Penan foragers in Borneo become the center of an international controversy, in turn impelling Malaysia to take a vehemently anti-environmental stand at the 1992 international Earth Summit in Rio. Refugees or immigrants from almost all the nations of Southeast Asia establish diasporic communities and networks—within the region and beyond—that may have substantial impacts both on host communities and at home. Previously unempowered or disempowered peoples in remote locales now engage in conversations, and perhaps even actions, with each other and with far wider communities than once had been imagined.

TOBY ALICE VOLKMAN

Southeast Asia Resources:
Asia Watch, 485 Fifth Ave., New York, NY 10017.
Southeast Asian Tribal Groups and Ethnic Minorities:
    Prospects for the Eighties and Beyond, Cultural Survival
    Report 22, 1987.
*Traditional Property Rights and Natural Resource
    Management Project,* World Resources Institute,
    Washington, D.C.

ACEHNESE OF INDONESIA

Aceh, located on the tip of north Sumatra in Indonesia, has a population of 3 million. It has all the attributes of a province, but since 1959 it has had "special region" status in recognition of its 30-year war (which began in 1873) against the Dutch colonial army, its fierce role in the war of Indonesia's independence (1945-49), and its determination to fight incorporation into a larger province in the 1950s.

Aceh's readiness to fight the central government has led to the emergence of armed guerrilla movements at various times. Most recently, the Aceh/ Sumatra National Liberation Front, better known as Aceh Merdeka, emerged in 1976. A brief period of activism in the late 1970s led to hundreds of arrests throughout the region.

In the late 1980s, the separatist movement reemerged, this time between guerrillas trained in Libya and an Indonesian army determined to respond with force. A bloody counterinsurgency campaign resulted in thousands of deaths between 1989 and 1991. Trials of suspected Aceh Merdeka supporters continue, and military control is tight, although the executions and disappearances associated with the 1989-91 military offensive have largely ceased.

Of Aceh's eight districts, East Aceh, North Aceh, and Pidie have provided most of the supporters for separatist movements. In recent years, industrialization has been heavy in these districts along the east coast of Aceh, and most of the jobs have gone to Indonesians from outside the region. Resentment toward the central government for exploiting Aceh's wealth without the Acehnese gaining much benefit fueled the resistance. The east coast industries include oil (PT Arun, developed in conjunction with Mobil Oil), fertilizer, pulp and paper, and logging.

Despite the dangers of speaking out, INGI, an Indonesian coalition of private organizations, has fought human-rights violations and environmental problems in Aceh. In a 1992 message to donor countries, INGI called for "an end to the continued practice of unacknowledged detention and the shooting of suspected 'security disturbers.'" The document noted the difficult situation of widows and orphans, urged Indonesia to guarantee a livelihood to victims of human-rights violations, and expressed concern about "acute environmental degradation."

SIDNEY JONES

Aceh Resources:

Asia Watch, 485 Fifth Ave., New York, NY 10017 (212)972-8400; fax: (212)972-0905.

TAPOL, the Indonesian Human Rights Campaign, 111 Northwood Rd., Thornton Heath, Surrey CR7 8HW, UK (44-81)771-2904; fax: (44-81)653-0322.

The Jakarta-based Indonesian Legal Aid Foundation (Yayasan Lembaga Bantuan Hukum Indonesia) has done the best reporting from Indonesia; fax: (62-21)330-140.

ASMAT OF INDONESIA

The Asmat occupy extensive tidal forests on southeast Irian Jaya, Indonesia's easternmost province. The Indonesian government has bludgeoned the fierce pride of these once head-hunting warriors since assuming authority over the western half of the vast island of New Guinea in 1963, renaming it Irian Jaya.

The impenetrability of the rich forest to all but its native people led officials who had been collecting kickbacks from the logging concessionaires to begin using threats, intimidation, and physical force to make the Asmat log their own trees. Beginning in the 1970s, whole villages were forced for months at a time to fell trees for "the Company." Routine reprisals for failure to meet demands for logs included beatings by local officials and the withholding of the legal minimum wage.

Although the Asmat own all the land within the logging concessions, they receive no compensation for the trees. Instead, the government arrogates to itself the right to dispense natural-resource concessions on native lands. Asmat who refuse are accused of subversion, a capital crime.

As brute force became less politically viable, it was discarded in favor of

Asmat Resources:
Asia Watch, 485 Fifth Ave.,
New York, NY 10017
(212)972-8400.
Environmental Defense Fund,
1875 Connecticut Ave., NW,
Suite 1016, Washington, DC
20009 (202)387-3500.

more subtle manipulation. The workers receive tobacco and food and are then told they "owe" the merchants, repayable with logs. The Asmat thus acquire needs that can be met only at company stores, with loans that can be repaid only by obtaining more logs. Sweeteners offered to soften opposed clans include credit cards for stores owned by logging merchants.

"What will my children do when the big trees are all gone and the sago and palm and fruit trees and all our foods from the forest are damaged or flooded and cannot grow?" asks "J." He and his clan are clearing a corridor through the jungle brush and paving it with saplings for an immense felled tree. It can take two days and hundreds of saplings to move a single log to the river.

"If we cut all the trees now, so we can get tobacco and things from the store now, what source of income will our children have left? And what food will they eat if the forest is destroyed?" Two decades of stripping the forest of trees has reduced the Asmat's ability to sustain themselves from the land. Erosion and silt increase flooding and reduce the variety and quantity of fish the rivers can support.

In the 1980s, it became common for government inspectors to reject logs felled by the Asmat, relieving logging merchants of the obligation to pay for them. Subsequently such logs were loaded for export as officials looked the other way. For example, in February 1992, villagers were told to bring in logs significantly smaller than regulations allow. When 1,000 logs were rejected, two months' work went uncompensated. But there was no trace of the logs at the local loading point in July.

> In Indonesia, over 100 companies have mining concessions in forest areas near rivers.

Experience and occasional workshops conducted by support organizations are helping awaken post-contact generations to their rights against exploitation. But without ongoing village programs and without phone, road, or reliable air links to the Asmat jungle, responsibility falls on the graduates of these workshops to stem the loss of control over their lives, the discrediting of their culture, and the growing marginalization and impoverishment of the Asmat on their own land.

RAÏSSA LERNER

BURMA'S INDIGENOUS PEOPLE AND THE MILITARY JUNTA

"The only thing that can save Burma, the people, and the environment is for the military to be replaced by the elected government and federal democracy introduced that will stop the war—and then my work begins." This statement was voiced by Pado Thaw Thi, a wildlife conservationist of Burma's Karen people. He was referring to the 1990 election in which the pro-democracy party of Aung San Suu Kyi, recipient of the 1991 Nobel Peace Prize, won an overwhelming majority. Burma's ruling junta, the State Law and Order Restoration Council (SLORC), has never allowed her party to take office and keeps Aung San Suu Kyi under house arrest.

A British colony when Japan invaded in World War II, Burma became independent in 1948, although its history of ethnic conflicts was never resolved. In 1962, General Ne Win took power. His army, the Tatmadaw, has ruled Burma ever since.

The Tatmadaw wages a brutal counterinsurgency campaign in frontier areas where ethnic minority people are in rebellion. As the ruling officers are mostly Burmese (the majority ethnic group), other ethnic groups are automatically suspected of being rebel sympathizers. Indigenous people are subject to torture for information or just to terrorize them. Tatmadaw troops systematically rape girls and women to terrify ethnic minority villagers into

133

EDITH T. MIRANTE

Burma Resources:

"B.U.R.M.A. Newsletter," P.O.
Box 1076, Silom Post Office,
Bangkok 10504, Thailand.

"Burma: Rape, Forced Labor,
and Religious Persecution in
Northern Arakan," 1992
report by Asia Watch, 485
Fifth Ave., New York, NY
10017.

obedience or into leaving the country as refugees.

The AIDS epidemic has spread like wildfire through the remote mountains of Burma due to the international trade in prostitution and heroin. Burma is the world's biggest producer of opium, the raw material for heroin. The SLORC is very much in control of the production areas, and drug money helps pay for the Tatmadaw's weapons.

Another major source of hard currency is the sale of natural resources. The SLORC sold the tropical forests of southern Burma, home to Karens and Mons, to Thai firms, which clear-cut them in a frenzy for valuable hardwoods. The SLORC has also sold fishing rights, allowing the marine habitat of the Andaman Sea to fall prey to Thai trawler fleets. Mon fishing villages were forcibly relocated to prevent interference with Thai fishing operations.

Reports indicate that ethnic minority people, including Shans, Kachins, Chins, Palaungs, Pa-Os, and Karennis, are being forced to build roads and prepare pipeline routes in areas where foreign multinationals have entered into ventures with the SLORC for oil exploration. In the Northeast, a "death railway" line is being built from Loikaw to Aung Ban, with the assistance of UN agencies. A SLORC officer said that the high death rate was because hill people were being brought to the plains for the railway work: "They sweat a lot, they lose weight and they have some health problems. . . . Every day people are dying. It's a normal thing."

EDITH T. MIRANTE

THE CORDILLERA PEOPLES OF THE PHILIPPINES

The Igorot of the Philippines' Cordillera Mountains in northern Luzon, once called the "aristocrat of savages" by journalist Edgar Snow, have been the subject of outsiders' awe and wonder for almost 100 years. Unlike the surrounding lowland Ilocanos, who during 350 years of Spanish rule adopted European dress and formed links to international markets, the loincloth-clad Igorot appeared to the Americans who colonized the islands in 1898 to be as pristine as the forested mountains they inhabited.

The U.S. creation of a 6,000-square-mile Mountain Province in 1908 brought together highlanders who spoke mutually unintelligible languages, embraced different belief systems, and generally identified themselves by local geographic terms of reference. The imposed colonial administrative grid made visible broad commonalties among highlanders, encouraging social and political interactions. By treating highlanders as a single kind of people requiring "protection," U.S. rule accentuated the highland-lowland divide and led many highlanders to view themselves as a unified Igorot minority population.

U.S. colonial rule also opened up the Cordillera region to world market forces. Gold attracted the most interest, and by the 1930s a mining boom was underway. Not only did industrial mining forever change the landscape, but it also brought in hundreds of Americans and thousands of lowland Filipinos. Road construction and the demand for such American staples as potatoes and carrots created a vibrant commercial vegetable industry. In addition, the U.S.-inspired Philippine colonial summer capital of Baguio City served as a post-World War II gathering place for highlanders to articulate political demands associated with Igorot-ism and to call for rights to ancestral domains in Igorot-landia.

Highlander efforts during the 1950s and 1960s to join with lowland Filipinos as equals under the banner of "national integration" ended abruptly when then-President Ferdinand Marcos imposed martial law in

134

1972. Widespread opposition to a Marcos-directed logging and pulp enterprise and to a project calling for construction of four hydroelectric dams along the Chico River united college-educated and village-based highlanders, giving voice to what became an international outcry against the projects. Within the Cordillera, some of the most talented young people joined the Communist Party's New Peoples Army (NPA) to prevent Marcos from implementing these schemes. Intensive military operations left scores of dead, and even larger numbers suffered from other human-rights abuses.

Corazon Aquino's assumption of the presidency led to the cancellation of the dam projects and a blossoming movement for Cordillera regional autonomy. The call for autonomy included a desire for Igorot self-determination and for a form of government that would embrace traditional social and political structures. However, hope for meaningful autonomy has faded, due in part to divisions among highlanders holding differing views about the role of a Cordillera autonomous region in relation to the nation-state. Moreover, efforts by some Cordillera organizations to sway international support and reallocate resources that had been used to oppose Marcos have further weakened highlander unity. The remaining elements of the Cordillera NPA continue their struggle against the government.

In the meantime, many Cordillera residents continue to "wager the land," in the words of George Washington University geographer Martin Lewis, with intensive use of chemical inputs for vegetable farming. Along with excessive logging and other dubious environmental practices, this poses a critical challenge for the Cordillera's 1 million residents. Moreover, scarce local health services, poor infrastructure, and overall neglect by Manila have left the Cordillera with a standard of living seen as well below that found in the lowlands. As hope for regional autonomy fades, so too does the potential for the Cordillera to offer a more solid footing to Filipino nationalism and an alternative path toward national development.

GERARD A. FININ

> U.S. rule accentuated the highland–lowland divide and led many highlanders to view themselves as a unified Igorot minority population.

EAST TIMOR

A former Portuguese colony occupied by Indonesia since 1975, East Timor is home to some 30 indigenous groups and an increasing number of Indonesian settlers. The word Maubere has come to be a collective nationalist term to describe the East Timorese people. According to the 1990 Indonesian census 742,700 people live in East Timor; as many as 100,000 of them may be Indonesian civil servants.

The Indonesian army poses the major threat to the political, economic, and cultural survival of East Timorese. No one knows how many people were killed in the Indonesian invasion or in the military offensives that followed it through the mid-1980s, nor how many died from war-related famine and disease. Most estimates are around 100,000. Mass executions and widespread disappearances took place through 1984.

Human-rights violations continued thereafter, although fewer mass incidents were reported. The arbitrary arrest and torture of East Timorese suspected of supporting the armed resistance movement, the Frente Revolucionaria de Timor Leste Independente (Fretilin), were routine. Because East Timor remained closed to outsiders, with access restricted to a few voluntary agencies and diplomats on flying visits, it was difficult to gather and verify information.

In January 1989, when Indonesia "opened" East Timor, information began flowing more freely. Also, the thousands of East Timorese students studying

East Timor Resources:
Amnesty International, 1
    Easton St., London WC1X
    8DJ, UK.
Asia Watch, 485 Fifth Ave.,
    New York, NY 10017.
East Timor Action, Network,
    P.O. Box 1182, White Plains,
    NY 10602 (914)428-7299.
TAPOL, 111 Northwood Rd.,
    Thornton Heath, Surrey, CR7
    8HW, UK (44-81)771-2904;
    fax: (44-81)653 0322.

in Indonesia facilitated the development of an international support network. The resistance movement began to emphasize *intifada*-like tactics, with frequent, large-scale demonstrations in Dili, the capital. At a demonstration on November 12, 1991, close to 100 people died and as many were missing when the Indonesian armed forces fired on unarmed marchers. Indonesia closed the territory again, and the military tightened surveillance.

East Timorese culture has suffered from the Indonesian presence. After the invasion, the government moved huge numbers of people from their traditional homes and resettled them in camps that, over the years, became Indonesian-style villages. Portuguese, the language of the elite, disappeared from schools and churches. Indonesian language, values, and history became standard in elementary schools, while East Timorese had little opportunity to learn about their own recent past. Tetun, the lingua franca of the territory, is still a language of instruction in the early grades of state schools but is gradually giving way to Indonesian.

The Roman Catholic church is the only major institution to survive the Indonesian onslaught. Before the invasion, the population was heavily animist, with Catholicism largely restricted to the elite. By 1984, about half the people in East Timor were Catholic, a proportion that has steadily risen because people see the church as the most important buffer against the government. East Timor remains under the direct supervision of the Vatican and is not part of the Indonesian Catholic Bishops Conference. Most priests are indigenous East Timorese, and many face constant harassment from Indonesian authorities. The government is training more East Timorese in seminaries in east Java and eastern Indonesia.

The economy is under the complete control of the military. Coffee, East Timor's major crop, is controlled by PT Denok, a military-run company. Australia and Indonesia have signed several agreements for offshore oil exploration in what is known as the Timor Gap. These agreements have led Portugal to file a suit (pending in the World Court) that charges that Indonesia has no legal authority over East Timor in international law.

SIDNEY JONES

HILL TRIBES IN THAILAND AND H.I.V./AIDS

136

The mountains of northern Thailand are home to many tribal minorities. Government censuses conducted from 1986 to 1989 counted over a half million tribal people, about 1 percent of the population of Thailand. The so-called "six tribes" are the Karen, Hmong (Meo or Miao), Lahu, Mien (Yao), Akha, and Lisu. There are also the H'tin, Lua (Lawa), and such smaller groups as some 150 Mlabri (Spirits of the Yellow Leaves).

For centuries, even millennia, trade and political relations have linked highlanders and lowlanders in mainland Southeast Asia and Southwest China. Links have intensified in recent decades as modern states have sought to incorporate peripheral peoples and territories. Since the 1950s, Thailand's hill tribes have been increasingly drawn into national and global systems. This has been facilitated by schools taught in the Thai language and by local, bilateral, and multilateral development projects that have built roads and introduced new cash crops to replace the opium poppy. Plantations and other capitalist ventures have entered the hills, and tourism has flourished.

Although H.I.V. reached Asia later than the Americas, Europe, and Africa, the Global AIDS Policy Coalition projects that by the year 2000, Asia together with Oceania will have the highest proportion of H.I.V. infections. According to World Health Organization reports on AIDS cases, Thailand is

Southeast Asia's hardest-hit country. Initial cases of full-blown AIDS, beginning in 1984, were found predominantly among male homosexuals. H.I.V. infection was next reported among intravenous drug users. However, the massive and pervasive commercial sex industry, geared to local clients as well as to sex tours from abroad, fuels heterosexual transmission, which may now be the primary route of H.I.V. spread. In 1992, over 10 percent of male army recruits in some northern provinces tested positive for H.I.V.

Never isolated from their Thai neighbors, the hill tribes are not immune to Thailand's exploding H.I.V./AIDS epidemic. A tribal infant infected perinatally was among the country's first 25 recorded AIDS deaths. Indeed, recent political and economic changes increase hilltribe vulnerability to H.I.V. infection. Despite the dollars devoted to development, impoverishment and marginalization are on the rise among highlanders. Land available to tribal farmers has decreased with the advent of roads, plantations, and government reforestation projects. At the same time, the population in the hills has increased through natural growth, illegal immigration of highlanders and lowlanders from war-torn Burma, and migration by landless lowland Thai peasants.

Increases in the cash economy have not offset the deterioration of the traditional subsistence economy. Thus poor tribal women are forced into prostitution in the lowlands, tribal men migrate to valley towns for wage labor, and demoralized tribal men and women alike become addicted to smoking opium or, lately, to injecting heroin. Due to migration patterns, trade networks, and the impact of development, H.I.V./AIDS seriously threatens tribal minorities throughout mainland Southeast Asia and Southwest China.

CORNELIA ANN KAMMERER AND PATRICIA V. SYMONDS

THE NEW KHMER ROUGE THREAT IN CAMBODIA

In April 1992, heavily armed Khmer Rouge troops stormed a central Cambodian village and killed seven ethnic Vietnamese civilians. When the UN Transitional Authority in Cambodia sent in a representative, villagers appealed to UNTAC to station 10 troops there. This was not done, and the Khmer Rouge struck again that May. "The people have lost hope," a local official said. According to Far Eastern Economic Review, nearly 1,500 people fled the village.

In July, near the Vietnamese border, Khmer Rouge gunmen massacred and mutilated an ethnic Vietnamese couple, their seven-day-old son, four other children aged 7 to 16—Cambodians whose grandmother was Vietnamese—and their uncle.

The Khmer Rouge threatened yet another racial pogrom after the U.S. Chief of Mission in Phnom Penh, Charles Twining, stated his fear that history might repeat itself and that bodies of ethnic Vietnamese would once again float down the Mekong River as they had in 1970. Khmer Rouge leader Khieu Samphan declared that "if the Cambodian people cannot see a peaceful resolution to the problem, they will seek other means."

Khieu Samphan has been as good as his word. In October 1992, the bodies of ten ethnic Vietnamese civilians were found floating off the Cambodian coast; a senior Khmer Rouge commander admitted that his guerrillas had kidnapped eight more. That December, reported Indochina Digest, the bodies of three more Vietnamese fishermen were found floating in the Mekong River. Soon after, in what the New York Times described as "the deadliest violation of the Cambodian peace accord," two boatloads of Khmer Rouge troops entered a fishing village and murdered thirteen ethnic Vietnamese, including six women and five children. According to a UN spokesperson, "They asked villagers to identify the Vietnamese. Those identified were summarily executed." The attackers also murdered two Cambodians and wounded thirteen others. In March 1993, Khmer Rouge forces murdered thirty-three Vietnamese civilians in another attack.

In July 1992, Khmer Rouge guerrillas mortared a Cambodian Buddhist monastery in Siemreap province, killing one monk and injuring three others. The temple was destroyed. According to Indochina Digest, defectors told UNTAC that "a Khmer Rouge general executed their company commander" for his willingness to respect the agreement on cantonment of troops under UN supervision. Nevertheless, the Khmer Rouge's longtime allies, two U.S.-backed parties, have also called for a virtual "ethnic cleansing" of Vietnamese from Cambodia.

The U.S.-backed Lon Nol regime expelled most of the country's 450,000 ethnic Vietnamese in 1970, when bodies first floated down the Mekong. Pol Pot drove out more in 1975. The rest were systematically murdered, and only after Pol Pot's overthrow in 1979 did some refugees return from Vietnam, along with some newcomers.

Khmer Rouge Resource:
Campaign to Oppose the
   Return of the Khmer Rouge,
   318 Fourth St., NE,
   Washington, D.C. 20002
   (202)544-8446; fax:
   (202)675-1010.

Since the October 1991 Paris Agreement, Pol Pot's Khmer Rouge has called the world's bluff, and the UN peace plan is in crisis. The agreement gave the Khmer Rouge time to expand their military control, move into the political arena, stockpile weapons, and collect vast sums of money.

Now, as the country's economy collapses under international pressure and continuing denial of aid, the Khmer Rouge again threatens Cambodia. Without resolute international action, it will be made an integral part of the country's political future, despite their genocidal record in power in 1975-79, when 1.5 million people died at their hands.

In 1988, Southeast Asian nations denounced "the genocidal policies and practices of the Pol Pot regime," but most Western diplomats have ignored the issue. In 1990, the great powers could only abhor unspecified "policies and practices of the past." The perpetrator of all these massacres, the Khmer Rouge, retains its place in the United Nations and in UN planning for Cambodia.

Legal action against the Khmer Rouge long faced Chinese and U.S. opposition. However, the United States has said it would help a newly elected Cambodian government bring the Khmer Rouge to justice.

BEN KIERNAN

KMHMU OF LAOS, VIETNAM, THAILAND, AND CHINA

For the half-million Kmhmu in Laos, Vietnam, Thailand, and China, life has long involved hard choices: between preserving a traditional way of life marked by social inequality or seeking equal opportunity and fuller civil participation; between gaining supplementary income working as sawyers and elephant drovers for Scandinavian and Thai lumber companies or seeing the forests preserved for their descendants; between continuing a difficult life as highland swidden farmers or moving to the lowlands and watching their children shun the ancestral culture to fit in with new neighbors. Sometimes the Kmhmu themselves make the choices; more often, the choices are made in Bangkok or Vientiane, Washington or Tokyo.

In Thailand and Laos, much of the forest where the Kmhmu traditionally lived has been destroyed. The situation is the same whether the forests were clear-cut by logging companies or napalmed and defoliated by U.S. and Thai planes targeting the Lao People's Liberation Army and the guerrillas of the

Kmhmu Resources:

A number of Kmhmu villages in Laos receive development assistance from the American Friends Service Committee, 1501 Cherry St., Philadelphia, PA 19102, and the Mennonite Central Committee, Box 500, Akron, PA 17501.

The Lao Kmhmu Association, 425 N. California St., Stockton, CA 95202, has begun reconciliatory aid to Kmhmu villagers in Laos.

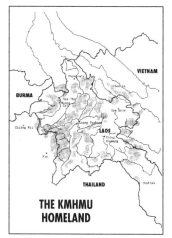

THE KMHMU HOMELAND

Communist Party of Thailand (CPT). A half-century ago, tigers were the biggest threat to a Kmhmu mountain village, but tigers disappeared decades ago. Now the biggest threat is hunger, as the productivity of swidden fields has diminished and forests no longer sustain fishing, game hunting, or the gathering of leaves, fruits, and herbs.

Between 1945 and 1975, many Kmhmu in Laos and Vietnam provided crucial support to the revolutionary cause, motivated by the hope of living as citizens of a multiethnic state. To a large degree, many of these aspirations have been fulfilled. In the Lao People's Democratic Republic, the constitution guarantees equality among ethnic groups, and Kmhmu have opportunities undreamed of by their predecessors: to become doctors and engineers, to study in Moscow or Tashkent, to develop a script for their own language. But Laos and Vietnam are impoverished, and northern Thailand is the poor outreach of a country only recently escaped from poverty. Resources are limited, and many promises go unkept.

For highlanders in Thailand, nothing is better than to be a former communist. Government services flow first to villages whose loyalty was once suspect in order to redress inequities and address needs that might otherwise inspire social unrest. Thus Kmhmu are perhaps fortunate to live so close to the border with Laos, in regions that provided a base for the CPT rebellion. All but one or two of the thirty Kmhmu villages in Thailand have electricity, water systems, good roads, and schools. Women and children no longer spend hours carrying water and processing rice and can instead learn to read and write.

High costs go along with benefits. Logging companies denuded the hills, and villages were relocated to the paved highways. Television brings news of the outside world, along with tastes that can't be sated—and monthly visits from the debt collectors. In the modern equivalent of a century-old custom, young men leave their home villages to work for months or years in Chiang Mai or Bangkok so they can earn a bride-price and begin a family. But today, when the men return, they may bring H.I.V. infections with them.

In Laos and Vietnam, material conditions for most Kmhmu remain much as they were in previous generations. The hardships of war have diminished, but extreme poverty in both nations has prevented electricity, roads, water systems, and schools from reaching all but a few villages. The environmental destruction from bombs and defoliants lingers in many areas. Increasingly, forests are logged for export to Thailand, Japan, or Europe. Rising rural populations, scarce land, and often-misguided government plans compel farmers to overuse fields; each year the yields drop. Educational opportunities have increased steadily, but those who complete secondary education return to their home villages only for visits.

FRANK PROSCHAN

139

LUMAD OF THE PHILIPPINES

Lumad, a generic term, refers to the non-Muslim indigenous peoples occupying the island of Mindanao in the Philippines before the Spanish conquest. These peoples have survived centuries of violence inflicted on them by migrant communities and by the Philippine government.

Composed of about 18 ethnic groups, the 2.1 million Lumad comprise the largest group of tribal Filipinos. In the name of development, the government has usurped their ancestral domains through force, intimidation, and the law. The Lumad have learned that "progress" is not synonymous with their economic well-being.

One example is the Bagobo's defense of Mt. Apo, the tallest volcano in the Philippines. The ancestral home and spiritual sanctuary of the Bagobo and several other ethnic groups, Mt. Apo is also the site of large-scale geothermal exploration by the government-owned Philippine National Oil Co. (PNOC).

Drilling operations, road clearing, and other infrastructure-building activities have destroyed large forests and their rich biodiversity. The situation is aggravated by the intervention of the Philippine Army, which facilitates the PNOC's operations by establishing checkpoints to harass or intimidate those who oppose the project.

The Philippine constitution, which recognizes the rights of indigenous communities to their ancestral domains, should provide a legal basis for protecting the Bagobo. However, that right is subject to other constitutional provisions and national development policies. Geothermal exploration seems to slip through these loopholes, as do pasture leases for wealthy lowlanders, agribusinesses, tree plantations, and logging and mining operations.

> Datu Tumutuas, a Manobo leader, witnessed members of the Citizens Armed Forces Geographical Unit protecting illegal loggers with government-supplied arms.

In another example, in 1991, Datu Tumutuas, a Manobo leader, witnessed members of the Citizens Armed Forces Geographical Unit—a government-supported paramilitary group that battles the communist-led New Peoples' Army—protecting the illegal loggers with government-supplied arms. Tumutuas has been deprived of his farm, and thus his ability to support his family. He is now in hiding after several attempts on his life.

In Trento, Agusan del Sur, the paramilitary force of the Paper Industries Corp. of the Philippines has threatened several Manobo families inside and outside the company's tree plantation. Those inside were pressured to discard farming and participate in the company's "social forestry." River blockades prevented those living outside from bringing farm products to market. Several tribal elders have been arrested and jailed for clearing a farm lot.

In Tagum, Davao del Norte, the North Davao Mining Corp. entered Mansaka territory and began operations without complying with environmental laws or consulting the community. The mine-tailings pond is located exactly on the tribal area. The company has not compensated the Mansaka, and the mountainsides and lakes have been destroyed and the people threatened with landslides and pollution.

ANTOINETTE ROYO

---

140   MUSLIMS OF THE PHILIPPINES

The Philippine polity emerged in parallel with the Christianization of the archipelago during three centuries of Spanish colonization. The process, however, was intensely resisted by Muslims in Mindanao, Sulu, and Palawan, which were incorporated in the polity only in the 1900s during the U.S. colonial period.

After Philippine independence in 1946, the Muslims saw Manila's national-integration policies as an attempt to assimilate them into the Christian majority. Because the government failed to recognize the Muslim's cultural and religious values, deployed the country's resources in favor of Christian communities, and fostered massive Christian migration to Muslim lands, the Muslims began to perceive themselves as second-class citizens.

In the late 1960s, the displacement of Muslim settlers from their ancestral lands and the loss of Muslim political control over large parts of Mindanao became catalysts for the formation of the Moro National Liberation Front. The MNLF fostered a new Moro national identity in order to unify various Muslim ethnic groups and aimed to establish an independent Islamic state. Financed by other Islamic countries, the front forced the Philippine army

*Muslims of the Philippines
Resource:*
Moro Human Rights Center,
  Manila, Philippines
  (63-2)922-9621.

into a war that claimed more than 50,000 Muslim lives and created thousands of refugees between 1972 and 1976.

As the conflict stalemated, a compromise reached in 1976 provided for an autonomous government in Muslim-dominated provinces. However, then-President Ferdinand Marcos enforced autonomy in terms convenient to Manila and used the power to appoint officials to break MNLF unity. Simultaneously, the central government promoted development programs for the Muslims and made provisions for recognizing the importance of Islamic culture and protecting Muslim land rights. Although few of these efforts materialized, the policy coopted Muslim moderates and weakened the MNLF's appeal. In the 1980s, the MNLF renewed its secessionist claim and war, but the movement was split into three factions, while support from abroad diminished.

Between 1986 and 1989, the MNLF renegotiated autonomy with the new Aquino administration, but again Moros got less than they wanted. In a 1989 plebiscite boycotted by two Moro factions, only four provinces, each with a Muslim majority, opted for autonomy. Muslims in provinces with Christian majorities remain subject to Christian administration. Moreover, the new autonomous region lacks natural resources, basic infrastructures, and an industrial base. Besides the radicals, also Muslim moderates who had put great hopes in the post-Marcos regime cannot hide a deep sense of frustration.

LANFRANCO BLANCHETTI-REVELLI

ORANG ASLI OF MALAYSIA

The 70,000 Orang Asli ("original people") of the Malay Peninsula face the loss of both their resource base and their cultural identities. Although the various groups traditionally lived by differing combinations of hunting, gathering, fishing, shifting cultivation, and trade, all shared a dependence on and attachment to the forests in which they lived. During the 1960s, Malaysian planners decided that plantations made better use of level or moderately sloping land than did forestry. State governments, which control all land not held under individual deeds, sold logging rights to most of the forest, and by 1990 only the most rugged and least accessible forests remained. Once the land was cleared, federal and state land-development agencies converted it to rubber and oil palm plantations, some of which were divided up and allocated to Malay homesteaders.

"Development" ignored the Orang Asli who inhabited the forests. Malaysian law considered them squatters on state land. Although some states set aside small "Aboriginal Reserves" or "Aboriginal Areas," these could be revoked at any time, and frequently were. The federal Department of Aboriginal Affairs was unable or unwilling to obtain secure tenure on any but a few token plots.

As a result, the Orang Asli have been arbitrarily moved, regrouped, or pushed off their land, and outsiders have taken over their traditional lands and their fruit trees. The Department of Aboriginal Affairs has developed some "regroupment schemes," in which Orang Asli are brought together and expected to adopt an economy based on rubber and other cash crops, but the land and facilities are far from adequate. Most groups must supplement their income by collecting forest produce, such as rattan, but that is rapidly disappearing along with the forests.

The Department of Aboriginal Affairs aims to absorb the Orang Asli into the Malay population by converting them to Islam and inducing them to

Orang Asli Resource:
Center for Orang Asli
  Concerns, 86-B Jalan SS
  24/2, 47301 Petaling Jaya,
  Malaysia.

Orang Asli Action:
It is probably useless for foreigners to contact Malaysian officials on behalf of the Orang Asli, as the government rejects such unwanted advice. It would be more effective to pressure agencies that finance development projects in order to get guarantees that displaced Orang Asli will receive appropriate assistance. Supporters can also contribute to the Center for Orang Asli Concerns.

141

adopt the Malay way of life. The department is now trying to do that with assistance from state departments of religion. However, the Orang Asli don't want to become Malays, and the low quality of the education they have received and their lack of economic resources have prepared them only for integration on the bottom rung of Malaysian society.

Some Orang Asli and other Malaysians have founded the Center for Orang Asli Concerns to fight for Orang Asli economic rights and their constitutional right to retain their religion and identity. COAC publishes "Pernloi Gah: Orang Asli News," a Malay-English newsletter.

KIRK ENDICOTT

PENAN OF SARAWAK

Penan Resource:
Sahabat Alam Malaysia (Friends of the Earth Malaysia), 43, Salween Rd., 10050 Penang, Malaysia.

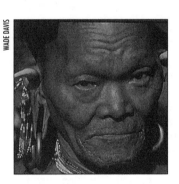

WADE DAVIS

The Malaysian state of Sarawak on the island of Borneo suffers from the world's highest rate of deforestation. In recent years, logging companies have moved into parts of Sarawak occupied by Penan hunter-gatherers.

The 6,500 Penan are divided into two distinct groups: the Eastern and Western Penan. Today, only 6 percent of Penan remain fully nomadic. Since 1960, nearly all the rest have settled and taken up farming.

The Penan landscape is filled with cultural significance. Some places are marked physically, others are marked in memory; some have direct relevance to subsistence, many don't. Rivers and river names form the skeleton around which Penan organize environmental knowledge. Rivers may be named for ecological or geographical features, for events, or for individuals. Penan refer to the deceased by the name of the river nearest to which they died. In this way, Penan preserve the memory of burial sites of long-dead ancestors and anchor genealogical knowledge in the physical landscape. These names form a sort of charter for each band.

The Penan also name specific trees, particularly productive stands of the staple sago palm. The key concept in naming and using such trees is the verb molong: to preserve or foster. Throughout the forest, each community has a collection of thousands of trees and sago clumps that particular individuals or households molong. The molong system underlies a long-term harvesting strategy that assures the continued availability of resources.

Although the international campaign on behalf of the Penan focuses on the physical impact of logging, the dispossession caused by the industry is more complex. By transforming the landscape, logging destroys those things that are iconic of Penan society. When bulldozers clear roads through the forest, they scour away the surface of the land and obliterate recognizable features. Once the forest canopy is opened, an impenetrable mass of thorny vines and shrubs appears. These areas are virtual deserts with respect to the availability of game, and the dense cover makes movement difficult and access nearly impossible. The cultural density of that landscape—all the sites with biographical, social, and historical significance—is hidden, producing a sort of collective amnesia.

Since 1987, the Penan have resisted logging companies by erecting blockades. Aside from ordering waves of arrests at blockade sites, the government has dismissed and trivialized the protests. It claims that Western environmentalists instigate the Penan, who don't know any better, transforming the civil disobedience of Penan into the misbehavior of children.

In any case, the government asserts, Penan can move to new areas. This is unrealistic and unacceptable. Logging is proceeding so fast that no undisturbed forest will remain in a few years. The proposed Adang and Magoh biosphere reserves are being logged. The proposed Pulong Tau National Park

142

has repeatedly been diminished in size by timber concessions, and roads are being pushed through into the area.

Recently, Sarawak declared the Melana Forest Reserve to be a "biosphere reserve" for the Penan, but nomadic Penan refuse to move there. Not only do they lack any historical connection to the area, but it has been logged already. To resolve the dispute over logging and Penan land rights, the government must acknowledge the existence and legitimacy of the cultural significance of the Penan's landscape.

J. PETER BROSIUS

ROHINGYA AND KAREN OF BURMA

EDITH T. MIRANTE

The military rulers of Burma (also known as Myanmar) justify their monopoly on power by sowing—and then "predicting"—ethnic discord. Historically, an unequal but workable relationship developed between the dominant Burman race and ethnic groups that include the Karens, Shans, Chins, Kachins, Arakanese, and Mons. British colonial rule and a brief wartime occupation by Japan exacerbated the tensions inherent in a multi-ethnic society. Upon independence in 1948, Burma stitched together a loose federal union, but little more than a decade later General Ne Win ended democratic rule. In 1988, the military justified its brutal suppression of a nationwide uprising for democracy in the name of unity.

The Burmese government's campaign against Muslim Rohingyas from Arakan State and the decades-long war against the Karens, Burma's largest minority, illustrate the plight of many less visible groups in this war-torn country. Human-rights groups such as Asia Watch and Amnesty International have reported on the military's campaign of repression against the Rohingyas, which has included systematic rape, torture, and religious persecution. The Rohingya exodus to Bangladesh has created a refugee nightmare, especially for women and children who bear an inordinate share of the hardship.

In the government's war against various minority groups living in timber- and mineral-rich areas, the campaign against Karens is the oldest and could even be regarded as a personal vendetta by army commanders. In 1987, a Burmese military government spokesman disclosed the intention to "eliminate the Karens in two years." Technically, he was referring to the armed rebels, but many civilian Karens are sympathetic to a cause defined by the fighters as "dying free rather than living like a slave."

A true reconciliation has been undermined by the junta's narrow definition of citizenship, its continuing civil wars against ethnic groups fighting for a genuine federal union, and its dominance over every aspect of life in Burma. Burma's political, cultural, and environmental integrity are all threatened by the prolonged rule of a military government determined to maintain its power by force.

Only coordinated international pressure will be effective against a stubborn military regime that spends most of its meager budget on arms for use against its own people. And the international community must continue to press the Burmese military government to allow an impartial international force, such as the United Nations, to supervise Rohingya repatriation.

MAUREEN AUNG-THWIN

143

YAMDENA ISLAND OF INDONESIA

Yamdena Resource:
NGO Network for Forest
Conservation in Indonesia
(SKEPHI), Tromol Pos 1410,
Jakarta 12160, Indonesia.

Yamdena Action:
Write a polite but firm letter to
the ministers of forestry and
the environment, telling
them that Indonesia's greatest asset is its rich, beautiful
natural resources. Say that
you will take your tourism
dollars elsewhere if these
resources are lost. Ask
Indonesia to respect and
enforce the 1971 decree
declaring Yamdena's forests
to have protected status.
Hasjrul Harahap, Forestry
Minister, Manggala
Wanabakti, Jl. Gatot
Subroto, Jakarta, Indonesia.
Emil Salim, Environment
Minister, Jl. Medan Merdeka
Utara No. 7, Jakarta,
Indonesia.

Yamdena Island in Indonesia's southeast Moluccas archipelago looks like an idyllic paradise, with lush rain forests and turquoise coral reefs. But the inhabitants of Yamdena face threats to their livelihoods, culture, and lives from a timber company that has been logging a large portion of the island's rain forest. In July 1991, the Indonesian Department of Forestry gave PT Alam Nusa Segar (PT ANS) permission to log 95 percent of the 425,000 acres of forests on Yamdena. The company's owner is President Suharto's eco-nomic advisor and head of the Salim Group, one of Indonesia's largest con-glomerates.

The Association of Tanimbar Intellectuals (ICTI) and the NGO Network for Forest Conservation in Indonesia (SKEPHI) are leading a campaign against the logging. They argue that in 1971 a portion of the area was declared pro-tected by the minister of forestry. This decree has never been rescinded.

Hasjrul Harahap, the current minister of forestry, has ordered a team to study the issue but says that logging will continue while the government completes the study. He says that stopping the company would show disre-spect to the local offices recommending the permit.

During the dispute, PT ANS has logged tens of thousands of cubic yards of wood. Although the cutting hasn't approached Yamdena villages, its effects are already being felt. PT ANS sealed shut a spring that feeds the Lorobunga River to make way for a logging road. Villagers in Tumbur and Lorulung say the river has since dried up. An ICTI study shows that forest degradation in Yamdena will cause erosion and further damage the island's delicate lime-stone ecosystem.

Logging has wrought serious social damage as well. Inhabitants of Yamdena accuse PT ANS and the Department of Forestry of violating custom-ary rights that establish how local resources may be exploited. Promises from PT ANS to build schools and health clinics have proven false. What the com-pany identifies as the health clinic is actually a private home containing no medical supplies.

In July and September 1992, frustrated Tumbur villagers took matters into their own hands. Attacking the PT ANS base camp, they burned a truck and destroyed several buildings. PT ANS retaliated by calling in the military, whose soldiers beat up villagers and arrested thirty-eight people, including two village leaders. Several islanders have been sentenced to prison terms.

In response, the Bishop of Moluccas issued a letter of protest concerning the physical harassment and intimidation of the islanders. Moluccan com-munities in Jakarta, Surabaya, and throughout the province have also asked Minister Harahap to stop the logging.

ICTI and SKEPHI have called for a halt to the logging based on Indonesia's Basic Environmental Law Article 5, which states the people's right to enjoy a healthy and decent environment. The people of Yamdena argue that logging benefits nobody but the company and the central government.

MARTHA BELCHER

The South Asian subcontinent remains a catalogue of serious rights violations: ethnic, religious, gender, cultural, ecological, and economic. Nevertheless, several important advances occurred this past year, particularly: the multiple, locally organized responses to the riots following the December 1992 destruction of the Babri Mosque in Ayodhya, India; Pakistan's agreement to allow the repatriation of Urdu-speaking "Biharis" from Bangladesh; the growing visibility of the women's movement in Pakistan in discussions of gender and religious rights; the appointment of a Commission on Human Rights in India to investigate misuse of police powers; and a consolidation of a few gains of tribal organizations in controlling their own destiny.

"Rights" language is premised on contractual or constitutional relationships through a state. But the state is part of the problem in protecting many of the rights listed above. Hence the importance of the local responses to the violence in India. "Rights" language as interpreted in the First World can also seem biased and parochial in the Third World: this has become an issue in India regarding both individual and social or group rights.

Amnesty International's March 1992 report on tortures, rapes, and deaths in custody generated considerable furor and accusations of bias. AI responded to one of these charges by beginning to acknowledge and list torture inflicted by "opposition" groups as well. In turn, India appointed a Commission on Human Rights. Torture and partisan involvement by Indian police in riots have been issues for some time, most egregiously lately in the December 1992 and January 1993 riots in Bombay. Quite apart from the sympathies of some police with the Hindu right, politicians have compromised police neutrality. The Chief Minister of Maharastra State did little during the Bombay riots, it is widely alleged, because he has been currying support from the Shiv Sena, the local Hindu right-wing organization.

The 1992 "Earth Summit" in Rio de Janeiro dramatized the differences between the rights perspectives of the First World—particularly the United States—and the Third World, with India taking a major role in the latter group. India charged the United States with "green imperialism"—for example, in seeking to protect U.S. industry from international regulation while imposing U.S. environmental standards on the Third World, and by promoting First World patent rights over agricultural gene banks taken from Third World plants. More problematically, India and Bangladesh face conflicts between social justice and large-scale development projects. Thus, India's Narmada Dam and Sardar Sarover Project will displace thousands of poor tribals and peasants. Similarly, population pressure, refugee resettlement, and competition over land are destroying the ecology of Adivasis, Andaman Islanders, and other forest and shifting-cultivators. In May 1993, 100 people died in Manipur when Naga rebels tried to protect land against the influx of Bengali Muslim peasants.

Wildlife reserves that cater to Western notions of conservation are also a problem because they sometimes displace and exclude the human beings who have depended upon these areas. The establishment by the Kattunaichens of what environmentalist Mahdiv Gadgil acknowledges as a biosphere reserve in the Chembakolly Forest demonstrates that traditional multicrop cultivation can modify and manage the forest rather than destroy it. This is a small but bright exception in the destruction of forest tribal groups. In contrast, the continuing Bhopal case poses an allied set of environmental issues. There, powerful economic interests overrode local ecological and safety regulations, which led in turn to efforts to downplay the epidemiological impacts of toxic releases and systemic illness.

The biggest story of 1992-93 is the struggle over the definition of the Indian polity, the relation between nationality and nation, and the efforts by the Hindu right to turn Muslims into second-class citizens and seize hegemony on behalf of the entrepreneurial middle and upper castes. Is India to be a secular democracy or a fundamentally Hindu state? This is a caste and class issue, not merely a Hindu versus Muslim one. Remember that India is the world's second largest Muslim society, so discrimination against Muslims is not the scapegoating of a small group. The Hindu right wishes to reconvert Muslims—some 200 Mir Muslims in Gujurat converted to Hinduism after the December and January riots out of fear. Rightist leaders such as Bal Thackeray of the Shiv Sena draw parallels with the treatment of Jews in Germany—and see Hitler as a hero.

The key 1992 event in regard to communalism, the term by which India's religious conflicts are known, was the destruction on December 6 of the Babri Mosque in Ayodhya, allegedly the birthplace of the Hindu god Ram. The Bharatiya Janata Party (BJP), Rashtriya Swayamsevak Sangh (RSS), Vishwa Hindu Parishad (VHP), and Dharam Sansad ("parliament of sadhus") have long planned to build a Ram temple there, as well as to remove all mosques at Mathura and Kashi. The history of the Hindu right goes back to the 1920s and the founding of the RSS, the core rightist organization of northern India. It is highly disciplined, recruiting young boys and molding them through sports and fighting exercises.

The RSS has tended to shun publicity, preferring to do "cultural work" behind a series of loosely connected front organizations. In a partially literate society, the RSS depends on visual communication, from rallies and marches to videos and ubiquitous

Paniya elder

stickers. The latter are emblematic of the RSS style. Easy to affix anywhere and filling visual spaces, the stickers contain no signature of the RSS, only its symbols: om, the saffron flag, the warrior figure of Ram, the temple to be built to Ram, and often a Maruti car—a symbol of the consumerism of its constituency. This is a movement not of the downtrodden but of small-scale traders and upper castes.

Through most of 1992, India seemed paralyzed by the campaign of the Hindu right to "liberate" the Ram Janambhoomi complex in Ayodhya. Both the march on Ayodhya and the rise of the BJP as a force on the national scene and in state politics seemed unstoppable. The central government was paralyzed (or complicit) and ineffectual in stopping the destruction of the mosque. State and city governments were paralyzed (or complicit) and ineffectual in stopping the killings in December and January. In Bombay alone, some 600 people may have died, some 200,000 fled the city, and the army was called in for the first time since independence.

Dharavi, a huge shantytown in Bombay, had never experienced major communal riots. The Shiv Sena had tried and failed to organize there in the 1970s. But Tamil Hindus in Dharavi had been abandoning the Congress Party for the past year. On December 6, over 750 homes were destroyed after the police allowed the BJP and Shiv Sena to

146

hold a "victory" procession in a 40 percent Muslim area.

Still, without being overly optimistic, a remarkable resistance to communalism has grown since the December and January debacles. A prime example is the Movement for Secular Democracy, based in Ahmedabad, a city troubled by communal riots almost continuously since 1985 when it was the flash point during India's version of affirmative action on behalf of the lowest castes and untouchables. The MSD held its first demonstration (disrupted by BJP sympathizers) on December 10, only four days after the destruction of the Babri Mosque.

Organized by Prakash Shah, an eminent journalist with a long history of oppositional politics, and Ashim Roy, a socialist union leader, the movement called on Muslims to ignore the boycott of Republic Day that had been urged by many conservative Muslim leaders, and instead demonstrate their loyalty to the idea of India. Indeed, thousands of tricolor flags festooned alleys and buildings in Muslim neighborhoods on Republic Day. An MSD conference drew 1,200 statewide activists, and, most importantly, the MSD formed Sainik Dals (peace committees) composed of Hindus and Muslims in sensitive areas. The MSD maintains a distance from all politicians—the state is the problem—both from BJP's communalism and the Congress Party's opportunism. With slightly different forms appropriate to each place, groups have formed in Kanpur, Bombay, Bhopal, Patna, and Delhi.

In an equally significant activity, liberal Muslims decided to rally rather than allow traditionalists to lead the Muslim community into self-destructive reactions to the Hindu right. (In April 1993, the Muslim Personal Law Board met with the prime minister in an effort to derail compromises being worked out over Ayodhya, such as the building of both a mosque and a temple at the site.) In January 1993, more than 500 Muslim intellectuals—including *Financial Express* editor A.M. Khusro, *Urdu Times* editor Sajid Rashid, screenwriter Javed Akhtar, actress Shabaana Azmi, and the revered poet, Kaifi Azmi—condemned and challenged the Muslim communal leadership.

The other critical development on the rights scene in India is in the Punjab, where 12 years of violence seem to have ended, and the country seems to have weathered its most serious separatist movement. Panchayat elections were held in 11,630 villages, and investment is returning.

On a much larger—so far unsuccessful—scale, Afghanistan and Sri Lanka are engaged in a long-term struggle to emerge from protracted violence, with profound implications for group rights. The collapse of the communist regime in Afghanistan has not led to stable peace among the contending ethnic communities. Nor does the continuing discord allow for the clearing of the Afghan landscape of mines, which would be critical to reestablishing traditional agricultural and pastoral economies.

In Sri Lanka, the assassinations of opposition leader Lalith Athulathmudali and President Ranasinghe Premadasa within a week of one another in the spring of 1993 seem to have fostered a measure of revulsion against the violence of the civil war and its manipulation by politicians. Meanwhile, the Tamil-majority city of Jafna in the North remains under siege, producing a stream of refugees both abroad and to the South. Muslims on Sri Lanka's east coast are also under severe pressure, caught between the Tamil Hindus and the Sinhalese Buddhists. Some 20,000 people are estimated to have died in the struggles by the Tamil Liberation Tigers to create a separate Tamil state in the North.

President Premadasa's funeral was sparsely attended, and even generated celebrations across the South because of his alleged Mafioso tactics. Widely suspected of being behind Athulathmudali's assassination, the president exercised political control through violent repression and intimidation. Part of his record is the extremely violent repression in 1989 of the People's Liberation Front.

Pakistan and Bangladesh likewise continue to struggle with political instability and social turmoil. In Pakistan, in particular, there has been a series of public charges of torture against the state

March for tribal rights

in its efforts to suppress "dacoits" in Sindh. The charges have been supported by such evidence as the tortured body of the leader of the National Democratic Party. Similar charges face opposition groups, including the neo-fascist Mohajir Quami Mahaz, whose leader, Altaf Hussain, is now in exile in London.

On the brighter side, Pakistan has agreed to accept Urdu-speaking refugees from the 66 refugee camps in Bangladesh. These Muslims fled to Pakistan during the 1947 partition of Pakistan from India, and they later sided with West Pakistan in the 1971 struggle over the separation of East Pakistan to become Bangladesh. In 1979, 50,000 refugees tried to march to Pakistan through India, but the Bangladesh army stopped them. Although some "Biharis," as they are known, have integrated into Bangladeshi society, many have lived in refugee camps since 1971. Under Zulfakir Bhutto, some of these Urdu speakers were allowed into Pakistan, and a few more entered under President Zia-ul-Haq, but none were allowed under President Benazir Bhutto.

A third major issue on the Pakistani docket is women's rights, especially regarding the use of rape as a political weapon. In fact, the emergence of a vocal and visible middle-class women's movement is reconfiguring the Pakistani landscape, not only in regard to gender issues but of religious rights as well.

In 1991, the Veena Heyat affair was made public. Ms. Heyat's father, a veteran politician, had asked the government for an investigation, but when it refused, he held an unprecedented press conference. Ms. Heyat accused the president's son and his friends of gang rape as part of a vengeance feud between families. Although no recourse was made available through the judicial system, the case gave voice to several issues surrounding the use of rape to dishonor the families of the abused women.

One problem is that women who allege rape are usually jailed themselves for adultery. If the accused man refuses to bear evidence and no other witnesses testify on her behalf, the woman is the only one who is "proven" to be adulterous. The celebrated case of Safiya Bibi, a blind 16-year-old, brought such abuses to light. The Women's Action Forum and other groups have used the cases of Veena Heyat and Safiya Bibi, as well as rising statistics on rape, to open discussion about the incoherence of Islamic laws put in place under President Zia-ul-Haq, laws that conflate rape, adultery, fornication, and obscenity. When a recent government commission attempted to clarify the definitions, however, it found its own document too obscene to publish.

MICHAEL FISCHER

South Asia Resources:
India Fund, 1616 P St., NW, Washington, DC 20036 (202)328-5187.
India Today, Living Media India PVT, Ltd., F14-15 Connaught Pl., New Delhi 110001, India.
Locayan Bulletin, 13 Alipur Rd., Delhi 110054, India.
South Asia Bulletin: c/o Department of History, State University of New York at Albany, Albany, NY 12222.

ADIVASIS OF THE CHITTAGONG HILL TRACTS AND THE PLAINS

The Adivasis, the tribal people of Bangladesh, are part of a much larger tribal population throughout the Indian subcontinent. Only about 1 percent of Bangladesh is Adivasi, but that is well over a million people. The word Adivasi means "original inhabitant."

There are many tribes, divided by language, ethnic origin, and religion. But all are seen, and see themselves, as different from the majority Bengali population. All Adivasis express their feeling in a communal way and maintain a strong relationship to the forests, hills, and rivers. According to tribal custom all land is the property of the tribe.

The largest tribes are the Santal and Mandi of the plains and the Chakma and Marma of the Chittagong Hill Tracts (CHT) of the southeast. For centuries, the Adivasis lived in the forests and the hills; the Bengalis, who traditionally cultivated the plains, are now encroaching on tribal lands.

Most Adivasis of the 13 tribes in the CHT came from Burma centuries ago but retreated to the hills when Bengali settlers arrived in the seventeenth century. Under British rule, they received some protection and autonomy. At independence in 1947, they asked to join India but were placed with Pakistan, which abolished the CHT's special status and built the giant Kaptai Dam, displacing one-sixth of the population and submerging 40 percent of the cultivable land.

After Bangladeshi independence, Adivasis unsuccessfully petitioned the government to restore their autonomy. A guerrilla war arose between government forces and the army of the Chakma's Jana Samhati Samiti (JSS—United Peoples Party). In part due to outside pressure, the government has made some attempts to settle with the JSS but without success.

Between 1977 and 1987, 300,000 Bengali peasants settled in the CHT; they now constitute over one-third of the population. Development projects haven't benefited the Adivasis, and the three district councils, established in 1989, operate under severe restrictions. Although outside observers can rarely enter the CHT, there are consistent reports of killings, torture, rapes, and illegal arrests by government forces. In 1990, at least 55,000 CHT refugees were in the Indian state of Tripura. The war in the CHT should be ended via a negotiated settlement. CHT Adivasis need some measure of autonomy and land reserved for their exclusive use.

In the plains, with 27 tribes, Adivasis have abandoned slash-and-burn cultivation and now depend mainly on settled agriculture. Only 50 years ago, forests covered a quarter of present-day Bangladesh; today they cover 6 to 8 percent. As the forests disappear, Adivasi languages, cultures, and lifeways face tremendous pressure.

The plains Adivasis lived unmolested on most of their traditional territories until the 1960s, when Bengali settlers began arriving in large numbers. The 1965 Vested Property Ordinance took land from non-nationals, but the Bangladesh government has since used it against ethnic and religious minorities. Many tribal lands have been listed as "enemy property" and taken away.

Today, land grabbing is the major problem for all Adivasi. Their land is taken by fraud, bribery, and force. It is difficult for Adivasis to protect their rights because most are illiterate and uneducated and have few resources to stand up to landlords and moneylenders and police, forest guards, or other government officials.

The struggle for survival is desperate for the vast majority of Bangladeshis, but Adivasis also face discrimination. Although Adivasis have equal rights

149

under the law, most Bengalis consider them to be "primitive" or "jungly" and regard their religion and culture as inferior.

Those tribes in which some members have gained basic education, such as the Mandi, are losing land less quickly than less-educated Adivasis. In addition, Tribal Welfare Associations preserve Adivasi culture and land rights.

Bangladesh is desperately poor and development is a priority, but it shouldn't come at the expense of Adivasis. International donors have a responsibility to ensure that aid benefits the poorest, including Adivasis. The Adivasis must participate in any development on their lands. Adivasi title to both individual and communal land needs to be strengthened, and land taken from them by fraud or force should be restored.

Bangladesh's remaining forests are both a national asset and home to the Adivasis. They shouldn't be destroyed for the sake of short-term gain, nor should they be used as resettlement areas for non-Adivasis.

ADAPTED FROM "THE ADIVASIS OF BANGLADESH: CHILDREN OF THE FOREST" BY THE MINORITY RIGHTS GROUP

AFGHAN NOMADS

The pastoral nomads of Afghanistan are victims of the long-term warfare that began with the Soviet invasion in 1979. The warfare continues despite the Russian withdrawal and the collapse of the communist regime in Afghanistan.

Many millions of land mines are scattered indiscriminately over the Afghan landscape, making many traditional migration routes and pasture lands dangerous. The war also sharpened ethnic lines: Pashtun nomads have found themselves deprived of grazing rights by Tajik and Uzbek villagers in the north and by Hazaras in the center of Afghanistan.

Since the nomads' way of life depends on mobility and secure access to far-flung resources, a culturally distinct way of life is at risk. Although nomads constituted between 15 and 20 percent of the pre-war population of Afghanistan, reconstruction plans have almost entirely neglected their needs. They are not politically organized as a group, and historically they have been at odds with whatever government ruled Afghanistan.

THOMAS J. BARFIELD

AFGHAN HINDUS AND SIKHS

The fall of the leftist regime of Najib Allah in 1992 was a joyous occasion for Afghanistan that lasted but a few days. The first Kabul residents to suffer under the new order, the Hindus and Sikhs, faced open religious and cultural persecution, and many were expelled to India. The fate of these minorities was even worse in Jalalabad, where Hindu and Sikh temples were burned and businesses were ransacked. In Kabul, Hindu and Sikh women were raped in public, and Hindu and Sikh houses were looted.

The UN General Assembly has raised the question of the rights of religious minorities in Afghanistan, indirectly referring to the Hindus and Sikhs, but it has taken no action. The argument is that the Hindus and Sikhs belong culturally and ethnically to India; that is the claim of the Afghans who are promulgating the expulsion and harassment of Hindus and Sikhs. Hindus and Sikhs living abroad are denied their right to obtain an Afghan passport.

Though the Hindus and Sikhs are a small minority in Afghanistan—250,000 and 150,000, respectively—their treatment by the authorities has a great impact on the survival of all minorities. The Hindus and Sikhs of Afghanistan are Afghans; any failure to respect their rights undercuts the unity of Afghanistan as a diverse nation.

AMIN TARZI

ANDAMAN ISLANDERS OF INDIA

Onge man

The four groups of indigenous people of India's Andaman Islands are part of the rapidly disappearing hunter-gatherer Negrito peoples of South Asia. Unlike the rapid violent demise they met with at the hands of the British, the islanders now face a slow death, brought about in large measure by administrative acceptance of ultimate extinction.

Only 33 Andamanese remain of what was once the largest group occupying the most territory. They bear the ravages of the longest duration of contact, and, until 1970, they were scattered in the bigger towns in the islands, in various degrees of addiction and ill health. In 1970, when the government settled them on Strait Island, it was assumed the Andamanese would resume their traditional way of life based on generations of inherited resource knowledge, anchored to an environment that had accumulated meaning. However, the Andamanese have no ties to Strait Island to sustain them, and their social ills persist.

The Onge of Little Andaman, too, have dwindled steadily, and now number about 100. Onges continued a semi-nomadic way of life unimpeded until 1967, when the government opened up Little Andaman to refugees from Bangladesh and Sri Lanka and moved the Onges into two permanent settlements at two corners of the island.

The Jarawas have been steadily pushed to the margins of their forests. For 20 years, India has tried to make contact with groups of Jarawas, who remain mostly hostile. Although the government halted the large-scale expeditions launched by the British on Jarawas, settlers, illegal encroachers, and the police have taken it upon themselves to initiate a small-scale war against them. At the same time, the administration allots land to settlers and periodically legalizes encroachments along the borders of the forest.

The Sentinelese, named after their island, are the most isolated indigenous group in the islands. In 1991, for the first time, a contact team wasn't met with the customary shower of arrows.

With the end of their nomadic way of life, Andamanese and Onges have become victims of development plans packaged in the welfare system. These plans were ostensibly designed to benefit the islanders—to assure them of health and gently assimilate them into the dominant population. The results have been disillusionment and cynicism. Infants continue to die at high rates, tuberculosis and respiratory diseases are common, every adult and child suffers from anemia and skin infections, and Onge men are becoming alcoholics. With the Andamanese and the Onges set on a course of dependency and dissolution, it appears to be only a matter of time before the Jarawas and the Sentinelese are forced onto the same track.

For the Andaman administration, development is a cloak for gaining access to the islands' forests. It makes little difference to the islanders whether it is an imperial power or the Indian government, since the forest is always perceived as virgin territory to be destroyed—along with its inhabitants—in the name of civilization and progress.

SITA VENKATESWAR

151

BHOPAL, INDIA

On December 3, 1984, a Union Carbide pesticide plant leaked 40 tons of toxic gas over the city of Bhopal, exposing 600,000 people. At least 3,500 people died immediately; at least 10,000 have died since. Many of the survivors suffer from permanent damage to their respiratory, reproductive, or immune systems.

Rehabilitation programs have been ineffective due to government corrup-

Bhopal Actions:

Until India reorients its relief programs for Bhopal victims, interim payments of $8 per person per month must continue. Address letters supporting victims demands for rehabilitation to The Prime Minister, North Block, New Delhi, India.

Challenging *forum non conveniens* dismissals would demonstrate support for Bhopal gas victims and set a precedent for other cases of multinational corporate abuse in the Third World. Contact the International Coalition for Justice in Bhopal, 777 UN Plaza, New York, NY 10017.

tion. To pacify the concerns of foreign investors, India settled its lawsuit against Union Carbide out of court for a sum of money that has proven inadequate for even health-monitoring costs. Plans to distribute the available funds are based on a categorization of victims that systematically denies continuing disabilities. For example, extraordinary rates of reproductive disorder aren't classified as exposure related. Children born after the leak who evidence learning disabilities aren't categorized as victims. No attention is given to the possibility of the long-term effects such as cancer.

Victims have demanded the establishment of a "National Commission on Bhopal," comprised of gas victims and independent professionals, that would oversee rehabilitation programs for 20 years to avoid the political vagaries of changing governments. In addition, victims insist that access to health care and economic aid be based on the geographical distribution of exposures rather than on fraudulent categorizations said to be based on symptoms. (A geographical determination of victims would allow resources to reach poorer sections of Bhopal through community-oriented programs for health care, housing, and vocational opportunity.) And victims have also called for a major reorientation of rehabilitation efforts, which would require both resources and political will.

In the United States, people should give support to efforts to restart the legal proceedings here. Thus far, U.S. courts have denied their jurisdiction on the grounds of *forum non conveniens* (inconvenient forum), assuming that Indian courts provide due process. However, there have been blatant failures of due process throughout the Indian litigation, finalized by an out-of-court settlement without the consent of the plaintiffs.

KIM LAUGHLIN

HAZARAH OF AFGHANISTAN

An estimated 1.3 to 1.7 million Hazarahs, a people of Mongol ancestry, inhabit most of central Afghanistan, which is called Hazarajat. Their language is a distinct dialect of Persian known as Hazaragi. They are not only an ethnic minority but also a religious one. Most Hazarahs are Shi'ahs of the Imami school; some belong to the Isma'ili Shi'ahs. There are also some Sunnis among the Hazarahs.

In the course of Afghan history, beginning in 1747, Hazarahs have been subjected to repeated attempts by the dominant Pashtuns to bring them under direct rule and to usurp their autonomy and cultural diversity. None of the campaigns against the Hazarahs was more destructive than the late-nineteenth-century wars of 'Abd al-Rahman Khan, who tried to end Hazarah autonomy through force and imposed integration. He also gave great portions of Hazarah land to the Pashtuns. Although 'Abd al-Rahman Khan abolished slavery in Afghanistan, this rule did not apply to the Hazarahs.

The Hazarahs survived and retained their different culture, despite immense difficulties, until the end of the leftist regime in Kabul in 1992. Now, however, they could face their toughest challenge, one that might mean the end of an entire group.

The Hazarahs are being systematically persecuted and killed by various non-Hazarah and non-Shi'ah groups. They are accused of having separatist ideas and of being bad Muslims. In the civil strife that has engulfed Afghanistan since the fall of Kabul, every group attacks its rival's military and civilian targets, but Hazarahs are attacked just for being Hazarah. They are systematically captured and killed, and there are many reports of rapes of Hazarah women in Kabul.

AMIN TARZI

KATTUNAICKENS OF INDIA

The lower Nilgiri mountains and forest are home to five tribal groups, the Kattunaickens, Bettakurumbas, Paniyas, Moolukurumbas, and Irulas. An ecologically sensitive region, the Nilgiris is the source of all the major rivers of southern India. However, the last 25 years have seen a relentless invasion of tribal territory by land-hungry migrants, mainly from neighboring Kerala State. The forests have been ruthlessly exploited and depleted.

Until the 1960s, possession of the land was proof of ownership, but the entry of a nontribal people rendered tribals landless and marginalized them in their own territories. Outsiders swiftly procured legal documents proving ownership. Tribals were exploited and cheated of their land through indebtedness and often outright fraud. A centuries-old tradition and way of life was overturned within two decades.

In 1986, ACCORD, a nongovernmental organization, began working in the Nilgiris. Clearly, the problems of the tribal people arose from one fact: indigenous lifestyles and cultures were rooted in the land and the forests. Kattunaickens practiced food-gathering with a little bit of shifting cultivation and traditionally moved from place to place fairly regularly.

Thus in the heart of the Chembakolly forest a group of Kattunaicken decided to put down roots in forest lands once owned by their ancestors. They realized that if they didn't settle down, they might soon be displaced permanently as the forests disappeared. A large settlement gathered. Huts were built, crops planted, and a thriving Kattunaicken community emerged, joined by a large group of Bettakurumbas.

In January 1993, Madhav Gadgil, an internationally renowned environmentalist, visited Chembakolly after rumors spread that tribals were grabbing forest lands and destroying the environment. Instead, Gadgil found over 30 species of tubers and plants on a single Kattunaicken plot, all collected carefully from the forest. The plot, the haven of centuries-old forest food-gatherers, contained chili plants, aubergines, dozens of varieties of tubers, greens, tomatoes, and wild forest species.

Such efforts are crucial to maintaining global biodiversity. And because protecting the cultural survival of the Kattunaickens means not just protecting one tribe, the Nilgiris have154

been declared a "biosphere reserve." A proposal has been made to divide the reserve into a core zone, which will have no human intervention; a middle zone, where certain land-use rights will be allowed; and an agricultural zone. For the Kattunaickens to survive in their forest homes, they need government permission to allow a certain amount of agriculture in the middle zone.

In Gujarat, Madhya Pradesh, Bihar, Bengal, Orissa, and Uttar Pradesh states, indeed throughout India, tribal communities live in forests that are steadily being depleted while people become pauperized. Instant solutions are not the answer, but wherever forests and tribal people exist together, there is scope for imaginative and innovative planning. The Kattunaickens of Chembakolly represent one ideal: tribal people entering the Indian mainstream on their own terms and with their culture, dignity, and pride intact. For most tribal groups, this is still a distant dream.

MARI THEKAEKARA

MEENA OF INDIA

About 500 Meena tribals in India are staging nonviolent direct actions, such as marches and road blockades, to oppose the illegal mining of dolomite in the Sariska Tiger Reserve, which covers 200,000 acres in the

Alwar District of Rajasthan. The tribals, who have formed themselves into a group called the Save Sariska Movement, are also attempting to expose corrupt officials who allow the illegal dolomite mining to go ahead. Much of the dolomite ends up in the West, mainly as talcum powder.

In 1991, the Indian Supreme Court outlawed all mining in the reserve, but as many as 267 mines have continued operating. In addition, the Rajasthan government has granted 117 new mining leases.

The impact on the Meena has been severe. Their grazing lands and fields are being destroyed, and wells and ponds are drying up. The tribals are suffering from harassment by forestry officials, who levy false fines against them for cutting the trees. The forest officials are known to collaborate with the mining department in the courts to let mining continue in tribal areas.

The miners are exploiting tribals as cheap laborers, including putting women and children to work. Tuberculosis and other respiratory diseases, a result of stone dust, are becoming common among mine workers.

AMAN SINGH

MOOLUKURUMBAS OF INDIA

Moolukurumba youths practicing archery

The Moolukurumbas inhabit the hills and forests of the Nilgiris in Tamil Nadu and Wynadu in Kerala State. Traditionally hunter-gatherers, they practiced agriculture enough to meet their grain requirements.

Twenty years ago, the area around Moolukurumba villages was densely forested. People grew rice, maize, and millet and bartered surplus rice for salt. Money was nonexistent. Once a year, traders arrived with bales of cloth, for which people traded grain. Three or four times a week, the men went hunting and the women fished. Their forest home met all their needs.

For the Moolukurumba, the threat is to their lifestyle and culture. The forest is now a closely guarded place where they are prohibited from their centuries-old tradition of hunting. The men still go on traditional hunts, but these have been reduced to a ritual. Although rich film stars, politicians, and executives routinely bribe forest guards so they can go on weekend shooting sprees, a Moolukurumba caught with a wild rabbit is fined or arrested.

Many Moolukurumbas have received modern education, but the cultural transition this entails is tragic. Where once they had enjoyed a proud existence, their new education gives them only clerical jobs at the bottom of the ladder in nontribal mainstream society.

Women are hit hardest. Tribal women had been free of taboos and the restrictions of surrounding societies, but now Moolukurumba women have adopted many customs from the neighboring Nair-Hindu culture. Consequently, they are less free than women of the other tribes in the region. This situation is likely to worsen if the tribe allows itself to be integrated into mainstream society.

MARI THEKAEKARA

NAGAS OF INDIA

The 1.5 million Nagas, belonging to 27 groups called "tribes," are the indigenous peoples living on the mountainous frontier between India and Burma. At the beginning of the Christian era, their Hindu neighbors identified them as Nagalogoe ("people in the realm of the naked"). Although the highlanders remained outside the valley political institutions of Hindu, Islam, and Buddhist religious systems, the Hindu kingdoms of Manipuris and Ahoms considered Nagas to be pariahs.

In the colonial era, the British appropriated huge tracts of Naga land and forest for cultivating tea, extracting coal, and logging. The British recognized that

154

Naga Resources:
Naga National Council, 56
   Landsdown Rd., Bromley,
   Kent BRI 3PQ, England, UK.
Naga Scholars' Society,
   Longterok Printing Press,
   Purana Bazar, Dimapur,
   Nagaland, India 797112.

a cultural gulf, and a high degree of antipathy, existed between the highland Naga and the lowlanders and thus maintained a small portion of Naga territory, the Naga Hills District, as a separate entity. Here the 1873 Bengal Frontier Regulation prevented non-natives from buying and speculating. The rest of Naga areas were considered to fall under the Crown's jurisdiction.

Later on, the British, in a cartographic feat, demarcated the nation-states of India and Burma, leaving the Naga divided in an alien political geography. This helped seal the fate of the Nagas when Britain hurriedly withdrew from the subcontinent. India and Burma each claimed to be successor states to the colonial power.

Today the Nagas are facing the ultimate test of survival in the wake of a development strategy alien to their social structure. In the early 1960s, India had made some promising moves, establishing cultural and land rights within a Nagaland state. But with the advent of this state, non-Naga merchants and cultural brokers began to penetrate Naga areas and even to expropriate tribal development funds. Current development plans compel Nagas to leave their traditional lands and move to urban "growth areas" in order to obtain employment and adopt a modern way of life.

Moreover, India's armed forces occupy all Naga-inhabited areas, a situation maintained by a number of special acts. These acts have the singular purpose of rationalizing a military response to three main concerns of the Nagas: amalgamation of fragmented Naga-inhabited areas under one administrative roof, the return to Nagas of all forests and territories transferred by the British, and the right to determine their own future, preserve traditional society, and pursue a new way of life molded on their own past. Thus the enormous power exercised by the armed forces is an explicit expression of India's determination to continue the colonial legacy.

C.L. IMCHEN

NARMADA VALLEY TRIBALS IN INDIA

In central India's Narmada Valley, violations of the rights of tribals have arisen in the context of a highly prestigious development project. For many years, the Sardar Sarover Project on the Narmada River in Gujarat State has been touted as a technologically advanced achievement, one that has unprecedented social and environmental standards. Officials call its resettlement and rehabilitation plans the most progressive in modern India. Yet the project differs little from others in its neglect of social and environmental impacts. Violations of a wide range of tribal rights contravene the policies of both the Indian government and the World Bank, a major funder of the project.

Consider one incident. In January 1993, without any prior notification, a survey team accompanied by a police party reached Anjanwada village in Madhya Pradesh State. A few villagers resisted this unannounced intrusion, which they saw as preparation for moving them from their homes. When a 15-year-old said they would not permit the survey and subsequent evacuation of their village, a police officer hit her with his rifle. Other women converged around her and themselves became the targets of the police. Many villagers gathered, and the police subsequently departed.

The next day over 100 police descended on Anjanwada. The villagers fled toward the Narmada River, where the police cornered and beat them. Meanwhile, other police entered the village and ransacked homes. Two days later, 25 armed police and some hired laborers converged on the village from two directions. The villagers fled again, and the police spent six hours destroying all they could lay their hands on.

*Tribals displaced by
Narmada Dam*

The next week, many activists and villagers were arrested on a range of false charges. The apparent reason was the resistance of the tribals to having their lands, homes, and belongings surveyed and their opposition to having their lands submerged by the dam.

The urgency of completing the surveys was necessitated by a March 31 deadline set by the World Bank. Intensive national and international pressure had impelled the bank to commission an unprecedented independent review of the project. Released in June 1992, the review unambiguously called for the bank to step back. Four months later, after an acrimonious debate, 42 percent of the World Bank's board, including directors from Japan, Germany, the United States, Canada, Australia, and Scandinavia, voted to suspend its $450 million loan. The bank decided to proceed anyway, but announced that the central and state governments would have to complete a series of benchmark studies within six months. It is this deadline that compelled the Madhya Pradesh government to push through the surveys.

This is not the first time the Sardar Sarover Project has violated the rights of tribals, nor is it the first time tribals have resisted. According to official estimates, the project will displace 199,500 people, almost 60 percent of them tribals. They predominantly belong to the Bhil community, including Tadvi, Bhilala, Vasava, Nayak, and several other distinct peoples.

Although a progressive resettlement policy exists on paper and the dam is almost complete, no comprehensive blueprint exists for implementing this policy. In fact, official estimates of the extent of tribal dislocation are too low because several attendant developments—a wildlife sanctuary, canals, and so on—have not been taken into account.

In the few resettlement sites, the condition of tribals is grim because of conflicts with the host community, relatively unproductive farm lands, and inadequate supplies of fuel, fodder, and water. In addition, resettled tribal peoples are unfamiliar with the culture and ecology of their new surroundings. Mortality rates have risen; several studies indicate psychological and physiological stress.

The first permanent submergence from the Sardar Sarover Project is due with the next monsoon season. The lands and homes of about 15 tribal villages will be permanently inundated. A majority of the residents have pledged to stand firm in the face of the rising waters.

SMITU KOTHARI

156

NYIMBA OF NEPAL

Some 1,200 Nyimba live in northwest Nepal near Tibet. The sunny, agriculturally productive valleys of the region have been home to several generations of Nyimba families, who trace their origins to western Tibet and Tibetan speakers in Nepal.

With the Chinese takeover of Tibet, the centuries-old salt and wool trade between Tibet and India has dwindled. Meanwhile, the eradication of malaria from Nepal's southern jungles has opened the area to foreign traders and eroded the Nyimba's market. To maintain their ancestors' wealth, some Nyimba resort to trading stolen religious articles and tiger bone, which Chinese regard as an aphrodisiac.

For the first time, a Nyimba represents Humla in the Nepal Parliament, but to gain political power, Nyimbas must deny their ethnicity—to the point of adopting Nepali names and changing their eating habits. Nepalis consider Nyimba to be dirty and scorn their culture.

Contact with ideas incompatible with traditional values—from trading, working, or studying elsewhere—poses an additional threat to Nyimba culture. Instead of polyandrous marriages, Western notions of love are becoming more prevalent among the Nyimba. Many younger brothers choose partition and break up the family and its property in order to have a monogamous marriage.

ADAPTED FROM *CULTURAL SURVIVAL QUARTERLY*

PANIYAS OF INDIA

STAN THEKAEKARA

Paniya woman

The Paniyas, the largest of the five tribes in their area, inhabit the lower Nilgiri mountains of Tamil Nadu State. Their earliest recollected oral legends recall their capture and enslavement by Chetty landlords.

With the Abolition of Slavery Act in the nineteenth century, slavery gave way to bonded labor. Under this system, a Paniya agreed to work for a Chetty employer on a one-year bond. The bonded person received clothes and some money at the time of the agreement. Subsequently, the Paniya received no cash, only a measure of unhusked rice every evening and a morning and midday meal of rice gruel.

In the early 1960s, settlers from neighboring Kerala State were encouraged to clear forests in the lower Nilgiris under the "Grow More Food" campaign. These Kerala Christians, known as Chetans, enticed Paniyas away from their Chetty bond-masters with offers of cash. This effectively broke the bonded labor system, but also created a new kind of slavery. The Keralans started little eating-houses and shops and encouraged Paniyas to buy on credit. They also introduced alcohol to the area.

Up until the 1970s, tribals still inhabited and owned the densely forested region. The Chettys occupied large tracts of low-lying areas, where they grew rice. Few people held actual ownership deeds; possession was proof of ownership. However, the Chetans began collecting money from the Paniyas who were indebted to them, and since the latter had no money, they had to give away tribal land instead.

Throughout the period of bonded labor, Paniyas continued their tradition of gathering food from the forest. By the 1980s, local forest cover was badly depleted. The Paniyas have never made a transition from their forest culture to the cash economy. They haven't adjusted to buying nutritious food, so their once-healthy diet, based on the abundance of forest food, lacks sufficient protein. The effects of this deficiency are seen most dramatically in women, especially during childbirth. There are many deaths from anemia. Children succumb to minor illnesses because they are malnourished.

Bonded labor also destroyed the Paniya family system, much the same way that slavery separated African-American families. This has caused a breakdown in the tribe's social structure. In recent years, there has been an alarming rise in suicides.

Despite tremendous odds, Paniyas have been remarkably resilient. Through their organization the Adivasi Munnetra Sangam, the tribals of the Nilgiris have regained much of their land. They have also begun to organize a cultural revival, bringing the five tribes together for the first time. The Paniyas are in the forefront of the movement, which they realize is the way to ensure their survival.

MARI THEKAEKARA

TRIBALS IN BIHAR AND ORISSA STATES OF INDIA

In early April 1993, 52-year-old Falguni, a tribal from Dhangaon village of Palamau District, Bihar, starved to death. Falguni was one of hundreds of thousands of tribals in the states of Bihar and Orissa in India who face a

157

steadily worsening famine.

There have been repeated warnings of this grim situation. The national and state governments have been negligent, if not apathetic, notwithstanding many visits by politicians to the "affected" areas and despite overflowing food reserves.

In the tribal majority areas of Kalahandi, Bolangir, and Malkangiri in Orissa, tribals are migrating en masse from their homelands as even the basics of a subsistence diet of wild roots, leaves, or dried mango kernels become scarce. Several newspapers have reported harrowing stories of tribals selling their children for $15 to subsist for a few days more.

In addition to official neglect, the primary causes of the famine are ecological and economic. Extensive deforestation in these areas, rapidly expanding tea plantations, and other land colonization processes have stripped communities of their access to and control over productive natural resources. The resultant cycle of drought, indebtedness, and impoverishment has affected many thousands of people in Bihar alone. Parasitic officials and local vested interests have compounded the situation by using the famine to appeal for more grains and money, little of which find their way to the starving tribals. Growing evidence suggests a correlation between escalating impoverishment and severe cutbacks in social spending owing to loan conditions set by the International Monetary Fund and the World Bank in 1992.

SMITU KOTHARI

TRIBALS' RIGHTS IN INDIA

UUA INDIA FUND

Tribals constitute 7.8 percent of India's population and occupy almost 18 percent of the country's geographical area. However, development models adopted by the government put them virtually under a state of siege. Forty-six years after independence, more than 55 percent of tribals live below the poverty line, according to official statistics.

Whenever the tribals rose in revolt, as they did in the eighteenth and early nineteenth centuries in the northwest part of India, the Rajput kings and the British rulers ruthlessly crushed the rebellion. There are ample signs even today of deep-rooted discontent among the tribals, such as the demand for a separate Jharkhand state and various movements in the northeast.

The rulers, whether Rajput kings, the British, or elected government officials, have treated tribals as intruders. This is evident from laws, enacted both by the colonial government and since independence, that have the ostensible objective of protecting forests and the environment. Millions of tribals have been uprooted and deprived of their means of livelihood when the forests in which they lived were acquired or submerged for government-sponsored irrigation schemes, power projects, and other development programs. The tribals lost the right to collect minor forest produce such as tendu leaf, mahua, and gum when the various forest areas were declared as wildlife sanctuaries and acts to protect the environment and wildlife were enacted. In some sanctuaries, tribals have been forcibly evicted from the core zone by forest officials, who are almost omnipotent. A forest official can arrest anyone on suspicion, can collect fines, and can confiscate tools and implements used by the tribals. Hence, development has deprived tribals of the use of forest, water, land, and mineral resources, exacerbating disparities between the tribal-inhabited regions and the rest of India.

No doubt various state governments have enacted laws to protect the interests of tribals, but these mostly remain on paper. Though the Indian Constitution provides guidelines to the states to initiate special measures for the economic development and rights of tribals, only lip service has been given to these principles. On the contrary, the condition of tribals has deteriorated over the years, with alarming increases in interstate and intrastate migration, the marginalization of farmers, and the incidence of bonded and child labor.

M.D. MISTRY

WANNIYALAETO OF SRI LANKA

PATRICK HARRIGAN

Wanniyalaeto Resource:
Cultural Survival Trust of Sri Lanka, 25 Galle Face Centre Rd., Colombo-3, Sri Lanka. (Note: This organization is not affiliated with Cultural Survival.)

Sri Lanka's Wanniyalaeto ("forest-dwellers")—or Vedda, as others call them—descend directly from the island's original inhabitants. These forest nomads preserve much of their stone-age culture based upon hunting, honey gathering, shifting cultivation, and, above all, a deep collective love for their ancestral habitat, the semi-evergreen dry monsoon forest.

Modern surveys speak of two categories of Wanniyalaeto. The large majority joined the many development schemes aimed at assimilating them into a more settled way of life such as those of Sinhalese or Tamil peasants. A minority continue their ancestors' way of life.

Under the colonial-era Fauna and Flora Protection Ordinance, indigenous Wanniyalaeto aren't considered endangered. Rather they are seen as a dire threat to the forests they have managed and protected for thousands of years. In 1977, the Accelerated Mahaweli Development Scheme was launched, leading to the evacuation of several Wanniyalaeto hamlets to create the 198-square-mile Maduru Oya National Park for such endangered species as elephants and leopards, but not for the threatened indigenous culture.

The 96-year-old Wanniyalaeto patriarch Uru Waruge Tissagami and seven tradition-minded families have adamantly refused to be evicted from their ancestral hunting grounds. Counseling nonviolence and adherence to traditional rights, Chief Tissagami has thwarted repeated attempts by state agencies to oust the last Wanniyalaeto from the forest. However, the Wanniyalaeto have been powerless to prevent unwelcome road construction, illicit deforestation, and commercial poaching, typically carried out in connivance with park officials.

In June 1990, following a meeting between Sri Lanka's then-President Ranasinghe Premadasa and Chief Tissagami and other Wanniyalaeto leaders, the Wannietto Trust was created with a mandate "to take specific measures to protect and nurture the Vedda Wannietto culture." Although the trust has representatives from relevant ministries and private organizations, including the Cultural Survival Trust of Sri Lanka, it is hamstrung by bureaucratic foot-dragging and an absence of funds.

159

Most resettled Wanniyalaeto are economically backward, socially isolated, and politically marginalized. They are demoralized at having exchanged the freedom of their forest culture for the trappings of a modern society that most Wanniyalaeto consider to be quarrelsome, cunning, greedy, and untrustworthy. Many have retained their indigenous identity and want to return to their ancestral way of life. In May 1992, armed police prevented 21 colonized Wanniyalaeto families from joining Chief Tissagami and his party.

Lasting gains could still result from plans for the culturally appropriate development of a Wanniyalaeto-administered forest sanctuary. But many Wanniyalaeto fear that the government is only waiting for Chief Tissagami to die before bulldozing through with an agenda more agreeable to commercial interests.

CULTURAL SURVIVAL TRUST OF SRI LANKA

SUB-SAHARAN AFRICA: ENVIRONMENT, POLITICS, AND DEVELOPMENT

The winds of change are blowing across Sub-Saharan Africa, a diverse region of 47 countries stretching from the rolling savannas south of the Sahara desert to the coastal mountains and valleys of the Cape. In hundreds of cities and towns, prodemocracy demonstrators have taken to the streets. In over a dozen countries, opposition to one-party rule has led to promises of open elections, and major reforms aim at improving relations between governments and their citizens.

Okiek woman

Despite these changes, over 70 percent of the people in Sub-Saharan Africa still lack basic civil liberties and human rights. Moreover, the region faces what amounts to a humanitarian crisis as a combination of drought, civil conflict, and economic decline threaten nearly 60 million of the region's 550 million people. Millions more, possibly a quarter of the total population, are poverty-stricken.

The forces of colonialism are partially responsible for Africa's difficulties today. In the nineteenth century, European powers drew political boundaries that cut across indigenous cultural and territorial divisions, exacerbating social tensions. Large areas of land were taken over by colonial administrations or European companies and individuals. Forced off their ancestral land, tens of thousands of Africans became laborers and migrant workers.

When the colonial era ended in the 1950s and 1960s, Sub-Saharan countries were left with few trained personnel and little infrastructure. Exploitative policies extracted Africa's minerals and other natural wealth for the benefit of outsiders. National economies were geared toward producing goods—including such cash crops as coffee, palm oil, and cocoa—for European markets. Colonial leaders, as well as those who replaced them, devoted little attention to improving the grain and root crops upon which most Africans have depended.

Living mainly in rural areas, many Africans now make a living through a combination of agriculture, domestic animal keeping, and wage labor. About 24 million herders raise livestock both for subsistence and for sale. On the other hand, the urban population is growing rapidly; Lagos, Nairobi, and other cities already have serious shortages of housing, employment, and social services.

One legacy of European-drawn borders is the ethnic diversity that characterizes almost every African state. Nigeria contains as many as 160 different groups. Even countries such as Swaziland that are occupied almost entirely by a single ethnic group are usually subdivided along lines of kinship and social affiliation. The picture is com-

160

RODERICK BLACKBURN

ELLIT FRATKIN

Rendille elder

improved in some rural areas, economic growth has been limited at best. Moreover, some government elites and their supporters have used large-scale projects for self serving political and economic purposes. River-basin developments, in particular, have transferred resources to those in power at the expense of indigenous peoples. For example, the erection of the Manantali Dam on the Senegal River boosted local land values. Backed by government troops, politically well-placed individuals then began registering plots of land in their own names, forcibly relocating local people and almost touching off a war between Senegal and Mauritania.

Many of the elite are reluctant to acknowledge the existence of distinct indigenous groups within their countries' boundaries. Rather than grant one group primacy, states maintain that all resident groups are indigenous. Thus, it is extremely difficult to obtain reliable census data broken down along tribal affiliation or ethnic group membership. Estimates of the number of indigenous Africans range from 25 million to 350 million.

Relatively few African governments have targeted development at improving the living standards of groups that are defined on an ethnic basis. One reason is that states understandably want to avoid South Africa's apartheid system of separate development. Thus, Botswana, one of

plicated by the fact that the various African societies speak as many as 2,000 different languages and have an array of religious beliefs. These countries are governed by indigenous elites who also vary greatly in size and cultural characteristics.

For the new African leaders, decolonization offered a chance to implement development programs that would benefit the citizens of independent states, although these countries faced several constraints in their efforts to develop, not least of which were access to capital and technical expertise. But with advice supplied by Western experts and loans from the World Bank, the International Development Association, and other international agencies, African governments embarked on ambitious programs of industrial and agricultural development. The projects they undertook ranged from state farms to large-scale efforts to develop river basins, from road-building to the establishment of schools and health services.

Unfortunately, many projects have yielded mixed results. While access to social services

Africa's oldest democracies, expanded its Bushmen Development Program to include all people in remote areas. In this case, as in many others, there was a less commendable reason as well. Botswana could now assist well-to-do people in the remote areas in addition to Bushmen. The program thus became a source of subsidies for wealthier people to develop cattle ranches and farms in out-of-the-way places.

Victims of Progress

At times, dependence on funds from international development agencies and multilateral development banks has resulted in the imposition of programs that are geared toward objectives

CLAIRE RITCHIE/NNDFN

Nyae Nyae woman confronts the South African military, 1989

162

defined by those agencies rather than by Africans themselves. For example, "structural adjustment programs" have meant drastic cuts in spending on social services, reductions in government subsidies, and increases in food prices.

Misguided development efforts and structural adjustment have hit hardest those at the bottom —the very poor, particularly those in urban areas. Per capita incomes declined at an annual rate of over 1 percent in the 1970s and 1980s in Sub-

Saharan Africa. Since the 1970s, unemployment has spread, especially among the growing numbers of young people. In many countries, half the population is 15 years old or younger, with profound implications for government expenditures on social services and economic assistance.

Competition for scarce resources has increased the pressure on governments to come up with sustainable long-term development policies. However, at the same time, Africa's external debt now stands at $255 billion. Much of the continent's export earnings now go to paying off these debts: African governments spend twice as much money on debt service as on health and education, even while they curtail investments in social and economic development.

The failures of development are not the only reason that African economies and living standards have deteriorated. One of the worst threats to Africa is militarization. During the Cold War, the superpowers poured billions of dollars worth of weapons and military assistance into the continent. Hundreds of thousands of Africans have died at the hands of state-supported military units. Governments such as those of Sudan and Ethiopia spent considerable sums—sometimes over half the national budget—on weapons and supporting armies. Scarce foreign currency was used for military hardware—money that could have been used for development or humanitarian aid.

In response to the crisis of survival that many Africans face, literally thousands of self-help organizations and multipurpose development associations have emerged at the grassroots level. In East Africa, the Organization of Pastoral People has been established to seek rights for Maasai and other herding peoples. In Swaziland, women have formed some 200 zenzele ("do-it-yourself") voluntary associations. These groups engage in activities ranging from day-care services to horticulture projects. Since 1986, a cooperative joining 32

Ju/'hoansi Bushmen communities in northeastern Namibia has undertaken farming activities and worked to establish secure rights to land and natural resources. Oromo in Ethiopia are actively conserving the range lands on which they depend.

Likewise, indigenous groups have resisted the establishment of certain development projects, as was the case with the Barabaig, a society of farmers and pastoralists in northern Tanzania. With financial support from Canada's International

Ogoni protest march, 1993

Development Agency, the Tanzanian National Agriculture and Food Corporation had acquired title to some 100,000 acres of the Barabaig's crucial dry-season grazing land for a wheat project. Tanzania didn't compensate Barabaig for their losses, even though the project reduced livestock numbers and milk yields. Police have arrested Barabaig for trespassing on what used to be their own land and saddled them with large fines for damage their cattle did to the wheat crop. With the help of the Legal Aid Committee of the University of Dar Es Salaam, the Barabaig are seeking to have the government recognize their customary rights.

The Barabaig case is but one of many instances in which indigenous groups have had to resort to legal action to press their claims. Many other ethnic and tribal groups in Sub-Saharan Africa have become vocal about infringements on their rights. G/wi and G//ana, assisted by journalists, have argued for continued rights of residence and resource use in Botswana's Central Kalahari Game Reserve, despite a 1986 government recommendation that these Bushmen peoples be relocated. In northeastern Namibia, Ju/'hoan Bushmen collab-

orated with film makers who documented their efforts to convince herders who had moved into their area to leave peacefully.

Long viewed as "victims of progress," indigenous peoples in Sub-Saharan Africa are moving to take control of their own destinies. They are protesting the ways in which governments, multinational corporations, and development agencies have treated them, and they are seeking redress through the media and the courts and in their own communities.

ROBERT K. HITCHCOCK

163

Sub-Saharan Africa Resources:
African American Institute, 833 United Nations Plaza, New York, NY 10017.
Africa News, P.O. Box 3851, Durham, NC 27702.
Africa Recovery Briefing Paper, United Nations Department of Public Information.
Africa Watch, 485 Fifth Ave., New York, NY 10017.
African Cultural Institute, 13 Avenue du Presidente Habib Bourguiba, Boite Postale 1, Dakar, Senegal.
Human Rights Internet, 1338 G St., SE, Washington, DC 20003.
International African Institute, Lionel Robbins Building, 10 Portugal St., London WC2A 2HD, England.
International Institute of Human Rights, 6 Place de Bordeaux, 67000 Strasbourg, France.
TransAfrica, 545 Eighth St., SE, Suite 200, Washington, DC 20077.

AWEER OF KENYA AND SOMALIA

The Aweer, commonly known by outsiders as the Boni, live in southern Somalia and the Lamu District of the Kenyan hinterland. They number about 2,000 in Kenya and 1,000-2,000 in Somalia, where they are called the Kilii. Traditionally hunter-gatherers, today Kenyan Aweer are turning to swidden agriculture and Somali Aweer are taking up pastoralism.

Aweer face two main threats: forced abandonment of hunting-gathering and political insecurity. Most Aweer country is unsuitable for agriculture because of poor soils, lack of water, and tsetse-fly infestations, which is why neighbors left the land to the Aweer in the first place.

Hunting-gathering is the most appropriate adaptation to the local ecology, and the Aweer subsistence and trade economy once provided them with food and outside goods. Aweer culture also revolved around hunting-related traditions. However, slash-and-burn cultivation is destroying wildlife habitats that a government ban on hunting was supposed to save, while variable crop yields due to infertile soils and highly fluctuating rainfall have resulted in chronic nutritional shortages, particularly for Aweer children. With the culture and economy of the people under great stress, men are moving to Lamu District and to villages in search of work, leaving women alone.

Political insecurity has existed at least since Kenyan independence in 1963 due to Somalia's territorial claims on northeast Kenya. It has increased considerably in the past three years with the war in and the subsequent disintegration of Somalia. Only sporadic "development" has taken place in Aweer country because of fear on the part of civil servants. No private group has ever worked in Aweer country. Schools have no teachers and health clinics no medical personnel. The dirt road leading into Aweer land is impassable during the rains, and no relief food can reach people. Old and young alike have high mortality rates due to nutritional problems coupled with a lack of health care. Moreover, the Aweer are watched closely by forest and wildlife rangers, and natural resources that once were critical for food, medicines, construction materials, household items, crafts, and so on are denied them in the name of conservation.

The Aweer need a management plan that would provide for the sustainable utilization of their forest resources. The forest contains many items that were once traded via local and international networks, and many could be traded again.

ANIEL STILES

164

BORAN OF KENYA

The 30,000 Boran in northern Kenya are an Oromo people, cattle herders who migrated from southern Ethiopia over the past two centuries to escape warfare and drought. Divided between Muslims settled along the Uaso Nyiru River in Isiolo District and non-Muslims to the north in Marsabit District, Boran herding lands have been restricted, and the Boran have been forced to take up sedentary lives in towns.

In the 1960s, Kenyan forces brutally suppressed the Boran during the ill-fated "shifta" secession movement, when the Boran allied with Muslim Somalis who attempted to secede. The Boran were confined to "strategic villages," and Kenyan forces confiscated or shot much of their livestock. By 1971, the Boran were starving and stayed alive only with the massive outside famine relief.

Today, most Boran live in poverty near urban centers, subsisting as charcoal burners, firewood gatherers, paid herders, night guards, or prostitutes.

Although a few have opened shops or found government jobs, urbanization has brought impoverishment and proletarianization as low-wage workers to most Boran. They lack political power or economic security; raids, warfare, and drought compound both problems. Development efforts based on livestock production, such as restocking herds with cattle, camels, goats, and sheep, could promote Boran self-sufficiency. In this arid region, livestock production is one of the few viable enterprises.

ELLIOT FRATKIN

BUSHMAN PEOPLES IN NAMIBIA AND SOUTH AFRICA

Ju/'hoan Bushman preschool

Bushman Resource:
!Kung San Foundation/Nyae Nyae Development Foundation of Namibia, c/o Cultural Survival, 215 First St., Cambridge, MA 02142.

For the Ju/'hoan and other Bushman groups in Namibia, progress on rights has been substantial in the last few years regarding land, education, and culture. However, glaring inequities persist, primarily in the areas of economic and political rights.

Labor and regional-government laws and structures are only now being created in Namibia to replace the institutionalized oppression that was apartheid. Attention to better communication and to addressing the conditions of unfairness that characterized the previous South West African administration under South Africa will have to take place on a massive scale.

Nowhere are injustice and cultural blundering more apparent than in the inability of the Roman-Dutch legal system, still reigning in Namibia, to address the needs and sensibilities of the Bushmen. The legal system pays little attention to the economic needs of communities, and Bushmen frequently run afoul of this system because it defines out of existence some of their bases of survival. Without land on which to farm or do hunting-gathering, Bushman peoples face a choice between starvation and poaching or cattle theft. In one 1993 case, a Namibian court sent all the men in one village to jail for violating hunting laws that remained unclear despite years of requests for clarification. The ownership of game and other wild natural resources on communal land is also still in question.

Cultural translation is partly, of course, a linguistic matter, and this area, too, needs urgent attention. Social and domestic crimes and legal rights involving theft are often tragically confused. The very existence of differing social codes is acknowledged only punitively: cultural assumptions about infanticide and senilicide clearly underlay a March 1993 murder conviction.

Cultural misunderstandings of a "blame the victim" variety abound and may be illustrated graphically in the case of the 4,000-plus Bushman people, many originally from Angola, who fled with the South African Defense Force after Namibia became independent in 1990. Fearing reprisals from the new Namibian government as former collaborators, Bushman soldiers and their families were enticed to flee with promises of training, education, and a secure place to live in South Africa. A scant couple of years later, the former Bushman soldiers are trying, in droves, to return. The SADF failed to anticipate their needs, and they have become an embarrassment to the South African government.

In South Africa, the African National Congress has taken up the issue of land rights in the regions where the government resettled Bushmen. Meanwhile, however, many exiles have asked nongovernmental organizations and citizen groups in Namibia to help them return. Clearly, multicultural understanding is in its infancy in the new nations of southern Africa.

MEGAN BIESELE

165

EFE OF ZAIRE

Efe Action:
The Ituri Fund seeks to support the training of local people as health-care providers, health educators, primary school teachers, and community organizers. Send checks, payable to Cultural Survival—The Ituri Fund, to Cultural Survival, 215 First St., Cambridge, MA 02142.

The Efe live in the Ituri rain forest of northeast Zaire, one of Africa's most remote regions. The Efe are among the groups of hunter-gatherers often called "Pygmies;" others include the Aka, the Mbuti, and the Sua.

Numbering about 3,000 today, the Efe population is dwindling. Such factors as seasonal hunger, sexually transmitted diseases, and a poor diet have made Efe fertility rates among the world's lowest. According to Harvard University anthropologist Peter Ellison and UCLA anthropologist Robert Bailey, nearly one-third of post-menopausal Efe women have never had a live birth. The infant mortality rate is nearly 12 percent. Researchers like Ellison are working to determine the causes of infertility so the Efe can achieve the modest goal of simply having children.

Medicines, food, and money seldom reach the Efe because of the poor condition of bridges and roads. The nearest hospital is 22 miles away, a one-day walk on a dilapidated and muddy road. The very ill must stay home. The Zairian government has no plans to repair the infrastructure of this remote region or to educate villagers about health care.

ROY RICHARD GRINKER

G/WI AND G//ANA OF BOTSWANA

"The government wants the Ju/wasi to leave their land with their cattle and go to a strange land, and people's hearts are sore because people will be destroyed. We will stay here."

/Xaesce G/=Oma, Ju/wasi, Namibia

The G/wi and the G//ana have subsisted in the center of the Kalahari desert for hundreds, if not thousands, of years by hunting and foraging for food. For several months of the year, water is so scarce that they must survive on wild melons or water roots. Even so, says John Marshall, who visited the G/wi in the mid-1950s, "Eventually the melons run out. . . . You get desperate for water, real water." In drought years, inhabitants would trek to springs near the present-day town of Ghanzi or to the Botletle River.

In the nineteenth century, Boer farmers moved into the Ghanzi area and started cattle ranches. G/wi and G//ana still visited the area during droughts, but within a few years of Marshall's visit, Ghanzi farms were being surveyed and would later be sold to entrepreneurs from South Africa and Gaborone, the capital of modern-day Botswana. Most of the new cattle corporations fenced off farms and threw out the resident Bushmen, including visiting G/wi and G//ana, who no longer had a "last defense" against thirst.

Three years after Marshall's visit, the Bechuanaland Protectorate Administration built the Kuke fence, a veterinarian cordon cutting across several hundred miles of the Kalahari, theoretically to stop the spread of hoof-and-mouth disease. The result was to interrupt the migrations of large herds that the G/wi and G//ana depended on for meat.

With the protectorate's establishment of the Central Kalahari Game Reserve, a fence almost entirely encircled G/wi and G//ana lands and kept cattle out. Bushmen who had traditionally hunted in the area now had to seek a permit and could hunt only in the traditional manner and dress.

A water borehole drilled on the reserve in the early 1960s drew a large settlement around the present community of Xade. During drought years, the settlement's numbers increased to more than 600 (1,400 to 2,000 people live in the reserve today). A drought-relief program, begun in the late 1970s, continues, as does its unfortunate side effect of fostering the dependence of many reserve inhabitants on state handouts of mealie corn, flour, and oil. While the intent of the program was to help "remote area dwellers" survive, it has become, along with the requirement of game licenses, a tool for keeping them sedentary and away from what Botswana hopes will become a lucrative safari industry.

Since 1985, government decrees have added to the threats looming over the G/wi and G//ana. First, the government required all native inhabitants to leave the reserve, but fortunately it didn't enforce this decree. In 1991, the Ghanzi District Council attempted to convince the central government to exclude the Xade region from the reserve under the guise of development for the people living in the reserve. This plan, which Botswana's president has yet to rule on, would reduce the land available to the G/wi and G//ana to one-fifteenth its traditional size and would encourage cattle programs in Xade. It is likely to benefit cattle ranchers around Ghanzi, who desperately need pasturage, more than the Bushmen of the reserve, and then, only temporarily, because grazing is sparse in this dry region.

Although a clinic and a primary school have come to Xade and the drought-relief program continues, no substantive development has succeeded in the region. G/wi and G//ana representatives have petitioned the government for real development programs. Embarrassed at past failures, the government has pledged to help in some way but seems locked in ambivalence. It must face the advocates of a burgeoning tourist industry, who favor protecting native game over native people, as well as the pleas of cattle ranchers.

Grazing is not tenable in the region, but the government could promote a Bushman wildlife ranger program. The G/wi and G//ana could cull game populations for a trial period. Bushmen would be appointed as game wardens; they are more likely than outsiders to do a good job at this task, in part because they stand to lose the most if the game disappears.

JOHN E. HUDELSON

HADZABE OF TANZANIA

Hadzabe Action:

Help the Hadzabe continue their way of life. Support the good will of the Tanzanian government and help fund a better flow of information between it and Hadzabe. Foreign help in spotting encroachment and providing transport and support personnel for local government enforcement is essential. Foreign hunters should persuade outfitters to employ Hadzabe as trackers and in conservation patrols.

About 700 Hadzabe live in the hills south and east of northern Tanzania's Lake Eyasi; another 250 to 300 live west of the lake. Most live by bow-hunting and gathering. Women and children have autonomy and excellent nutrition. The Hadzabe have maintained their unique language over many centuries.

Hadzabe occupy an important corridor of wild country between the major conservation areas of northern Tanzania. Many Hadzabe say they want to protect their country and wild animals for the future, but their way of life is threatened by encroachment on their territory, the felling of trees for the charcoal trade, and invasions of the hilly, forested savanna by livestock.

Overcrowded neighbors seek to farm or herd in the rocky forests, exploiting the grass and water sources. For example, Datoga recently began to herd cattle into the hilly forests, having devastated their own lowland pastures. Such encroachments drain game and plant resources and affect water supplies. Near desertificaton results in many places, which are already parched from lack of rain. Outsiders have taken up all the irrigation sites. In 1992, missionaries, without government permission, began to construct a church at the most productive hunting water hole in Hadzabe country. Outsiders began moving in within weeks.

The Tanzanian government has tried to help the Hadzabe, and local government makes many concessions. Game laws are interpreted liberally in the East (although harshly in the West). A lasting obstacle is the worthy refusal to discriminate according to tribe. Discrimination by traditional economy might be an option.

The new land laws might help. Canadian Universities Service Overseas has helped set up a Hadzabe village (an administrative unit, not a cluster of houses) that includes a large section of Hadzabe country. More recognized

167

villages are needed to capture more land, but time is running out. Hadzabe need help in enforcing a village's right to exclude new settlers. It is too easy for outsiders to buy their way in, and remoteness handicaps government supervision.

Another obstacle is disagreement among Hadzabe—some favor a single farming settlement. However, repeated attempts at settling the Hadzabe—some funded by international charities—show that it results only in the loss of more land, epidemics and weight loss among children, and drunkenness and violence.

Other Hadzabe suggest a voluntary mixture of a village for "development" and a large bush area for a "traditional economy" to include trade in artifacts, honey, and other forest products. More Hadzabe favor this approach but dislike any forceful leader. Most wish everyone else would go away.

NICHOLAS BLURTON JONES

HERERO OF BOTSWANA

Northwest Botswana's Herero, like the closely related Mbanderu, are cattle and goat pastoralists. They are a very distinct group, marked by the Victorian dresses and turbans of the women and the walking sticks of the men. They maintain a determined ethnicity and cultural identity while fully participating in the country's economic, political, and educational systems.

The Herero in Botswana descend from refugees from a genocidal campaign waged by German troops in South West Africa between 1904 and 1907. Given haven by the Tswana chiefs, the Herero gradually rebuilt their herds. By the 1930s, they had reestablished their way of life in widely dispersed homesteads, each associated with a family herd of cattle and small stock.

The Herero are not threatened in the same ways many other groups in Africa are threatened. They are prosperous, even wealthy, by the standards of the country. Botswana is a parliamentary democracy with natural resources that support rapid economic development and the extension of government services. It has a solid environmental awareness, and the press and local councils monitor development schemes for their ecological consequences.

Ironically, the worst threat to the Herero is a consequence of improved health. Until the 1960s, they suffered from high levels of sterility, a problem shared with groups from northern Namibia up to the Sudan in the so-called "infertile crescent" of central Africa. Since antibiotics became widely available in the 1960s, the sterility has been greatly reduced. The fertility rate has more than doubled, and women now average over seven births in their lifetime. The consequent rapid population growth strains schools and health facilities. Because limited water and grazing land essentially fix the number of cattle, everyone is impoverished.

Government services are oriented to the settlement pattern of the Tswana—the dominant ethnic group—who tend to live in a large town and to visit their dispersed herds and fields only periodically. The Herero, by contrast, live in isolated homesteads and so benefit less from public services. Schools and clinics are often far from home. Moreover, Herero women don't enter the cash labor force as much as women from other ethnic groups. As a result, the decline in fertility that usually comes with education and wage work is likely to be delayed for them.

HENRY HARPENDING

HIMBA OF ANGOLA AND NAMIBIA

Himba Resource:

Margaret Jacobsohn, with Peter Pickford and Beverly Pickford, *Himba: Nomads of Namibia*, Struik Publishers, 1990.

Himba Action:

Contributions can be made to Integrated Rural Development and Nature Conservation, c/o Palamwag, Box 339, Swakopmund, Namibia and to Endangered Wildlife Trust, Private Bag X11, Parkview 2122, Transvaal, South Africa.

The semi-nomadic, pastoralist Himba live in the rugged mountains and sandy plains of southwest Angola and the Kaokoland region of northern Namibia. Over the past two decades, the approximately 9,000 Himba have had to cope with drought, poaching, war, and rapidly changing political and economic circumstances.

Himba had ranked among Africa's richest pastoralists, but a drought from 1979 to 1982 destroyed up to 90 percent of some herds, along with parts of the Himba's social fabric. Some Himba engaged in wage labor, others turned to foraging, and still others moved to the peripheries of settlements so that they could get food from relief agencies.

Warfare was a major threat. In the early 1980s, a new front opened in the conflict between South Africa and the South West African Peoples Organization, or SWAPO. Land mines along the border between Namibia and Angola caused many casualties. Guns became much more accessible, with a resulting increase in poaching of elephants, rhinoceros, and antelopes.

As livestock numbers declined and predators were killed off, the need for herders fell. Himba men left home to find other work, while the new market economy altered gender relationships. Men had better access than women to cash and participated more in political activities.

One response of Himba women was to intensify their efforts to make and sell crafts to tourists. Some families stayed year round at places tourists frequented, a trend that had a severe impact on local vegetation. Conflicts arose as Himba competed among themselves for tourist money.

In response to such problems, an innovative development program was set up in Namibia through the combined efforts of Himba communities and Integrated Rural Development and Nature Conservation (IRDNC), a nongovernmental organization. The Himba were not averse to tourism—as long as they received some of the benefits and had some control over it. Now tourists pay a daily levy of about $10 per person, which is divided among the lineages that have traditional rights to the area.

IRDNC was also instrumental in establishing a game guard system in which local people, selected by the Himba, monitor wildlife and detect poachers. Since local people now benefit more from wildlife, they are more willing to conserve this resource, and elephant, rhinoceros, and other wild animal populations are rising. Such efforts have succeeded in part because Himba themselves planned and implemented them. But if the programs are to remain viable, the right of Himba communities to resources needs to be backed up with legal protection.

ROBERT K. HITCHCOCK

169

KÉLÉ OF GABON

Formerly semi-nomadic hunter-gatherers, the Kélé have been sedentary since French colonial rule in the 1930s. In the village of Makouké in central Gabon, economic modernization seriously threatens the Kélé's health and way of life.

In 1977, the French-Belgian company Agro-Gabon expropriated over 18,500 acres of Kélé farmland in order to establish a palm-tree plantation and palm-oil factory near Makouké. As a consequence of losing their land, the Kélé must either cultivate poor soils or travel long distances to find productive farmland. At the same time, vital hunting forests have been destroyed due to the company's activities. The factory also regularly dumps excess palm oil into the Ogooué River, endangering aquatic life and eliminating another important food resource for the Kélé.

With the destruction of their habitat and economic bases, many Kélé have grown despondent and turned to alcohol. This trend has sown discord in Makouké, leading to frequent verbal and physical fighting. Many children are now born with fetal alcohol syndrome or with a propensity for becoming alcoholics in later life. Air pollution caused by the factory attracts flies whose stings often cause serious allergies and ulcers and can even kill children.

Humanitarian organizations should pressure Agro-Gabon and similar international developers to reform their land-use and waste-management policies. Unless action is taken soon, further damage to the culture and health of the Kélé people will amount to ethnocide.

FRANÇOIS NGOLET

KOFYAR OF NIGERIA

Kofyar Resources:
For information on the questions concerning property institutions and land tenure that the Kofyar and many developing societies face, refer to: *The Ecologist*, July/August 1992; International Association for the Study of Common Property, Woodburn Hall 200, Bloomington, IN 47405; and the Land Tenure Center, University of Wisconsin, Madison, WI 53706.

The Kofyar, a group of some 142,000 people, live on the southern escarpment of the Jos Plateau and in the Benue Valley lowlands of Plateau State, Nigeria. In the last 40 years, about 30,000 Kofyar have moved from traditional subsistence farming of manured terraces into producing cash crops of yams, rice, millet, and sorghum for urban markets. At the same time, smallholder households still practice hoe farming, and the Nigerian government has provided no agricultural extension, credit, or mechanization for development.

An all-weather road and the oil-boom-fueled expansion of motorized transport have furthered the largely successful and spontaneous transition of the Kofyar to a mixed subsistence-cash economy. However, increasing state control of land tenure and agricultural inputs could threaten this change, which has improved Kofyar access to modern medical care, education, and consumer goods.

Traditional Kofyar property rights include private, inheritable control of homestead farms and village common property in fallow lands and forests. Any state attempt to unilaterally register land would interfere with the Kofyar's system of socially recognized boundaries, transactions, and adjudication of competing claims. Existing government statutes also make no provision for collective administration, protection, and conservation of community land and other resources. Nor do statutes cover the creation of such rights in a frontier area. Autonomous local control is generally more equitable, better informed on ecology, and more conducive to sustainable land use than are the legal codes and machinery of state and federal bureaucracies.

Similarly, the government's distribution of such necessary agricultural inputs as chemical fertilizers has been grossly inefficient. Kofyar farmers prefer dealing with a market economy, even though that would mean the end of state subsidies and storage facilities.

In the past, Kofyar have benefited from a lack of government interference in indigenous development of agriculture and the absence of large foreign-financed projects. Increased external control in the form of land-tenure regulations or large-scale agricultural development would be counterproductive.

ROBERT MCC. NETTING

MAASAI OF KENYA AND TANZANIA

The 500,000 Maasai of East Africa, affiliated into 14 independent groups, inhabit the savannas of southern Kenya and northern Tanzania. In the late nineteenth century, these cattle herders lost much of their livestock to internal warfare and rinderpest disease, and they were unable to resist British appropriation of their Kenyan grazing lands. After 1911, the British limited the Maasai to Kajiado and Narok districts in southern Kenya and prohibited them from selling livestock, milk, or beef in the European-dominated markets.

170

Due to both good rainfall and improved health services for humans and livestock, the population of the Maasai and their herds grew in the 1950s. However, the proportion of Maasai living on the land declined as poor Kikuyu and Kamba peasants expanded onto marginal farming lands. At the same time, larger-scale landowners developed wheat and beef estates on the better lands. In the 1960s, the Kenyan Maasai accepted land partitioning on "group ranches" to protect themselves from losing more land to farmers or expanding game parks. In Tanzania, the government confined many Maasai to "ujamaa" villages and restricted them from grazing livestock, particularly in the Serengeti and other game parks.

In recent years, Kenyan Maasai have begun dividing their land into individual ranches. This privatization has been a mixed blessing. It has helped prevent the encroachment of agriculture on Maasai grazing land, led to better marketing for livestock, and fostered settlements that provide elders and children with better access to schools and health clinics. But it hasn't created economic security and, by fostering an elite of landholders, it contributes to separating a formerly cooperative people into the haves and the have-nots. Furthermore, growing competition between farmers, herders, and wildlife hastens land degradation and overgrazing.

Development efforts, such as improving veterinary resources, should aim at helping Maasai to market their livestock. Maasai could also benefit more from the tourism industry—for example, they could become joint owners of game parks. Finally, political empowerment would promote the fair distribution and management of shared grazing resources.

ELLIOT FRATKIN

MIKEA OF MADAGASCAR

DANIEL STILES

Mikea hunter-gatherer

The Mikea live in the dry forest of southwest Madagascar, north of the provincial capital of Toliara. Their population is unknown but probably numbers about 1,000. They are hunter-gatherers and also practice low-intensity swidden cultivation. Mikea live part of the year in semi-nomadic villages and camp for about four months in the deep forest. Some Mikea have settled in coastal villages to fish, and others have settled permanently in inland villages and farms. The Mikea are outside mainstream Malagasy life, and academics and government officials even debate their existence.

Mikea are not under serious threat of survival today because the population density in their area is very low and their land is poor. In fact, they are largely ignored by the government and development workers, although Christian missionaries are trying to convert and settle them in villages. Mikea obtain food from the forest and from their fields, and hunger is unknown.

Their main problems are health, sanitation, and the availability of water. For several months of the year, some parts of Mikea country are totally devoid of water, and they depend on moisture from tubers for survival. Health conditions are very poor due to lack of sanitation and high levels of parasitic infection. Children in the camps don't attend school, and almost all Mikea are illiterate. They seem content with their lifestyle, however, except for the health and water problems. Some Mikea may resume hunting-gathering, leaving settled villages for camps in the forest, where food security is more assured and government officials don't bother them for taxes or other civic duties.

The main long-term threat to the Mikea is environmental degradation by slash-and-burn farming and encroachment by agriculturalists. People are migrating into the Mikea country due to chronic drought in the south.

The surface soils of Mikea lands are mainly sand, and deforestation fol-

171

lowed by livestock grazing could eventually cause serious damage. Thus increased population and livestock pressures could lead to problems in the future, creating the need for a forest reserve or park. Hunting-gathering would be allowed within sustainable limits to ensure the conservation of resources for Mikea subsistence.

DANIEL STILES

NHARO BUSHMEN OF BOTSWANA

Nharo Resources:
First People of the Kalahari, P.O. Box 173, Ghanzi, Botswana.
KURU, P.O. Box 219, Ghanzi, Botswana.
Mathias Guenther, *The Nharo Bushmen of Botswana: Tradition and Change,* Helmut Buske Verlag, 1986.

The Nharo, numbering about 6,000, live in the Ghanzi District of western Botswana and in eastern Namibia. Most work as laborers on European-owned cattle ranches; in Botswana a few hundred live at settlements set up by the government. In the Ghanzi farm block, an area of about 3,000 square miles, game and wild food plants have been depleted, so hunting-gathering can no longer meet people's subsistence needs. Hunger and malnutrition are serious problems; especially during droughts, many Nharo depend on the government for food.

The Nharo and their Bushman neighbors lost their land a century ago through treaty negotiations in which they played no part. Land remains the Nharo's principal problem, even though the government, in the mid-1970s, set aside a number of farms for the Nharo and other Ghanzi Bushmen groups to set up ranching cooperatives and several other development projects. However, some of these farms may revert back to the government for private ranching schemes.

A 1992 letter to the Botswana central government by the "First People of the Kalahari," signed by several Bushman spokespeople, identified three urgent needs. Land was the first. The other concerns were the absence of development officials and programs that "meet the special needs of the N/oa khwe" (the "red people," the Nharo's new self-designation) and the need for a national council of Bushmen as "a legitimate negotiating partner" with government.

A significant catalyst to developing such self-directed initiatives is KURU, a grassroots organization that grew out of the Dutch Reformed Church mission in D'Kar in 1986. *Kuru* is a Nharo word meaning to make or accomplish, reflecting the organization's aim to promote self-managed schemes among the Nharo and other farm Bushmen. Projects include a vegetable-garden operation, a tannery and leather workshop, a district-wide preschool program of eight schools, crafts marketing, a contemporary-art project, and a highly promising cochineal harvesting project that will incorporate 32 family garden units.

KURU strives to loosen the ties of dependency of the Nharo and other farm Bushmen, but its limited resources and lack of recognition and support on the part of the district and federal governments reduce its effectiveness. Moreover, only the government has the authority and capacity to meet the three demands of the farm Bushmen: land, political representation, and empowerment.

MATHIAS GUENTHER

NUER OF SUDAN

Occupying 22,000 square miles of savannah and marshland along the central southern tributaries of the White Nile, the Nuer are the second largest cultural-linguistic group of Southern Sudan. Numbering more than a million, they are transhumant agro-pastoralists whose economy centers on sorghum and cattle.

Since the second Sudanese civil war in 1983, the Nuer have been trapped in a vortex of violence, famine, and disease that has claimed the lives of 600,000 Southern Sudanese and displaced at least 3 million people and possibly many more. An uneasy 11-year truce in which the central government granted the South "regional autonomy" separated this war from the first Sudanese civil war (1955-1972).

The current conflict began after the Northern-dominated government decided to construct a massive, environmentally disruptive canal through the central marshlands of the Upper Nile; to deny the Southern regional government's claims on the massive oil deposits discovered in its territories in the mid-1970s; to dissolve the Southern Regional Assembly and redivide the South into three provinces; and to impose a particularly brutal version of Islamic *Shari'a* law.

Because Nuer territories contain the richest known oil deposits in the South, they were among the first to be devastated by raids by government-sponsored Arab militias. Beginning in late 1983, these raids destroyed or dislocated scores of Nuer and Dinka villages. The raiders captured and enslaved hundreds of women and children.

Since the post-1985 buildup of the Sudanese People's Liberation Army, these raids have largely been contained, but the western Nuer were next overwhelmed by an epidemic of visceral leishmaniasis that has claimed more than 60,000 lives. Although Médicins Sans Frontièrs has tried to check the epidemic by opening small treatment centers, medical supplies are urgently needed, as are fishing equipment, agricultural tools, cattle vaccines, mosquito nets, sorghum seed, and school materials.

Between 1983 and 1988, the central and eastern Nuer regions were subjected to extensive government offensives and periodic air bombardments. Some 400,000 Southerners, including many Nuer, sought refuge in Ethiopia, only to be driven out after the fall of Mengistu's Dergue government in May 1991. In addition, 2 million more Southern Sudanese, camped on the outskirts of Northern cities, desperately need relief and protection. Beginning in the late 1980s, the government has systematically bulldozed these enclaves and has dumped some 500,000 of the inhabitants in distant camps devoid of adequate water, food, and medical supplies.

Barred by bureaucratic rules from obtaining national identity cards, displaced Southerners are subject to arbitrary arrest, torture, murder, and forcible conscription into the army. Because only government-backed Muslim organizations can work with this population, formal allegiance to Islam is a principal criterion in who gets what little relief is available.

Unless concerted pressure can be brought to bear for a political solution to the war, the plight of the Nuer and other Southern Sudanese is unlikely to be relieved in the foreseeable future.

SHARON HUTCHINSON

173

OGONI OF NIGERIA

Ogoni have farmed and fished on the fertile alluvial plains of the Niger Delta in southern Nigeria for hundreds of years. After 30 years of oil exploitation in their territory, however, the 500,000 Ogoni can no longer fish, farm, or hunt because the rivers are polluted and the farmlands have been rendered unproductive.

Almost all of Nigeria's oil, which accounts for 94 percent of the country's GNP, comes from the delta and its fringes. Since 1958, Shell and Chevron have extracted $30 billion in oil from Ogoni land, yet Ogoni communities lack telecommunications, hospitals, electricity, roads, pipe-borne water,

Ogoni Resource:

Movement for the Survival of Ogoni People, 24 Aggrey Rd., P.O. Box 193, Port Harcourt, Nigeria (234)84-331763.

Ethnic Minority Rights Organization of Africa, 63 Tejuosho St., P.O. Box 696, Surulere, Lagos, Nigeria (2341)832218.

> "Indigenous people often do not realize what is happening to them until it is too late. More often than not, they are the victims of the actions of greedy outsiders."
>
> Ken Saro-Wiwa, Ogoni Nation, Nigeria

industry, and well-equipped schools. Their unemployment rate is as high as 85 percent. Oil exploration has resulted in respiratory diseases, hearing problems, and air-borne diseases in Ogoni communities. The companies flare gas 24 hours a day—and have done so for 33 years—in defiance of Nigerian law.

Oil extraction has profoundly affected Ogoni society as well. Innumerable oil spills from outdated equipment have driven fish offshore, where the Ogoni are not equipped to fish. In this former "food basket" of the Niger Delta, people must now violate traditional taboos against buying food because acid rain has destroyed the productivity of the land. Environmental degradation is so severe that over 20,000 Ogoni migrate annually to Gabon and Cameroon to work, leading to family breakups and other social stresses.

In recent years, more Ogoni die annually than are born. Ogoni languages are on the verge of disappearing, and public institutions compel Ogoni to speak English and other dominant languages. Ogoni have little representation in Nigerian federal institutions and virtually no political power. A new constitution, intended to usher in a democratic government in 1993, doesn't protect the rights of the smaller minority populations.

To better redistribute delta oil wealth, in 1991 Nigerian president Ibrahim Babangida created 11 new states and greatly increased the number of local governments. Although variable in size, these local governments receive equal sums of money from the federal administration. This leaves highly populated areas like Ogoniland short of funds for primary schools while other districts have a surplus.

In August 1990, the rulers of the five Ogoni kingdoms signed a draft bill of rights demanding political autonomy, political representation at the federal level, local control of development resources, and religious and cultural rights. Federal inaction on the bill of rights prompted the Movement for the Survival of the Ogoni People to issue an ultimatum in 1992 to Shell, Chevron, and the Nigerian National Petroleum Corporation—the area's major oil companies—demanding $6 billion in royalties. The companies' answer was to seek the protection of the government, which promptly sent troops and armed police into Ogoni.

In January 1993, 300,000 Ogoni protested their situation throughout Ogoniland. Since then, tension has been building, and law-enforcement officials are keeping round-the-clock surveillance in Ogoni communities.

JENNIFER RATHAUS

OKAVANGO DELTA PEOPLES OF BOTSWANA

The Okavango Delta of Botswana is inhabited by five ethnic groups: Hambukushu, Dxeriku, Bayei, Bugakhoe (Basarwa), and Xanekwe (River Basarwa). The total population of these groups is about 100,000 people; they inhabit both the swamp in the center of the delta and the desert on both sides of the Okavango. People fish, farm, hunt, gather wild foods, and raise domesticated animals.

Tourism is concentrated in the central and southern parts of the delta, which contains the Moremi Wildlife Reserve and several large safari concessions. Most of the former inhabitants have relocated to a few large, new settlements, and most of the men work as guides or boat operators.

In the northern, narrow sections of the delta, development has occurred mainly on the western side. People on the eastern side still live a traditional lifestyle, but they face a major threat from South Africans taking over islands for vacations. Indigenous people set up overnight camps on these islands while they fish and hunt. Without the use of those islands, people can't journey more than a half-day from their villages, and the prime fishing grounds are at least a day's journey away.

Non-local people acquired many islands in 1992, purportedly for tomato farms, and this cuts the number of islands available for camping in half. Because fish are the major source of protein for many villages, the loss of any more islands will have a dramatic effect, especially on the health and welfare of children.

The people intent on leasing the islands use state-of-the-art communications, helicopters, powerboats, and other technology. The indigenous people, who have no motorized transportation, telephones, or radios and little political influence, are at a great disadvantage in learning about and resisting such threats.

Nevertheless, in 1992 people in one village banded together to stop the acquisition of their main island. Access to transportation and communication will help them address this threat and also would greatly improve access to health care. In addition, agencies in Botswana need to be made more aware of the consequences—to people and wildlife—that the loss of the unique ecosystems on these islands will have in the northern Okavango.

JOHN BOCK

OKIEK OF KENYA

RODERICK BLACKBURN

Okiek man

The Okiek, comprised of about two dozen groups numbering in all about 40,000, are a hunting and gathering people living in or near most of the highland forests of central Kenya. In this century, the Okiek increasingly depend on cultivation and pastoralism while retaining their traditional forest adaptation and ethos. They have a complex but effective territorial system that regulates kin group access to forest resources and reduces competition.

Throughout much of this century, under first the British and later the independent Kenyan government, the Okiek were not officially recognized as a distinct ethnic group. Therefore, they were denied legal rights to their traditional forest territories. Several groups were evicted repeatedly from their territories or were denied use of forest resources.

The current Kenyan government favors the preservation of native trees, and, in conjunction with a British aid program, is beginning to recognize that the Okiek are both a distinct people and effective forest conservators. A pilot development program in the Mau Forest, the largest forest of native trees in East Africa, aims to foster sustainable uses of honey, wax, fruits, natural medicines, and other forest resources by traditional forest dwellers as a way to both preserve forests and meet essential food needs. The National Museums of Kenya also sponsor a "Guardians of the Forest" program to recognize the conservation ethic of traditional hunter-gatherer peoples.

If they succeed, these projects are a cause for hope, yet current government policies also encourage the conversion of communally owned nonforest lands to individual ownership. Few Okiek have a tradition of individual land ownership. As a result, Okiek families are selling off land to members of other ethnic groups for short-term gains, jeopardizing their long-term well-being. If the Okiek become landless and fragmented, efforts to protect their culture by preserving their use of forests may be to no avail.

RODERIC H. BLACKBURN

175

RENDILLE OF KENYA

Rendille Resource:
Elliot Fratkin, *Surviving Drought and Development: Ariaal Pastoralists of Northern Kenya,* Westview Press, 1991.

Rendille are pastoralists whose economy is based on raising camels. The 21,000 Rendille occupy desert lowlands in Marsabit District, northern Kenya, where over a period of 60 years, they have seen their herding lands reduced from about 22,000 square miles to about 3,000. First, the British colonial government imposed "tribal boundaries;" later, political insecurities followed Kenyan independence in 1963 as Rendille faced raids by Somali and Boran secessionists.

During the 1970s and 1980s, Rendille suffered extensive droughts and periodic famine. As a result, over half the population have settled in mission towns that distribute famine relief. Although these towns provide physical security and access to health care and schools, mechanized boreholes (wells) and increased demand for firewood have led to serious overgrazing. Today, most settled Rendille lack direct access to their milk animals, which are herded far away by adolescents and young men in mobile camps.

In addition to settling near mission towns, Rendille have experienced several large-scale development projects. In 1976, UNESCO's Man and the Biosphere Program and the UN Environment Program established the Integrated Project in Arid Lands in Marsabit District to monitor the spread of the desert. The project became a multi-million-dollar effort to encourage Rendille and Ariaal nomads to establish settled lives and to increase the marketing of their livestock as a way of reducing environmental degradation.

Today, the Rendille are becoming a sedentary people, isolated from their mobile herds. Increasingly, they get food by selling their herds or depending on mission relief.

Recently, northern Kenya's stability has weakened with the large influx of refugees from Sudan, Ethiopia, and Somalia, many of whom have traded guns for animals. Inter-ethnic livestock raiding is sharply higher, but the government does little to stop the fighting.

Although Marsabit District has received considerable amounts of famine aid and international development funds, these have largely focused on distributing foods, not on investing in the region's long-term productivity. Although the basis of Rendille economy is camel pastoralism, very few efforts by international donors or by the Kenyan government have aimed at improving veterinary care or other supports for livestock production and marketing, the food system best adapted to the region.

ELLIOT FRATKIN

176

SOMALI OF SOMALIA, ETHIOPIA, KENYA, AND DJIBOUTI

Somali Resource:
I.M. Lewis, *A Pastoral Democracy: A Study of Pastoralism and Politics Among the Northern Somali of the Horn of Africa*, Africana Publishing Company for the International African Institute, 1982.

The Somalis of the Horn of Africa are pastoralists who herd camels, sheep, and goats. Numbering an estimated 6 million, they recently have faced severe difficulties as a result of drought, disease, and war.

Somalia, where most Somalis live, has become a potent symbol of human suffering: 150,000 people have died in the past two years, most of them civilians caught in fierce fighting. In early 1992, 1,000 people died every day from starvation and disease; 2 million of Somalia's 7 million people were at severe risk from lack of food, water, and health care.

The tragedy of Somalia is an outgrowth of two decades of internal and external policies. Some efforts aimed at assisting the people of Somalia to become self-sufficient, but militarization overshadowed these projects. The Somali military of President Siad Barre, trained first by the Soviets and later by the United States, fought pitched battles in the late 1980s with such rebel organizations as the Somali National Movement. Countless civilians suffered,

Somali Action:
Relief Agencies working in Somalia include CARE International, 660 First Ave., New York, NY 10016; Médicins Sans Frontières, 30 Rockefeller Plaza, Suite 5425, New York, NY 10012; Save the Children Fund, 54 Wilton Rd., Westport, CT 06880; UNICEF, 331 East 38th St., New York, NY 10016; and World Concern, Box 33000, Seattle, WA 98133.

and hundreds of thousands of refugees fled to neighboring Djibouti, Ethiopia, and Kenya, where they lived in appalling conditions.

Open warfare and a harsh counterinsurgency campaign resulted in the deaths of tens of thousands of Somalis, many of them women and children. Men were forcibly conscripted; those who refused to fight were detained and tortured. Water points and other infrastructure were destroyed, livestock killed, and development projects shut down. After Barre fell in January 1991, the country divided into a number of clan-based fiefdoms that continued the struggle for dominance.

One of the greatest problems facing the people of Somalia was the chaos in the countryside. In many places, no stores, clinics, schools, or wells remained. Some markets had literally tons of food, but it was available only to those with cash. Somali children suffered and died within sight of stockpiles of food. Lack of potable water exacerbated health problems. Medicine was scarce. Looting of relief convoys by armed factions disrupted the flow of aid into areas most in need. By mid-1992, the famine in Somalia was perhaps worse than the one in Biafra in the 1960s or in Ethiopia in 1984-85.

Despite these difficulties, many Somalis and relief agencies have collaborated in an effort to save as many people as possible. CARE International has handled logistical operations, and a number of international relief agencies operate feeding centers. In early 1993 peace talks among 15 Somali factions led to a somewhat tenuous cease-fire. Somalis hope they can now return to a semblance of a normal life and rebuild their economy and institutions. There are now plans to set up 18 regional governments, each with three representatives. One of the three will be a woman.

ROBERT K. HITCHCOCK

TURKANA OF KENYA

Turkana are the most isolated and mobile of Kenya's pastoralists. Numbering 250,000, they inhabit the arid semi-deserts of northwest Kenya, where they subsist on cattle, small animals, and camel herding, as well as on fishing, hunting-gathering, and low-paid work in the towns.

Since the 1980s, drought, famine, and warfare with competing Pokot, Gabra, and Samburu pastoralists have been the major forces affecting Turkana life. A 1980 drought cost the Turkana over 90 percent of their cattle, and 80,000 Turkana sought famine relief in Catholic missions at Kakuma and Lodwar. After the drought, the Kenyan government and European countries—particularly Norway, the Netherlands, and Germany—established the Turkana Rehabilitation Project (TRP). By 1982, this multi-million-dollar project was providing about 200 tons of grain per week to destitute Turkana, leading to the formation of large, settled famine camps in which surviving livestock soon overgrazed limited pastures. Seeking to reduce food dependency, the project also initiated small-scale irrigation schemes to settle pastoralists, and Norway built a disastrously unsuccessful fish-processing plant on Lake Turkana. More successful was a Food for Work program initiated by TRP that contributed paid labor to ongoing irrigation, rural road, and tree-planting projects in Turkana District. Many Turkana recovered and built up their herds, and by 1985 only 15,000 Turkana received famine relief, although one-third of the district's pastoralists now live in or near the famine camps.

Turkana society remains extremely poor. More and more people are leaving the pastoral economy and migrating to towns, where they find low-paying jobs—the men as watchmen, herders, or construction workers, the

177

women making charcoal, brewing illegal beer, selling mira'a (or khat, an illegal stimulant), or engaging in prostitution.

The Turkana need to improve their ability to compete in Kenyan markets. Thus assistance efforts should encourage livestock production through better veterinary services, marketing infrastructures, and appropriate education.

ELLIOT FRATKIN

TYUA OF ZIMBABWE

Tyua Resource:
Robert K. Hitchcock,
   "Settlement, Seasonality, and Subsistence Stress Among the Tyua of Northern Botswana," in Rebecca Huss-Ashmore, ed., *Coping with Seasonal Constraints*, Museum Applied Science Center for Archaeology, University of Pennsylvania, 1988.

Tyua Action:
Zimbabwe Trust, a private organization, is assisting the community-based resource-management and rural-development efforts of the Tyua and other rural Zimbabweans. Contributions can be sent to Zimbabwe Trust, P.O. Box 4027, Belgravia, Harare, Zimbabwe; Kalahari Support Group, c/o Keizersgracht 682, 1017 ET Amsterdam, The Netherlands; or Kalahari Peoples Fund, 3100 9th, NW, Albuquerque, NM 87131.

The 1,000 Tyua Bushmen in western Zimbabwe and 6,000 in northeast Botswana were known in the past as skilled elephant hunters. Today, many Tyua derive some of their income and subsistence through work for others as agricultural laborers, herders, and hunting guides.

In the 1930s, the establishment of the Wankie Game Reserve (now Hwange National Park) displaced hundreds of Zimbabwe Tyua from their traditional territories. In the 1940s, the Bechuanaland Protectorate Administration forcibly resettled northern Botswana Tyua into villages. The process of dispossession was nearly completed with the appropriation of grazing land in both Zimbabwe and Botswana for a private ranching and agricultural scheme.

During the Zimbabwean war for independence in the 1960s and 1970s, some Tyua joined the liberation struggle against Rhodesia. Others worked for government ministries or private companies as building roads and fences. Some Tyua became specialized hunters for safari companies, and a few took part in wild-animal-eradication efforts aimed at stemming the spread of diseases.

The 1989 imposition of an international ban on ivory trading has hurt those Tyua households that engaged in commercial hunting and ivory carving. Ironically, elephant populations in western Zimbabwe and northern Botswana were rising when the ban began; in fact, crop damage by elephants is now a major problem. Tyua and other rural Zimbabweans can't kill animals raiding their fields and must depend instead on Department of National Parks and Wildlife Management game scouts to deal with problem animals.

Beginning in 1991, two districts in which Tyua reside, Tsholotsho and Bulalima Mangwe, became part of Zimbabwe's Communal Areas Management Program for Indigenous Resources. Under CAMPFIRE, as it is known, rural peoples have the authority to manage local wildlife and to benefit from the revenues deriving from such wildlife-related activities as hunting and tourism.

Although the Tyua and their neighbors have rights to the benefits from local wildlife, most revenues have gone to the district councils and haven't been distributed to communities. Worse, some district-council projects have had significant environmental impacts. For example, with the refurbishing of a dam, some people keep their cattle in one place year-round. As a result, overgrazing has reduced some of the grasses that Tyua women need for thatching their homes or for selling to raise money for children's schooling.

ROBERT K. HITCHCOCK

With the end of the Cold War, the Middle East and North Africa have become more—not less—polarized, and more violent. Ethnicity, rather than political affiliation or ideology, increasingly determines social and economic position. As a result, it is not only small, remote indigenous communities that are at risk but whole nations.

In North Africa's Magreb region, renewed war threatens to break out in the former Spanish Sahara. Moroccan settlement policies, designed to thwart a long-deferred UN-monitored referendum on the contested territory's future, are reducing indigenous Saharawis to a minority.

In Algeria and Tunisia, basic democratic rights are under suspension due to challenges to the state from Islamic fundamentalist movements that seek to appropriate a nationalist mantle to themselves. Egypt, too, is under growing attack from radical Islamic minorities. The same is true across much of the Middle East as radical Islamicists challenge secular nationalists in many countries and within national movements, such as that of the Palestinians.

At the same time, the Horn of Africa is a cauldron of clan- and ethnic-based violence. Somalia is in a state of almost complete disintegration; Sudan is rent by a brutal but largely unreported civil war; rival ethnic groups periodically battle one another in Djibouti; and sporadic fighting threatens to erupt into renewed civil war in southern Ethiopia. Only in the newly independent state of Eritrea are the guns silent.

To the northeast, Kurds, divided among six countries, contend with threats ranging from cultural suppression in Turkey to outright extinction in Iraq, while Palestinians grapple with a steadily shrinking set of political options. Any peace agreement with Israel is at best likely to serve only those Palestinians residing in the occupied West Bank and Gaza Strip, ignoring fully half the Palestinian population, which is scattered throughout the surrounding region. Even Israeli society suffers from internal ethnic divisions—between the Ashkenazim (Jews of Eastern European origin), the Sephardim (Jews of Middle Eastern origin), and Israeli Arabs—that increasingly define that country's domestic political landscape.

Meanwhile, within stable countries in the Arab core, including Jordan, Syria, and Saudi Arabia, the status and very survival of certain privileged ethnic minorities could be threatened by a sudden change in the regimes in their countries. This is the case for the Alawites, indigenous to northern Lebanon and Syria, and the Circassians, imported by the Ottoman Turks from Eurasia in the late 1800s.

Instability most insistently affects the periphery of the Arab world, where non-Arab minorities in what might be termed border states face diminishing access to resources or protection against incursions and expropriations by their societies' dominant groups. Chronic, structural economic crisis is exacerbating a crisis of legitimacy in political entities at many levels of these societies. For example, in Algeria, the government suspended elections in 1992 to prevent Islamic fundamentalists from coming to power.

As established institutions fail to command widespread popular support, whole societies verge on breakdown. In some cases, criminality fills the vacuum, although less so in the Arab world than in, for example, Eastern Europe or South Asia. In other cases, such as Sudan and Lebanon, narrowly based communal or confessional groups impose order through coercion and terror. Though economic forces drive these crises, cultural factors give them particular shape. Under these circumstances, previously marginalized peoples become more vulnerable than ever, as pressure increases to appropriate what limited resources — particularly land—they may have and as concern for and attention to minority rights evaporates.

Rich and Poor

This turmoil is both a legacy of the Cold War and a harbinger of the "new world order" that is succeeding it. The abrupt pull-back of the United States and the former Soviet Union from much of the region outside the oil-producing states, coupled with the weakening (or outright collapse) of unpopular regimes that the geopolitical giants had propped up, has triggered a scramble for power that has little to do with once-dominant political and economic philosophies. Ethiopia and Somalia are the most prominent examples but not the only ones. Throughout North Africa and the Middle East, the main contending ideologies of the twentieth century—communism and capitalism—no longer grip the popular imagination. The region's socialist-oriented experiments have been abandoned in all but name, and crushing debt, grossly unfair terms of international trade, local corruption, and chronic mismanagement render capitalist development an unreachable objective for most poor countries.

Nor has oil wealth brought political democracy to the richer countries. Instead, it has enhanced ethnic stratification and inequality through the use of large migrant populations in local work forces as well as in military and security forces. In Kuwait, recognized citizens with full political and economic rights constitute less than one-third of the population.

The disenchantment that accompanies this new set of realities creates an ideological vacuum that is increasingly filled by militant ethnic or religious revivalism, both of which are distinctly intolerant of minority rights. As economies decline and political legitimacy evaporates, many people grasp at what is closest and most familiar—asserting religious, ethnic, clan, and even sub-clan identities with a terrifying ferocity toward "outsiders" and little or no tolerance toward dissenting members of the groups themselves.

Feeding this bigotry in many countries is an increasing concentration of social control over economic resources and political power. Scarcity is breeding scapegoating and fostering even more social exclusion of cultural minorities within and between societies. Indigenous peoples, already denied access to political and economic power, find themselves threatened not only with isolation or discrimination but with outright destruction, as with the forced relocation of Ethiopian and Egyptian minorities in the 1980s.

Ethnic hierarchies are perhaps most pointed in the oil-rich Gulf states, where the highly stratified migrant labor forces perform much of the work for a privileged sector of the indigenous population. Most of the foreign workers in Kuwait, eastern Saudi Arabia, the Arab Emirates, and Oman are drawn from Asia, with significant numbers also coming from Africa and elsewhere in the Middle East. The 1991 Persian Gulf war brought this issue to a head as ethnicity became the basis for wholesale deportations of Yemenis, Palestinians, and Sudanese by the Saudi ruling family as punishment for their governments'—in the case of the Palestinians, their political leadership's—support for Iraq.

Elsewhere, in the Magreb region of northeast Africa Arab-based regimes use indigenous minorities to manipulate and divide the labor force. For the Khabyls in central Algeria, under these circumstances, a prime interest is consistent inclusion in the country's political and economic life. In contrast, the main desire of the Jews of Yemen is to be left alone and to maintain their long-standing cultural and economic autonomy.

Shaping the Future

The most innovative social experiments in the region are underway in Eritrea and Ethiopia, where sweeping revolutionary upheavals have dismantled narrowly based political structures. The Transitional Government of Ethiopia is seeking to reconstitute the former Amhara-dominated empire on the basis of voluntary association through the devolution of power to the country's many major ethnic groups. The new government has redrawn Ethiopia's internal boundaries and made extensive regional autonomy official policy. However, moves in this direction have unleashed powerful nationalist sentiments among formerly dominated groups that may not fold back into attempts to reunify the country. It is also not yet clear to what extent and in what ways the rights of smaller ethnic and tribal minorities within these autonomous regions are to be protected.

The newly independent state of Eritrea is considerably more unified, following a bitter 30-year war and a 1993 UN-monitored referendum in which 99.8 percent of the voters opted for independence from Ethiopia. Eritrea's provisional government, like the new government in Ethiopia, has committed itself to extensive regional autonomy. New laws guarantee all nine ethnic groups the right to be educated in their indigenous languages. In addition, new civil and criminal codes recognize local customs and systems of land tenure. Yet to be seen, however, is the extent to which traditional land claims will be protected as tens of thousands of refugees and exiles return to the war- and drought-ravaged land.

In the volatile political and economic environment of the 1990s, then, threats to indigenous peoples will vary widely depending upon the particular circumstances of the people at issue. Economic factors will play a growing role in defining problems and shaping potential solutions. For the Saharawis and the Palestinians, the right to an independent state is the main goal of the political movements representing them on the local and international stages. For the Kurds in the Middle East, as for the Tamacheq in the Sahel region of north-central Africa, the demand is for some form of secure local autonomy. For the Nubians in upper Egypt, as for the Marsh Arabs of southern Iraq, it is for inclusion in the dominant society, while for the Kunama in Eritrea it is for a balance between local autonomy and national inclusion.

In this constantly shifting context, calls for "democratization" on the part of the industrial states of Europe and North America must be tempered by a comprehensive and clear grasp of local political, social, and cultural issues. Similarly, foreign governments, multilateral institutions, and private donor agencies operating in these countries need to respect the rights of indigenous peoples on terms that reflect their specific circumstances.

Of course, no formula or simple checklist applies universally. Nevertheless, the growing political instability across much of the Middle East and North Africa, coupled with shrinking economic prospects, will add weight and complexity to the threats to the rights of indigenous peoples—even as these tendencies obscure the same people from public view.

DAN CONNELL

Middle East/North Africa Resources:

Africa News, P.O. Box 3851, Durham, NC 27702.

Grassroots International, 48 Grove St., Somerville, MA 02144.

Middle East Journal, 1761 N St., NW, Washington, DC 20036.

Middle East Resource and Information Project publishes the bimonthly *Middle East Report* and other topical papers. MERIP, 1500 Massachusetts Ave., NW, #119, Washington, DC 20005 (202)223-3677.

The Middle East Studies Association publishes "MESA Bulletin" and the *International Journal of Middle East Studies*. MESA, Department of Oriental Studies, University of Arizona, Tucson, AZ 85721.

One World Action, 59 Hatton Garden, London EC1 UK.

BEDUIN ARABS IN ISRAEL

Beduin Arabs in Israel are a minority within a minority; they comprise about 15 percent of Israel's Arabs, who in turn form about 18 percent of the population. Like all Arabs in Israel, the beduin community derives from Arabs in the parts of Palestine that became Israel in 1948.

Israeli authorities distinguish between beduin and other Arabs, but the beduin are only distinguished by roots in tribes that were once nomadic, whereas other clans lived in villages and towns. Yet even before the British rule that preceded the state of Israel, beduin were no longer nomadic livestock herders in most of Palestine. According to the 1931 census, almost 90 percent of beduin in the Negev depended on agriculture. Today, dependence is equally pronounced on wage labor, with beduin Israelis concentrated in low-skilled, low-paying jobs.

Behind the transformation of the beduin economy from agriculture to wage labor lies the issue of land, the crux of the conflict between the state and Arab citizens. Before 1948, land ownership in Palestine was often unregistered. In the Negev, in particular, few people had registered titles, although many had other proofs of long-standing ownership, occupation, and use. After 1948, Israeli authorities rejected these proofs. One law made the land of the 1948 refugees state lands; another expropriated lands not in possession of their owners on April 1, 1952, even if the absence was due to forced evacuation.

> About 15 percent of beduin in the Galilee and about half in the Negev live in unauthorized villages and hamlets or in isolated groups of dwellings spread over their traditional lands.

Almost all beduin lands now belong to the state and may be leased for farming. Jewish settlements (communal *kibbutzim* and cooperative *moshavim*) have long leases and can rely on automatic renewal, but beduin farmers may only lease land for six months each year and have no guarantee of leasing the same land, or any land, the next year. Moreover, they don't receive allocations of irrigation water that *kibbutzim* take for granted. In these circumstances, beduin use farming only as a sideline.

The government intends for all beduin to live in a few planned settlements, but about 15 percent of beduin in the Galilee and about half in the Negev live in unauthorized villages and hamlets or in isolated groups of dwellings spread over their traditional lands. Their houses are illegal and are demolished regularly, including in areas where beduin have registered land titles. Even homes built before 1948 have been demolished.

The government settlements have no industry and provide almost no employment. Their infrastructure is far inferior to that in nearby Jewish localities due to the much smaller budgets granted to Arab local councils. Instead of elected councils, most beduin Arab towns have government-appointed ones. In a 1982 survey of 160 families in Rahat in the Negev—the largest government settlement—155 were ready to give up their new town life immediately.

ADAPTED FROM "PLACES OF BITTERNESS" BY THE MINORITY RIGHTS GROUP

BEGA OF ETHIOPIA

Land degradation, uncertain rainfall, and growing population in Ethiopia's northern highlands have led the government and aid planners to envision resettling people from there to the country's less-populated southwest. In one experiment, the government forced over 40,000 drought victims to move from Wollo and Shoa provinces 500 miles to Wollega on the southwest border.

Inevitable, sometimes bloody, clashes over resources have occurred between settlers and the Bega already living in Wollega. The Bega have practiced shifting cultivation, leaving some land fallow for regeneration, but the settlers use the fallow land. At the same time, the demand for fuel and building materials for the rising population has hastened deforestation, in turn leading to some climatic changes, damaging the ecological base, and reducing the diversity of plant and animal life.

Population and land pressures in the North mean that planners will continue to consider resettlement as an option. If it is to be a viable alternative, it must be voluntary. Aid must assist the settlers in their new homes and must help host communities such as the Bega expand their opportunities, as compensation for the resource demands of the settlers.

JOHN PRENDERGAST

BERBERS OF NORTH AFRICA

Calling themselves *Imazighen* (Free Men), Berbers live in North Africa in the Sahara desert and the Sahel. Most Berbers are Sunni Muslims, but their religious practices include elements—such as saint worship—that predate the spread of Islam across the region.

A group of 15 million people, Berbers nonetheless basically identify with their tribes; most other forms of identification—including language—differ among and even within tribes. However, Berbers have lost some of their particularism since the independence of the countries in which they live.

Berbers form most of the population in the Western Sahara, 35 percent of the population in Morocco, almost a fourth of the population in Algeria, 20 percent in Mauritania, and fewer than 10 percent in Burkina Faso, Mali, and Libya. As the indigenous group of North Africa, Berbers share oral traditions but have organized no distinct political entity in modern times except for a "state" led by Abd al-Karim al-Khatibi in a struggle against Spain and France in the early twentieth century.

183

Berbers were marginally successful in resisting incorporation into contemporary society until recently, but extensive rural-to-urban migration and the decline of traditional agricultural resources have forced them to adapt. Only one Berber group—the Tamacheq (Tuareg)—remains truly transnational, but government policies in Burkina Faso, Mali, southwest Libya, and Algeria increasingly restrict even their traditional migrations. Algeria in particular has tried to settle its Tamacheq.

The larger communities in which they live will most likely absorb Berbers; arabization policies, changing economic patterns, and the economic power of central governments make self-reliance and distinctiveness difficult. These policies and processes provoke occasional resistance—such as violent demonstrations against Algeria's arabization—but Berbers possess neither the political cohesion nor the economic power to prevent absorption. Only in Morocco, where they still play an important political role, are Berbers likely to maintain a privileged position—as long as the country's political structure isn't altered.

DIEDERIK VANDEWALLE

BIDOON IN KUWAIT

During the Iraqi occupation, bidoon soldiers suffered a disproportionate number of deaths and formed the majority of the prisoners of war.

The bidoon (meaning "without") are a community of up to 200,000 stateless people living on the margins of Kuwaiti society. Some bidoon have nomadic (beduin) ancestry and others are villagers; an unknown number immigrated in recent decades from surrounding countries. They contrast with the 600,000 full Kuwaiti citizens and, prior to August 1990, the 1.2 million foreign workers in Kuwait on temporary permits.

The situation of the bidoon first became an issue in 1959, when the royal family began preparing Kuwait for independence by drafting a constitution and codifying citizenship. Amiri Decree #15 accorded Kuwaiti citizenship only to people and their descendants who had resided in Kuwait prior to 1920 and had maintained residence since then. Many bidoon, not understanding the value of citizenship, failed to register in 1959. Kuwait had made no distinction previously in access to education, health care, and jobs.

In 1970, the Kuwaiti Parliament passed a liberal naturalization law, in large part to regulate the anomalous status of the bidoon, but the citizenship problem escalated. The oil boom attracted many people to Kuwait, and some Iraqis fled to Kuwait in the 1980s to avoid the Iran-Iraq war.

In 1986, Kuwait took a drastic step to reduce the number of bidoon by eliminating their civil identity cards. The government required foreign citizens to produce passports before they could get this identification, which was needed for civilian employment. Bidoon who could produce foreign passports could work, but, ironically, the "real" bidoon lacked passports and could no longer find jobs.

With the elimination of civil IDs:

• bidoon couldn't work in the civil service, banks, or the private sector;

• bidoon couldn't own property or a car, get a driver's license, or obtain certificates of marriage or divorce;

• bidoon children couldn't attend government schools and their access to health care was restricted;

• bidoon could only travel abroad for special medical treatment or for one-way exit;

• bidoon could be deported as aliens if they committed a misdemeanor or a serious crime.

Women had no legal job options, and men were channeled into the lower ranks of the armed forces and police. Their military IDs enabled them to gain access to housing, education, and marriage, but those privileges would be revoked if they left the service. By August 1990, bidoon comprised 95 percent of the army's lower ranks.

Bidoon who didn't join the armed forces or police faced an intolerable situation. To obtain property, they had to have it registered in the name of a Kuwaiti. And yet the bidoon would have no legal recourse if the Kuwaiti "owner" seized that property or goods. Social discrimination increased because their parish status was emphasized by the legal and employment distinctions.

During the Iraqi occupation, from August 1990 through February 1991, bidoon soldiers suffered a disproportionate number of deaths and formed the majority of the prisoners of war. Nonetheless, many Kuwaitis made them the scapegoats for the army's failure to stop the invasion and accused them of aiding Iraq.

In fact, if stopped at an Iraqi checkpoint, bidoon either had no ID or only a military ID, and so Iraqis tried to force them to collaborate. After liberation,

Bidoon Resources:

Lawyers Committee for Human Rights, 330 Seventh Ave., New York, NY 10001.

Kuwaiti Association to Defend War Victims, P.O. Box 2211, Salmiyah, Kuwait.

Middle East Watch, 485 Fifth Ave., New York, NY 10017

bidoon were harassed by Kuwaiti officials and civilians. Returning bidoon POWs were denied the same benefits as the Kuwaiti POWs and lost their military or police jobs.

In May 1991, the Committee to Support the Stateless in Kuwait appealed to foreign human-rights organizations, arguing that the only solution was citizenship. The human-rights committee in the Parliament, elected in October 1992, has begun reviewing citizenship criteria, but powerful vested interests oppose incorporating the bidoon. The number of citizens would rise by nearly one-fourth, diluting the benefits available to citizens and widening the arena of political struggle. The government—and many citizens—prefers to ignore the voiceless bidoon and to pretend they are really foreigners.

ANN M. LESCH

JEWS OF YEMEN

About 1,500 to 2,000 Jews live in three areas in the north of the Republic of Yemen. Descendants of between 1,000 and 3,000 Jews who chose not to emigrate to Israel in 1948, they have synagogues, maintain Torah-Talmud schools, marry other Jews, and own property and vehicles. Men are identified by sidelocks and the lack of a dagger, which most other Yemeni men wear. Many are successful artisans and work in markets with Muslims.

Throughout the 1980s, and probably since, Muslim tribal leaders have guaranteed Jews protected status. International Jewish organizations, among others, visit these communities and provide Hebrew books. Although opinions differ regarding the status of Yemeni Jews, they appear not to be persecuted, to move freely in the country, and be as secure economically as other Yemeni. Those wishing to emigrate do so for economic or kinship reasons.

THOMAS B. STEVENSON

KURDS OF ARMENIA, AZERBAIJAN, IRAN, IRAQ, SYRIA, AND TURKEY

The historic homeland of the Kurds, popularly known as Kurdistan, is a mountainous region extending over parts of Armenia, Azerbaijan, Iran, Iraq, Syria, and Turkey. About 60 percent of the estimated 18 to 22 million Kurds live in Turkey, traditionally in its East. Since 1960 voluntary migration and forced resettlement have resulted in hundreds of thousands of Kurds moving to urban centers in Turkey's West.

About 35 percent of Kurds live in Iran and Iraq, 4 million in the former and 3 million in the latter. Fewer than 5 percent of Kurds live in other countries, including in Europe, which is home to as many as 400,000 Kurdish "guest workers," and Turkmenistan, to which the Soviet Union deported most of the Kurds of Azerbaijan in 1944.

Kurds speak a language that is related to Persian and have cultural traditions that are distinct from those of their Arab and Turkish neighbors. Most Kurds are Muslims and adhere to Sunni Islam. There is also a sizable Shi'ah minority, especially in Iran, as well as Kurdish followers of several Islamic schismatic sects and a few Kurdish Jews.

For more than 50 years, the chauvinistic nationalism promoted by various Arab, Iranian, and Turkish governments tended to alienate, rather than assimilate, Kurds and reinforced aspirations for autonomy or independence. These governments responded to Kurdish demands for political freedom with a panoply of rights abuses, including efforts to suppress Kurdish culture, especially in Turkey prior to 1990 and in Azerbaijan during the Soviet period. Among the assaults on Kurdish culture were official (in Turkey) and de facto (in Iran and Iraq) prohibitions on research and publication about the Kurds. Consequently, little literature is available about one of the world's largest national communities.

The most brutal repression of Kurds occurred in Iraq during the 1980s. An official campaign, code-named Anfal, aimed to eradicate the rural support base for Kurdish resistance movements by destroying whole villages and removing their people to government-controlled compounds. In some cases, the entire populations of villages were killed. An estimated 300,000 Kurds "disappeared" between 1983 and 1988. The campaign included the bombing of Kurdish villages with chemical weapons during 1988. In the most sensational incident, at least 4,000 Kurds died when Iraqi military forces dropped chemical weapons on Halabja in 1988.

Memories of the Anfal prompted a mass exodus of more than 2 million Kurds from northern Iraq after their 1991 rebellion against Saddam Hussein collapsed. Their flight to Iran and Turkey commanded international attention (at least temporarily). Media images of foodless, shelterless women and children trudging through snow-covered mountain passes elicited an outpouring of humanitarian assistance.

This popular sympathy tended to complicate the policies of governments that for years had ignored the repression of Kurds. The United States and some of its European allies, for example, had ignored Kurdish aspirations during the Cold War, preferring to maintain their ties with Turkey, which denied that its Kurdish minority constituted a distinct ethnic group.

In 1991, Turkey's unwillingness to provide security for hundreds of thousands of Kurdish refugees from Iraq prompted the United States, Britain, and France to create a protected zone in Iraqi Kurdistan. Most Kurdish refugees had returned by early 1992, and they have worked since then to create an autonomous region within Iraq. However, Iran, Syria, and Turkey insist that they won't permit Iraqi Kurds to create an independent Kurdish state.

ERIC HOOGLUND

Kurdish Resources:

Badlisy Center for Kurdish Studies, 2413-A Willow Ave., Tallahassee, FL 32303.

Institut Kurd de Paris, 106, Rue LaFayatte, 75040 Paris, France.

Kurdish Human Rights Watch, P.O. Box 1354, Fairfax, VA 22030.

NUBA OF SUDAN

PETER MOSZYNSKI

Nuba woman

There is growing concern for the plight of the Nuba, one of the largest of many non-Arabic speaking indigenous groups in northern Sudan. With a vibrant and distinctive culture, these hill-farmers predate the arrival of their Arab neighbors.

Sudan has been engaged in almost constant internal war since before independence in 1956, when the African south of the country rebelled at the prospect of being ruled by the Arab north. Nuba are caught in the middle of an increasingly vicious civil war.

After suffering decades of government attempts to clothe, Islamicize, and "civilize" them, Nuba now face cultural and perhaps physical elimination. While the current government of Sudan may be prepared to exempt the south of the country from the full rigors of Islamic law, it will allow no such compromise for anyone in the north. Many Nuba have converted to Islam, but still attempt to retain their traditional customs.

Nuba are often moved to "safe" areas in the desert to the north. Large numbers of women and children are living in displaced camps in the deserts of North Kordofan, known as "peace villages," but very few men in evidence: local Nuba suggest that they have "disappeared."

Meanwhile, the government is selling land titles in the Nuba Mountains to absentee landlords and investors in mechanized agriculture. Traditional sustainable farming methods are being replaced by overintensive monocultivation, a very destructive form of agriculture, using displaced Nuba as a pool of cheap labor. Planning Minister Ali el Haj has boasted that 40,000 applica-

Nuba Resource:
Nuba Mountains Solidarity
Abroad, c/o Sudan Update,
BM CPRS, London WCIN
3XX England.

tions have been received for parcels of Nuba land.

As the situation of the Nuba illustrates, the war in Sudan isn't simply between an Arab and Muslim north and an African and Christian south. In both the North and the South, large minorities have been marginalized by successive central governments in Sudan. As ecological pressure threatens northern Sudan, Arabized groups there encroach on the lands with higher rainfall to the south. These groups have formed militias.

Now, as the government and the rebels in the South once again discuss the possibility of a peace settlement, the Nuba and other northern minority groups fear they will lose all their lands and their distinctive culture if they are left as marginal groups in the north of a divided country. Their future will be very bleak indeed, unless the United Nations or other representatives of the international community can gain access to the Nuba Mountains and set up some form of "safe havens."

PETER MOSZYNSKI

NUBIANS IN EGYPT

The High Dam forced resettlement of all Egyptian Nubian villages between Aswan and the Sudan border. By 1963 the Nubians had been relocated in a 12-mile crescent of houses above reclaimed agricultural land east of Kom Ombo, 20 miles north of Aswan. The resettlement population has grown from 50,000 to an estimated 300,000 today, including other Egyptians who have gradually settled among the Nubians. Egyptian schools and Egyptian television have also brought mainstream Egyptian culture to the Nubian settlement. Older customs and lifestyles are no longer possible.

The loss of Nubian languages seems inevitable. Arabic terms are increasingly part of Nubian speech. Most young people use Arabic among themselves. Although related dialects are spoken in the Sudan, Nubian languages may soon disappear in Egypt. Young women, like thousands of men, are finding jobs in cities near the settlement. Many Nubian men work outside the country. Thus far, Egypt hasn't permitted Nubians to formally sell the government-issue homes or agricultural real estate. The number of non-Nubians living in Nubian communities may increase sharply once this becomes possible.

However, a new sense of identity is growing among many Nubians. They see themselves now as descendants of Kush, the black kingdom of ancient Egypt, thus making them related to other African people. There is talk of Nubian political interests, and a new Nubian popular music is performed on national radio and in local concerts. Before the High Dam, Nubian men migrated from isolated villages where most women and children lived and Nubian culture was reproduced; today, in their settlement and in the cities, Egyptian Nubians are forming a self-conscious minority while they gradually lose their ancient cultural heritage.

ROBERT A. FERNEA

187

NUER AND ANUAK OF ETHIOPIA

Surrounded by the mountains, swamps, and deserts of the Lower Omo Valley, one of Africa's few remaining wildernesses, the Bumi, Mursi, Surma, Anuak, and Nuer are largely cut off from the day-to-day affairs of Ethiopia. However, this isolation does not leave them immune to the region's rising ethnic strife.

One of the bloodiest conflicts in Ethiopia today is being waged between the Nuer and Anuak peoples. The regime of Mengistu Haile Mariam armed and favored the Nuer, and thus often led to atrocities against and repression of the Anuak. The Anuaks formed the Gambela People's Liberation Front (GPLF) to protect their interests from the central government and from hostile Nuer militia. After Mengistu's overthrow in 1991, the GPLF massacred large numbers of Nuer militia members and civilians.

Since the most intense fighting in late 1991 and early 1992, the situation has stabilized somewhat, but the potential for conflict remains. If the Sobat Basin in Sudan becomes a target of offensives by that government, thousands of Sudanese Nuers will escape into Ethiopia, exacerbating an already tense situation. The Ethiopian government and the UN High Commissioner for Refugees will be key to preventing a further deterioration of the situation.

JOHN PRENDERGAST

PALESTINIANS IN THE OCCUPIED TERRITORIES

Saharawi Resources:
Minority Rights Group, "Saharawis of Western Sahara."
Task Force, Western Sahara Coordination Office, c/o Barbara Simons MEP, EP 79-113 rue Belliard, B-1040 Brussels, Belgium.

The conflict between Palestinians and Israelis is over land and people. Palestinians have been dispersed since the 1948 war during which the Israeli state was established. At that time, some 770,000 Palestinians fled their land and were not permitted to return. Over 400 of their villages were razed to the ground.

A second exodus came with the 1967 war between Israel and Arab states. Israel deported 200,000 West Bank Palestinians to Jordan and established a military government in the territories it acquired: the West Bank, the Gaza Strip, and East Jerusalem, as well as the Golan Heights and Sinai Peninsula. Since then, the struggle over land and people has intensified in what are known as the Occupied Territories and today threatens the survival of Palestinians as a nation living on their own land.

Palestinians descend from the biblical Canaanites. Like other peoples in the region, they were "Arabized" in the Muslim conquests of the seventh century and retain a distinct Arabic territory, culture, and dialect. Israel hasn't carried out a census since 1967, but there are an estimated 1.8 million Palestinians in the West Bank, 750,000 in the Gaza Strip, and 130,000 in East Jerusalem.

Unlike previous rulers of the region, Israeli policy since 1967 has been to declare ever more land off-limits to Palestinians and to encourage Jews to move to their land. Palestinians in the Gaza Strip have lost control over 45 percent of their land; West Bank Palestinians lack access to 65 percent of theirs. Since the late 1970s, thousands of Jews from Israel and other countries have moved onto Palestinian land. In 1991, over 110 settlements in the West Bank and Gaza Strip housed 110,000 Jewish settlers; 120,000 settlers have moved to high-rises in East Jerusalem.

Palestinians can't build on much of the land they retain, and Israeli authorities often demolish any house built without a license. In addition, the military has destroyed an estimated 120,000 fruit and olive trees since 1987. Olives, olive oil, and citrus fruits are among the mainstays of the Palestinian economy.

The settlers in the Occupied Territories are supported by military legislation, which also criminalizes a host of Palestinian political, economic, and cultural activities. Moreover, the government uses sweeping emergency regulations to demolish homes for punitive reasons and to deport without due process those Palestinians it considers inciters. Thus many Palestinians speak of a "creeping, de facto annexation" of their land and express fears that ultimately they will be subject to "transfer" to other Arab countries, as right-wing Israelis threaten.

Only with the popular uprising—the *intifada*—after December 1987 have

188

Palestinians slowed this creeping annexation by drawing world attention to their plight. They persuaded the U.S. government, which helped bankroll Israeli settlements, that a solution to the Palestinian-Israeli conflict must be found. Direct peace negotiations began in 1991, and a new Labor government froze new settlement construction in 1992.

In the absence of a peace agreement, however, settlers continue to move to the Occupied Territories; deportations and other punitive measures against civilians proceed unabated. The Palestinian nation continues to be fragmented and dispersed.

JOOST R. HILTERMANN

SAHARAWIS OF THE WESTERN SAHARA

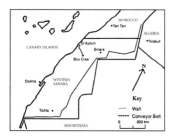

Key
— Wall
••••• Conveyor Belt
0   200 km

The home of the Saharawis is the former Spanish colony of Western Sahara, but since 1975 they have been a people divided, with some living in refugee camps in the harsh desert of southwest Algeria, others living in liberated areas of the Western Sahara, and the remainder living in their land under a brutal and illegal Moroccan occupation.

The current Western Sahara roughly corresponds to the land of the *ahel es-Sahel*, the people of the coastal Sahel. Nomadic pastoralism was the basis of the society and economy. Spanish colonialism (1884-1976) and Saharawi society were transformed with the 1962 discovery of vast phosphate reserves at Bou-Craa. Urban employment grew and by 1974 over half of Saharawis lived in the three main towns. Some family members abandoned nomadic pastoralism, a change reinforced by severe droughts from 1959 to 1963 and 1966 to 1974.

The Saharawis consistently resisted exploitation and in 1973 established the liberation organization known by its acronym POLISARIO. Colonial rule ended in 1976, but instead of transferring power to an independent Saharawi state Spain ceded the northern two-thirds of the Western Sahara to Morocco and the rest to Mauritania. In 1976, the POLISARIO declared the Saharawi Arab Democratic Republic; the state is now a member of the Organization of African Unity and is recognized by 76 countries.

The Saharawi government is one that has yet to control all its land. Despite a string of UN resolutions after 1966, the Saharawis were denied their right to self-determination. War broke out, and many Saharawis fled to southwest Algeria near Tindouf, where refugee camps were established. About 200,000 refugees remain there today.

After a brutal war, Mauritania sued for peace in 1979. Morocco, with increasing Western support, began to occupy more and more of the Western Sahara. The POLISARIO continues to control part of the territory.

After much negotiation and following resolutions in 1990 and 1991, the United Nations launched a peace plan that included a free and fair referendum. A UN peacekeeping force was deployed and a cease-fire started in September 1991, but the referendum, scheduled for December 1991, has not been held. Morocco has repeatedly violated the cease-fire and has blocked progress on the peace plan. Arrests, harassment, and "disappearances" continue in the Moroccan-occupied Western Sahara.

ANDY RUTHERFORD

189

SIDAMA OF ETHIOPIA

The Sidama include many peoples of southern Ethiopia, including the Alaba, Bako, Gibe, Gimira, Janjero, Kafa, Kambata, Maji, Ometo, Tambaro, Walamo, and others. As far back as Emperor Menelik's time in the first decade of this century, the Ethiopian state has forcibly annexed the Sidama. Their lands and those of the Oromo formed the economic base of the Ethiopian Empire, and land-hungry settlers from the north and central parts of the country seized the best property. Lands that had produced a wide variety of crops for the Sidama now yield only coffee.

Beginning in the 1960s, liberation movements in the region have aimed toward self-determination. In the 1980s, the Sidama Liberation Front sought national independence, identifying the Sidama as a conquered and colonized nation.

Today the Sidama still want to liberate their land and labor from state control. The government that deposed Mengistu Haile Mariam in 1991 has promised self-determination and decentralization along ethnic and regional lines. If the government carries through on this promise, matters could improve dramatically for Sidama communities, raising the possibility of self-government and the restoration of local control over resources.

JOHN PRENDERGAST

TAMACHEQ OF MALI

Focusing more on the needs and biases of development planners and the international market than on herders, the government of Mali consistently favors sedentary agriculture over nomadic herding.

In the early 1970s and the 1980s, severe drought forced hundreds of thousands of Tamacheq nomadic herders of northern Mali to abandon their traditional migratory routes. Most Tamacheq (who are also known as the Tuareg) fled to urban centers or neighboring countries for food and employment; others settled not far from home and hoped to attract food relief and development assistance.

In 1990, a rebellion instigated by a militant Tamacheq faction led to civil war and a second wave of displacement. This time, inter-ethnic hostilities and an oppressive military response forced urban and settlement Tamacheq either into hiding or to seek protection in overcrowded refugee camps in Algeria and Mauritania. These displacements are but the most recent in a pattern of abuses that began under the former colonial administration.

Focusing more on the needs and biases of development planners and the international market than on herders, the government of Mali consistently favors sedentary agriculture over nomadic herding. For example, there were numerous failed attempts between the 1940s and the 1970s to increase milk and meat production through privatizing pastures and creating Western-style ranches. Environmental incompatibility and desertification resulted.

As political stability and favorable rains return, Tamacheq are attempting to determine how and in what capacity they will return to their homelands. The threat of recurring drought and restrictions on migration due to occupied lands, combined with diminished livestock productivity, indicate a need for a new direction. Within the settlements, many established in the last 10 years, community organizations have been collaborating with foreign and indigenous development organizations. The objective is to work toward a more drought-resistant and diversified economy that is synchronized with other economic activities and ethnic groups in the region.

LARRY CHILDS

190

Although European societies have frequently trumpeted their tolerance for minorities, recent events demonstrate all too clearly the inflammability of hatreds old and new. The savage slaughter of Muslims in Bosnia, the harassment of Roma (Gypsies) across the continent, the vandalism of Jewish cemeteries in France, and several cases of language suppression at least at the level of petty officialdom all attest to attitudes and practices that recall—and threaten at times to reproduce—repressions of earlier periods.

At the same time, immigrant groups face increasing bitterness, as in debates over whether Sikhs in Great Britain should be allowed to wear turbans with their work uniforms or whether North African Muslim girls in France could wear head kerchiefs to school. Meanwhile, legal theory and practice often underscore the ambiguous identity and patriotism of members of religious groups, like Jehovah's Witnesses in Greece, that reject military service or the wearing of secular uniforms. In most cases, such conflicts, while born of postcolonial and postmodern conditions, reproduce many of the features of older battles over exclusion and inclusion.

These features reproduce the post-Enlightenment premise of a collective European identity. Whether through linguistic homogenization as a basis of building or reconstructing nation-states—as in post-Revolutionary France or post-Independence Italy—or through the attempt to create ethnically homogenized nation-states—as in the Balkans—most European nationalisms rested on the presupposition that all Europeans were intellectually and culturally superior. What made them so was their capacity for internal differentiation—"national genius," "individualism," etc., which was conceptually contrasted with the supposed inability of other peoples to act with inventiveness or originality. Colonialism rein-

forced this ideology, which superficially resolved an apparent paradox: while European states claimed to be culturally homogeneous, local cultures often maintained strong identities and even nurtured political separatism.

However, tolerance of internal difference among local European populations varied enormously and often entailed assessments of the degree to which specific groups were accepted as "genuinely" European. The nomadic lifestyle and distinctive appearance of the Roma, for example, were not accepted. Instead, the Roma were treated as both out of place and unclassifiable in terms of residence, an unpardonable sin in a world organized according to the cultural logic of bureaucracy.

Even whole sedentary regional peoples can fall afoul of such categorical resentments. Northern Italian hostility to the Mezzogiorno, now embodied in openly racist political action, feeds on stereotypes of an "African" heritage. Even in the immediate afterglow of reunification, many West Germans sneered at "Ossies" as lazy and unintelligent "Slavs," while the economically depressed eastern part of the country has proved especially fertile ground for racist sentiment largely directed against non-German immigrant workers (notably Turks).

Despite claims to the contrary, European bureaucratic nationalism does not embody a transcendent rationality, but rather must be seen as a manipulable symbolic system of inclusion and exclusion. Only thus is it possible to avoid the constraints of that European exclusivism whose practical expressions are the prejudices and repressions documented here. Viewed in this way, European exclusivism—both in a pan-European sense and at the national level—is clearly laden with ideas that, while they are presented as grounded in universal principles of logic, actually derive from local ways of symbolizing identity.

Especially durable in this regard has been the ideology of "blood." Consider the Bosnian tragedy, in which Muslim women sometimes kill the children conceived as a result of their rape by Serbian soldiers. In the view of the women, the

WILLIAM G. LOCKWOOD

Encampment of Muslim Roma from Bosnia at Rome, Italy

192

logic of patrilineal descent apparently makes the children members of the enemy's "blood line." This tragedy shares remarkable similarities with recurrent resuscitations of Indo-European concepts of the blood line in Nazi ideology and in various European incarnations of the eugenics movement, which has often played an insidious role in pseudoscientific defenses of restrictive immigration laws.

Such ideas have certainly not died. Even in

the absence of significant Jewish populations, for example, Poland, Romania, and other countries are hosting renewed bouts of anti-Semitism, doubtless fueled by economic and social stress. In Russia, the open expression of anti-Semitic sentiments has occasioned widespread concern. The absence of a large target population does not diminish concern, since the progressive erasure of any cultural and ethnic difference leads to a generalized contempt for, and identification of, "outsiders."

Stereotyping is not always consistent. In Greece, where sympathy for Jews afforded many of them generous protection from the Nazis—a sympathy that has not been fully eroded by more recent support for the Palestinian cause—issues of linguistic and cultural identity seriously plague Slavo-Macedonians. On the other side of the border, this situation is further exacerbated by the Macedonian government's territorial expansionism and ethnic nationalism, stances that also threaten the status of ethnic Albanians both there (about 40 percent of the population) and in Serbian-controlled Kosovo (about 90 percent of the population).

A constant source of ethnic tension lies in the dynamics of frontiers. Even in countries with histories of relative tolerance toward minorities, the presence of a significant minority with ethnic ties across contested borders is often the catalyst for repression or harassment. The status of ethnic Hungarians in Romania is a case in point.

This issue is especially sensitive in the Balkans and the former Soviet Union, where once coexistent minorities are now in a state of war with one another. Until recently, the Sarakatsani, Vlach, Pomak, Albanian-speaking groups, and other migrant agricultural communities that once had relied on freedom of passage across what became sealed borders found themselves dispossessed of a major element of their cultural identity—their mode of subsistence. But today, even with relative freedom of travel restored, these groups have long since lost an important component of their ability to survive as cultural entities. In the Balkans, especially, scholarly disciplines such as philology and folklore have long served to help create "national" identities while denying the cultural affinities of minority peoples with communities in other nation-states.

Even where repression has abated, as in the case of the Basques or the Bretons, other factors threaten cultural survival. Assimilationist tactics and the political predominance of a majority language serve the interests of central governments, even if a degree of regional autonomy exists on paper.

On the other hand, in the Basque case, and in Brittany, Eire, and Wales, attempts to revive a language thought to be in decline can also result in excessive purism and localized repression. While the Corsican language fights for recognition, its local variants increasingly merge into a standardized form; much the same can be said of Catalan. On Cyprus, the future of the local language—treated for political reasons as a "dialect" of Greek—must contend with the official use of standard Greek, while its previous currency among Muslims has been radically eroded by the latter's identification by both sides of the conflict as "Turks."

Extremely small groups, such as the Jewish community of Yannina in Greece, the "secret Jews" of Portugal, or the Maronites of Cyprus, face special challenges to their distinctive identities either through emigration or through absorption into the host country's majority culture. Pockets of isolated groups with known connections elsewhere—the Saxons of Romania, for example—may have more cultural resources for maintaining a separate identity but face active discrimination precisely for that reason.

The future for minorities in Europe is unclear. The European Community appears committed to defending local cultures, raising the prospect that unification may coexist with increasing reinforcement of local identities. The European Court has already challenged in some instances the repression of minority populations and religions. On the other hand, the rise of fascist movements in several countries—skinhead violence in Germany and the inflammatory rhetoric of Jean-Marie Le Pen in France are notable flashpoints—combine with post-communist disintegration and ethnic nationalism to raise a terrifying specter of "ethnic cleansing" throughout large sections of the continent. The term itself points up the symbolic as opposed to rational character of current events.

The very assumption that Europe is somehow "above" such things is itself an expression of the premise of European superiority, a superiority that more powerful groups apportion according to their own preferences. It is also an echo of the widespread pre-World War II refusal to contemplate the unimaginable—which then took place.

MICHAEL HERZFELD

193

ASHKENAZIC JEWS IN FRANCE

Ashkenazic Jews have been immigrating to France from various Central and Eastern European countries since the late nineteenth century. About 250,000 to 300,000 now live in France, including descendants of the ancient Alsatian Jewish community, whose members received French citizenship soon after the 1789 revolution.

Decimated by deportation and genocide under the Nazi occupation during World War II, France's Ashkenazic Jewish community today lacks generational depth. Family memories remain shattered. Although Ashkenazic Jews have integrated into French society, culture, politics, and economic system, the trauma of the genocide was long a taboo subject in French public discourse. In 1993, President François Mitterrand officially designated July 16 as a national day of remembrance for victims of racism and anti-Semitism. The decision represents a major symbolic event, recognizing the active collaboration of French authorities in the genocide of the Jews.

JOËLLE BAHLOUL

ABKHAZIANS OF GEORGIA

Abkhazian Resources:
Unrepresented Nations and Peoples Organization, San Francisco Coordination Office, 347 Doloros St., Suite 206, San Francisco, CA 94110 (415)626-0995; fax: (415)626-0865.
Abkhazian-American Human Rights Committee, 268 Derrom Ave., Paterson, NJ 07504.

Abkhazians are among the first people known to have settled on the rich seacoast and farmlands bordering the Black Sea in the former Soviet Union. Mentioned by Pliny Major in the first century A.D., Abkhazian history and culture were affected by the domination of Greeks, Romans, Turks, Russians, and Georgians. Today, this distinct Caucasian ethnic group, with a population of 90,000, is on the verge of extinction.

Under the Soviet state, Abkhazians governed their own republic until Stalin and Beria (both from Georgia) changed that status in 1931 and designated Abkhazia an autonomous republic of Georgia. For all practical purposes, Georgia then administered Abkhazian affairs until the collapse of the Soviet Union. In just a few decades, Abkhazians had dwindled to 17 percent of the population on their ancestral lands, primarily due to Stalin-era mass deportations, executions, and programs to settle Georgians on their territory.

Since Georgia's separation from the Soviet Union, its leaders have tried to incorporate the Abkhazian Autonomous Republic into a unitary Georgian state. Abkhazians and all the other minorities in Abkhazia, who together constitute a narrow majority, have resisted. In response to moves to "Georgianize" Abkhazia—all too reminiscent of the Stalin era's bans on the Abkhazian language and cultural institutions—Abkhazia declared its sovereignty and attempted to negotiate a federal relationship with Georgia.

On August 14, 1992, the Georgian government moved troops into Abkhazia. Since then, Georgian forces have terrorized Abkhazian civilians. Georgians have pillaged or destroyed every Abkhazian cultural institution in the Abkhazian capital of Sukhumi, including its history archives and museum. The primary sources of Abkhazian history and culture no longer exist.

Convulsions such as this one in the mini-empires of the old Soviet Union derive largely from trampled minority rights. Governments and citizens of other countries can help by refusing to tolerate the use of force against minorities and by offering to help shape equitable pluralistic states.

PAULA GARB

BALTICS

Estonia, Latvia, and Lithuania regained their independence soon after the dissolution of the Soviet Union in 1991. They had been independent in the period between the two world wars, until 1939, when Hitler and Stalin signed a secret pact effectively placing the Baltics in the Soviet sphere of influence.

Under Soviet occupation, the Baltic population suffered heavy losses due to flight, war casualties, deportation, and the execution of political prisoners. The Sovietization of political, economic, and social structures brought in many non-native (mainly Russian) officials and workers. By 1989, ethnic Estonians and Latvians barely comprised a majority in their republics. Lithuania fared better, maintaining 80 percent of the population. These figures have improved slightly since 1991 as some Russians have left.

All three Baltic nations are in the process of restructuring their political, economic, industrial, medical, and educational systems. Success in the transition largely depends upon economic, political, and humanitarian aid and expertise from the West. Improved economic conditions in the Baltics will help curb "brain drain" to the West, decrease mortality, and increase birth rates.

Russia presents another potential threat to the people of the Baltics. The sensitive issues in negotiation with Russia include borders, natural resources, the rights of Russians living in the Baltics, and the continuing presence of the Russian military. Many Balts feel that political and economic stability in Russia will ensure Baltic freedom, but if conservatives regain power in Russia, the Baltic nations could be vulnerable to military intervention. That makes international recognition and support for the Baltic states vital for the survival of Baltic societies.

SUZANNE L. MULLIN

Baltic Resources:
Association for the Advancement of Baltic Studies, 111 Knob Hill Rd., Hackettstown, NJ 07840.
Soros Foundation, 888 Seventh Ave, Suite 1901, New York, NY 10106.

BASQUES OF SPAIN

Together with Catalans and Galicians, Basques make up the three "historic" ethnolinguistic minorities of the Iberian peninsula. Located in the western Pyrenees, the Basques have a unique and ancient cultural heritage and language that distinguish them from surrounding Castilian and French speakers. They also have one of the most active popular cultural movements in Western Europe today.

Nationalism and separatist sentiment have been a part of Basque life since the late nineteenth century. The victory of the fascist Franco regime in the Spanish Civil War in the 1930s inaugurated the darkest period for Spanish Basques. For over three decades, Spain virulently repressed political dissent and all public expressions of Basque language and culture. Particularly in the 1970s, police took advantage of "antiterrorist" laws to systematically arrest and torture individuals suspected of sympathizing with the underground Basque independence movement.

Spain's transition to democracy since Franco's death has improved the situation for Spanish Basques. The plight of political prisoners continues unresolved, but the worst abuses of police power have ceased. Basque nationalist political parties are now legal, and, since 1979, Spanish Basques have enjoyed limited self-rule.

Perhaps the greatest threat to Basque cultural survival is the erosion of Euskara, their unique non-Indo-European language. Compared to Catalonia or Galicia, where most native residents still speak the indigenous language, the percentage of Basque speakers has declined drastically and hovers at about 30 percent of the population today compared to 90 percent a century ago.

Basque Resources:
Robert Clark, *The Basques: The Franco Years and Beyond*, University of Nevada Press, 1979.
For publications on the status of the Basque language, write the Servicio Central de Publicaciones del Gobierno Vasco, Duque de Wellington, 2, 01011 Vitoria/Gasteiz, Spain.
For information on activities to protect the rights of linguistic minorities in the European Community, contact European Bureau of Lesser Used Languages, 10 Sráid Haiste Iocht, Baile Atha Cliath 2, Ireland.

195

Since the 1960s, popular interest and mobilizations have aimed at turning those numbers around. In Spain, Euskara is now an official language alongside Spanish, and the autonomous Basque government and various independent cultural organizations are helping introduce it into the educational system, media, and public administration. These efforts have made some headway, but much more needs to be done to gain the support of the private sector, especially the entertainment industry and other businesses.

While the future of Euskara is unclear, the European Parliament, via the European Bureau of Lesser Used Languages, is taking steps to establish general guidelines to protect the rights of linguistic minorities. As yet, there are no means for enforcing compliance.

JACQUELINE URLA

CELTS OF THE BRITISH ISLES

"We do not wish to break existing nations up, but we also do not wish to become assimilated into a culture, language, or lifestyle that is not ours. We are specific peoples, regardless that we do not have an independent state. This must be accepted.

Lars Emil Johansen, Greenland Government
Presentation at the United Nations, December 9-10, 1992

The term Celts refers to speakers of the language family shared by the inhabitants of the British Isles at the time of the Viking and Norman conquests a millennium and more ago. Today the term has lost much of its original meaning owing to English domination and capitalist modernization.

Linguistically and historically, the Celtic regions of the British Isles include Ireland, Wales, and the Highlands and islands of Scotland, as well as Cornwall and the Isle of Man. With each generation, fewer people speak the Celtic languages of Welsh and Irish and Scottish Gaelic; Cornish and Manx are virtually extinct. Issues of cultural survival are most acute for Celts in Scotland and Wales.

Attempts to promote nationalist consciousness and ethnic distinctiveness can be seen in Welsh-language television and radio (about 20 percent of the population of Wales speaks Welsh), as well as in the program of Plaid Cymru, the Welsh Nationalist Party. In Scotland, only about 80,000 people (1.6 percent of the population) speak Gaelic. Here Celtic identity is identified exclusively with the Highlands and islands, which the more prosperous Lowlanders and Anglicized landholders denigrate as backward.

Language is only one side of the picture. Divisions of economic power play themselves out as well. The Celtic regions of both Wales and Scotland are beautiful but poor and sparsely populated. Soils are ill-suited to cultivation. Regional economies depend heavily on sheep farming and extractive industries—mining, fishing, forestry, and, recently, offshore oil.

The loss of control over resources to absentee owners and multinational corporations is a point of contention. The fortunes of the Scottish National Party rose with its advocacy of Scottish control of oil production. When London blocked that in the late 1970s, the SNP turned part of its focus to preserving crofting, the rural way of life in the Highlands and islands. Crofters combine subsistence tenant farming with fishing, weaving, bed-and-breakfast tourism, and other sources of income. Crofter tenancy has been protected by law since 1886, but since 1976 people have been able to buy their crofts. However, ownership may threaten Celtic culture by creating class divisions within communities.

Many people in Scotland and Wales see themselves as part of a "fringe," an underdeveloped periphery created by centuries of English domination. Although not everyone in the marginal regions calls themselves Celtic, this is sometimes called the "Celtic Fringe." In the Highlands and islands of Scotland, "Celticness" is a metaphor for a way of life at odds with British urbanism and industrialization.

The consequences of marginality range from the actual demise of communities to inadequate health and educational facilities. Perhaps the most famous case is that of St. Kilda, an island west of the Outer Hebrides. The St. Kildan crofters were forced to move to the mainland in 1930 after London decided that the cost of providing social services to this remote place was too high.

Depopulation—due to lack of local jobs or affordable housing and to perceived opportunities elsewhere—is perhaps the greatest threat to the survival of a Celtic culture. While the global recession may actually slow some forces of "modernization," an expanding European Community is likely to increase economic polarization through a more tightly structured division of labor. This would make it harder for rural people to preserve their way of life.

JANE NADEL-KLEIN

CORSICA

Corsica Resource:
Unione di U Populu Corsu, B.P. 177, 20288 Bastia, France. Its 1992 publication *Autonomia* costs 60F.

The Mediterranean island of Corsica, which is part of France, has a population of about 280,000, over half of which is clustered around Bastia and Ajaccio. Geographic isolation and a history of government neglect have disadvantaged the island both economically and culturally. By the turn of this century, no alternatives to subsistence agriculture and small-scale pastoralism had been promoted on the island. The Corsican diaspora began, stripping the villages in the mountainous interior of their populations.

The flight to continental France for work and education had serious repercussions for Corsican culture and language. Today, the language is in significant danger. The economy, concentrated in tourism and services, is extremely fragile and threatened by both the specter of international property speculation for tourism and economic harmonization in the European Community, which will reduce or eliminate tax and transportation advantages that partially compensate for the island's isolation.

Cultural rights, too, are at risk. France's Constitutional Council declared the formal recognition of the "Corsican People" unconstitutional, and France refuses to sign the European Convention for Regional or Minority Languages.

France must give Corsica the same recognition extended to other European autonomous regions. In addition, it should shield Corsica (at least temporarily) from European Community policies that could damage this peripheral region. In short, Corsica needs the economic and political resources to sustain its population, language, and culture.

ALEXANDRA JAFFE

197

MARONITES AND ARMENIAN CYPRIOTS

Maronites and Armenian Cypriots, the two smaller minorities of Cyprus, each constitute about a half percent of the population. The major threat to both, as well as to the Greek Cypriot majority, comes from 30,000 or so Turkish troops in the occupied north of the country.

Although hostilities ceased in 1974, the occupying army denies Armenians and Maronites, as well as Greeks, access to their villages and properties in the north. The United Nations has made repeated attempts to resolve the Cyprus problem, but it has found it impossible to overcome Turkish intransigence. Talks at the United Nations in 1992 ended in a stalemate.

Prior to 1974, most Maronites lived in villages in the north. When Turkey invaded in 1974, Maronites, like Armenians and Greeks in the north, were forced to move to the south, becoming refugees in their own country.

VASSOS ARGYROU

IBERIAN CRYPTO-JEWS

Most Iberian Crypto-Jews live in eastern Portugal, although some may live in Mallorca. These scattered groups are the vestiges of a once-thriving Jewish society. Beginning in the fifteenth century, Jews became subject to increasingly discriminatory laws, expulsion—from Spain in 1492, Portugal in 1496—and, finally, forced to convert to Christianity.

Crypto-Jewish communities came into existence as Jews began observing their religion in secret. This practice became perilous when the Inquisition began to hunt down Jews who hadn't accepted conversion. Over the next centuries, the terror of the Inquisition made these communities ever more secretive.

Jewish fears abated in the 1920s when Iberia's fledgling republics promised religious freedom. People began declaring their religion publicly, and institutions were set up to help them. But the Franco and Salazar regimes and their support of the Catholic backlash against the Crypto-Jews crushed this tentative opening.

Today, with Iberian democracy and religious freedom apparently firmly rooted, Crypto-Jewish communities are again coming forward. Now, however, the threat comes from tourists, missionaries, and publicists drawn to this dramatic history. Particularly distressing—to both the Jews and their Catholic neighbors—are writers and filmmakers who promise scholarly portrayals but produce sensationalist copy for the popular media. These works inevitably make their way back to the community and cause much distress. This kind of attention threatens these people's rights to emerge publicly in their own way and time and to maintain amicable relations with their neighbors.

ROBERT ROY REED

MACEDONIA

After the Balkan Wars in 1913, the region known as Macedonia was divided among Serbia (later Yugoslavia), Bulgaria, and Greece. Since the establishment of the Peoples Republic of Macedonia as one of six Yugoslav republics at the end of World War II, the existence of a distinct Macedonian nationality, language, and culture has been recognized virtually everywhere in the world—except in Bulgaria and Greece.

Nevertheless, the Republic of Macedonia failed to receive widespread international recognition as a political entity when it declared its independence in 1991 because Greece insists that only Greeks, not Slavs, have the right to call themselves Macedonians.

The survival of Macedonian minority culture in northern Greece and southwestern Bulgaria is threatened because these countries deny that any such minority exists within their borders. In both countries, long-standing policies of discrimination and assimilation ban the use of the Macedonian language (a South Slavic language) in schools, church services, and newspapers, radio, and television. Macedonian cultural organizations, such as Ilinden in Bulgaria and the Center for Macedonian Culture in Greece, cannot register because they are said to be separatist and a threat to national security.

Macedonian activists from both countries have been harassed and persecuted for traveling to meetings of the Conference for Security and Cooperation in Europe to protest violations of their rights. On such occasions, they have formed part of international delegations that included Macedonian representatives from Greece, Bulgaria, Albania (which also has a small Macedonian minority), and the Republic of Macedonia, as well as from Macedonian diaspora communities in Canada and Australia.

Macedonian Resources:
Country Reports on Human
Rights Practices for Greece
and Bulgaria, United States
Department of State, 1990
and 1991.
Macedonian-Canadian Human
Rights Committee, P.O. Box
99504, 1095 O'Connor Dr.,
Toronto, Ontario, M4B3N1,
Canada.

In Greece, the Central Organizing Committee for Macedonian Human Rights, formed in 1984, seeks to overturn two specific laws. One denies the validity of university studies undertaken in the Macedonian language; the other covers the rights of political refugees who fled Greece after a civil war in 1949. Only refugees "of Greek descent" can return to Greece and reclaim their confiscated property. The committee has also protested the fact that Greece may deny entry to Greek-born Macedonians who live abroad and have been active in Macedonian organizations.

To insure the survival of Macedonian culture in Greece and Bulgaria, the governments of these two countries must be persuaded to protect the rights of Macedonians and other minorities, including the right to preserve and develop their language, identity, and culture. These rights are specified in such international agreements as the June 1990 Document of the Copenhagen Meeting of the Conference on the Human Dimension of the Conference for Security and Cooperation in Europe.

LORING M. DANFORTH

POLAND

Historically multiethnic and multireligious and the homeland of much of the world's Jewry, Poland is now 95 percent Polish Catholic due to the Nazis' mass extermination of Jews and to the shifting borders and mass deportations following World War II.

The primary ethnic minorities are Germans, Byelorussians, Ukrainians, and Lithuanians, as well as Polish Gypsies. In addition, the collapse of communism encouraged a mass influx of Romanian Gypsies who lack legal status and hence lack basic human rights. Except for Gypsies, all groups live predominantly in mixed settlements, with bireligious and bilingual families common.

Individual minorities sometimes are the object of local antagonism, but thus far any tensions have been confined to the local level. Since 1991, the Polish government has signed treaties of cooperation with Germany, Ukraine, Belarus, and Lithuania (in progress) that include provisions to guarantee the rights of these minorities.

Anti-Semitic epithets surface periodically. These tend to refer to stereotypes rather than to actual relations among non-Jewish Poles and the very few remaining Jewish Poles, who are assimilated into the general population and are seldom the individual targets of anti-Semitism.

The Polish Catholic Church aspires to have the country's domestic and foreign policies reflect the views of its hierarchy. Already enacted is Church-initiated legislation banning abortion and mandating Catholic instruction in the public schools. Not only Poland's minorities but many Catholics as well are displeased with this role for the Church.

JANINE R. WEDEL

POMAKS/ BULGARIAN MUSLIMS

The term Pomak refers to Bulgarians who converted to Islam during the Ottoman period while continuing to speak Bulgarian. Of at least 400,000 Pomaks, perhaps 250,000 live in southeast Bulgaria. Others live in Greece and Turkey, and a related group, Torbeshi (Macedonian-speaking Muslims), live in Macedonia. Pomak culture blends Muslim, Christian, and pre-Christian elements to preserve some of the oldest layers of Balkan culture, including patrilineal extended families and folk rituals.

From 1944 to 1989, the communist government severely curtailed Pomak ethnic rights as part of a campaign of "Bulgarization." In the late 1960s, it forced Pomaks to assume Slavic names, closed mosques, and banned circumcision and Pomak clothing and music. Pomaks were subject to government harassment at home and at work. Those who refused to comply lost their jobs, were imprisoned, or were even tortured or killed.

The campaign drove Pomak culture and ethnic identity underground, but it survived. Since 1989, Pomak culture—religion, music, costume, and self-identity—has revived. Yet, after being forced to assimilate for a generation, many Pomaks do not readily identify themselves as such.

At the same time, Pomak culture now faces the danger of being assimilated into Bulgarian Turkish culture. Bulgarian Turks, who are much more numerous and better organized than Pomaks, speak Turkish and are ethnic Turks. The Movement for Rights and Freedoms—the so-called Turkish Party—has emerged as a viable representative for Bulgarian Turks, and hopefully for Pomaks as well.

CAROL SILVERMAN

ROMA

The worst-abused people in Europe are the Roma (or Gypsies—a term many consider pejorative). Roma have been endangered, both culturally and individually, since soon after their arrival in Europe from India some 900 years ago. The Nazis butchered some half million Roma, the only people other than Jews scheduled for genocide on the basis of race. Now Roma appear to be facing another period of intensified repression in Eastern Europe's newly independent states.

There is no accurate census of Roma in Europe, but the best estimate seems to be five to six million, roughly half the total number outside India. Some two-thirds live in Eastern Europe, with another concentration in Spain. Despite stereotypes, most Roma have been sedentary since soon after their ancestors came to Europe. Many Roma speak a language closely related to modern Hindi, but it is divided into many dialects.

During the Cold War, clear differences developed between Eastern and Western Europe in terms of conditions for Roma. In the West, general discrimination continued but there was no strong effort to force radical cultural change. Prohibitive regulations and the decreasing availability of campsites made a traveling lifestyle increasingly difficult.

Though all Eastern European regimes were committed to assisting under-developed groups, most sought to accomplish this through forced assimilation. Every communist regime in Eastern Europe except Yugoslavia's made a nomadic lifestyle illegal. Romania, with one of the largest Roman populations, refused to recognize Roma as a distinct ethnic group.

"Democratization" in Eastern Europe has created an even worse situation as nationalism has often translated into xenophobia. For example, in June 1992, 200 people in Romania set fire to a Romani hamlet. The Ethnic Federation of Roma in Romania, in a formal complaint, enumerated 24

Roma Resource:
International Romani Union,
U.S. Office, Manchaca, TX
78652.

attacks during the first half of 1991 alone. Events such as these have taken place in every Eastern European state.

The disintegration of explicitly multicultural Yugoslavia has been a particularly heavy blow. Yugoslavia had provided a model for both East and West in its treatment of Romani citizens. In 1981, Yugoslavia granted Roma nationality status, thereby giving them the same constitutional rights as other minorities. Routes of upward mobility and integration were provided for those Roma who sought these. Today, however, Yugoslav Roma—the largest population in Europe—are suffering from a particularly virulent form of the same persecution that nationalism has meant elsewhere in Eastern Europe.

Roma throughout Europe have organized since World War II. In the West, groups usually have formed to struggle for civil rights. In the East, where explicitly political organizing was impossible, Romani groups had worked to preserve their linguistic and cultural heritage. With the advent of democratic systems in Eastern Europe, Roma began forming a variety of political parties, including at least seven in Romania. These parties tend to ally with major political parties, a strategy that has resulted in several Roma representatives in most Eastern European governments.

Standardization of language is a primary task that leaders of the Roman movement have set themselves, but this is only indicative of the even greater problem of unifying a dispersed and highly differentiated people. In 1971, the first World Romani Congress was held, and delegates agreed to use the term Roma to describe themselves, adopted a flag and the slogan *Opre Roma!* (Roma Arise!), and established commissions for social affairs, education, war crimes, language, and culture. Out of this grew the International Romani Union, an association of over 70 organizations in 28 countries. Three subsequent world congresses have been held.

WILLIAM G. LOCKWOOD

SAAMI OF SCANDINAVIA

Area of traditional Saami settlement in the 1900s

Southern limit of year-round reindeer herding

0   200   400 km

Formerly called Lapps, Saami reside in four countries, interspersed with Scandinavians (Norwegians and Swedes), Finns, and Russians. Most Saami share the occupations of others in their Arctic and sub-Arctic regions, including fishing and farming, but a visible minority of this minority herd reindeer. Altogether, perhaps 40,000 self-described Saami live in Norway, 15,000 in Sweden, 4,000 in Finland, and fewer than 2,000 in Russia. About two-thirds of these 60,000 people speak Saami (a Finno-Ugric language). On average, these Saami constitute 1 percent of the population in their respective nation-states. Only in a few homogeneous areas and in recent years have public schools featured Saami-language instruction.

Incursions on indigenous Saami rights to use land and water intensified in the seventeenth century when colonization, missionaries, forced acculturation, taxation, trade, and plunder by outsiders increased in proportion to geographic accessibility, territorial competition among northern European nation-states, and the attraction of such Arctic resources as furs, forests, and ores. All these trends were amplified by population pressure from the south and the introduction of firearms. Another dramatic turning point came with the expansion of hydroelectric power after World War II.

Most recently, the 1986 nuclear disaster at Chernobyl disproportionately affected Saami regions. Until Chernobyl, debates over Saami rights pivoted on the phrase "land and water," with the greatest concern voiced on behalf of Saami engaged in reindeer herding and husbandry, even though virtually

201

Saami Resources:

Saami Institute, 9520 Guov'dageai'dno, Norway.

Myrdene Anderson, "Transformations of Center and Periphery for the Saami in Norway," *Anthropologica*, 1987.

Hugh Beach, "Perceptions of Risk, Dilemmas of Policy: Nuclear Fallout in Swedish Lapland," *Social Science and Medicine*, 1990.

Hugh Beach, Myrdene Anderson, and Pekka Aikio, "Dynamics of Saami Territoriality Within the Nation-States of Norway, Sweden and Finland," in *Pastoral Nomad Territoriality*, Berg Publishers, 1991.

Robert Paine, *Dam a River, Damn a People: Saami (Lapp) Livelihood and the Alta/Kautokeino Hydroelectric Project and the Norwegian Parliament*, International Work Group for Indigenous Affairs, 1982.

The Saami People and Human Rights, Charta 79 and Affiliated Interest Groups.

all Saami into the twentieth century relied on primary subsistence activities and hence suffered from colonial settlements and resource extraction. Since Chernobyl, notions of indigenous rights to land and water have expanded to encompass, as it were, air, reflecting the less-visible radioactive contamination of the food chain.

Although Saami and others have responded with alarm to the fallout from Chernobyl, and before that from Soviet atomic bomb testing in Siberia, government-established safety thresholds for ingesting contaminated foodstuffs have been arbitrary and contradictory, confusing homemakers, hunters, and herders. After Chernobyl, some heavily contaminated foods—from berries to fish, meat to milk—had to be destroyed. However, this stopgap only temporarily detours the radioactivity in the food chain; the situation remains serious, considering the long half-life of some contaminants.

The more familiar threats to Saami culture continue to be the dominant cultures' resource-extraction industries, tourism, transportation, media, and military maneuvers. The Saami, like others in northernmost Europe, are divided in their responses to such intrusions. One consequence is the emigration of many younger people to southern Norway, Sweden, and Finland. A surplus of males remains in the north because more women move away than men. The decisions of women in particular to emigrate are fueled by job opportunities elsewhere and weighed against hard-to-maintain subsidized housing in the North and the ten-month, nine-year compulsory schooling of children. Both factors restrain women and divorce them from their more active traditional roles in child-rearing and subsistence.

Despite the historical stumbling blocks to Saami exercising their rights, only since the 1970s have Saami successfully resisted outside manipulation of northern natural resources. In Norway, grassroots demonstrations against one proposed dam expanded when the next major dam proposal arose into activism aimed at the country's Parliament and international human-rights and nature-conservancy groups. Hydroelectric dams interrupt reindeer migration routes, change the water table, and even modify temperature patterns.

Beginning in the 1970s, Saami organizations advising state bodies have helped alert the public to the erosion of Saami control over their traditional regions. Also in the 1970s, a pan-Saami alliance launched the Saami Institute to promote indigenous research and cultural protection. It receives support from the governments of Norway, Sweden, and Finland.

MYRDENE ANDERSON

SEPHARDIC JEWS IN FRANCE

Numbering between 300,000 and 400,000, Sephardic Jews comprise about 55 percent of France's Jewish population. The community is diverse, made up of immigrants from the whole Mediterranean basin who began settling in France at the beginning of the century. The largest part comes from France's previous North African colonies.

Sephardic Jews are among the best-integrated immigrant communities in Western Europe, yet they constitute a distinctive ethnic identity based on diverse forms of expressing their cultural identity. Despite recent anti-Semitic attacks targeting French Jews as a whole, Sephardic Jews are neither physically threatened nor subject to official discrimination. Instead, the dilemma they now confront is how to secure their integration into French society while maintaining their distinct culture.

JOËLLE BAHLOUL

SLOVENIA

Slovenia Resource:
Society for Slovene Studies, c/o Henry Cooper, President, Russian and Eastern Europe Institute, Indiana University, Bloomington IN, 47402. The society publishes a newsletter, a journal (*Slovene Studies*) and a supplement (*Research and Documentation: Slovene Studies*).

Slovenia declared its independence on February 20, 1991. Although almost everyone in the republic speaks the same language and is Roman Catholic, tensions could arise between Slovenes and enclaves of Serbs, who have been peaceful so far. An external threat could occur if Serbian forces cross the Kupa River. An internal threat to the new republic comes from the renewed political power of the former communist party.

Foreign powers have dominated Slovenia for most of its history. Following the Slovene proclamation of independence, the Yugoslav army invaded in July 1991 but was defeated. Economic support from the United States, the European Community, and the International Monetary Fund would help Slovenes maintain their independence, as would admission to the European Community.

IRENE PORTIS-WINNER

THE VLACHS OF THE BALKANS

KONFERENCA E I E SHOOATES
TE ARUMUNEVE TE SHQIPERISE

Vlach Resource:
Society Farsarotul in America, P.O. Box 753, Trumbull, CT 06611. This is the oldest and largest Vlach organization in the United States.

The Romans conquered Macedonia in the second century B.C. and intermarried with the indigenous Balkan peoples. The Vlachs are the Romance-language-speaking descendants of this union. Their language is similar to Romanian. The Vlachs are also known as Koutsovlachs, Arumanians, Macedo-Romanians, and several other names.

Once wholly contained within the Ottoman Empire, at the turn of this century the Vlachs were divided among Albania, Bulgaria, Greece, and Serbia. At the time their population was estimated at 500,000; recent estimates cite less than half that number. Today there are organized groups of indigenous Vlachs in Albania, Greece, and Macedonia and diaspora groups in Romania, Germany, and America.

The greatest threat to the Vlachs is rigid nationalism in the Balkan states, which have done their best to assimilate minorities. Between 1860 and 1945, Romania sponsored a nationalist movement among the Vlachs, but it tried to foster a Romanian nationalism. The movement never had a large following; opposed by Greek nationalists, it collapsed after World War II.

In the last half century, Vlachs have adopted fairly assimilated lifestyles. Little prevents their disappearance. The Vlachs still have no schools or churches in their own language, although this lack of institutions may soon change in Albania, which claims the largest Vlach population of any Balkan state. From the standpoint of the Vlachs, a Balkan peninsula united on the model of the European Community would be the best possible development because it would eliminate the arbitrary borders separating the Vlachs and make diversity less threatening to the Balkan states.

NICHOLAS S. BALAMACI

203

The Anglo-European invasion of North America and the subsequent destruction and dispossession of its indigenous societies began early in the seventeenth century. It has left a legacy of injustices under which American Indians and Inuit peoples suffer continuing threats to their existence as distinct peoples. Specific issues arise in the areas of political rights, land rights, religious freedom, rights against taxation, and development projects that affect all the indigenous peoples within the territorial boundaries claimed by the United States and Canada.

In the United States, an elaborate body of laws dealing with Indians and Alaskan and Hawaiian natives pretends to offer fair treatment while facilitating the transfer of wealth and power from the hands of indigenous groups to the hands of those in power. This transfer is often only thinly veiled under laws and legal doctrines that have legalized seizures of indigenous lands that would be illegal in the case of non-indigenous people. In the United States, only indigenous groups are subject to the taking of their land without due process of law and with either no compensation or compensation set at rates that amount to theft.

Since 1899, the "plenary powers doctrine," which applies to powers unrestricted by the Bill of Rights, has held that Congress has unlimited powers in relation to Indian peoples and that, in essence, indigenous peoples have no collective rights. Although many Indian nations entered into treaties with the United States in apparently honorable nation-to-nation exchanges, this doctrine provides that the United States can abrogate the treaties at any time in what amounts to a raw use of power.

If, indeed, power corrupts and absolute power corrupts absolutely, the plenary powers doctrine must be one of the supreme symbols of corruption. The courts have applied this doctrine with what can only be described as indifference to indigenous

life and society. A group of Native Americans in California sued to stop the building of a logging road through public lands to cut down public forests, arguing that the proposed road would disturb their sacred sites and make it impossible for them to practice their religion. After rejecting arguments that the road would cost taxpayers more than the market value of the timber to be harvested, the U.S. Supreme Court did agree that the development would destroy the Indians' religious practice. However, it said that the Constitution guarantees only that the U.S. government will not *found* a religion but provides no protection should it *destroy* one. The road was built.

A second legal principle, derived from the 1955 case of the Tee-hit-ton Indians of Alaska, provides that the U.S. government may encroach on Indian lands in the absence of a treaty, thus upholding many cases of what amounts to land theft. Although the Constitution provides that the government can take land only for public purposes, federal agencies have taken land for such private purposes as sales to local speculators, mineral developers, and logging companies. The courts have determined that the Indian lands in question are not protected by the Bill of Rights.

In 1955 the Supreme Court extended the *Rule of Tee-hit-ton* to Indian lands "protected" under treaties, as in the case of the Western Shoshone in Nevada. In 1863, the Western Shoshone signed the Treaty of Ruby Valley with the United States, apparently guaranteeing their tribal land titles to much of present-day Nevada. However, the Department of the Interior claims that it "encroached" on Western Shoshone land. Therefore, says the department, the Indians can't regain their own land but only have a right to compensation for it. In other words, theft is legal, the United States is the thief, and the cloak of public indifference obscures the raw exercise of power. In the case of indigenous peoples, the state apparently feels it has no need to place even a veneer of fairness over its exercise of power.

To "settle" Indian claims and decide on compensation for peoples like the Western Shoshone, Congress created the U.S. Indian Claims Commission. Although the courts and the commission have decided that in many instances Indians lost property through blatant fraud, the commission can't order the return of the stolen property to its rightful owners. Indians can only seek compensation based on the value of the land—an amount to be determined based on market value *at the time of the taking*. In other words, real estate worth billions of dollars, seized over a century ago in dealings recognized as outright theft, is to be compensated for at its original, long-ago market value. Thus the Western Shoshone have refused to accept their $26 million award—supposedly equal to the 1872 value of most of Nevada. New York Indian nations have been compensated for lands in the western part of the state at pennies per acre. This process has been repeated hundreds of times.

These and other doctrines essentially determine that indigenous peoples enjoy the rights guaranteed in the U.S. Constitution only as individuals, not as societies, let alone as sovereign nations. Indeed, indigenous peoples experience even individual rights differently than other citizens of the United States. When oil companies detected promising energy resources on Hopi and Navajo land, they urged the federal government to obtain leases from the Indians. Realizing that traditional governments were unlikely to agree to the leases, the federal government created U.S.-style electoral systems for the Hopi and Navajo; after the elections, which were ignored by most Hopi and Navajo, the new tribal governments signed the leases.

Every kind of natural resource has been treated in this manner, even grasslands. In 1934, Congress passed the Indian Reorganization Act, ostensibly to provide a structure for governance for Indian reservations. One result of this act was that the Department of the Interior began to act as trustee for Indians. In other words, in the eyes of the law, the government would treat Indians the same as it would mental incompetents. At that time, many Indian peoples had only grasslands, which they used for horses and cattle and a subsistence economy. Since the mandate of a trustee is to use the assets of the ward in a way that maximizes income, the government fenced off these grasslands into range units so it could lease the land, usually to white ranchers (almost always at bargain-basement prices). This provided some immediate income for Indians but also destroyed their subsistence economy and threw many into poverty.

Subsistence hunting and fishing in rural Alaska

To compensate for this "side effect," the government eventually provided public assistance (welfare) but deducted the lease income to pay for it. White ranchers received the use of Indian land for very little cost, Indians became paupers and trespassers on their own lands, and Indian wealth was transferred to the hands of non-Indians, all under a cloak of legality.

When development companies began exploring Alaska after World War II, they were able to remove all indigenous claims to most of this territory by persuading Congress to pass the Alaska Native Claims Settlement Act. Billed as a measure to bring the blessings of modernity to indigenous peoples, the act's practical result has been to give developers unimpeded access to Alaskan resources, at the same time phasing out native governments as legal entities.

The legal framework differs slightly in Canada, but conditions for indigenous peoples are not significantly better. In Quebec, for example, the Liberal Party has framed its own designs for sovereignty around developing much of the northern part of the province. During the 1970s Quebec built a massive hydroelectric project, and it now has plans to add a huge network of dams that will flood some Inuit lands and most of the territory of the James Bay Cree.

Quebec's claim to these lands amounts to little more than the ancient claim of right of discovery. At some point in Canadian history, politicians in Ottawa drew lines around lands they hadn't visited; in the arbitrary drawing of these borders, the territory of the James Bay Cree was allocated to Quebec. Today, politicians in the province claim that a few Indians have no right to stand in the way of projects that would benefit millions, implying that the raw exercise of power has no moral content. Quebec intends to do everything in its power to go forward, although it is proposing massive ecological dislocation and is using a technology that not only could become obsolete in a few decades but is based on market projections that display more wishful thinking than business sense.

Outside Quebec, too, Canada appears unwilling to take serious steps to settle Indian claims. Under dispute are hundreds of parcels of land that compose substantial segments of Ontario, Manitoba, Saskatchewan, Alberta, and British Columbia, as well as the Northwest Territories and parts of the Maritime Provinces. At its present rate of addressing these questions, Canada will take more than two centuries to settle all pending claims.

This foot-dragging is accompanied by a discussion of Indian rights in the courts that reads like pages out of a nineteenth-century U.S. legal history. In a recent case in British Columbia, one court fell back on European feudal law. Indians are to be treated as serfs, with the government essentially acting as lord of the manor. This is essentially where U.S. Supreme Court Justice John Marshall derived his language in the founding Indian law cases in the United States. The logic is that indigenous people have no inherent political or property rights, only those rights bestowed by the European sovereign. If the sovereign did not bestow particular rights on a specific group, such rights do not exist.

Indeed, in both Canada and the United States, the rights of indigenous peoples in the Anglo world rest on flimsy legal principles. Native groups find themselves at a disadvantage regardless of whether they choose to play the game by asserting their rights through the prevailing government channels. This ancient game of heads-you-lose tails-I-win is the most persistent threat to the continued existence of indigenous societies.

JOHN MOHAWK

United States/Canada Resources:
Aboriginal Rights Coalition, 151 Laurier Ave. East, Ottawa, Ontario K1N 6N8 Canada (613)235-9956.
Akwe:kon Journal, Cornell University, 400 Caldwell Hall, Ithaca, NY 14853 (607)255-4308.
Canadian Alliance in Solidarity with Native People, P.O. Box 574, Station P, Toronto, Ontario M5S 2T1 (416)972-1573.
Cultural Survival Canada, 1 Nicholas St., Suite 420, Ottawa, Ontario, Canada K1N 7B7 (613)233-4653.
Indian Country Today, P.O. Box 2180, Rapid City, SD 57709 (605)341-0011.
Indian Law Resource Center, 601 E. St., SE, Washington, DC 20003 (202)547-2800.
Indigenous Women/Indigenous Women's Network, P.O. Box 174, Lake Elmo, MN 55042.
Inuit Circumpolar Conference, 170 Laurier Ave. West, Suite 504, Ottawa, Ontario K1P 5V5 Canada (613)563-2642.
Native American Rights Fund, 1506 Broadway, Boulder, CO 80302 (303)447-8760.
News from Indian Country, Rt. 2, Box 2900-A, Hayward, WI 54843 (715)634-5226.
Seventh Generation Fund for Indian Development, P.O. Box 10, Forestville, CA 95436 (707)887-1559.

ALGONQUINS OF BARRIÈRE LAKE, CANADA

Algonquin Resource:
Algonquins of Barrière Lake,
  408 Queen St., Ottawa,
  Ontario, KIR 5A7.

Several hundred miles north of Ottawa, the 450 Algonquins of Barrière Lake are fighting for their survival. The community is located in the middle of Quebec's La Verendrye Wildlife Refuge. Four years ago, realizing that the forest in the reserve had been half clear-cut, the Algonquin took to the barricades to block further logging until a plan for sustainable development could be agreed upon.

The Algonquins argued that the logging compromised their traditional activities—hunting, trapping, gathering medicines and other plants, and foraging—as well as logging. The wildlife park allows commercial and sport hunting, another concern to Algonquins because hunters could go up to the border of the community's 59-acre reserve, endangering life and limb and making certain traditional activities impossible.

In August 1991, the Canadian and Quebec governments signed an historic agreement with the Algonquins, pledging to meet their demands for ecologically sustainable logging. Unfortunately, Quebec has failed at every turn to honor the agreement. The logging companies continue to operate, despite commitments that areas considered "sensitive" by the Algonquins would have interim protection while a long-term management plan was being developed. In February 1993, the Quebec government suspended the agreement, claiming a deadlock in negotiations over the Algonquin demand for a buffer zone between logging operations and streams.

CULTURAL SURVIVAL CANADA

ANISHINABEG OF THE UNITED STATES

In the United States between 1887 and 1932, more than 60 percent of the 140 million acres in indigenous lands were lost, leaving them with only 50 million acres of marginal land.

Andrew Gray

The White Earth Reservation in northern Minnesota is home to the Mississippi band of Anishinabe (also known as the Ojibway), who reserve this land under an 1867 treaty. Ironically, the reservation's wealth has become its source of poverty. Land speculators, timber barons, and unscrupulous Indian agents took most of this land for its rich soil, the beauty of its lakes, and the bounty of its forests.

Today, non-Indians hold 90 percent of the reservation, and most Anishinabeg are refugees on their own lands, condemned to live in poverty for almost three generations. Of 20,000 tribal members, most would like to come home.

For 70 years, through numerous federal and state lawsuits and seven federal investigations, Anishinabeg have sought the return of their land. Although they have seen no justice, they continue to rely upon the land for sustenance—half of the Anishinabeg people harvest wild rice, three-fourths hunt, and many garden, collect medicines, or make baskets from birch trees. Members of the tribe face arrests and the continued frustration of seeing the land degraded by clear cutting, pesticide misuse, and agriculture policies that strip it of indigenous medicines. (The reservation is so rich with medicines that it is known as the medicine chest of the Ojibway.)

Formed in 1988, the White Earth Land Recovery Project buys about 750 acres of burial grounds, maple sugar groves, and medicinal plant habitat each year and holds these lands in trust. The project is negotiating with large absentee landholders, including government agencies, which hold one-third of the tribe's land, and is reestablishing traditional land-management knowledge and practices. In 15 years, White Earth hopes to secure one-third of the reservation for future generations.

At the same time, two local collectives—Ikwe and Manitok (owned by the tribal government)—market wild rice, wild fruit preserves, and baskets to

207

national markets, capturing some of the value added for tribal products. Each step is small, but it is the Anishinabeg's own.

WINONA LADUKE

THE CANADIAN CONSTITUTION AND ABORIGINAL RIGHTS

The past dozen or so years have been historic ones for aboriginal rights in Canada. In 1982, an amended Constitution Act came into effect. Section 35 "recognized and affirmed" the "existing treaty and aboriginal rights of the aboriginal peoples of Canada."

In court, the federal and provincial governments argued that these words didn't revive rights that had been the subject of past legislation but only protected rights that had avoided any infringement by legislation, inconsistent government policy, or Euro-Canadian settlement. However, in 1990 in *Sparrow v. The Queen*, Canada's Supreme Court confirmed that the constitutional provisions were meaningful and active and part of a general fiduciary relationship between the Crown and aboriginal peoples. Legislation that infringed significantly upon aboriginal or treaty rights would have to be carefully justified, both as to its legislative purpose and the means of implementation, and would have to have as little impact as possible on those rights.

In cases since *Sparrow*, Canada and the provinces have sought to limit the extent of the fiduciary obligation and the power of the constitutional protection. The Supreme Court has yet to act on any of these cases.

In 1990, the federal and provincial governments drafted a series of constitutional amendments to deal with these and many other issues. However, the reforms failed to receive the necessary approval of every provincial legislature that they would need to become law. In Manitoba, Elijah Harper, a Cree member of the provincial legislature, was largely responsible for the rejection of the amendments. The legislatures of Newfoundland and Manitoba also declined to ratify them.

In 1992, a second constitutional process, this one including Canada's three major aboriginal organizations—the Inuit Tapirisat, the Assembly of First Nations, and the Native Council of Canada—resulted in a consensus that was put to a referendum vote in August. Known as the Charlottetown Accord, the 1992 reforms included provisions for recognizing the "inherent right of self-government" of aboriginal peoples, although the accord made these provisions subject to relatively vague federal and provincial laws for "peace, order and good government." The accord failed to get the support of voters. A separate aboriginal vote was also negative, revealing the refusal of many indigenous people to recognize the jurisdiction of the federal system in any way.

PAUL WILLIAMS

CREE OF JAMES BAY, CANADA

Cree Resources:
Grand Council of the Cree, 24 Bayswater, Ottawa, Ontario K1Y 2E4 (613)761-1688

In northern Quebec, along the rivers that flow into James Bay, the Cree are fighting both the provincially owned utility and the government to block one of the world's largest hydroelectric schemes. The first phase of megaprojects in the James Bay region has already seriously disrupted the lives of the 9,000 Cree.

In the early 1970s, Hydro Quebec began constructing massive dams and diversions. The Cree first learned of the project from newspapers and challenged it in court. Although they were granted an injunction, construction stopped for only one day, and the Cree were forced to accept a negotiated settlement that allowed construction to continue. They won protection of as much of their traditional activities as they could, but their rights in a newly created reservation turned to ashes:

they found that submerged and rotting vegetation was leaching methyl mercury, making fish unsafe for consumption.

The hydroelectric mega-projects have been devastating in other ways. One entire community was relocated. At their new home in Chisasabi, Cree adolescents hang out in a forlorn shopping mall, built for them by Hydro Quebec. Alcoholism and other substance abuse is on the rise. Roads built for the project have brought in hunters from southern Quebec, as well as more social stresses. The traditional fabric of life is unraveling.

In the late 1980s, the Quebec government and Hydro Quebec launched plans for a series of further mega-projects. All told, the three phases of James Bay projects would include three dozen dams and hundreds of dikes, changing the course of every free-flowing river into James Bay and affecting a watershed roughly the size of France.

This time, Hydro Quebec is finding the Cree to be a more effective adversary. Led by Grand Chief Matthew Coon Come, the Cree have garnered support in New York State, in New England, where exported power was destined for sale, and from sympathetic Canadians. But despite cancellation of a contract between Hydro Quebec and the New York Power Authority, Hydro Quebec is still intent upon building the dams on the Great Whale River that flows into Hudson Bay.

The Great Whale project is now undergoing environmental review. The Cree are committed to saving the rivers and are active in the courts, the environmental review process, and their appeal to the court of public opinion.

CULTURAL SURVIVAL CANADA

GROS VENTRE AND ASSINIBOINE OF THE UNITED STATES

Home to the Gros Ventre and Assiniboine peoples, Fort Belknap Reservation in the Little Rocky Mountains of central Montana is only a few miles northeast of a gold mine that threatens the local environment. If the Zortman-Landusky gold mine, a subsidiary of Pegasus Gold, Inc., completes its next expansion, more than a billion gallons of cyanide solution could be released over the next few years into the main watershed that feeds Fort Belknap's aquifer.

Not only the environment but the survival of the Gros Ventre and Assiniboine cultures is at stake. For many years, the Little Rockies have been a source of subsistence, water, and healing medicines for many Native Americans, as well as the location of traditional ceremonies. For example, participants in the "vision questing" ceremony, which requires quiet and solitude, fast and spend four days and nights alone in the mountains. With bulldozing, dynamite explosions, and bright lights that remain on throughout the night as miners work, a vision quest is difficult, to say the least.

The first gold rush in the Little Rockies started around 1864 and continued intermittently until the 1950s, when high-grade ores were exhausted. The current rush began in the late 1990s with the advent of new processes that make it possible to profitably mine low-grade ore but that potentially endanger the environment. Water samples taken in 1991 showed elevated levels of lead on the reservation just below the mines. Elevated levels of arsenic, cadmium, selenium, manganese, and nitrates have also been reported.

NEILLY BUCKALEW

GWICH'IN OF THE UNITED STATES

The Gwich'in are the northernmost Indian nation in North America. Their territory spans the U.S.-Canadian border in the Yukon and Alaska. For 10,000 years, the Gwich'in have retained a way of life based on the land, primarily the porcupine caribou, whose numbers are around l70,000. They have sur-

209

vived by the caribou the same way the Plains Indians to the south once survived by the buffalo.

The future of the Gwich'in is threatened by proposed oil drilling in the Arctic National Wildlife Refuge (ANWR) in Alaska, the birthplace and nursery grounds of the Porcupine River caribou herd. Every year, the Gwich'in harvest up to 10,000 animals.

Especially since the Persian Gulf war, pressure has been intense to open the 19-million-acre refuge and its complex Arctic ecosystem to oil exploitation. The 105 miles of coastline in the refuge is the only part of the Alaska coastline that is off limits to oil leasing.

Just to the north, Prudhoe Bay and the Beaufort Sea now supply around 2.2 million barrels of oil a day through the Trans Alaska Pipeline to Valdez, Alaska. This represents about one-fourth of the domestically produced crude oil in the United States, and one-eighth of total U.S. daily consumption. Oil in the Gwich'in territory of the ANWR represents possibly fewer than 200 days of U.S. oil needs. If this oil is exploited, it will devastate the calving grounds of the porcupine caribou herd.

In the fall of 1991, Congress took some remedial action. For now, at least, it narrowly defeated legislation that would have sacrificed the caribou-calving and nursery grounds to oil drilling.

DONNA CARROLL

HAVASUPAI OF THE UNITED STATES

GRAND CANYON AREA URANIUM DEVELOPMENT

ACTUAL MINES
PROPOSED MINES
MINES OPERATED 1950s-1960s

Havasupai Resource:
"Uranium Mining at the Grand Canyon: What Costs to Water, Air, and Indigenous People?" *Workbook*, Spring 1991.

The U.S. government created a tiny reservation for the Havasupai people at the bottom of the Grand Canyon Reservation. About 300 members of nine bands of Pai found themselves grouped together under the name Havasupai on a land base that was too small to sustain them.

Most Havasupai live in Supai, a small village at the bottom of the Grand Canyon. Historically, the canyon has provided Havasupai with some protection from the incursions of miners and soldiers, but canyon walls afford no protection against new diseases. After a series of epidemics ripped through Supai, its population sank to 166 in 1906. Today, there are more than 500 tribal members.

The Grand Canyon Enlargement Act of 1975 expanded the reservation and, at least in the eyes of tribal members, guaranteed their rights of access to off-reservation lands for ceremonies. But in 1986, the Havasupi people discovered that Energy Fuels Nuclear (EFN) was interested in mining uranium ore from lands adjacent to the reservation, lands that are central to Havasupai spiritual beliefs.

The Grand Canyon has hosted uranium mines on both rims since 1951. The abandoned Orphan Uranium Mine superstructure still stands in the national park on the South Rim. Energy Fuels Nuclear's Canyon Mine, which threatens Havasupi sacred lands, is located on U.S. Forest Service land south of the park. In addition, the Forest Service granted EFN 12 additional drill-exploration permits near the Canyon Mine in 1990. Just six months later, the Havasupai discovered that a second uranium mining company was exploring and staking claims in the same region.

By 1993, uranium mining in the Grand Canyon area had come to a standstill. EFN closed its operations, at least temporaraily, when a glut of uranium on the world market caused uranium prices to bottom out. How soon the northern Arizona uranium industry will revitalize is open to question. The tribe has worked to stop the looming threat on the rims of their canyon since 1986 in the courts and Congress. Havasupai hopes for religious protec-

Havasupai Actions:
The tribe is losing as much as $18,000 a day in tourist revenues because its entire tourist operation was shut down after the flood. The Havasupai are continuing to repair the damages, but they are in urgent need of financial help. An emergency relief account has been established. *Havasupi Canyon Disaster Relief Fund Trust*, First Interstate Bank, P.O. Box 970, Scottsdale, Arizona 85252-0970.

Urge government officials, including Secretary of Interior Bruce Babbit, (U.S. Department of the Interior, 18th & C Sts. N.W., Washington, DC 20240) to support a moratorium on new mining at the Grand Canyon, at least until a cumulative environmental impact statement that measures the levels and impacts of radioactivity is completed.

tion in the courts were dashed when the Ninth Circuit Court denied their pleas to protect the area of the Canyon Mine. The Supreme Court has refused to hear the case.

In 1991, the Havasupai banned uranium mining, milling, and transport on reservation lands when they revised their tribal constitution. However, this measure does not have any power over off-reservation lands managed by the U.S. Forest Service. Therefore, it cannot block uranium mining south of the Grand Canyon.

Should the uranium mining industry come back to life, it will threaten the Havasupai religion and their environment. Specific environmental threats include contamination of ground and surface water, transport accidents, and airborne radioactive contaminants. According to the Forest Service Environmental Impact Statement on uranium mining at the Grand Canyon, the mine would release as much as a ton of arsenic and uranium oxide dust annually.

Surface waters would also be contaminated by uranium mines in operation. EFN said that there was only a remote danger of flooding. But in 1990, a flash flood ripped across the surface of the desert and down into Supai village. After the flood, water had also filled a uranium tailings pond at the mine site that was empty at the time. Had the pond been full of radioactive waste, it would have overflowed.

In February 1993, another flash flood from a different direction poured into Supai, devastating their crops and housing and destroying the configuration of their world-famous waterfalls. This flood was more devastating than the one in 1990, and tribal members are struggling to repair their way of life in the bottom of the Grand Canyon.

CATE GILLIS

HAWAII

Hawaii Resource:
Ka Lahui Hawaii, P.O. Box 4964, Hilo, HI 96720.

When Capt. James Cook sailed into the Hawaiian archipelago in 1778, he found a community of 800,000 people who were economically self-sufficient and fed and clothed themselves off the land. Within a generation, 770,000 Hawaiians were dead from venereal disease, flu, and pox, from *mai haole*—the sickness of the white man.

Hawaii was then welcomed into the family of nations and signed over 20 treaties, including treaties of friendship and peace with the United States. But in 1893, the U.S. Marines overthrew the kingdom of Hawaii; 1993 marks the 100th anniversary of the abolition of the right of Native Hawaiians to govern themselves.

In 1959, Hawaii became the 50th state in the nation. In every other state, the U.S. government set aside land for the native people as reserves, and other Native Americans can maintain their nations and pass certain laws to protect the land. In Hawaii, the government gave native lands to the state to hold in trust and made the 200,000 Native Hawaiians perpetual wards of the state. They can't form governments, nor can they control their land base.

In 1920, Congress did set aside some land for homesteads for individual Native Hawaiians. Some 24,000 families are now on lists waiting for their land entitlements. Since 1920, 30,000 individuals have died waiting for homeland awards.

Native Hawaiians have pursued their land claims through the courts, which have consistently ruled that, as wards of the state and federal governments, they can't sue to protect their trust lands and assets. Hawaiians are thus the only Native Americans—the only class of U.S. citizens—who can't

211

"We share the same river of life, what befalls me befalls you and downstream in this river of life our children will pay for our selfishness, greed, and lack of vision."

Oren Lyons, Onondaga Nation

appeal to the federal courts to redress a breach of trust.

Tourism is a major threat to the islands and their native people. Besides taking land from rural Native Hawaiian communities, the hundreds of thousands of tourists that come to the islands each year seeking paradise leave behind millions of tons of sewage. Because this sewage is deposited into the ocean, reef fish, squid, and turtles have disappeared in many places. In many other areas, the state and federal governments have established public parks that restrict native people from exercising traditional subsistence-gathering rights.

A further threat comes from the specter of geothermal energy development. For 25 years, efforts to tap this underground resource have contributed to destroying Wao Kele o Puna Forest, the last tropical rain forest in Hawaii. This forest is sacred to the lands of Tutu Pele, the grandmother Pele, who erupts and gives birth to the earth. Geothermal development thus denies Native Hawaiians their right to worship.

Extensive U.S. military installations also present a substantial threat to Native Hawaiians and their land. For example, in Lualualei, Oahu, the U.S. military converted 2,000 acres of the territory set aside for Native Hawaiian homelands into a nuclear storage facility.

In 1987 Native Hawaiians took the initiative to reorganize their sovereign nation: Ka Lahui Hawaii. Ka Lahui Hawaii has the support of over 18,000 native citizens in Hawaii.

MILILANI TRASK

INNU OF LABRADOR, CANADA

The Innu are the traditional people of northern Quebec and Labrador, Newfoundland. The 1,200 Innu in Labrador live in some of the poorest of Canada's communities, with epidemic rates of substance abuse, teen suicide, and domestic violence.

The community of Davis Inlet, in particular, has been the focus of national attention. First, over a year ago six children died in a house fire. They had been left alone with a small and inadequate heater. Then in early 1993 several adolescents tried to commit suicide by sniffing gasoline. The community lays the blame for their desperate condition on the government's decision 20 years ago to uproot the community from its traditional lands and move it to Davis Inlet. Due to a recent outcry about Third World conditions at Davis Inlet, both the provincial and federal governments have relented and agreed that the community can be moved.

The Innu Nation also includes the community of Sheshashit, near Goose Bay. Its members have had to oppose the Canadian government and NATO in an attempt to stop high-speed, low-altitude military flights over their lands. The flights subject the Innu to sonic booms, scatter the caribou they hunt, and catch them unawares while they are whale fishing. When they blocked the airstrip, a Newfoundland judge found they were within their rights to do so. But routine and fairly constant low flights continue, despite the abandonment of government plans for a larger training base at Goose Bay.

The Innu also face a threat from the expansion of hydroelectric power projects. Newfoundland first developed Churchill Falls as a hydroelectric facility in the 1950s as a way to provide cheap power to the province of Quebec. Recently, Newfoundland has decided to further exploit the falls, threatening the Innu with more flooding and loss of their territory.

CULTURAL SURVIVAL CANADA

INUIT OF CANADA

The Inuit of Canada's frozen tundra number some 30,000 people, living in the Yukon and the Northwest Territories. For over three decades the Inuit have struggled for self-government and more autonomy, and they have achieved significant victories in recent years.

When it became clear that a comprehensive agreement for all Inuit wasn't possible, the 17,500 Inuit of the eastern Arctic began negotiating for their own territory in 1982. Their efforts bore fruit in 1991. The most extensive self-government settlement in Canadian history affirms the Inuit's rights to what was the eastern half of the Northwest Territories, 770,000 square miles known as Nunavut (Inuk for "Our Land"). The agreement includes mineral rights as well as wildlife-management accords.

The Inuit have suffered from efforts to assimilate them into Western lifestyles. They have been encouraged to settle in wooden houses on reserves and mimic the lives of southern Canadians, except that store-bought food is far more costly for the Inuit than it is in southern Canada. High unemployment and other social stresses have contributed to high levels of alcoholism, suicide, and sexually transmitted diseases. The loss of hunting, due to Southern fur boycotts, further isolates them from their traditional activities.

The Inuit also face an invisible threat. The Arctic is unaccountably contaminated with heavy metals and toxic chemicals. Polychlorinated biphenols (PCBs) heavily contaminate mothers' milk. The contamination had been attributed to the long-range transport of air pollutants, but recent information about irresponsible dumping by the former Soviet Union suggests another explanation.

CULTURAL SURVIVAL CANADA

MOHAWK NATION OF CANADA AND THE UNITED STATES

In 1975, 100 percent of all federally produced uranium in the United States came from Indian reservations, so that Indians were the fifth largest producers of uranium in the world.

Winona LaDuke in *Threshold*

The Mohawk Nation is the easternmost of a confederacy of nations known to the English as the Six Nations and to the French as the Iroquois Confederacy. Perhaps 30,000 Mohawks live in the United States and Canada, primarily on seven reserves in Canada and one in the United States. The latter, known as Akwesasne to the Mohawk, straddles the U.S.-Canadian border. The most populous Indian reserve in Canada is Kahnawake, a Mohawk territory near Montreal.

The Mohawk Nation is engaged in a long-standing contest with the state of New York, the United States, Canada, and the provinces of Quebec and Ontario over political rights and land claims, as well as other issues. The United States and New York State claim almost all Mohawk aboriginal country under treaties and land cessions dating from the end of the eighteenth century. However, these constitute nothing less than land thefts. For example, in the Treaty of 1797 a single individual "sold" millions of acres of land for $1,000, which he received as personal compensation. A long list of U.S. sanctions for such land seizures underlie the tensions between the Mohawk Nation and New York State.

One hotly contested issue is the right of Canada or the United States to levy taxes and otherwise exercise jurisdiction on Mohawk country. This conflict led to armed resistance in 1990, when Mohawks protesting the taking of land for a golf course at Oka, Quebec, were attacked by Quebec Provincial Police. One officer died in this incident.

The historic injustices suffered by the Mohawk people, including the supplanting of traditional forms of government with elected systems operating under state and provincial laws, have created an extremely complex environ-

213

ment. As a result, Mohawks find themselves in an intense internal dispute. Without community approval, individual Mohawk entrepreneurs have operated lucrative tax-free tobacco and gasoline businesses and, until 1990, casinos. At Akwesasne, Mohawk "warriors" organized a paramilitary group, ostensibly to keep state jurisdiction at bay but in reality to keep state authorities from closing the casinos.

Traditional Mohawks protested the casinos as illegal operations that went against community morality and operated solely in the interests of a few individuals and their non-Indian business partners. Anti-gambling demonstrations led to a fierce war that pitted the Mohawk "warriors" against traditionalists. Two Mohawk men died in a gun battle.

These internal problems have an external source: New York State officials failed to close the illegal casinos. When Mohawks protested the gambling, state officials turned a blind eye. Eventually, federal authorities moved in and arrested the casino owners. Nevertheless, the Mohawk case illustrates the shortcomings of a federal policy that legalizes reservation gambling without ensuring that casinos operate in a democratic political environment, free from criminal influence.

JOHN MOHAWK

NAVAJO OF THE UNITED STATES

"If they come and drag us all away from the land, it will destroy our way of life. That is genocide. If they leave me here, but take away the community, it is still genocide."

Roberta Blackgoat

Archeologists think the Navajo reached the U.S. Southwest sometime after 1300. Although the Spanish explored the region in the 1500s and 1600s, the Navajo had little contact with them until almost 1700. The Spanish lost control of the region in the late 1600s, but during the reconquest of 1696, Jemez, Tewa, and Keresan Pueblo Indians retreated with the Navajo to what is now northeast Arizona and northwest New Mexico.

Until the 1850s, the Navajo were independent of colonial, political, and missionary controls. They maintained an informal, decentralized political, social, and economic system centered around clan, domestic, and genealogical affiliations.

With the discovery of oil on Navajo land in 1922, non-Navajo companies needed local authorities with whom they could negotiate contracts. In 1923, the U.S. government appointed three Navajo men as a business council to deal with lease grants, and in 1938 instigated the formation of the Navajo Tribal Council. Since the 1930s, conflicts over U.S.-directed change—involving acculturation, relocation, livestock reductions, and land disputes—have raged between the Navajo and Washington.

Land disputes are the Navajo's most pressing problem. In 1974, Congress passed Public Law 93-531, ostensibly to resolve a land dispute between the Hopi and Navajo in Arizona. The law called for relocating almost 11,000 Navajo. Although the deadline for relocation was July 1986, about 1,000 Navajo still occupy the disputed land on Big Mountain. The police harass the remaining Navajo, say Navajo leaders, and federal agents have confiscated their sheep. Although they do not deny that a dispute exists with the Hopi, Navajo leaders contend that oil companies and the government have exaggerated the situation for political expediency and financial gain. The area in question has a rich vein of coal and evidence of oil deposits.

The dispute extends to attacks on Navajo religion. In October 1989 the courts dismissed a Navajo suit that claimed the relocation violated their First Amendment right to freedom of religion. The Navajo religion is integrally related to the land they inhabit.

ADAPTED FROM *CULTURAL SURVIVAL QUARTERLY*

POHLIK AND KARUK OF THE UNITED STATES

CHRIS PETERS

A 1988 U.S. Supreme Court decision seeks to destroy the sacred high country and the spiritual lives of the Pohlik and Karuk people of northwest California. The case, *Lyng vs. the Northwest Indian Cemetery Association*, further set a legal precedent to destroy sacred places and similar age-old spiritual wisdom of native people across the United States.

For thousands of years, the Pohlik and Karuk people have used the sacred high country of the Siskiyou Mountains for medicine making and vision quests. After long periods of fasting, sweating, and other training rituals necessary to purify the mind, body, and soul, spiritual leaders complete pilgrimages to such places as Doctor Rock, Peak 8, Chimney Rock, and Little Medicine Mountain. At these places and through age-old formulas that can include intense prayer, fasting, dancing, jumping, singing, and continuously driven thought, spiritual leaders articulate with the spiritual side of the universe and acquire the wisdom and knowledge to reaffirm the religious ideology and spiritual existence of tribal communities.

The most important use of the high-country prayer places is for preparing and performing ceremonies to heal and renew the earth. The Jump Dance and the White Deer Skin Dance in particular are central and indispensable to the religious ideology and unique world view of the Pohlik and Karuk. Both are 10-day ceremonies (or community prayers) that personify a tribe's spiritual existence; the need to perform such community prayers is ingrained in people's very souls. Medicine women from the two tribes also use the sacred high country to receive healing powers and gather medicinal plants and herbs used for healing ceremonies.

Use of the high country and sacred prayer places is restricted to a very few religious leaders who have attained the knowledge of high mountain medicine and who live pure and clean lives. Spiritual leaders are always cautious to use the process of medicine making in a good and careful manner; the misuse or abuse of such spiritual powers can cause significant emotional or physical harm to themselves, their families, and their villages. In fact, among many tribal groups medicine making, vision quest, and the use of high-country sacred places are very secretive acts, and the mere discussion of these processes is forbidden.

Through the ritual of high mountain medicine and the reaffirmation of earth spiritual wisdom, there has evolved among tribal people of northwest California an ecological-centered consciousness and a unique world view. This earth-renewal paradigm drastically departs from contemporary Euro-American thought. It defines their relationship to the earth and within the cycle of life. Through this understanding, Pohlik and Karuk people see beyond anthropocentric paradigms and comprehend the value of the sacred high country for the survival of all forms of life. Accordingly, sacred prayer places house the power or spirituality for the earth's natural systems. The knowledge acquired through the process of medicine making sets forth the principles for sustainable lifestyles.

In its 1988 *Lyng* decision, the Supreme Court denied Pohlik and Karuk spiritual leaders their First Amendment right to the free exercise of religion. The Court permitted the U.S. Forest Service to construct a road that would dissect the sacred high country and to implement a timber-cutting plan that would destroy the spiritual life of the tribal people. Congress has since included the sacred high country in the Siskiyou Wilderness Area, and the spirituality of northwest California tribes continues uninterrupted. The impact on other tribal groups, however, is analogous to an everlasting death sentence.

CHRIS PETERS

215

SAN CARLOS APACHE OF THE UNITED STATES

Apache Indians of Arizona's San Carlos Reservation are contesting the $200 million Mount Graham International Observatory being built on an Apache sacred site. The seven telescopes designated for the observatory will cover 24 acres on top of Dzil Nchaa sí án ("Big Seated Mountain"), the Apache name for Mount Graham. In an ironic insult, the centerpiece telescope for the observatory is named the "Columbus Project."

Mount Graham, which was taken from the Apaches in 1873, lies at the heart of an ancient 615-acre spruce-fir forest in Coronado National Forest. The Apache presence on the mountain dates back hundreds of years and includes its use as a source of medicines and as a site for worship healing, and burials and traditional rites of passage. The mountain range is also one of the most unique and diverse in North America.

In 1988, the University of Arizona at Tucson, the lead partner in the project, pressured Congress to exempt the observatory from federal environmental laws. Congress responded with the Arizona-Idaho Conservation Act, but the hearings and debate over the issue have not been made public. *The Congressional Record* does not mention that Mount Graham is a sacred site.

A 1990 resolution by the San Carlos Apache Tribal Council unanimously opposed the project, declaring the mountain "essential to the continued practice of physical and spiritual healing by Apache medicinemen/women." The next year, the Apache Survival Coalition—a group of Apache elders, medicine men and women, and their supporters—filed suit in U.S. District Court, contending that the congressional action is unconstitutional. The suit also charges the U.S. Forest Service with violating the American Indian Religious Freedom Act, the National Environmental Policy Act, the National Forest Management Act, and other federal laws in allowing construction of the observatory. The Apache are now appealing initial court rulings that went against them.

Seven U.S. institutions have dropped out of the controversial project. Remaining partners are the Max Planck Institute in Germany, the Vatican Observatory, the University of Arizona, and Italy's Arcetri Astrophysical Observatory. The city of Rome recently passed a resolution asking Italian partners to withdraw, but Rev. George Coyne, director of the Vatican Observatory, dismisses claims that Mount Graham is a holy site.

Site construction commenced in October 1990. To date, Vatican and German teams have built a road, leveled trees and earth on the mountain, and poured concrete molds for the foundation.

JENNIFER RATHAUS

TRADITIONAL SEMINOLE NATION OF THE UNITED STATES

In the late 1800s, the Traditional Seminole Nation retreated in the Florida Everglades after one of the longest and most brutal wars in U.S. history. The 300 members of the nation continue to follow their original instructions and to care for the land, people, and animals as they were directed by the Creator. Many members of the Traditional Seminole Nation come from the Panther Clan whose struggle, like that of the panther, is a struggle against extinction.

For over 250 years, the traditional Seminole people have used a ceremonial ground north of Lake Okeechobee. Since 1850, they have used this land with the permission of the state of Florida and non-Indian landholders, but now citrus groves, sod farms, and cattle ranches are destroying the Green Corn Dance grounds, threatening this traditional religious and cultural ceremony.

With recent encroachment into the cypress swamp and pine forest, most of the land has been converted to farming. Wetlands have been drained and dredged, cypress stands bulldozed, roads constructed, and much of the land denuded of vegetation.

Many hundreds of Seminoles participate in the Green Corn Dance ceremony, an annual renewal that, explains Danny Billie, spokesperson for traditional Seminoles, "defines who we are and what we are as traditional people. It is the heart and soul of the traditional Seminole way of life."

To save the Green Corn Dance ceremony, Seminoles are searching for a new site of several thousand acres north of Lake Okeechobee that could become a permanent ecological reserve and ceremonial site. This project would protect some of south Florida's remaining wild lands, the Seminoles, and all who rely upon their ceremony and caretaking of the earth.

WINONA LADUKE

WESTERN SHOSHONE OF THE UNITED STATES

STATE OF NATIVE AMERICA

Western Shoshone Resource:
Western Shoshone Defense
Project, General Delivery,
Crescent Valley, NV 89821
(702)468-0230.

A legal battle over traditional Shoshone territory—concerning about 80 percent of Nevada—has continued for over five decades. In the most recent ruling, on October 5, 1992, the U.S. Supreme Court let stand rulings that had stripped the Shoshone of all hunting and fishing rights in Nevada.

The legal maneuvering by the U.S. government to seize the land of the Western Shoshone (or Newe nation) of eastern Nevada centers on the ranch of Mary and Carrie Dann. For two decades, the Dann sisters have fought the government over questions of grazing rights and land ownership. The sisters and the Western Shoshone National Council maintain that the Danns are running their livestock on tribal land, subject to Indian not federal law. They say their land title is guaranteed by the 1863 Treaty of Ruby Valley. The Danns remain on their ranch despite continued harassment from the U.S. Bureau of Land Management.

The conflict is far from resolved. Despite economic hardship, the Western Shoshone refuse to accept cash for land that they believe is theirs and that provides them with their economic, cultural, and spiritual identities. The government awarded them some $26 million in 1979 for lands they had never sold or relinquished. According to the Claims Commission Act of 1946, the Western Shoshone's acceptance of the money would effectively result in their permanently losing the land title and would bar Indians from seeking further compensation. The government has placed the funds in a trust account on behalf of the Western Shoshone.

The BLM has also taken four Western Shoshone leaders to court for authorizing a 1990 roundup of wild horses to prevent overgrazing. Under federal law, it is illegal to round up wild horses without BLM authorization. The Western Shoshone contend that they authorized the roundup based on their religious beliefs to protect Mother Earth. The BLM has been widely criticized by both Indians and ranchers for failing to come up with a plan to control the growing wild horse population in Nevada and the rest of the West.

JENNIFER RATHAUS

217

The image of Central America that has taken shape over the last 15 years—one of death, civil war, and progressive economic disintegration—is unfortunately entirely real, as those living in the region can bear witness. Yet there are two other critical, and interrelated, realities in Central America, although both are little known and even less understood.

The first is geographical and derives from Central America's location between the Western Hemisphere's two major terrestrial ecosystems. A land bridge connecting North and South America, Central America's 200,000 square miles run diagonally northwest to southeast in a thin strip separating the Pacific Ocean from the Caribbean Sea. In this extremely heterogeneous mosaic of climate, land forms, soils, vegetation, and animal life, species from both North and South America intermingle. As a result, this isthmus is one of the world's richest zones of biological diversity. The tropical forests, in particular, are repositories of a multitude of species of flora and fauna. More than 850 species of birds, for example, have been recorded for Costa Rica and Panama alone, and some 225 types of birds use Central America as a seasonal migratory corridor.

The second reality is human. Among the diversity of Central America are the indigenous people who first began filtering into and settling the isthmus as much as 20,000 years ago. Although they suffered severe depopulation through warfare and disease with the arrival of the Spaniards, many Indian societies have managed to survive into the present century with their ethnic identities intact. With an estimated population of about 5.6 million at the time of the Conquest, their numbers have even increased steadily in recent decades and are beginning to approach pre-Columbian levels. Today there are over 43 distinct indigenous/linguistic groups in Central America, making up a total population of between 4 and 5 million people.

At the same time, however, Indians throughout the region have been marginalized politically, economically, and even geographically to the point where they are a silent, virtually unknown minority. Although they make up as much as 20 percent of the region's total population, few people, even in Central America, know much about where Indians live or how they go about organizing their lives. Even during the Columbus Quincentenary in 1992, few activities involved live Indians.

At first glance, Guatemala appears to be an exception. Its Indians are visually striking and numerous, comprising about half the country's 9 million people. They are arrayed among some 22 different Mayan linguistic groups in Guatemala's Central and Western Highlands: they have been heavily studied, written about, and photographed, and countless tourists have admired their colorful weavings. The story of the bloody repression and outright massacres suffered by Indians at the hands of the Guatemalan military from the mid-1970s through the early years of the 1980s has been vividly documented in books, articles, and films.

Despite all this coverage of Guatemala, few interpretations of these events have come from the Indians' point of view; their thoughts and feelings are largely missing. Likewise, their participation in the national political arena remains minimal. Moreover, the violence escalated anew in the early 1990s, and many highland areas are still heavily militarized. Brutal killings of indigenous peoples erupted openly once again, and continue even as the first refugees returned to Guatemala in 1993 after living in exile in Mexico for as long as a decade. Understandably, the prevalent atmosphere of tension and uncertainty

Kuna of Panama

has severely curtailed Indian organizing around social or political issues or for community development.

El Salvador has more than half a million Indians, yet this community is not only little known but its existence is often flatly denied. Since the sixteenth century, Indians have been stripped of virtually everything that underlies their culture: their native languages, much of their traditional culture, their autonomy, and their lands. Today they eke out a meager existence, supplementing subsistence crops they grow on rented parcels of land with wages from seasonal labor on coffee and sugar-cane estates.

Most of the other indigenous groups of Central America live along the lowland coastal Caribbean plain. These are the truly invisible peoples of Central America. With the exception of the Miskito—who came to prominence in the early and mid-1980s through their conflicts with the Sandinistas in Nicaragua—and the Kuna of Panama—who have been popular with tourists for their colorful mola blouses and with anthropologists for their unique culture—the Indians of Central America's Caribbean slope generally drew a blank with outsiders.

In fact, many Indians chose this exile, while others were pushed into rural backlands by hostile forces. Until recently, the indigenous peoples of Central America lived in relative isolation in their "regions of refuge," largely protected from the incursion of the outside world by thick stands of forest, heavy rainfall, and a generally inhospitable environment.

Living in small communities hugging desolate mountain slopes or tucked away in the folds of tropical rain forests, even subsistence has been difficult and hardship and deprivation the rule. Roads, schools, health care, and electricity are substandard or absent. Those Indians who have migrated to cities and towns in search of jobs in recent years tend to remain isolated, squatting along the periphery of urban society, eking out a tenuous existence through occasional manual labor.

Now even the possibility of isolation is disappearing. Since the 1940s, exponential population growth throughout Central America, capitalist schemes utilizing new technologies for exploiting natural resources, and advances in public health have combined to open up these areas to the mass immigration of landless peasants, cattle ranchers, and entrepreneurs in search of lumber. The population of Central America has grown from about 3.7 million at the turn of the century to more than 25 million today; it is projected to double by 2010. At the same time, multinational companies are extending their tentacles into the last remaining hinterlands in search of cheap timber, oil, and precious minerals.

The point has been reached where most of the remaining wilderness has run out, and there are no backlands into which indigenous peoples can retreat to avoid outsiders. As all these forces advance, the forests are cut down and burned off at a steadily accelerating pace, and the native inhabitants are deprived of their resources, displaced, and driven into cultural extinction. Fully two-thirds of the lands covered by forests since the first settlement by aboriginal peoples thou-

219

sands of years ago have been cleared since 1950, and the pace of deforestation has accelerated every decade during the last 40 years. On the Atlantic Coast, Central America's last remaining stands of tropical rain forest—with the Indians living inside them—are falling before the advances of loggers, cattle ranchers, and peasant farmers forced from their overpopulated, degraded home territories on the Pacific side.

If people in industrialized countries are concerned over the fate of Central America's shrinking tropical forests, the Indians living in them—often the sole inhabitants—are expressing a good deal more than concern: they are terrified. If the forests disappear, so, too, will their way of life, their cultural identity, their economic base, their autonomy.

At the same time, a second, more positive trend has grown up alongside this pattern of environmental and human destruction. The indigenous peoples of the increasingly threadbare Caribbean coastal forests have begun to organize around the issues of land protection and natural

DERRILL BAZZY

Guatemalan refugee

resource management. For example, in southern Belize, the Toledo Maya Cultural Council is lobbying for the government to establish a Mayan homeland. In Honduras, the Tol, Pech, Tawahka Sumu, Lenca, Garífuna, and Miskito are all forming federations to defend their territories. In Nicaragua, the Miskito of the Atlantic coast are setting up a "protected area" that would ensure their control over the wealth of natural resources in their region. In Costa Rica, the Bribri and Cabécar peoples are forming "Councils of Elders"

in an effort to play a leadership role inside the La Amistad Biosphere Reserve, a bi-national forest park that spans the Costa Rica-Panama border.

In Panama, the three major indigenous groups —Guaymí, Kuna, and Emberá—are engaged in a difficult campaign to demarcate and patrol their tribal lands and protect their resources. Open violence has broken out on several fronts in Panama, with the most prominent between non-Indian colonists from the interior provinces and the Kuna of the Madungandi region in eastern Panama.

Virtually all these groups have been stirred into action over the last five or ten years, as the sound of approaching chain saws has come closer and closer. Many of these indigenous groups are small, but they are beginning to join together to revitalize their cultures and defend their rights to land.

This profusion of activity is a promising beginning. Yet the movement of Indians to organize to protect their lands has not received the outside support it needs. As they seek to guard their cultures and their homelands, they are engaged in a race against time and the powerful forces of destruction. With their living spaces shrinking and their escape routes blocked, Central America's indigenous peoples face difficult odds in their fight for survival.

MAC CHAPIN

Central America Resources:
Indian Law Resource Center, 601 E St., SE, Washington, DC 20003 (202)547-2800.
Mac Chapin, "The Coexistence of Indigenous Peoples and the Environment in Central America," map, co-produced by Cultural Survival and the National Geographic Society, 1992.
"Central America and the Caribbean," *Cultural Survival Quarterly*, 13(3), 1989.
Tom Barry, *Roots of Rebellion*, South End Press, 1987.
Tom Barry, *Central America Inside Out: The Essential Guide to Its Societies, Politics, and Economies*, Grove Weidenfeld, 1991.
Tom Barry and Kent Norsworthy, various country guides published by the Inter-Hemispheric Education Resource Center, Albuquerque, NM.

BRIBRI AND CABÉCAR OF COSTA RICA

MARCOS GUEVARA

TALAMANCA REGION

Bribri and Cabécar Action:
In Costa Rica, one path to gaining respect is to get the Congress to approve international conventions regarding human rights. One form of support that can be effective is the pressure that individuals and organizations can establish from the outside on Congress and the executive branch of the Costa Rican state.

The 17,000 Bribri and Cabécar are the most numerous indigenous peoples of Costa Rica. They live on the slopes of the Cordillera de Talamanca (Talamanca Mountains), above the country's principal national park. Because the Bribri and Cabécar languages are closely related, the two groups are known generically as Talamancas.

Talamancas have been stripped of much of their territories little by little, partly by Creole peasants and partly by large-scale cattle owners. This is plainly evidenced in the southern part of Costa Rica. In addition, North American enterprises claim they acquired lands in the Talamanca region from United Brand Company, which in the past had thrown people off the land to produce bananas.

The most urgent threat to these lands concerns mining. Canadian and North American enterprises are soliciting the Costa Rican Congress to grant them land rights covering 70 to 80 percent of Costa Rica's indigenous reserves. The Costa Rican government is participating in mining in conjunction with the Costa Rican Oil Refinery, which is soliciting concessions to exploit coal in two indigenous reserves. Congress is revising various concessions, which could produce environmental and social deterioration without precedent in these regions.

The threats facing Talamancas are so numerous that people have organized to confront them and to strengthen their rights to the land and their culture. For example, the Codebriwak Association (Committee for the Defense of the Rights of the Bribri and Cabécar), a federation of smaller groups, aims to unite all the local efforts into one voice to counter projects it considers negative.

MARCOS GUEVARA

BRIBRI, TERIBE, GUAYMÍ, KUNA, EMBERÁ, AND WOUNAAN OF PANAMA

Panama's more than 200,000 Indians are divided up into six groups: Bribri, Teribe, and Guaymí in the West; and Kuna, Emberá, and Wounaan to the east. Virtually all these groups live inside the few remaining stands of rain forest in the country.

In contrast to most Central American countries, Panama has a tradition of recognizing indigenous homelands dating back to 1938, when the Kuna of San Blas received their own *comarca,* or autonomous reserve. The Emberá and Wounaan Indians of the Darién region were granted a *comarca,* called *Emberá Drua* (Emberá Territory) in 1983. The Kuna of the Madungandi region in eastern Panama and the Guaymí in the Northwest are seeking legalization of their territories as well.

In recent years, all of Panama's indigenous peoples have had their forest lands threatened by the massive incursion of non-Indian colonists, the spread of cattle ranches, and illegal and semi-legal logging operations. Open violence has occurred with greater and greater frequency in both Kuna and Emberá regions in eastern Panama. Land is now the key issue for indigenous groups throughout the country.

Over the past five years, Kuna, Emberá and Wounaan, and Guaymí have organized around the issues of natural resources and land. The Kuna pioneered these efforts in 1983 with the creation of the Project for the Study of the Management of Wildlife Areas in Kuna Yala (PEMASKY), which set up a forest park as a buffer against settlement on the southern border of their *comarca.* This was followed in 1989 by the First Inter-American Indigenous Congress on Natural Resources, held in Panama City. Increasingly, other Indians are following suit.

221

The present Panamanian government has shown virtually no interest in protecting either indigenous rights or the remaining forests. Two examples of this lack of concern—coupled with capitalist greed and corruption—are a recent concession granted to Texaco to explore for oil in wildlife and indigenous areas of the Bocas del Toro region of western Panama and the upcoming battle over completing the Pan-American Highway through the Darién to connect Central with South America. Both projects threaten the way of life of countless Indians, as well as some of Panama's most valuable surviving stands of untouched forest. The Texaco concession has been withdrawn, temporarily at least, after considerable lobbying from environmentalists in Panama and in other countries.

MAC CHAPIN

CAKCHIQUEL MAYA WOMEN OF GUATEMALA

"When I am out working in my farm, if I see a little *mastate* tree or *guarumo* growing, or one of the plants we use to make thatch, I take care of them. I don't chop them down. Only people who don't know the uses of these plants destroy them."

Enriqueta Martínex, Cabécare, Costa Rica

The 12 indigenous communities along the shores of Lake Atitlan, Guatemala, represent a spectrum of the changes associated with development. The Tunecos of San Antonio Palopó, a Cakchiquel-speaking town of 2,800, are typical. They are wrestling with the loss of lakeside land to *ladino* (non-Indian) owners of vacation homes, the daily invasion of tourists searching for cheap souvenirs, and the unreality of television and videos.

Accompanying this modernization package is the pervasive embrace of the global economy, which is replacing traditional highland Maya life. For generations, life in San Antonio revolved around corn production. What little cash Tunecos needed came from selling anise and onions, plus some seasonal work on coastal cotton plantations.

In the late 1970s, the people of San Antonio revamped their economy. With the help of the Catholic Church and the Peace Corps, they bought footlooms, learned to weave, and reoriented production around commercial textiles. Nearly half the households now have looms, and incomes have risen considerably. The benefits of this new industry have not been spread equally, however. In particular, women find themselves economically vulnerable and more dependent on men.

When the survival of these Cakchiquel Maya families was based on *milpa* (corn), men and women shared work. Household needs quickly absorbed the little cash generated. Because life would be extremely difficult without their wives, men treated women as valuable and relatively equal partners. Even in the 1980s, as the cash economy was expanding, women weavers played important roles in efforts to establish a textile cooperative. Today, however, men dominate the more lucrative footloom weaving industry, and women play secondary roles as back-strap weavers. Urged on by Westerners with orders to fill, middlemen hesitate to hire women, whose non-paying family tasks prevent them from easily meeting production deadlines. Men can spend all day at the looms while wives prepare meals and keep children occupied.

This sexual division of labor affects the quality of life for the whole family. Women's small earnings go to satisfy family consumption needs because men express their economic prowess by buying such conspicuous goods as watches, tape decks, and houses. Entrepreneurs invest their earnings in stores or boats but not in family diets. As their fortunes rise, men may even provide less for their families, ostentatiously spreading their money around through parallel marriages and a second or third set of children.

These skewed gender relations are expressed at the community level as well. Some men forbid their wives to leave the home, especially at night. Only men go to the video theater, and no women are members of commu-

222

nity organizations like the PTA or the church council. Nor do women serve as officers in the textile co-op, although they outnumber men as members.

This pattern is reinforced by assumptions that women, as dedicated homemakers, do not need, or want, an education. As a result, monolingualism and illiteracy add to women's subordination, exacerbating their economic vulnerability.

TRACY BACHRACH EHLERS

CARIB TERRITORY OF DOMINICA

Carib Resource:
Carib Council, Carib Territory, Salybia, Dominica, West Indies.

The Carib of Dominica hold the only legally recognized reserve of indigenous land in the Caribbean islands. The 3,700-acre Carib Territory on the northeast coast of the island of Dominica is guaranteed to the 5,000 Indo-Dominican people. About 3,000 Carib residents live on the territory.

Carib Reserve Act Number 22, enacted in 1978, vests control of the territory with the Carib Council and the Carib chief, which are elected every five years. The act resulted from years of demands by Carib leaders, particularly the elder women. The leaders continue to call for the land in the reserve to be held communally, something they consider central to the survival of the Carib people.

Most Caribs are cash-crop and subsistence farmers. In addition, a steady group of hardy fishers—many of whom face rough Atlantic waters in dugout canoes—keeps fishing traditions alive. Herbal medicine is prevalent among Carib families, as is midwifery. Although the Carib language is nearly gone in Dominica, it is spoken in Guyana and Belize.

During the 1970s, ethnic consciousness and cultural revitalization movements began growing among the Caribs of Dominica. In the Carib Territory, the cultural troupe Karifuna formed to help preserve Carib arts, crafts, and culture. Karifuna gets youngsters involved under the guidance of veteran Indian dancers, musicians, and culture-bearers, and the group has performed throughout North America and Europe.

During the 1980s, the Carib chief and members of the Carib Council traveled abroad to meet with other native peoples and participate in hemispheric events. Since 1988, the Caribbean Organization of Indigenous Peoples has brought together Carib descendants from Dominica, the nearby St. Vincent Carib community of Sandy Bay, Garifuna from Belize, and Arawaks and Carib representatives from Guyana.

Although the Carib communities in Dominica and St. Vincent are now established native enclaves, they face serious cultural and physical threats. The prevailing danger in Dominica comes from proposed legal measures to divide the Carib Territory into individual landholdings. Such a division could erode the Carib land base and wipe out the community culture it supports.

Another danger comes from the loss of the Carib rainforest habitat due to erosion and the clearing of land for banana cash crops. The community depends on the forest for housing, boats, herbs, grasses for baskets, and other needs. Carib farmers are good producers, but they need better access to markets and other resources to help them diversify their agriculture. The importance of Dominica's protected banana market within the British Commonwealth diminishes with competition from Honduras and other major Central American banana producers within the European Community.

Most important, the effort to preserve and revitalize Carib culture and language, led by the Carib Council and its chief and buttressed by Karifuna,

223

deserves international recognition. Carib leaders, including Chief Irvince Auguiste and Parliamentary Representative Worrell Sanford, are pressing for much-needed community-development projects, such as a gravity-fed water system and agricultural extension. In St. Vincent, the 6,000 or so Carib descendants lack a land base and want the government to return to them 3,500 acres as a reserve.

JOSÉ BARREIRO

CHORTÍ OF HONDURAS

The heart of the Chortí Maya settlement in Honduras has historically been Copán, the site of the ruins of a famous Mayan ceremonial center in the far west of the country. Although significant numbers of Chortí still inhabit the nearby Guatemalan municipalities of Jocotán and Camotán, few people in Honduras could be classified culturally as Chortí.

Descendants of the Chortí in Copán are almost completely acculturated. In 1988, in only four of the forty-three villages surrounding the town of Copán Ruinas were there any Chortí speakers, usually only one or two people. In only two villages did any inhabitants identify themselves as Chortí. No Hondurans wear indigenous Chortí clothes.

In the mid-1980s, some Guatemalan Chortí residents of Copán (along with some non-Indians) had to leave Honduras because they lacked the proper documentation required by immigration laws. This exodus further reduced Chortí ethnic presence in the country.

The 1988 Honduran census underscores the decline of Chortí culture. For the first time since 1945, the census collected data on ethnicity by recording the native language spoken by citizens. The results do not include Chortí among the indigenous languages spoken in Honduras.

JAMES R. SAMSON

EL SALVADOR

El Salvador's more than 500,000 Indians (10 percent of the total population) are virtually invisible. Their existence is commonly denied inside their own country, even though they make up sizable majorities in the western departments of Sonsonate, Ahuachapán, La Libertad, and La Paz, as well as populating Morazán in the Northeast. In recent years, their absolute numbers have risen, but the government hasn't taken a census of the indigenous population since the early 1930s.

The Indians of El Salvador are heavily acculturated. Virtually all of them spoke Spanish by the turn of the nineteenth century, and today no more than a handful of elders have even partial knowledge of an Indian language. Few of the trappings of indigenous culture can be seen. Native dress has disappeared except for a few older women in rural villages who wear tattered *huipil* blouses and wrap-around skirts. To all appearances, little distinguishes the Indians of El Salvador from the *ladinos* surrounding them.

Yet in certain pockets, they are clearly identified, both by themselves and by others. They are defined by the manner in which they speak Spanish, their control of the *cofradía* religious system, their low self-esteem, and their abject poverty. Virtually all the Indians are landless peasants who spend a large part of their time working as peons on coffee and sugar-cane estates.

El Salvador's recent civil war has left Indians collectively more economically depressed than ever. Because they are chronically mired in poverty, they lack the resources to migrate to the capital or provincial cities, much less the United States. Even their fledgling attempts to gain control over collective pieces of land under the nation's agrarian-reform program have been stifled.

Despite these difficulties, El Salvador's Indians have formed representative organizations to pressure for their rights. The oldest, most prominent example is the National Salvadoran Indigenous Association.

MAC CHAPIN

GARÍFUNA OF BELIZE

The Garífuna, also known as Caribs or Black Caribs, are not native to Central America but can be classified as an Indian element on the basis of their genetic makeup and their use of a language indigenous to the Americas. Of mixed African and Carib Indian descent, the Garífuna originated on St. Vincent Island in the Lesser Antilles. Garífuna were deported by the British to Honduras in 1797 and reached Belize during the early nineteenth century.

Garífuna are concentrated in six villages in southern Belize near the Caribbean coast—Dangriga (formerly Stann Creek), Hopkins, Georgetown, Seine Bight, Punta Gorda, and Barranco. The British established agricultural "reserves" on the outskirts of Dangriga and Punta Gorda during the 1930s for subsistence-oriented farmers and fishing people. In recent decades, the number of Belize Garífuna has remained relatively stable. The most numerous Indian group in the country, they number about 11,000, accounting for 8 percent of the population.

Some Garífuna are migrating from coastal villages. This trend reaches throughout Belize and beyond to large Garífuna communities in Los Angeles, Houston, New Orleans, and New York. However, the homelands remain strong Garífuna territory.

WILLIAM V. DAVIDSON

GARÍFUNA OF HONDURAS

Garífuna speakers occupy the Caribbean coast between southern Belize and northeast Honduras, plus a small enclave at Pearl Lagoon, Nicaragua. Of the 54 Garífuna settlements in Central America, 44 are along the coast of northern Honduras. Garífuna are the majority rural people of the country's northern coastal fringes.

Official population estimates for Honduran Garífuna are between 70,000 and 80,000, but Garífuna leaders often suggest a figure of 200,000 to 300,000. A 1988 Honduran language census lists 27,745 Garífuna speakers, certainly an undercount.

Garífuna are unified and characterized primarily by language and rituals. Women normally dominate agriculture and food preparation, which centers on bitter manioc. Men engage in fishing-related activities and wage labor away from the villages.

Although the distinctive Garífuna culture, including dance, folk stories, songs, death, and rituals, remains strong in the home beach lands, out-migration throughout Honduras and abroad is increasing. Maintaining the language and traditions is more difficult away from the villages. In addition, *ladino* encroachments onto traditional Garífuna lands present the possibility of cultural dissolution.

WILLIAM V. DAVIDSON

225

GUAYMÍ OF COSTA RICA

The Guaymí in Costa Rica, numbering about 4,500 people, live in four indigenous reserves near the Panamanian border. Unjustly considered to be foreigners—specifically immigrants from Panama—the Guaymí have lived on the edge of Costa Rican society for decades, unable even to obtain recognition as citizens or to organize formally.

Recently, the Guaymí demanded recognition as Costa Rican citizens, not only for themselves but for other indigenous peoples who had also been denied this right. They brought a delegation to protest in the streets of the capital, San José, and occupied the courtyard of the cathedral there for several days.

Out of this experience the Ngobegue ("people") Association emerged. Since winning the battle of citizenship, it has fought for other basic rights for the Guaymí, such as land rights, the right to health, the right to have a traditional organization recognized by the state, and the right to maintain traditional forms of administering justice.

The Guaymí experience the same problems as other Costa Rican indigenous peoples, including deforestation of their lands, the destruction of the natural resources upon which their culture depends, and the imposition of foreign culture through schools and other state institutions.

MARCOS GUEVARA

HUAVES OF MEXICO

Huaves Resource:
Instituto Nacional Indigenista (National Indigenous Institute), Av. Revolucíon # 1279, 2 Piso, Col. Tlacopac, Mexico City DF, Mexico.

About 15,000 Huaves—peasant farmers, artisans, market women, and fishermen—inhabit sandy dunes adjacent to two large lagoons on the Tehuantepec Isthmus in southern Mexico. The Huaves have received scant attention from scholars or the public because of their remote location, far from major highways and tourist attractions. Nevertheless, pollution of the lagoons and of the Pacific Ocean by an oil refinery in Salina Cruz, Oaxaca, operated by PEMEX, Mexico's state-owned oil company, threatens their livelihood.

Oil spills have killed large numbers of fish and shrimp, the Huaves' primary sources for food and market products. PEMEX could remedy the situation by paying more attention to environmental safety and clean-up. However, it has shown little interest in helping the Huaves except to pay a small indemnity.

Historically, the Huaves have also been disadvantaged by their subordinate relationship to the much larger and more politically powerful Isthmus Zapotec who surround them. Zapotecs dominate local markets and have challenged Huave control of agricultural land.

HOWARD CAMPBELL

IXILS OF GUATEMALA

Until recently, the Ixils of Quiché Department were known chiefly for their devotion to Mayan tradition. But as they lost land to coffee plantations and their population grew, many became dependent on seasonal labor migration.

In the late 1970s, news of government assassinations began to filter out of Quiché, along with reports of a Guerrilla Army of the Poor (EGP). Started by outsiders recovering from revolutionary defeats in other parts of Guatemala, the EGP's presence triggered Guatemalan army reprisals against Ixils, pushing many of them into the guerrilla movement. In 1982, the army gained the upper hand by burning down rural settlements, corralling survivors into army-controlled "model villages," and drafting all the men into anti-guerrilla "civil patrols."

Ixil Resources:

Guatemala News and
Information Bureau, P.O.
Box 28594, Oakland, CA
94604 (510)835-0810.

Network in Solidarity with the
People of Guatemala, 1500
Massachusetts Ave, NW,
Washington, DC 20005
(202)223-6474.

David Stoll, *Between Two Armies
in the Ixil Towns of
Guatemala*, Columbia
University Press, 1993.

A decade later, some 12,000 Ixils—about 15 percent of the population—still hold out against army offensives in "communities of population in resistance" (CPRs), along with 5,000 refugees from elsewhere in the country. About 70,000 other Ixils live in army-controlled towns and resettlements, where they customarily blame both sides for the war. While resenting the army's mandatory civil patrols, many Ixils also say these patrols are necessary to ward off contacts with the still-active EGP and any consequent army reactions.

Now that Rigoberta Menchú, who hails from nearby Uspantán, has received the Nobel Peace Prize, human-rights organizations are moving into the Ixil area. However, they will have to balance the demands of CPR militants with the much larger number of Ixils who have accommodated themselves to army rule and pursue their objectives through less confrontational methods. Given the urgent wish of most Ixils for peace, human-rights groups should press both the guerrillas and the army to withdraw so that peasant families can give full attention to the formidable ecological problems they face.

Aid agencies have already flooded the area, but they need to focus on helping Ixils find new income sources. Owing to the diminishing land per capita available for burgeoning families, subsistence maize farming no longer meets nutritional needs.

DAVID STOLL

K'ICHE' MAYA OF GUATEMALA

K'iche' Maya resources:

Guatemala Scholars Network,
Route 1, Box 55, Friendsville,
MD 21531 (301)746-4057.

Guatemala News and
Information Bureau, P.O.
Box 28594, Oakland, CA
94604 (510)835-0810.

Perhaps no one better embodies the Maya resolve to survive adversity than Rigoberta Menchú, a K'iche' woman who received the Nobel Peace Price in 1992. But although answers to the needs of the K'iche' and other Maya in Guatemala are imaginable—land reform is the top priority—the clout to translate them into reality is not apparent.

The K'iche' Maya of Guatemala place great spiritual value on their links to the land, links that transcend Western conventions of territorial ownership and management. If land belongs to anyone, it belongs to the ancestors; the living must care for the earth as the dead did before them.

The Spanish conquest of 1524 dramatically altered traditional bonds between K'iche' and the land. The most disastrous consequence was demographic collapse. K'iche' constituted about half of Guatemala's estimated 2 million people at Spanish contact, a number that had withered to 130,000 a century later. Old World diseases were primarily responsible, but warfare, enslavement, exploitation, forced resettlement, and culture shock played a part.

The growing demand for coffee in Europe and North America during the nineteenth century led to radical changes for the Maya, creating demands for good land and cheap labor as well. With the so-called Liberal Revolution of 1871, a mind-set emerged intent on creating a "coffee state" by deploying native lands and hands to the ends of export agriculture. In the next few decades, the K'iche' lost prized land to aggressive planters, who also established large estates in the less fertile highlands to corral a work force that could be diverted, when needed, to the plantations. Forced-labor laws made up for any slack in this system.

The most onerous aspects of this political economy were dismantled between 1944 and 1954, but hope for sustained material progress and land reform disappeared with a CIA-orchestrated coup in 1954. Since then, regimes dominated or manipulated by the military have ruled Guatemala to

227

the detriment of the K'iche' and other Maya. Moreover, recent rapid population growth has resulted in more and more families struggling to survive on ever-smaller parcels of land.

Today, the K'iche' constitute about one-third of Guatemala's 5 million Maya. The largest of more than 20 groups, the K'iche' spread throughout several departments of western Guatemala, primarily El Quiché and Totonicapán. They remain part of the most vicious landholding inequality in all of Latin America: 90 percent of the farms work 16 percent of the land under cultivation, but 2 percent of farm operators control 66 percent of all cultivable land.

Human pressure on highland land is enormous, with subsistence needs often not remotely met, even with fertilizers and pesticides boosting yields. Guatemala, where corn was domesticated millennia ago, now imports this staff of life, while the best land is devoted to coffee, cotton, sugar, and nontraditional vegetables for export. At the same time, the forest cover is disappearing due to the practice of using firewood for cooking. Survival for the K'iche' is thus an interrelated set of environmental, demographic, and socioeconomic problems.

To these conditions must be added the counterinsurgency war. Armed rebellion in the 1980s met with a brutal response, which often failed to distinguish between guerrilla insurgents in rural areas and the people who lived there. The human costs of the war—massacres, village abandonment, lingering fear of intimidation and violence in a militarized society, and refugee flows within Guatemala and beyond to Mexico, the United States, and Canada—are borne by all Maya groups.

CHRISTOPHER H. LUTZ AND W. GEORGE LOVELL

LACANDON MAYA OF MEXICO

The Lacandon Maya live in the Selva Lacandona in the Montes Azules Biosphere Reserve of southeast Chiapas, Mexico. Most of the 500 Lacandon live in three communities, Lacanha, Mensäbäk, and Najá. They subsist mainly by swidden farming and supplement their diet by hunting small game. They also buy goods with money earned by selling arts and crafts to tourists at Palenque, a Classic Period Maya city.

The Lacandon were relatively isolated until after World War II, when much of the forest was opened to colonization and Maya from the Chiapas Highlands migrated to the region. Because of population pressure and land shortages, this flow from the highlands continues, severely affecting the Lacandon and their forest. The newcomers introduced cattle and pig husbandry, and abandoned *milpas* ("swidden fields") are now seeded with grass for grazing livestock rather then letting fields lie fallow to regenerate naturally.

As the forest is cut, the supply of game animals dwindles. As the Lacandon's wildlife resources are exhausted, they are forced to rely more on such processed foods as canned sardines and tuna. The need for manufactured goods makes it necessary to generate income. Men and women spend more time making arts and crafts for tourists, leaving people with less time for traditional practices and less control over their livelihoods.

Industrial concerns have also targeted the homelands of the Lacandon. In the past decade, these concerns have included oil exploration, but perhaps the most significant event was the bulldozing of a road through the Selva Lacandona in 1979 by companies seeking to exploit the jungle's timber. Today the supply of valuable timber is almost exhausted, but the road remains and fosters immigration directly into the heart of Lacandon territory. Mexico declared the Selva Lacandona a national park in 1971—with the Lacandon as its only legal residents—and expanded it to include all three Lacandon communities in 1975, but the government doesn't enforce the park boundaries or protect the Lacandon's right to the land.

Thus the Lacandon face a twofold threat. First, losing their land to immigrants from the highlands, along with the accompanying degradation of the forest, endangers the Lacandon's traditional way of life. Second, this threat to their traditional subsistence practices makes them more dependent on processed foods and goods whose production and prices they do not control.

Enforcing the boundaries of the Selva Lacandona would be one effective step toward protecting the Lacandon's traditional way of life, as would stopping, or at least slowing, industrial exploitation of the forest.

JON MCGEE

LENCA OF HONDURAS

The Lenca inhabit the pine-forested volcanic mountains of western Honduras. These heavily acculturated Indians live in *ladino* towns, along major transportation arteries, and occasionally in isolated mountain *caserios* (hamlets) in the departments of Santa Barbara, Lempira, Intibuca, Comayagua, and La Paz.

Before Spanish contact, the Lenca were divided into four territorial entities: the Care, Cerquin, and Lenca in Honduras and the Poton in El Salvador. In Honduras, they occupied an estimated 10,000 square miles in 1550, an area that has since contracted to about 4,200 square miles. Population estimates range from 50,000 to 95,000.

Linguists have had little success in finding Lenca speakers since the 1970s. Their religion, which fuses Catholicism and traditional practices, is harder to maintain as priests become less tolerant of syncretism. Still, despite such challenges to their culture, Lencas are trying to preserve what remains of it by continuing some of their religious practices and artisanry.

T. SHAWN MITCHELL

MALEKU OF COSTA RICA

The 520 Maleku are among the indigenous peoples who have suffered most in Central America. They live in the Guatuso Indigenous Reserve but possess only 15 percent of its land. They must dedicate themselves to work-by-the-day, selling their labor to cattle owners who occupy land that was once theirs.

229

The history of the Maleku is particularly dramatic in that they had long maintained their territorial and cultural autonomy despite Spanish conquerors and colonists. In the short space of 100 years, however, the Maleku have suffered impressive indignities, among them slavery to rubber collectors at the end of the nineteenth century. Since then, Maleku culture has been transformed by the plundering of their lands and natural resources.

Today Malekus are almost totally dependent on assistance from the Costa Rican state. *Palenques*, traditional homes made of bark and palm leaves, have disappeared. Instead, the state has built dismal houses of cement, wood, and zinc, without taking into account such Maleku customs as burying their dead in the house.

Malekus constantly confront the state's institutions as they fight to regain part of their lands, subsist, and gain respect for their customs and language. Nevertheless, Malekus outwardly appear very acculturated because their traditions are spiritual, not material.

A new organization, the association of Indigenous Maleku Farmers of Guatuso of Alajuela, tries to change the very negative destiny with which "progress" has saddled them. Among other things, this organization has started to take back the Maleku lands that are now occupied by cattle owners inside their indigenous reserve. Likewise, the group works toward cultural revitalization through bilingual classes and through access to protected lands, where Malekus can fish for turtles in a sustainable way.

MARCOS GUEVARA

MAYA OF GUATEMALA AND EDUCATION

Maya Education Resources:
Guatemala Scholars Network,
  Route 1, Box 55,
  Friendsville, MD 21531
  (301)746-4057.
Maya Educational Foundation
  (in formation), P.O. Box 38,
  South Woodstock, VT
  05071-0038 (802)457-1199;
  fax: (802)457-2212.

Guatemala, a country of over 9 million inhabitants, is home to some 5 million Maya. These numbers, however, do not afford Maya equal status in Guatemalan society. They have endured discriminatory treatment under colonial and post-independence governments, dominated by elites of European and mixed descent.

Gross discrimination in the provision of government services—except for an exaggerated and unwanted granting of "military aid" to the highlands—is especially noteworthy in terms of educational opportunities. The Maya tend to live in rural hamlets and small towns. Because central governments have traditionally concentrated social services in Guatemala City and, to a lesser extent, in departmental or state capitals, the Maya have limited access to secondary education. Their only recourse is to send students to distant state-run or Catholic Church schools, where they board or find lodging in private homes. For every quetzal (about 18 cents) the government spends in the western highlands, where most Maya live, three go to the eastern, largely *ladino* region. Ten quetzales go to Guatemala City.

Even with scholarship support, secondary education is beyond the dreams of all but a few Maya. University training is obtained only in a few inferior provincial centers or in Guatemala City. In the capital, the choices are between the large public university, San Carlos, several religiously affiliated institutions, and two private, non-sectarian universities. Most Maya fortunate enough to enter a university study at San Carlos; relatively few attend institutions with religious affiliations, and fewer yet go to non-sectarian schools.

The highest Maya participation—25 percent of all students—is in primary education, reflecting a wider distribution of small rural schools. Maya constitute 10 percent of all secondary-school students. Only 5 percent of Guatemalan university students are Maya. Because of costs, distances from home towns, and an often unfriendly ambiance, most of this 5 percent never graduate.

This educational deficit bodes ill for Maya to one day participate as equals in Guatemalan society, nor is the government seriously disposed to improve Maya educational opportunities. Any initiatives must first come from the Maya community itself, and then from international institutions. Some small efforts to support Maya higher education are underway, but much more needs to be accomplished.

The Maya will lose as they win, however, if they can't retain their own languages and cultures as they attend *ladino*-dominated schools. For centuries central authorities have attempted to hispanicize the Maya, but these efforts have been resisted. In these times of surging population, land deprivation, and immigration to urban centers, the key to Maya cultural survival may well be in gaining the education needed to compete in non-agricultural sectors of the economy while simultaneously retaining a distinct identity.

CHRISTOPHER H. LUTZ

230

MAYA REFUGEES IN GUATEMALA

Maya Refugee Action:
The returnees are counting on the international community to maintain vigilance in monitoring the actions of the Guatemalan government and military. Some groups active in the region are Witness for Peace, 2201 P St., NW, Washington, DC 20037, Americas Watch, 485 Fifth Ave, New York, NY 10017, and the American Friends Service Committee, 1501 Cherry St., Philadelphia, PA 19102.

In January 1993, nearly 3,000 Guatemalan Maya living in refugee camps in Mexico returned to their home country, the first of a projected series of repatriations agreed upon between the Guatemalan government and elected refugee leaders. The refugees are politicized, well organized, and aware that the prestige of Nobel laureate Rigoberta Menchú, a Guatemala Mayan exile herself, helps their position. The effort is financed by international donations and administered by the United Nations.

Maya anticipation of the return created fear and enthusiasm—the latter rare among these usually stoic people. Despite the amnesty implied by the agreement, President Jorge Serrano and his defense minister have stated that the returnees were clearly subversives because they would have had no reason to flee otherwise.

The first returning families have been settled in a remote part of El Quiché Department, squeezed between the remaining guerrillas and a Guatemalan army camp. This seems a formula for disasters similar to those they had fled. Since settlement, army patrols have maintained a constant presence, much to the discomfort of the returnees. Yet the success or failure of these returnees will determine whether refugees still in Mexico will follow in their footsteps.

The repatriation agreement promised land and money for tools, seeds, construction materials, and food until the first harvest, but the chances for sustainable agriculture are small in that part of El Quiché. Not only are the soils poor in quality, fragile, and shallow, but there are no roads, schools, health services, communications facilities, or sources of potable water. The area harbors some slash-and-burn cultivators, who worry that their own subsistence will be endangered.

All this suggests that the Serrano government is less than serious in its peaceful intentions. Apart from the purely political problem they face, Guatemala's Maya people are already too numerous to live well on the limited lands left to them after centuries of fraud, semi-legal encroachment, and outright confiscation. The "green revolution" has provided some respite, although at a high cost to Mayan health due to heavy use of pesticides. Massive land redistribution seems politically impossible for the foreseeable future, yet, for these people, to be without land results in both impoverished bodies and spirits.

NANCIE GONZALEZ

231

MAYA REFUGEES IN MEXICO

As a result of massive counterinsurgency campaigns in the indigenous regions of western Guatemala that took place largely between 1982 and 1984, at least a quarter of a million Maya fled their home communities or recently established colonies to settle in refugee camps, rural communities, and cities in Chiapas, Mexico's poorest state. Many were relocated in 1984 and 1985 to the states of Campeche and Quintana Roo, due in part to border attacks from the Guatemalan military, but thousands resisted relocation outside Chiapas. Thousands more became hidden agricultural workers, especially near the Pacific coast and in remote tropical *ejidos* (agrarian collectives).

Relatively few refugees have returned to Guatemala. Some have continued north to Mexico City or the United States, and over 50,000 remain hidden in rural and urban areas as unrecognized refugees ("illegal aliens"). These groups try to preserve their Mayan identity but find that the need to "become Mexican" is strong, due to their precarious legal status and the fear of being detected and deported. Some unrecognized refugees never tell their own children of their origins.

Human-rights groups have frequently complained about the treatment of official refugees, but little notice has been made of the thousands who have slipped into the least desirable labor niches. Mexico needs to declare an amnesty for Guatemalan refugees now integrated into the Mexican society and economy and allow them to live as open refugees without having to reside in camps or be pressured to return.

No formal support organizations exist for the unofficials because publicity would constitute a threat of discovery. Only the reform of Mexican law can end their lives of fear and cultural denial. In the meantime, their suffering continues. As one refugee said, "We must live a lie every day."

DUNCAN EARLE

NAHUA OF MEXICO

The Nahua, who speak Nahuat and Nahuatl, live in the Mexican states of Puebla, Tlaxcala, Veracruz, and San Luis Potosí. They have experienced serious human-rights abuses, particularly where they have lost their land to a Spanish-speaking minority and live in communities with rival armed insurgency groups.

Both problems affect Huitzilan de Serdán, a community in the northern sierra of Puebla. The Nahuat of Huitzilan lost most of their land when Spanish-speaking immigrants from Tetela de Ocampo settled in the community after 1900. Losing land lessens the Nahua's ability to grow food and particularly hurts women, who inherit less of their family estates when land becomes scarce.

Violence in Huitzilan has been especially severe since 1978, when the Unión Campesina Independiente (UCI—Independent Peasants Union) appeared and took over a pasture owned by a Tetela immigrant. The organization aimed to improve the economic position of its members by restoring to them the land they had used for growing corn. The situation turned violent when UCI members killed other Nahuat who were allied, through patronage and ritual kinship, with the migrant families from Tetela. A second insurgency group, La Antorcha Campesina—"Torch of the Farmer"— emerged, and violence escalated as the members of the two organizations sought vengeance on each other. The state and federal governments intervened first on the side of the landowners, who had lost some land to the UCI, and then on behalf of Antorcha. Government soldiers temporarily drove the UCI out, and Antorcha has established itself as the ruling group.

Women and children as well as men have died in armed clashes between UCI and Antorcha. Now firmly in power, Antorcha has become an oppressive force, intimidating, killing, and arresting those affiliated with its rival. Some of those arrested have received very long prison terms based on confessions extracted under torture. For example, Gerónimo Aco, Francisco Galindo, and José Hernández, arrested for murdering an Antorcha-affiliated municipal president, signed confessions under torture and are serving 20-year sentences. Puebla officials threatened to rape Aco's wife if he didn't sign a confession.

JAMES TAGGART

PECH OF HONDURAS

Most Pech (known as Paya until recently) live in pine-savanna-covered upland valleys in the Department of Olancho, Honduras. Tropical hardwood forests occupy the surrounding mountain slopes. Two outlying zones of Pech settlement are found in lowland areas. About 1,850 Pech live in 11 main communities.

Archaeological and historical data indicate that the Pech inhabited about 10,000 square miles of northeastern Honduras when Europeans arrived. Since then, the Pech region has contracted to a fraction of its former size and fragmented into isolated parcels associated with individual Pech villages.

The reduction of Pech territory occurred as the Honduran frontier moved eastward, initially forcing the Pech to retreat eastward in front of the advancing frontier, and later infiltrating and fragmenting the core of the remaining Pech lands. The colonization front has now overtaken the main Pech settlements, separating them from one another by lands occupied by *ladinos*.

The increasing integration of the Pech into Honduran society has led to the loss of much of their traditional culture. The older generation is bilingual, but there is concern that too few among the younger generation are learning the native language. Typical *ladino* clothing has replaced traditional dress. The traditional subsistence lifestyle is giving way to a peasant one, with increasing connections to the Honduran economy.

JAMES R. SAMSON

TAINO NATION OF THE CARRIBEAN

Taino Resource:
Nacion Taina, P.O. Box 883, New York, NY 10025 or Res. Jaguas C5, Ciales, Puerto Rico 00638.

Although the genocide against the native peoples of the Caribbean was nearly total, several Indo-Caribbean enclaves have survived. Five or more small communities remain in Cuba, St. Vincent, and Dominica. In the past decade, a revitalization of Taino cultural and family identity has occurred among *mestizo* descendants in Boriquen (Puerto Rico), Cuba, and Quisqueya (Santo Domingo). An estimated one-third of Puerto Ricans have strong Taino ancestry.

The resurgence of Taino identity among *boriquas* in Puerto Rico has resulted in several study groups, organizations, and cultural events on the island and in the United States and in the ceremonial restoration of the Taino Nation on November 19, 1992. The nation has gathered a core of families that have maintained rural and indigenous traditions. Its Council of Nitaynos has initiated a cultural-recuperation project that publishes a newsletter and organizes educational and cultural events, and it is promoting a major Taino conference scheduled for 1994.

JOSÉ BARREIRO

233

TAINO OF CUBA

Taino Resources:
Community contact: Cacique Francisco Ramirez Rojas, Caridad de los Indios, Municipalidad de Yateras, Guantanamo, Cuba.
Museo Matachin, Ciudad de Baracoa, Provincia Baracoa, Cuba.
Casa del Caribe, Santiago de Cuba, Cuba.

Caridad de los Indios and La Escondida near Guantanamo City are perhaps the best-known enclaves of aboriginal Indo-Cuban peoples. These two communities of Taino descendants, extending among several principal families, include over 1,000 people. Many *guajiro* homesteads in this part of Cuba identify as *"Indios"* and claim roots in Cuba's Taino and Arawak cultural legacy. Agricultural and herbal medicinal traditions persist, and several hundred Taino Indian words anchor the Spanish spoken in the area.

The Taino descendants in eastern Cuba survived war, slavery, disease, and 500 years of relocations into ever more remote mountain valleys. However, full assimilation is Cuba's official developmental norm for native ethnicities. Three decades of socialist government have brought medical centers and schools to their communities, but have also fostered intermarriage with other ethnic groups. Nevertheless, people in the region express a desire to meet "as Indians" and form cultural associations with other Indians even while Cuban researchers surmise that Cuban Indian families "tend to disappear."

The Cuban Indians of the Oriente region and their *guajiro* relatives in Camaguey Province and other parts of the interior remain isolated from each other and from the hemispheric trends of native peoples of recent years. They are a rural, farming, and fishing people, and they express strong identity with their land.

JOSÉ BARREIRO

TAWAHKA OF HONDURAS

Numbering fewer than 1,000, the Tawahka of eastern Honduras are being devastated by aggressive colonization, threatened by corporate plans for oil exploration and logging, and largely ignored by environmentalists who want to protect the tropical forests in which the Tawahka have lived for centuries. The Tawahka are struggling for legal rights to territories in a proposed reserve that bears their name.

The Tawahka lands comprise about 1,600 square miles of the Mosquitia, one of Honduras' most remote and biologically diverse areas. In 1992, President Rafael Callejas agreed to set aside some 3,500 square miles of the Mosquitia as a Tawahka Biosphere Reserve. In addition to the Tawahka's homelands, the region includes two national parks. Soon afterward, Callejas and Nicaraguan president Violeta Chamorro agreed to establish "La Solidaridad," a system of reserves in the Mosquitia region of both countries. The Tawahka Biosphere Reserve would form the central piece of the larger system.

These plans fall far short of the Tawahka's needs. Callejas' declaration of a reserve doesn't have the force of law. Even worse, the Tawahka have no legally recognized land rights in the proposed reserve, so they have no guarantee of protection for their communities and traditions.

In response, the Indigenous Federation of Honduran Tawahka (FITH) is seeking legal title to Tawahka lands. Creating a Tawahka *indigenous* reserve would allow FITH to work with the Tawahka to manage resources and protect the forest from invading colonists and corporations, something conservationists have been unable to do. Unfortunately, Honduran and international conservationists have lent only weak support to FITH's efforts.

In the meantime, colonists continue their destructive intrusion into Tawahka territory and resist efforts to establish any reserve, which could prevent their stripping the forests for cattle ranches. They are telling the Tawahka that the establishment of any reserve would deprive the Indians of *all* rights to the land and are pressuring them to oppose a reserve completely. But the alternative—no reserve—would only leave the Tawahka vulnerable to the abuse of colonists who already physically harass them and force them to work without pay clearing their own forests for cattle.

ADAPTED FROM "ACTION FOR CULTURAL SURVIVAL"

234

TOL OF HONDURAS

The Tol-speaking people (who are also known as Tolupan or Torrupanes and are better known to outsiders as Jicaques), live in north-central Honduras, primarily in Yoro Department. Their population is estimated at 7,000 to 18,000, with the lower figure probably more accurate. The 1988 Honduran language census lists 1,959 "Jicaque" speakers.

Researchers recognize 23 Tol "tribes" in distinct places in Yoro; two very small clans live more isolated in pine forests in Francisco Morazán Department. Virtually all these people are small-scale agriculturalists who have communal land titles. Those of Yoro gained lands in the mid-nineteenth century; those of Montãna de la Flor acquired two titles in 1928.

Unfortunately, few Tol, for a variety of reasons—especially *ladino* immigration—live on their lands today. Tol territory, over 6,000 square miles at Spanish contact, has been reduced to about 1,600 square miles today. The Tol are still a distinctive, identifiable population of Honduras, but they are becoming more assimilated into the dominant culture daily.

WILLIAM V. DAVIDSON

TZUTUJIL MAYA OF GUATEMALA

ROBERT CARLSEN

Elite soldiers on patrol in Santiago Atitlán

Santiago Atitlán is the only community in Guatemala free from political violence. Yet problems wrought by the peace in this Tzutujil Maya town unmask challenges faced by all Guatemalans.

In marked contrast with the present, the 1980s was a decade of horrific violence in Atitlán. Virtually nobody was spared the murder of family members or close neighbors. Although some early responsibility lay with left-wing guerrillas, by 1989 all political violence was attributable to the Guatemalan army, known to residents as the *Kiks* ("the bloody ones"). The situation peaked on December 2, 1990, when soldiers from the local garrison turned their weapons on several thousand unarmed residents, killing 13.

The ensuing national and international outcry forced the army's exit. The 15-mile area surrounding Atitlán is now Guatemala's only demilitarized zone, and not a single murder has occurred in Santiago Atitlán since the army vacated the area.

However, the very success of this peace threatens the Guatemalan military, and the situation remains unstable. During incidents in which the army has been directly implicated, an unusually high number of Santiago Atitlán residents have been targeted for robbery, rape, and murder while traveling outside the area. On several occasions, the army has mounted incursions into the demilitarized zone—in pursuit of "insurgents" whom no one else has seen. Said one military spokesperson, "By law, we have the responsibility to protect every part of the national territory."

ROBERT S. CARLSEN

235

South America is home to about 15 million Indians. Despite government efforts to present their countries as blended populations, magically converting Indians to such non-ethnic classifications as *campesinos, mestizos,* or *cholos,* most observers still see Indians as significantly "different," both from each other and from non-Indian society in general.

For most non-Indians, all first inhabitants are indios, connoting anything from inferior to subhuman. Ironically, Indians have begun to refer to each other as indios, a unifying category denoting "colonized people." This new sense of unity and shared situation has evolved into one of the region's most significant social phenomena: a broad, grassroots, indigenous social movement that has seized a place on the political landscape of almost every South American country. At the same time, the hundreds of small and large Indian societies are maintaining their unique ethnic identities.

They have done so with great difficulty. When Columbus sailed from Cadiz in 1492, about 20 million people lived and worked in South America. Within 100 years, European-introduced diseases had decimated over 90 percent of that population, while slavery and murder added to the tragedy. Half a millennium later, the total number of descendants of those colonized and subjugated by European conquerors is still short of the pre-contact population. Moreover, their problems with colonizers have changed only in scale and nature.

Throughout the continent, two major trends characterize today's indigenous human-rights picture. First, the dominant society no longer regards Indians simply as sources of cheap labor but, more importantly, as troublesome claimants to coveted land and resources. Second, in response to outside threats, South American Indians are no longer passive victims. Over the past 20 years, most indigenous peoples have organized themselves and entered the national and international political arena to defend their rights to land, resources, and the right to organize.

Shuar bicultural school

From Commodity to Claimant

From the sixteenth century to the mid-twentieth, most of the non-Indian elite viewed South America's original inhabitants primarily as cheap labor for factories, landholdings, and public-works projects. Secondarily, Indians were seen as weak claimants to land and resources.

Historically, land and labor conflicts have been most acute in the Andean highlands, where almost 90 percent of South American Indians live. In some parts of the Andes, Indian communities now occupy only the most isolated and relatively unproductive areas. In most countries, non-Indians have whittled away and absorbed the best lands progressively. Where landowners need a supply of periodic labor, a common pattern has emerged: small Indian communities have been allowed to remain but usually on holdings too small to provide basic subsistence. This assures wage labor for the larger-scale landowners.

Attempts to recover Indian lands have continued and expanded into the 1990s. The most noticeable cases may be in the Mapuche territory of south-central Chile and by a variety of indigenous groups throughout much of the highland areas of Colombia and Ecuador. The conflict has been dramatized by regular assassinations of Indian leaders in Colombia's Department of Cauca and in its Sierra Nevada de Santa Marta, as well as by an Indian-led strike for land rights and self-determination that paralyzed Ecuador in 1990.

First National Indian Conference in Colombia, 1982

Similar problems exist in Peru, even though many communities recovered lost lands during the 1970s through a progressive *Ley de Communidades Indigenas* (Law of Indigenous Communities). However, since 1980 the land question in Peru has been overshadowed by the Sendero Luminoso (Shining Path) guerrilla movement. It first appeared in the region around Ayacucho and subsequently spread to much of the central and southern Peruvian highlands. Although this movement recruits heavily among local Indians, it is an anomaly in its odd mixture of Andean and Maoist symbolism. Moreover, its expressed goals and methods of intimidation and recruitment more resemble those of Cambodia's Khmer Rouge

and Pol Pot than the democratic grassroots organizing characteristic of the ethnic federations that have evolved throughout South America.

Shifting Resources

Although Sendero Luminoso had its beginnings in isolated areas of the Andes, the movement still draws direct and indirect support from Peru's frustrated and angry urban unemployed. It also illustrates the growing urbanization of South America's Indians. Beginning in the 1960s, there has been a pronounced demographic shift from the countryside to cities. Highland Indians of Bolivia, Colombia, Chile, Ecuador, and Peru previously made up the rural agricultural labor force. Today, many live in squatter settlements in the region's major urban areas, at best surviving through formal and informal labor.

At the same time, the interests of the dominant sectors of South America have shifted from the labor of Andean Indians to using Indian land and resources in the lowlands. For that reason, human-rights reports focus mainly on the situation of land-based Indian societies. The cases document abuses ranging from health needs to physical violence, but land is the primary concern. For several years, land issues have dominated the political landscape.

Recently, governments have issued many promises, decrees, and statements regarding Indian lands. On April 23, 1988, for example, President Virgilio Barco signed documents formally turning over more than 30 million acres to the Indians of Colombia's Amazonian region, with the largest area—over 10 million acres—being the Predio Putumayo. In Bolivia, following a dramatic 44-day march in July 1990 by Indians from the Amazonian region to La Paz, President Jaime Paz Zamora issued three presidential decrees setting aside over 7 million acres as formal Indian territories. In 1992, Venezuela fol-

237

ASHANINKA ORGANIZATIONS IN PERU

Organization	Location	# of member communities
Apatyawaka Nampitsi Ashaninka (ANAP)	Pichis and Pachitea rivers	107
Central de Comunidades Nativas dela Selva Central (CECONSEC)	Perene and Satipo rivers	77
Federación de Comunidades Nativas Campas (FECONACA)	Perene River	5
Organización Ashaninka del Gran Pajonal (OAGP)	Gran Pajonal	33
Consejo Nomatseguenga y Ashaninka del Pangoa (CONOAP)	Pangoa River	25
Central Ashaninka del Rio Támbo (CART)	Tambo River	35 (inactive due to the violence)
Organización Campa del Rio Ene (OCARE)	Ene River	15 (inactive due to the violence)
Organización Indígena Region Atalaya (OIRA)	Tambo and Ucayali rivers	108

Over the past 20 years, South American Indians have organized to protect their rights.

lowed suit with the formal declaration of even more extensive Indian lands for its Yanomami and Yecuana. Brazil did the same for its Yanomami and Kayapo, granting them over 25,000 square miles, as did Ecuador for the Quichua (Runa), Achuar, Shuar, and Zaparo of Pastaza Province.

It would appear that 1992 was a banner year of respect for Indian land rights. However, the declarations of intent in Bolivia, the demarcations in Brazil and Venezuela, and even the formal titling in Colombia and Ecuador raise as many questions as they appear to resolve. In Bolivia, the government has moved very slowly to implement the decrees, and 1993 elections could easily lead to a reversal of the promises. In Venezuela, the lands have been declared a biosphere reserve, a category that permits the government to exploit the rich natural resources of the indigenous areas. In Brazil, local governments as well as military officials challenged the legality of President Fernando Collor de Mello's agreements even before he was impeached for misusing funds. In Colombia, the large tracts of land awarded in Amazonia are extremely isolated, and the security of Indian tenure on the land has yet to be tested in the face of other claimants or invaders.

Indian rights are still commonly neglected or violated. As such, there is ample reason to maintain vigilance regarding any examples that suggest vastly improved respect for indigenous human rights. In this task, one of the brightest lights is the growing number, strength, and sophistication of Indian organizations, which now cover the South American landscape. These include ONIC (National Indian Organization of Colombia), AIDESEP (Inter-Ethnic Association for the Development of the Peruvian Amazon), CONFENIAE (Confederation of Indian Nations of the Ecuadorian Amazon), CIDOB (Indian Confederation of the Bolivian Oriente), and COICA (Coordinating Body of Indigenous Peoples' Organizations of the Amazon Basin: the Amazonian regional coordinating group). As a result, Indian organizations can not only sound the alarm when human-rights violations occur, but they can position themselves to resolve, and even prevent, such situations from arising through information networks and land-use programs that will secure indigenous tenure rights and generate essential income.

THEODORE MACDONALD, JR.

238

ACHÉ OF PARAGUAY

The 700 Aché occupy three small parcels of land in eastern Paraguay. Deforestation and privatization on their foraging areas is making them dependent on missionaries and the government.

Two Aché communities—Ypetimi and Yñaró Puerto Barra—face threats from Proyecto Caazapa, a rural development project. After an international outcry over agro-industrial logging in the forests of the Ypetimi community, where 140 Aché live, the World Bank halted funding and about 5,000 acres were demarcated for the Aché. The land is being held by the Instituto Nacional del Indígena (INDI—National Indigenous Institute) with the stated intention of providing title to the Aché. However, this parcel is only a fraction of the area needed to maintain Aché hunting and gathering. Moreover, road building and deforestation are rapidly destroying the forest adjacent to the colony, and the Aché have sold the remaining mature timber on their land to buy machinery for commercial agriculture.

The second Aché community in the project zone, Yñaró Puerto Barra, with 50 Aché, has been administered by an American missionary for 15 years. Its 10 families have a relatively high standard of living, producing most of their subsistence and some cash in agriculture.

After leaving the forest in 1972, the 286 northern Aché settled at a Catholic mission called Chupa Poú. Another group of 50 Aché reside at a German mission nearby, where they await the receipt of their own land. A final group of 200 remains at Cerro Morotí, a Catholic mission.

Given the expanses of accessible forest nearby, these groups have spent most of their time hunting and gathering. However, this independence is threatened by the 1992 purchase of most of the Aché foraging area by The Nature Conservancy for a biosphere reserve. Aché attempts to acquire some of the land for themselves have stalled, and their access to foraging area remains at the will of The Nature Conservancy.

RICHARD REED

AMUESHA OF PERU

The *cornesha'*, or prophet-priest of the Amuesha, blows across a gourd bowl of specially brewed manioc beer and raises it toward the early morning sun. Sitting on an elaborate wooden bench, surrounded by his "brother's sons" inside the round, palm-thatched temple, he initiates the morning prayers to the Sun god and all the other powerful forces in the Amuesha cosmos. The macaw feathers in his wicker crown flutter, in play with the shimmering of the silver plugs in his earlobes and the gold disk hanging from his nose septum. He speaks of the approaching mellapo, or sacred time, and reminds his followers of the moral codes of their ancestors, exhorting them to put those codes into practice. He is the spiritual and moral guide of his people.

239

Since Micllatareñ died in 1975, abandoned by his "brother's sons," his temple in ruins, no prophet-priest has arisen to speak of the Sun's word and provide moral guidance. Some Amuesha have joined the Seventh Day Adventists or the Evangelical church, both of which condemn the spiritual and moral basis of the traditional culture. Others have gone to the city to try on new professions as servants, house guards, and prostitutes.

For moral and spiritual leadership, most Amuesha look to FECONAYA (Federación de Comunidades Nativas Yanesha'—the Federation of Native Yanesha Communities), which brings together 30 Amuesha communities in a common search for a future. The head of the organization, elected every two years, is called the "*cornesha'*," an unfortunate malapropism. During the past decade, foreign donations have become available to FECONAYA, and some of its leaders have been involved in fraud, scams, and outright appropriation of community funds. A recent *cornesha'* used a scholarship fund to finance high living in Lima, leaving students to fend for themselves.

"We are in a moral crisis," one Amuesha confides. "If our leaders behave this way, we are lost. We need a real *cornesha'* to guide us." The cultural and moral foundations are still there for the Amuesha, but they need to be rediscovered, as they have before in times of crisis.

RICHARD CHASE SMITH

ASHANINKA OF PERU

"We want the preservation of our culture, our language, our spirituality, and to retrieve our dignity that was lost during the last 500 years."
Eliane Potiguara, Brazil

240

Since 1980, Peru has faced growing internal violence. Some of the violence is the product of two armed political movements: Shining Path (Sendero Luminoso), which espouses an authoritarian Maoism, and Tupac Amaru Revolutionary Movement (MRTA), which is more nationalist. Some results from conflicts among drug cartels for control over the lucrative drug trade or between the cartels and the U.S.-backed anti-narcotics police. Hundreds of indigenous and non-indigenous communities are caught up in both kinds of violence.

In the Amazon, the Indian people most affected are the 50,000 Ashaninka (Campa), Peru's largest lowland Indian group. Today 80 percent of the Ashaninka live in officially titled and recognized communities that are represented by one of the eight organizations to have arisen in the past 20 years.

Renowned warriors since the seventeenth century, the Ashaninka are no strangers to violent incursions. The latest chapter in this history began in 1979 with a massive, well-planned invasion of the Ene River by "colonization cooperatives" from the Ayacucho region. Many co-ops became centers of drug production linked to the Colombian cartels. However, by 1985 Shining Path had established effective control over 70 percent of the valley as well as over the drug trade. With the notable exception of those settled near the Franciscan Mission at Cutivireni, most Ashaninka moved away from the main river to avoid confrontation with the drug traffickers or with Shining Path. A nervous calm reigned.

In 1988, MRTA quietly moved into the Pachitea and Pichis valleys; Shining Path moved into the upper Perene and Satipo areas and expanded down the Tambo as far as the town of Atalaya. Both armed groups, often battling each other, used communities as sources of food and shelter. Those living along the footpaths used by guerrillas received occasional indoctrination and pressure to join the movements.

By 1989, their traditional hospitality worn thin, their gardens emptied of subsistence crops, their children forcibly recruited into guerrilla ranks, and unwilling leaders executed, the Ashaninka shifted from uncooperative indifference to resistance. In December, MRTA executed a respected leader in the Pichis Valley, but within two weeks ANAP had raised an Ashaninka army of 1,000 armed with bows, arrows, shotguns, and hunting rifles. Within three months, ANAP had driven MRTA out and had assumed control of the region. In a paid announcement in a Lima paper in March 1990, ANAP announced that "the struggle of the Ashaninka people of the Pichis Valley has met with its objectives . . . but we remain alert and prepared to prevent anyone from abusing our people again."

Peru's armed forces didn't enter the fray until mid-1990 when they established permanent bases in Puerto Inca, Puerto Bermudez, Atalaya, and Satipo. An initial tense standoff between the Ashaninka and the armed forces has been replaced by an apparent understanding as the army respects the autonomy of the Indian communities.

From 1990 to 1992, the Pichis action produced similar responses among the Ashaninka of the Perene-Satipo area. However, this Ashaninka army confronted a far more complex situation, given the massive numbers of colonists in the area, the ease of local transport, and the fanaticism of Shining Path. Despite armed confrontations between guerrillas and Ashaninka resulting in many deaths and refugees, and despite Peruvian army actions, both Shining Path and MRTA maintain a threatening presence in this region.

After 1988, Shining Path initiated a campaign to control the Ashaninka in the Ene and Tambo valleys. Between 1989 and 1992, most Ashaninka abandoned their village sites, many living as wandering refugees in the forest. At least 700 Ene Ashaninka have made the arduous journey by foot across the Vilcabamba Range and resettled in the lower Urubamba Valley. Since early 1992, a new army garrison at the former Franciscan Mission in Cutivireni has permitted some Ashaninka to reestablish residence there, but constant Shining Path harassment makes life precarious.

President Alfredo Fujimori has promised to pacify the country by 1995 and taken some important steps in that direction. But the Ashaninka are preparing themselves for a prolonged struggle, not only against today's guerrilla movements or the occupying army but against any aggressor who fails to respect their territories, their culture, or their rights.

RICHARD CHASE SMITH

AYMARA OF CHILE

Aymara women

Of the approximately 2 million Aymara, about 30,000 to 50,000 live in northern Chile. The differing estimates between 30,000 and 50,000 represent those who maintain the Aymara language and culture as opposed to those who regard themselves as *mestizos*, combining indigenous and Spanish ancestry.

In the past centuries, the Aymara have migrated seasonally between the high grasslands (*Altiplano*) for pastures and the valleys for farming. This mobility also allowed them to become major merchants, traveling in caravans of cargo-bearing llamas from the Pacific coast to the jungles of Peru and Bolivia. Aymara migrants now also live along the coast, mainly in the cities of Iquique and Arica.

Major changes in Aymara migrations arose after 1973, as the Pinochet dictatorship imposed "forced Chileanization" on the *Altiplano*. To protect the frontier, the government established a new town on the site of the old hamlet of Colchane, replacing the traditional, ceremonial center with a new "Chilean" town. *Carabineros* (national police) were relocated from Isluga to Colchane.

Education was central to Chileanization. Forming a cultural enclave in the heart of communities, schools played an anti-Aymara role, with programs and teachers foreign to the Andean social and physical landscape. The impact has been critical. For example, Spanish-language education has been closely tied to the loss of the indigenous language.

Chileanization derived its logic in part from perceived national-security needs. Beginning in 1973, Chile set up military stations all along the frontier with Peru and Bolivia. Aymara pastoralists often were injured or killed while searching for lost llamas or simply crossing the border along traditional trails. The armed forces frequently shot at domestic animals and regularly inspected the persons, goods, and baggage of residents and travelers.

241

Recent improvements have come about with the formation of Aymara organizations, although the Aymara have long maintained flexible relations with authorities. Neither with the dictatorship nor with the new democratic government have they held either a confrontational attitude or one of mere dependence. They often support the government or negotiate with officials to obtain space for development and growth.

As a result, the government has provided the Aymara with relatively large amounts of resources. In addition, Chile's parliament recently banned mining companies from interfering with the water resources of Aymara communities and pastures.

Nevertheless, many ethnic needs remain unfulfilled. In particular, the old Aymara world is dying. Today's ethnic affirmation is a reaction to the destruction that can accompany so-called community development and a way for the Aymara to appropriate that process for themselves.

JOSÉ BENGOA

BRAZILIAN INDIGENOUS LAND POLICY

Brazil's 215,000 indigenous people, representing over 180 groups, can acquire legal land titles through a purchase or gift, the establishment of a reserve on land the state takes from private owners, or the setting up of an official indigenous area based on traditional land tenure. Indigenous areas, comprising 90 percent of the total so far titled, belong to the state but are reserved for occupation by indigenous people.

FUNAI (the National Indian Foundation) initiates the process to create an indigenous area, but it is chronically short of funds, and only 20 of its 4,500 employees are qualified to identify indigenous lands. In 1987, half the 93 million acres in question had only reached the first stage, identification. About 43 percent had been delimited; a mere 6 percent were registered indigenous areas.

At two recent periods, political bottlenecks slowed the allocation of land to indigenous groups. During Brazil's "democratic opening" in the late 1970s and the early 1980s, FUNAI went in the opposite direction to the rest of the country and hired many retired officers, just as military rule was waning. Meanwhile, the armed forces declared all land questions to be matters of national security, due to unrest in rural areas.

Next, between 1986 and 1989, José Sarney, Brazil's first civilian president in 22 years, put the Amazon region under military supervision. His Projeto Calha Norte (Northern Drainage Project) stressed the "natural vocation" of the Amazon for extracting minerals and timber, as well as its "strategic vocation" to be highly militarized. The military blocked any consideration of "excessively large" indigenous areas. It also allowed registration of land only on behalf of "unacculturated Indians," a definition applied so rigorously that the Yanomami were the only ones in the Amazon to qualify.

After President Fernando Collor de Mello took office in 1990, the National Security Council was incorporated into a new Secretariat for Strategic Matters, which interfered much less in indigenous affairs. FUNAI, however, persisted with the old procedures; action on indigenous areas remained virtually paralyzed until Collor visited the Yanomami. He ordered landing strips constructed by gold miners to be dynamited and gave miners six months to leave Yanomami territory. He also revoked an order confining the Yanomami to 17 separated areas.

FUNAI and police carried out Collor's orders haphazardly at first, but this soon changed. First, Collor came under intense pressure from human-rights and environmental groups because of the plight of the Yanomami. And he did not want Brazil to appear as a villain while hosting the 1992 Earth Summit in Rio. Between late 1991 and June 1992, 46 directives led to the delimiting of 36 million acres. Almost 23 million acres were registered as a Yanomami indigenous area.

Despite FUNAI's improved policies, Brazil's indigenous people face several immediate dangers. Because FUNAI has meager funds, it needs support from the World Bank and other international bodies. Meanwhile, an October 1993 constitutional deadline for regularizing indigenous areas looms. And with Brazil's constitution due to be revised in 1993, Congress may assume control of the process of setting up indigenous areas and make it easier to carry out mining on indigenous lands.

Under the present administration of President Itamar Franco, private organizations are FUNAI's main allies. Its opponents, the governors of northern states, particularly Amazonas and Roraima, claim that advocates for recognizing large indigenous areas are part of an international conspiracy to take over the Amazon region.

JOÃO PACHECO DE OLIVEIRA

CHIRIPÁ OF PARAGUAY

The expansion of agriculture and cattle ranching into their forests threatens the 5,500 Chiripá. About 85 percent of their communities have some land guaranteed by the Instituto Nacional del Indígena (INDI—National Indigenous Institute), and over half have title to the land they occupy, but the allocated land is insufficient to maintain indigenous production.

Most Chiripá divide their time among gardening, hunting, and wage labor, often harvesting forest crops for future sale. This affords Chiripá independence from the larger society, while providing them access to the marketplace. Paraguayan law allocates each indigenous family a minimum of about 25 acres, an area that will only support a family that engages in intensive commercial farming. Anthropologists estimate that families need about 10 times that amount of land to maintain indigenous agroforestry.

Most communities actually have far less than even the government minimum, a situation that makes Chiripá dependent on the market and threatens them with a concurrent loss of ethnic autonomy.

RICHARD REED

243

COYAIMA OF COLOMBIA

For over 100 years, the Coyaimas of Yaguara in Tolima Department have confronted the owners of cattle *haciendas*, who have done everything possible to expropriate Indian *resguardos* (community land). In the 1950s, similar confrontations escalated to such a point that massive conflicts known as *La Violencia* swept Colombia. Official persecution and the formation of armed opposition groups left those Indians of Yaguara who survived in a tenuous position.

In 1964, this Coyaima community agreed to relocate to the Department of Caqueta, on the Yari savannahs, where it would extend the Indian territory into the Amazon jungle. INCORA, the regional development agency, committed itself to titling a section of savannah and scrub forest where Coyaima could reproduce traditional agricultural and social systems.

Thirty years later, the Coyaima are still waiting for INCORA—along with other national authorities, the army, the Catholic Church, the U.S. Embassy, and private companies—to honor commitments to helping this Indian colony. Instead, during the past 10 years, new inhabitants have arrived and asked for titles to lands they claim are unoccupied, unowned state territory. Members of the Coyaima Community Council have gone to Bogotá many times to try to convince the government to survey and title Indian lands before open conflicts with the new colonists arise.

ADOLFO TRIANA

HUAORANI OF ECUADOR

Huaorani Resource:
Rainforest Action Network, 301 Broadway, Suite A, San Francisco, CA 94133.

Bearing presents and promises, Maxus Energy Corp. continues to push its oil road toward the land of the Huaorani. Taking advantage of divisions among the Huaorani over the issue of oil development, the Dallas-based company has given communities outboard motors and portable generators and promised to build schoolhouses and community centers—in exchange for extracting perhaps billions of dollars worth of heavy crude oil from Huaorani territory.

Particularly disturbing are reported attempts by Maxus to bribe leaders of ONHAE, the Huaorani Indian organization. The company's strategy has been to divide and conquer the Indians, and it has resisted calls by CONAIE and CONFENIAE, the national and regional indigenous organizations, for serious negotiations that would lead to involving native people in assessing and mitigating the environmental and cultural impacts of the road. CONFENIAE has called for a halt to road construction until such negotiations take place.

Although Maxus appears confident that it has won the Huaorani over, it is doubtful that it has informed many Huaorani of the probable impacts of plowing a 100-mile road into their land or of pumping millions of barrels of oil. Furthermore, agreements between the Huaorani and company or government officials are of dubious value, because the indigenous group has had no access to technical advisors or legal representation.

GLENN SWITKES

HUITOTO AND BORA OF PERU

In the 1920s, during the waning years of the rubber boom, two Peruvian administrators of the disintegrating Arana rubber empire forcibly moved about 6,000 Huitoto and Bora Indians from Colombia's Caquetá River to the southern bank of the Putumayo River in Peru. However, in 1933, with continuing skirmishes between Colombian and Peruvian forces and a measles epidemic said to have killed half the population, these same economic lords, now organized as a company, moved the remnants of the Huitoto and Bora, about 1,200 Indians, further south to the Ampiyacu River, where they were settled according to ethnic and clan affiliation.

The company established a large store and warehouse near where the Ampiyacu empties into the Amazon, a strategic location for controlling the Ampiyacu basin and for taking advantage of the Amazon's traffic. The store was the center of operations: goods moved from it into the hands of the captive Indian residents at exorbitant prices but with an aura of generosity. Indians paid off the debts by collecting such forest products as rosewood, rubber, resins, oils, wild-animal skins, dried fish, and palm fiber. The company shipped these to the regional commercial center of Iquitos.

In the late 1950s, the company owners, old and ailing, closed down the Ampiyacu operations and moved to Iquitos. River traders, or *regatones*, took over the exchange of forest products for manufactured goods and, for the first time, cane alcohol. Lumber companies in Iquitos sent in work teams or hired Huitoto and Bora to cut hardwood trees and drag them to the river. Commercial hunters began ranging the forests, seeking game animals to sell the meat in Iquitos.

With a 1974 law protecting native communities, Huitoto and Bora communities along the Ampiyacu received legal recognition and title to their lands. Armed with land titles and easy credit from the government agrarian bank, the Indians planted jute, rice, and corn for sale to the state marketing concern. Members of a crafts project organized through a state-sponsored women's movement made hammocks and tote bags out of palm fiber, yielding a new source of income for Indian women. Craft production went hand in hand with the arrival of tourists from Iquitos on elegant boats.

These changes brought a new sense of autonomy and economic independence to the Huitoto and Bora. By the late 1980s, the 13 communities of the Ampiyacu had organized the Federación De Communidades Nativas del Rio Ampiyacu (FECONA—Federation of Native Communities of Rio Ampiyacu River), a federation that gave them the political strength to demand more territory, reduce exploitation by the *regatones,* and stop the illicit extraction of timber and wild game. For three years, a FECONA crafts marketing project eliminated the *regatones* and raised craft prices.

However, a nationwide recession, brought on by government-dictated high gasoline prices, hit the Amazon region particularly hard. Easy credit disappeared, tourism fell to a trickle, and the bottom dropped out of the crafts market. Many Huitoto and Bora now recall the company era as a golden past, when they had access to trade goods and could pay for them over months or years.

With few alternatives, the Huitoto and Bora of the Ampiyacu are returning to the subsistence economy that has always been the basis of their survival. Small, diversified gardens, rotated regularly to rebuild the soils, and hunting, fishing, and gathering of forest products provide food and shelter. But they yearn for cash. Even amidst a traditional celebration of the *ungurabe* palm fruit, when two clans ritually exchange forest products for garden produce, Bora men dream of chain saws and of pastures full of cattle. The challenge is to build a sustainable local economy based on a balance of subsistence and cash-generating activities.

RICHARD CHASE SMITH

INGANO OF COLOMBIA

On December 6, 1992, a knife thrust to the heart killed José Homero Mutumbajoy, an Ingano leader from Putumayo Department. The murder symbolizes a cycle of colonization in the Amazon piedmont within which Inganos, Kofanes, Sionas, and Pastos now fight for survival.

On that day, Homero and other indigenous leaders had gathered near the department capital of Mocoa to prepare for meetings with government bodies. They hoped to resolve various needs afflicting their communities, including damage wrought by the activities of Ecopetrol, the Colombian oil company, complaints about Indian programs established by the government development agency, and the situation of the indigenous people of Mocoa.

Born in Yunquillo, Homero had become a leader of his Ingano community. Since childhood, he had traveled around Putumayo and seen the dislocation that oil production had caused among Indians of the Colombian frontier. This critical situation led to the formation of the Regional Organization of Putumayo, which later joined the National Indian Organization of Colombia. At the time of his death, Homero was president of the regional organization and a candidate for the Putumayo Departmental Assembly. He had initiated negotiations with Ecopetrol to have that company indemnify communities for the loss of their lands and the displacement of their people,

245

now reduced to living as uprooted urban dwellers.

Such actions failed to spark local authorities to defend Indian communities. Eventually, 130 families seized 15 acres of Catholic Church land in Mocoa, and Homero was elected president of the Committee for Indian Housing of Mocoa. Such work on behalf of Putumayo's Indians created concern among local authorities to the extent that they associated his organizing with such problems as armed insurgency and drug trafficking.

ADOLFO TRIANA

KAYAPÓ OF BRAZIL

More nations have disappeared during the twentieth century than at any other time in history. Brazil has lost one Indian nation per year since the turn of the century—one third of its cultural groups.

Jason Clay, *Hunger 1993*

About 3,500 Kayapó live in 15 villages, located at some distance from one another in southeastern Para between the Tocantins and Xingu rivers. Their traditional way of life contrasted with the one they are now encouraged to adopt in the name of progress. They had an intimate knowledge of the possibilities and limitations of the ecosystems in their lands. They knew the jungles and the savannas that not only supplied their physical needs but also formed the basis of their world view, kept alive by the intense ritual life they still maintain.

Until the 1960s, outsiders considered the Kayapó as "wild" and "jungle Indians." In the 1980s, drastic changes began in southeastern Para that had both direct and indirect effects on the Kayapó. Their lands were invaded and their forests cut down. Roads were built, bringing in ranchers and loggers. Mining activities and hydroelectric projects were introduced. Also, a race for mahogany started as prices for it soared on the world market. This wood became the "green gold" of Amazonia, while Kayapó country became a typical frontier region: chaotic, violent, and lacking infrastructure.

By the middle of the 1980s, logging took place on Indian territory more and more intensively, with FUNAI, the government agency for indigenous peoples, acting as intermediary with the loggers. In 1983 the agency's president started signing contracts with logging concerns to cut wood on Kayapó territory. The first Kayapó village on whose lands logging was permitted was Kikretum, led by chief Tutu Pombo. Soon logging operations expanded to the villages of Kokraimoro, Kubenkranken, and Aukre.

Gradually, the loggers gave up dealing through FUNAI and negotiated directly with the leaders of the two or three factions found in each Kayapó village. These indigenous representatives were young men who spoke some Portuguese and were more familiar than their elders with Brazilian society. This approach proved so effective that loggers repeated it elsewhere and, with the help of their Kayapó contacts, expanded their operations to the closely related Xikrin in the villages of Cateté, Bacaja, Kararaô, Bau, and Mekranoti.

No formal control is exercised over the amount of wood cut on Kayapó land, either by FUNAI, the Brazilian Institute for the Environment (IBAMA), or Indians themselves. Contracts with logging companies, when they exist at all, are filled with clauses showing clearly that the loggers' intentions are detrimental to the Indians. Such contracts usually state that the companies have been contracted by the Indians to cut wood. This clause gets around the rare inspections carried out by IBAMA and protects the companies against legal actions, since Brazilian law ostensibly protects indigenous lands and forbids logging on them, except under very specific circumstances.

The harm done to the health of the Kayapó, to their forests and rivers, and to the flora and fauna of their territory by the uncontrolled extraction of timber is profoundly affecting the way of life of this people. The Brazilian state, which is responsible for the arrival of loggers and miners in Kayapó territory, has never offered the Indians either qualified mediators or serious economic alternatives. Instead, the Kayapó have achieved a kind of illusory autonomy, accepting a model of development that will inevitably destroy the environment that has sustained them since time immemorial.

ISABEL VIDAL GIANNINI

MAKUNA OF COLOMBIA

Makuna Resources:
Coordinating Committee of the Amazon Basin, Jiron Almagro 614, Lima 11, Peru.
National Indigenous Organization of Colombia, Apartado Aereo 32395, Bogota, Colombia.

The Makuna, 600 people strong, live in Colombia's Vaupes region near the headwaters of the Comena River in the Amazonian rain forest. Makuna religion is a kind of ecosophy. They consider salt licks and fish-spawning spaces to be sacred, and their shamans carefully mediate the reciprocity among humans, fish, and game animals to keep it in balance. Traditionally, therefore, Makuna managed their environment and did not plunder it. Thus gold miners threaten the Makuna's sense of cosmological well-being as they endanger their traditional livelihood by indiscriminately cutting the forest, polluting the rivers, and killing fish.

Another secular threat comes from the cocaine industry. Involvements with cocaine dealers have brought money into Makuna society, and with it economic differentiation. Similarly, traders bring goods and indebtedness, and some Makuna have been forced into a state of debt bondage.

Since the 1970s, the Catholic Church has supported extensive missionary activities, as the name of the Makuna village of Santa Isabel suggests. Under the Church's influence, Makuna are abandoning the traditional longhouse for individual homes, weakening the ties of clan membership and reciprocity. Education in Catholic schools teaches Makuna children to ignore ecological and food taboos. Other religious groups have proselytized among the Makuna, although with less effect.

Missionary work does not always go unchallenged. One headman sends only alternate sons to Catholic schools and trains the others in traditional beliefs. Recently, major rituals such as the Spirit Dance have been held more often as the Makuna consciously attempt to reemphasize their cosmology and culture.

ADAPTED FROM *CULTURAL SURVIVAL QUARTERLY*

MAPUCHE OF CHILE

In 1979, the government of Augusto Pinochet overruled the legal existence of Mapuche reservations in Chile and enacted laws encouraging the transformation of the community-owned land-tenure system into individually owned private property. Since then, about 98 percent of community lands have been divided into individual plots through a legal process inherited and sustained by the current government of Patricio Aylwin. In the name of progress, indigenous language, marriage customs, and religion are under attack from crusading agencies, missionaries, and individuals.

The primary target of change is land. The attempt to integrate the Mapuche into Chilean society and economy has shrunk their reservations to the point where many are inadequate to support the population by traditional means. Many Mapuche have sold their land to developers or farmers. In other cases, landfill projects have infringed upon Mapuche terrain near large cities. The remaining communal lands are likely to be legally disbanded in the near future, which will probably drive more landless Mapuche to the cities.

Recently, the government has been focusing on writing a new indigenous law that Mapuche organizations could support through participation in the

247

government-affiliated Special Commission of Indigenous Peoples (Commision Especial de Pueblos Indigenas—CEPI). The proposed law would create indigenous development territories and establish a fund for expanding land under collective ownership. During a review in the Chilean parliament, however, the project met strong opposition—both from officials within the Aylwin government and from opposition parties—and it is being modified. The failure to enact a new indigenous law, or to amend the Chilean Constitution to include indigenous peoples, has helped erode an agreement first made with Mapuche leaders to support Aylwin's 1990 presidential candidacy.

The Mapuche have followed legal procedures in dealing with the government, but the judicial system has failed to respond in kind. Mapuche may turn to violent resistance as their only alternative. Thus in June 1992 the Consejo de Todas las Tierras (Council of All Lands), the only Mapuche organization that refuses to participate in CEPI, attempted to seize lost lands in several areas, including Carahue, Lautaro, Cunco, Panguipulli, Collipulli, and Nueva Imperial. As a result, council leaders were jailed. Government officials have accused them of forming an illegal association, have denied them access to the press, and have restricted them from traveling outside Chile.

Nevertheless, the council has received much support from rural Mapuche communities, other indigenous groups, and people abroad. Regional organizations such as the council, as well as more established groups, have taken on critical tasks, the most significant of which may be the dual role of sustaining Mapuche culture and organizing the often widely displaced Mapuche into a united force.

ALEJANDRO HERRERA AND TOM D. DILLEHAY

MBYÁ OF PARAGUAY

Over 7,000 Mbyá occupy the forests of eastern Paraguay. Until recently, they avoided missionaries, loggers, and yerba mate gatherers by dispersing into small groups and moving frequently. Now the Mbyá are encountering pressures from deforestation and commercial agriculture. Unless action is taken quickly, the last of their small communities will be exposed directly to these changes.

Land titling is hampered by inefficient and unwilling bureaucrats, and the problems are exacerbated by the dispersion of Mbyá communities. Small communities resist relocation to large reservations, and titling small parcels to each group creates islands of forest in what is becoming an ocean of soybeans.

As early as the 1970s, several Mbyá communities in the department of Caaguazu attracted international attention when Mennonite farmers displaced them. Recent development threatens the final refuge of the Mbyá, the forested highlands of Caazapá and Itaipua. Since 1985, settlers and corporations, intent on producing cotton and soybeans, have invaded these highlands.

From the west, the invasion is facilitated by a rural-development project initiated in the early 1980s. The project, which would have covered almost 1 million acres, was financed with World Bank loans until it became clear the effort would hurt the Mbyá. Still, land clearing in Caazapá reached the San Rafael highlands in 1990, leaving only a narrow corridor of forest for the Mbyá.

From the east, the Mbyá are threatened by commercial agricultural expansion on the fertile Parana flatlands. Most lower areas surrounding the Parana River were cleared by multinational agribusinesses a decade ago. The

Paraguayan government is now seeking loans to build roads into the last uncleared areas, including the heights of San Rafael.

Already, roads come within 10 miles of 90 percent of Mbyá communities. Peasant invasions have forced perhaps half of the communities to relocate to the highlands. Even in the highlands, logging has decreased Mbyá hunting returns. And skyrocketing land prices both force peasants into this frontier region and exacerbate the problems of guaranteeing Mbyá land or increasing their holdings.

Mbyá in the San Rafael have only tenuous control of the land they occupy. The government recently guaranteed a tract of about 20,000 acres in the San Rafael highlands to the Mbyá, but this is an unhappy compromise intended to provide the dispersed groups with a final, permanent refuge as their communities are stripped of their resources. The acreage set aside represents less than a third of the land needed to maintain the indigenous society and its hunting and gardening economy.

A larger Mbyá reservation could be created in the highlands adjacent to a proposed biosphere reserve. The Nature Conservancy is interested in preserving an area capable of sustaining the biological diversity of one of South America's last remaining subtropical deciduous forests.

RICHARD REED

MOJO, CHIMANE, SIRIONO, AND TRINITARIO OF BOLIVIA

In 1990, the Central de Pueblos Indigenas de Bení (Organization of the Indigenous Peoples of the Beni Region), an ethnic federation in Bolivia's eastern tropical lowlands, marched to defend the territorial rights of a number of small ethnic groups in the Amazon basin. In a journey that lasted for over a month, 700 Mojos, Chimanes, Siriono, and Trinitarios crossed 400 miles of jungle and rugged mountains. The march raised awareness in Bolivia of tropical forests and the need to protect indigenous rights in them. Its biggest prize was the transfer, by executive decree, of territorial rights covering over 11,500 square miles to some 10,000 Indians.

In 1993, however, many official promises made after the march remain unfulfilled. The Chimane, who live in the forest of the same name, have been unable to dislodge the timber companies that are removing valuable mahogany. The companies have ignored a decree that was supposed to suspend cutting and timber concessions in Chimane Forest. Although using new practices, the pattern of deforestation continues unabated in Chimane territory.

For the Siriono, conditions are little better. In mid-1992, cattle ranchers occupied one-third of the Siriono's 75,000-acre territory, despite a government pledge to send a boundary commission. The government demonstrated little political will to compensate or resettle the ranchers until the Siriono burned down an empty ranch house and began demarcating the territory themselves. At that point, the government acted on its pledge.

Other ethnic groups, too, face encroachments into their territory from cattle ranchers and colonists, although demarcation of the borders of the Isobore-Secure National Park where they live is complete. With the help of CIDDEBENI, a Bolivian nongovernmental organization, the indigenous peoples of the region have launched a training program and are developing plans to manage social and economic development within the park. They have also established an indigenous forestry guard to protect its resources.

KEVIN HEALY

249

PAI-TAVYTERÁ OF PARAGUAY

Almost 90 percent of the Pai-Tavyterá have title to community lands, but, like those of other Paraguayan Indians, their environment suffers from serious degradation. In addition to land loss, which has reduced the Pai to living on less than 2 percent of their original area, they have lost much of the standing timber and fauna on the remaining land.

Throughout the 1980s, the federal Instituto Nacional del Indigena (INDI—National Indigenous Institute) contracted with Pai colonies to sell their timber. The minister of defense and other INDI officers acted as intermediaries, selling timber at below-market rates and often smuggling it to Brazil. The Pai had to accept this practice in order to secure land titles. National exposure of the practice has halted overt timber sales, but not before the loss of timber had destroyed the hunting and agricultural potential of the forests.

RICHARD REED

PEWENCHE OF CHILE

Subsisting on a combined economy of livestock raising, piñon (a type of chestnut) collecting, and some agriculture, Pewenche communities are highly adapted to the environmental constraints of the Andes. Since 1991, however, seven Pewenche communities have been affected by the Pangue dam project of the National Electricity Company (ENDESA) in Chile's Upper Bío-Bío River area.

Although the World Bank-funded project won't displace Pewenche, the plans to develop the upper Bío-Bío area could affect them in various ways. Pewenche haven't participated in any aspect of the ENDESA project, and the government has conducted no social impact assessment. And because the government is determined to promote large-scale development, the series of dams is likely to be built.

Nevertheless, international resistance to constructing the dams continues, and environmentalists and others who want to save the river have had more success than the Pewenche in preventing total transformation of the area. International publicity has also forced the government to take limited action on behalf of the Indians. For example, the government has bought the community lands of the Quinquen Pewenche from Chilean landholders to legally restore the territory to the Pewenche.

As a result of its actions and international pressure, the World Bank has mandated to ENDESA that the Pewenche participate in the development programs planned for the area. On the Pewenche side is the Consejo de Caciques del Alto Bío-Bío (Upper Bío-Bío Council of Chiefs), which has emerged as a representative organization to confront the issue.

ALEJANDRO HERRERA AND TOM D. DILLEHAY

PIAROA OF VENEZUELA

The population of the Piaroa has grown 60 percent in the past decade, according to data recently released by the directors of the 1992 Venezuelan Indian Census. That news should cause cultural-rights advocates to rejoice, but the growth is highly uneven and favors the heavily acculturated Piaroa communities located at the margins of non-Indian society.

Piaroa pursuing a more traditional lifestyle in the remote heartland are suffering zero growth. In 1982, they accounted for 10 percent of the Piaroa population, a proportion that was cut in half by 1992. Numerical marginality intensifies pressure on traditional Piaroa to abandon their physical and cultural independence.

One of the main reasons for the demographic gap is unequal access to

250

modern medicine. The acculturated Piaroa enjoy better access to hospitals, clinics, pharmacies, itinerant doctors, vaccinations, nutritional supplement programs, medical dispensaries, and resident native nurses. These services are concentrated in the contact zones near the non-Indian towns, leaving the hinterland Piaroa out of the loop of contemporary health care. The result is higher mortality and emigration to communities where modern services are available. Special medical programs aimed at the interior peoples are desperately needed to bring traditional Piaroa back from the brink of extinction.

At the same time, a government attempt to reverse predatory logging threatens about a thousand Piaroa in the upper Suapure-Quanimo area of Bolivar State. The Environmental Ministry has adopted a new commercial-logging policy that calls for large-scale, long-term land leases in the hope of stimulating better forest-management practices, including the rotation of cutting zones and the replanting of tree species.

Despite the good intentions, the policy may mean that the Piaroa will be replaced by Licaima, a multinational consortium of logging companies, as the forest managers. Licaima has entered a petition for a 35-year land concession of almost 300,000 acres. In the meantime, the consortium has begun cutting trees.

Much of the concession land is inhabited. According to census figures, 886 Piaroa, distributed in nine communities, claim ancestral roots there and vigorously protest Licaima's invasion of their territory. The Piaroa use the land for agriculture, hunting, fishing, and gathering and for extracting palm oil, a highly marketable product. They have formed a multi-community business to facilitate their economic development.

It is ironic that this development-minded group may lose a large part of its land to outside developers. It would be contradictory for the Environmental Ministry, in the name of appropriate development, to favor Licaima, which has yet to present a forest-management plan, over the resident Indians, who have demonstrated their capacity to manage the forest.

STANFORD ZENT

RUNA, ACHUAR, SHUAR, AND ZAPARO OF ECUADOR

In April 1992, Ecuador's Organization of Indigenous Peoples of Pastaza (OPIP) won a stunning victory. After the Indian federation led a dramatic march from the Amazon rain forests over the Andes to the capital of Quito, Ecuadorian president Rodrigo Borja awarded the indigenous people of Pastaza Province a land grant the size of Connecticut. OPIP thus secured for its members the largest Indian land claim yet attained in Ecuador.

The march was spearheaded by 2,000 indigenous men, women, and children from 148 communities. As they made their way over the Andes, their ranks swelled to 10,000 by the time they reached the capital. Despite the pivotal outcome, however, the 1992 march is proving to be just one step in a long struggle for indigenous land rights. Many OPIP claims remain unrecognized.

The arduous march followed three years of Indian organizing to gain government recognition of their land rights. In 1989, OPIP and government representatives signed an agreement to gain legal recognition of Indian territorial rights and to revise plans for oil exploration in Pastaza. The government failed to fulfill its end of the agreement, and in August 1990 200 delegates from Indian organizations addressed a final demand to the president to legalize Indian territories in Pastaza. The government opposed this demand, claiming that Indian organizations wanted to acquire the whole province

Oil-well fire in the Ecuador Amazon

and set up a separate state. The situation deteriorated when the government militarized the oil-exploration zone.

Even Borja's 1992 declaration fails to meet some key demands of OPIP and the Indian organizations. The march had two objectives: to legalize Runa, Shuar, and Achuar territories in Pastaza and to reform the constitution to recognize Ecuador's cultural diversity. Borja referred the latter point to Congress.

In the end, Ecuador has legalized a total of 59 percent of the area claimed by OPIP—but not as Indian territory. Instead, IERAC, the land-titling agency, awarded communal titles to 19 blocks that include many of the 148 indigenous communities of Pastaza. The Achuar secured rights to 57 percent of their territory, while Zaparo (mixed with Runa) received title to less than 50 percent of their claim. Shuar people in Pastaza were denied 63 percent of their land.

The settlement included many compromises. To please the international community, Borja's award appeared to be a significant concession to indigenous peoples. To placate environmentalists, it enlarged the Yasuni National Park to include a block of Runa territory in Pastaza.

The biggest concession was to the military, which was granted a 24-mile-wide swath of land along the Peruvian frontier as a "security zone." This zone constitutes 30 percent of the territory claimed by OPIP. Indian nations within it find themselves without the means to legally secure their ancestral lands.

Now that legal titles have been signed for the 19 community blocks, their physical delimitation must be completed. This is proving difficult as IERAC places obstacles in the way of Indian organizations. Only two blocks are in the planning stages for delimitation. Moreover, IERAC has continued its practice of granting land titles within these blocks to non-Indian colonists. The Indian organizations of Ecuador now plan to approach the United Nations to have the entire territory claimed by OPIP for the four indigenous nations of Pastaza—including the 19 blocks, the security zone nations and the Yasuni Park extension—declared as an internationally recognized reserve.

DOMINIQUE IRVINE

MARCHING TO QUITO: INDIGENOUS TERRITORY IN PASTAZA PROVINCE, ECUADOR (SQUARE MILES)

	Total Claimed As Indian Territory	Legalized Titles		Titles Not Legalized	
		Before April 1992	After April 1992	Redesignated Park	Security Zone
Runa	6,269 (101%)	238 (4%)	3,626 (58%)	1,051 (17%)	1,354 (22%)
Achuar	1,434 (100%)	607 (42%)	210 (15%)	0	617 (43%)
Shuar	708 (100%)	0	262 (37%)	0	446 (63%)
Zaparo	445 (100%)	0	209 (47%)	0	236 (53%)
Total	8,856 (101%)	845 (10%)	4,307 (49%)	1,051 (12%)	2,653 (30%)

Note: percents do not necessarily total 100 due to rounding.

WAYUU OF COLOMBIA

Some 128,000 Wayuus live in La Guajira Department on the peninsula of the same name. Since 1891, when Colombia and Venezuela split up the peninsula, the Wayuu, like their land, have been divided between the two countries.

Covered by sand and wind, the semi-desert landscape required the Wayuu to move continuously in search of limited water supplies. Each family had several residential sites that it visited cyclically, following water and ancestors. The Wayuu pastoral community had a strong element of anarchism that enabled them to get along with different peoples.

Colonization, mining, tourism, and water pollution now threaten Wayuu culture, as does the introduction of private property. In order to survive, many Colombian Wayuu will have to move to Venezuela or other regions of the country, taking with them their rakes, shovels, and wheelbarrows, their families, and their traditions.

In the 1960s, colonists, miners, and merchants reached La Guajira and demanded individual land titles, which in turn shrank Indian landholdings. At the same time, economic systems and rules appeared that were alien to the Indian culture and its matrilineal clans. So-called bonanzas, including a period when the Venezuelan oil industry attracted Indians, left the Wayuu with little or nothing.

Today, in the El Cerron-Zona Norte Complex, exploited by Intercor, a subsidiary of Exxon, the Indians observe a daily parade of 40,000 tons of coal crossing their territory on its way to international markets. The Wayuus rarely work in the coal mine, but the acidification of the soil due to mineral dust that emanates from the open pits threatens their culture with extinction. Skin and lung problems from the dust have begun to devastate the Wayuu as well.

Intercor has responded with some assistance that alleviates but doesn't resolve the issue. Some settlements have had to relocate. The government has tried to resolve some of the water problems by demarcating *resguardos* (Indian landholdings) to guarantee Wayuu lands, but these include none of the mining zones. In addition, the mine has split Wayuu land in two and has eradicated several clan cemeteries, while the government has delayed formally establishing some *resguardos* in hope of assuring mining concessions and creating tourism zones.

Another threat comes from beef-jerky producers. Traditionally, 3,000 Wayuu families set up temporary residence in Manuare to sell beef jerky to people who collected salt there and used the income to buy maize, brown sugar, coffee, lard, and plantains. Of the 3,000 families, only 800 remain. In 1970, the "Salinas Concession" appeared, introducing the industrial-level exploitation of jerky. At first the company agreed to indemnify local people for their losses, but later it created a two-tier system—a small one, managed by Wayuus, and a mechanized one run by the company.

The salt industry presents a related danger. The state-run salt company, afflicted with a chronic deficit, has begun to liquidate itself in anticipation of privatization. It has offered people a chance to buy in, promising that the transformation would better allow the company to export salt, improve the use of the port of Bahia Honda, and provide long-term benefits to both Wayuus and consumers. The owners committed themselves to building an experimental garden for the Wayuu, maintaining a system of potable water, and establishing a store and a health system. The company has followed through on few of these promises. Meanwhile, "salt lords," who regard themselves as owners of large extensions of land and resources, have appeared,

> "At first I thought I was fighting to save rubber trees, then I thought I was fighting to save the Amazon rainforest. Now I realize I am fighting for humanity."
>
> Chico Mendes,
> Brazilian rubber tapper

253

bringing in workers from Cordoba, Bolivar, and Sucre departments.

In 1990 several hundred Wayuu protested construction of a highway that posed a severe danger to their cultural identity. This state project could usurp Wayuu land and provide easy entry for colonists. Even without the road, cultural penetration into many communities has damaged Wayuu clan structures.

Colombia's new constitution fails to address many Wayuu concerns. For example, territorial restructuring offers some political jobs to individuals but fails to recognize Wayuu lands.

ADOLFO TRIANA

YANOMAMI OF BRAZIL

Between 1987 and 1990, Brazilian governmental policies left the Yanomami Indians with no medical care or outside help of any kind in the face of a gold rush of genocidal proportions. This led to the deaths of no fewer than 1,500 Brazilian Yanomami (over 15 percent of the total population) from violence, malnutrition, malaria, and other epidemics brought in by gold panners (*garimpeiros*).

The international outcry over this grave situation led Fernando Collor de Mello, Brazil's newly elected president, to order the expulsion of the *garimpeiros* from Yanomami lands using the federal police in "Operation Free Jungle," which cost the government nearly $2 million. Furthermore, after the completion of the physical demarcation of a 68,000-square-mile area of Amazon rain forest, and despite strong objections from the military and from mining interests, President Collor created the Yanomami Indigenous Reserve. The Yanomami's future seemed assured after 20 years of struggle by Brazilian and international organizations.

However, local authorities and the military undercut these measures, and scandals forced Collor to resign. No sooner had the park been established than *garimpeiros* began reinvading Yanomami lands. By early 1993, an estimated 11,000 gold prospectors were working illegally within the reserve. Their presence seriously threatens the lives of the Yanomami and is destroying the environment. The situation is again critical.

A new operation, dubbed "Free Jungle II," was begun at the end of February to evict the *garimpeiros* from the reserve, dynamite their clandestine landing strips, and impose stricter controls over the airports from which they embark. Although over 4,500 gold miners were reported to have left or been forcibly removed from indigenous lands by mid-March, the removal operation is not bringing the expected results.

The authorities are reportedly unable to control the air traffic of *garimpeiro* planes. The Yanomami leader, Davi Kopenawa, reported to *O Estado de Sao Paulo* on March 24, 1993, that many prospectors were still hidden in the jungle and that others had buried their equipment and food supplies before leaving, with the intention of returning after the rains, when "Operation Free Jungle II" is over. According to *CCPY Update 65*, upon arriving in Boa Vista several gold miners said "that they would be staying in the region to reoccupy the reserve once the present blitz is over."

It is clear that a permanent solution needs to be found to prevent reinvasions and to protect the Yanomami Reserve in the future. Such a solution will have to provide alternative forms of economic development for Roraima and other states in the impoverished northeast of Brazil. The Brazilian government needs to evaluate its mining and Indian policies in order to formulate coherent guidelines that can be effectively enforced. Until this is accomplished, Yanomami land tenure remains tenuous. Yanomami lives depend on it.

GALE GOODWIN GOMEZ

YE'KUANA AND YANOMAMI OF VENEZUELA

About 3,600 Ye'kuana live in Venezuela's Amazonas and Bolivar states. Their neighbors are 13,000 Yanomami Indians, whose plight in the face of development is well known.

For 40 years, Yanomami and Ye'kuana have lived a strained but peaceful coexistence. Now they are trapped in the same web. Since the late 1960s, private entrepreneurs and government legislation and economic policies have led to steady encroachments on their ancestral lands.

In the 1960s, Venezuela decided to colonize the "empty" lands of southern Venezuela, where tropical rain forests and rivers, mineral, and timber were supposedly waiting to be conquered. Of course, these Amazonian lands were not really empty. They are the homeland of the Ye'kuana and Yanomami and 10 other indigenous peoples.

In the early 1970s, a new policy emerged to help the Indians survive this "Conquest of the South." Indian villages received land grants in the form of provisional titles. Then, in the mid-1970s, a new administration replaced the Conquest of the South with a "conservation" policy that designated many protected areas exempt from economic development.

Neither the Conquest of the South nor the protected-areas policy had the rights of indigenous people in mind. The former aimed at the short-term exploitation of the region's resources; the latter merely bought time for new groups to enter the competition for exploiting the Amazon's untapped resources.

The official policies of the 1990s are similarly ambiguous. Gold mining is banned in Amazonas, but the new governor has promised to open up the state to miners. In fact, large-scale gold mining, illegally practiced on the Orinoco River in Yanomami territory, is polluting the river and threatening widespread deforestation. Gold mining is also practiced on a small scale in several other forest tracts throughout Amazonas.

This geological imperative makes the efforts of Indians to secure their land especially critical, but they are trapped by environmental laws. The government claims it can't allocate land titles in protected areas, including those established on ancestral lands. On the other hand, Indians are seeking a reinterpretation of this law so that it could become a weapon in their struggle for land rights.

Some Ye'kuana villages are investigating another possibility: setting boundaries to their territory themselves. The Ye'kuana argue that the government didn't ask their opinion before transforming parts of their ancestral land into a national park in 1979 or into a biosphere reserve in 1991. Thus, they say, they need no permit to establish the limits of their own lands.

NELLY ARVELO-JIMÉNEZ

255

BIBLIOGRAPHY

Russell Lawrence Barsh, "An Advocate's Guide to the Convention on Indigenous and Tribal Peoples," *Oklahoma City University Law Review*, Spring 1990.

John H. Bodley, *Tribal Peoples and Development Issues: A Global Overview*, Mayfield, 1988.

Julian Burger, *Gaia Atlas of First Peoples: A Future for the Indigenous World*, Anchor Books, 1990.

Julian Burger, *Report from the Frontier: The State of the World's Indigenous Peoples*, Zed Books Ltd., 1987.

Gerard Chaliand, ed., *Minority Peoples in the Age of Nation-States*, Pluto Press, 1989.

Jason Clay, *Indigenous Peoples and Tropical Forests: Models of Land Use and Management from Latin America*, Cultural Survival, 1988.

Cultural Survival Quarterly (especially "At the Threshold: An Action Guide for Cultural Survival," 1992; "A Decade of *Cultural Survival Quarterly*," 1991; and "Organizing to Survive," 1984).

Alan Thien Durning, "Guardians of the Land: Indigenous Peoples and the Health of the Earth," Worldwatch Paper 112, Worldwatch Institute, 1992.

Barbara F. Grimes, ed., *Ethnologue: Languages of the World*, Summer Institute of Linguistics, 1992.

Don Hinrichsen, Geoffrey Lean, and Adam Markham, *Atlas of the Environment*, Prentice Hall, 1990.

"IWGIA Newsletter," International Work Group for Indigenous Affairs, Copenhagen, Denmark.

Peter Knudtson and David Susuki, *Wisdom of the Elders: Honoring Sacred Native Visions of Nature*, Bantam, 1992.

"Minority Rights Group Reports," Minority Rights Group, London, England.

Roger Moody, ed., *The Indigenous Voice: Visions and Realities*, Zed Books, 1988.

Roger Moody, *Plunder!* Partizans/Cafca, 1991.

Norman Myers, ed., *Gaia: An Atlas of Planet Management*, Anchor Books, 1984.

U.S. Department of State, "Country Reports on Human Rights Practices for 1992," Report Submitted to the Committee on Foreign Affairs, U.S. House of Representatives.

"World Refugee Survey, 1992," U.S. Committee for Refugees.

Indigenous Organizations with Consultative Status in the United Nations Working Group on Indigenous Populations:

Four Directions Council
Eskasoni Indian Reserve, Eskasoni, Nova Scotia
BOA 1JO Canada
Tel./fax: (902)379-2361

Grand Council of the Cree
2 Lakeshore Rd., Nemaska, Quebec
J0Y 3B0 Canada
(819)673-2600; fax: (819)673-2606

Indian Council of South America
Apartado Postal 2054, Correo Central, Lima 100
Peru
Tel./fax: (51-14)236955

Indian Law Resource Center
601 E St., SE, Washington, DC 20003
(202)547-2800; fax: (202)547-2803

Indigenous World Association
275 Grand View Ave., #204, San Francisco, CA 94114
(415)647-1966

International Indian Treaty Council
123 Townsend St., Suite 575
San Francisco, CA 94107-1907
(415)512-1501; fax: (415)512-1507

International Organization of Indigenous Resource Development
P.O. Box 370, Hobbema, Alberta
T0C 1N0 Canada
(403)585-3038; fax: (403)585-2025

Inuit Circumpolar Conference
170 Laurier Ave. West, Suite 504, Ottawa, Ontario
K1P 5V5 Canada
(613)563-2642; fax: (613)565-3089

National Aboriginal and Islander Legal Services Secretariat
201 Cleveland St., Redfern, New South Wales 2016
Australia

National Indian Youth Council
318 Elm St., SE, Albuquerque, NM 87102
(505)247-2251; fax: (505)247-4251

Nordic Sami Council
SS-99980, Utsjoki
Finland

World Council of Indigenous People
100 Argyle Ave., 2nd Floor, Ottawa, Ontario
K2P 1B6 Canada
(613)230-9030; fax: (613)230-9340

INDEX OF PEOPLES

257

ABOUT THE CONTRIBUTORS

Maureen Aung-Thwin, a free-lance writer, serves on the boards of Asia Watch and the Burma Studies Foundation.

David Akin is a doctoral candidate in anthropology at the University of Hawaii.

Myrdene Anderson is an associate professor of anthropology at Purdue University.

Vassos Argyrou has a doctorate in anthropology from the Indiana University.

Joëlle Bahloul is an assistant professor of anthropology, Jewish studies and women's studies at Indiana University.

Nelly Arvelo-Jiménez is professor of anthropology at the Venezuelan Institute for Scientific Research.

Nicholas S. Balamaci is secretary of the Society Farsarotul and a speech writer for New York City Mayor David Dinkins.

Marjorie Mandelstam Balzer teaches in the Russian Area Studies Program at Georgetown University and edits *Anthropology and Archaeology of Eurasia*.

Thomas J. Barfield heads the Department of Anthropology at Boston University.

José Barreiro teaches in the American Indian Studies Program at Cornell University.

Martha Belcher has worked at the Indonesian Forum for the Environment and is an editor for Rainforest Action Network.

José Bengoa is an historian and coordinator for the Chilean government's Special Commission on Indian Affairs.

Megan Biesele is the liaison for documentation for the Nyae Nyae Development Foundation of Namibia.

Roderic H. Blackburn is a research associate at the American Museum of Natural History in New York.

Lanfranco Blanchetti-Revelli is a graduate student in anthropology at the Johns Hopkins University.

John Bock is doing doctoral research in Okavango peoples at the University of New Mexico in Albuquerque.

J. Peter Brosius is an assistant professor in the Department of Anthropology at the University of Georgia, Athens.

Neilly Buckalew has been an intern at Cultural Survival.

Howard Campbell teaches in the Department of Sociology and Anthropology at the University of Texas at El Paso.

Robert S. Carlsen is a research associate in the Department of Anthropology at the University of Colorado at Boulder.

Donna Carroll is a project assistant at the Gwich'in Steering Committee.

Laurence Marshall Carucci is an associate professor of anthropology at Montana State University.

Norman Chance is a senior fellow at the Institute of Arctic Studies at Dartmouth College and research associate in the Department of Geography at McGill University.

Emily Chao is a doctoral student in the Department of Anthropology at the University of Michigan, Ann Arbor.

Mac Chapin directs Cultural Survival's Central America Program.

Larry Childs advises Mali and Tamacheq on community development.

Dan Connell founded Grassroots International and is the author of *Against All Odds: A Chronicle of the Eritrean Revolution* (Red Sea Press, 1993). He teaches journalism at Simmons College.

Loring M. Danforth is a professor of anthropology at Bates College.

William V. Davidson teaches in the Department of Geography and Anthropology at Louisiana State University.

Wade Davis is executive director of the Endangered Peoples Project.

Tom D. Dillehay is a professor of anthropology at the University of Kentucky, Lexington.

Bill Donner teaches in the Department of Anthropology at Millersville University.

Don E. Dumond teaches in the Department of Anthropology at the University of Oregon.

Duncan Earle teaches in the Department of Anthropology at Texas A & M University.

Tracy Bachrach Ehlers is an associate professor of anthropology at the University of Denver.

Kirk Endicott is a professor of anthropology at Dartmouth College.

Robert A. Fernea teaches in the Department of Anthropology at the University of Texas, Austin.

Gerard A. Finin is a fellow of the East-West Center in Honolulu, Hawaii.

Michael Fischer is a professor in the MIT Science, Technology, and Society Program.

Gail A. Fondahl is a research fellow at the Institute of Arctic Studies, Dartmouth College, and an associate professor of geography at Middlebury College.

Judith Fitzpatrick teaches in the Department of Anthropology and the Tropical Health Program at the University of Queensland, Australia.

Elliot Fratkin is associate professor of anthropology at Pennsylvania State University.

Jan S.N. Furukuwa is a free-lance writer and a member of the Chamoru Nation.

Paula Garb is a researcher in global peace and conflict studies at the University of California, Irvine.

Elizabeth Garsonnin works at the Public Media Center in San Francisco, California.

Cate Gillis is a reporter in Arizona.

Isabel Vidal Giannini is an anthropologist in Brazil.

Nancie Gonzalez is an anthropologist and fellow at the United States Institute of Peace.

Gale Goodwin Gomez, a linguistic anthropologist, is a researcher and indigenous-rights advocate with CCPY.

Bruce Grant is a doctoral candidate in the Department of Anthropology at Swarthmore College.

Roy Richard Grinker is an assistant professor of anthropology at George Washington University.

Mathias Guenther is an associate professor of anthropology and sociology at Wilfrid Laurier University.

Marcos Guevara is an ethnologist at the University of Costa Rica.

Henry Harpending is a professor of anthropology at Pennsylvania State University.

Kevin Healy is a senior representative for Bolivia with the Inter-American Foundation.

Alejandro Herrera is an anthropologist at the Universidad Austral de Chile.

Peter H. Herlihy is a geographer at the University of Kansas.

Michael Herzfeld is a professor in anthropology at Harvard University.

Joost R. Hiltermann is the author of *Behind the Intifadah: Labor and Women's movements in the Occupied Territories.*

Robert K. Hitchcock is an assistant professor of anthropology and coordinator of African studies at the University of Nebraska, Lincoln.

Eric Hooglund is the editor of *Middle East Journal.*

Antony Hooper is a senior fellow in the Pacific Islands Development Program of the East-West Center in Honolulu.

John E. Hudelson is an anthropologist and writer based in Middlehope, NY.

Sharon Hutchinson is an assistant professor of anthropology at the University of Wisconsin at Madison.

Dominique Irvine is program director for Indigenous Resource Management at Cultural Survival.

C.L. Imchen is a reader for the Department of Sociology, North Eastern Hill University, Shillong, India.

Alexandra Jaffe is an assistant professor in the Department of Sociology and Anthropology at the State University of New York, Cortland.

Nicholas Blurton Jones is a professor in the Graduate School of Education at the University of California, Los Angeles.

Sidney Jones is executive director of Asia Watch.

Cornelia Ann Kammerer is a research associate at Brandeis University and a visiting assistant professor of anthropology at Hampshire College.

Marion Kelly is an associate professor in the Ethnic Studies Program at the University of Hawaii.

Ben Kiernan is an associate professor of history at Yale University.

Stuart Kirsch is a visiting assistant professor at Mount Holyoke College.

Alexander Kostyakov is chair of the Khakass Peoples Association "Tun" in the Republic of Khakasia.

Smitu Kothari is an editor of *Locayan Bulletin.*

Winona LaDuke directs the White Earth Land Recovery Project.

Brij V. Lal is a Pacific historian at the Research School of Pacific Studies of the Australian National University.

Kim Laughlin teaches anthropology at Rice University.

Raïssa S. Lerner is studying law and human rights at Harvard Law School.

Ann M. Lesch is a professor of political science and associate director of the Center for Arab and Islamic Studies at Villanova University.

Herbert S. Lewis is professor of anthropology at the University of Wisconsin in Madison.

Lamont Lindstrom is a professor of anthropology at the University of Tulsa.

William G. Lockwood teaches in the Department of Anthropology at the University of Michigan, Ann Arbor.

W. George Lovell is professor of geography at Queen's University, Kingston, Ontario.

Christopher H. Lutz directs Plumsock Mesoamerican Studies.

Theodore Macdonald, Jr., directs the Center for Cultural Survival at Cultural Survival.

R.T. Mahuta directs the Centre for Maori Studies and Research at the University of Waikato, New Zealand.

Chief Willie Bongamatur Maldo is curator of the National Museum of Vanuatu and former president of the Blong Malvatumauri.

Jon McGee is an associate professor of anthropology at Southwest Texas State University.

Carole McGranahan has worked for the International Campaign for Tibet.

Samuel F. McPhetres is a former archivist for the Trust Territory of the Pacific Islands in Saipan, Northern Marianas.

Marc S. Miller, project director for *State of the Peoples,* is author of *Irony of Victory* (University of Illinois Press, 1988) and the editor of *Working Lives* (Pantheon, 1981).

David I. Minkow is a San Francisco-based free-lance writer.

Edith T. Mirante directs Project Maje, based in Cranford, NJ.

M.D. Mistry is coordinator of DISHA in India.

T. Shawn Mitchell teaches in the Department of Geography and Anthropology at Louisiana State University.

John Mohawk teaches in the American Studies Department of the State University of New York, Buffalo.

Peter Moszynski coordinates the London-based Nuba Mountains Solidarity Abroad.

Jane Freeman Moulin is an associate professor in the Department of Music of the University of Hawaii.

Suzanne L. Mullin teaches at Indiana University.

Jane Nadel-Klein teaches at Trinity College.

Karen L. Nero teaches in the Department of Anthropology of the University of Auckland, New Zealand.

261

Robert McC. Netting is a professor of anthropology at the University of Arizona, Tucson.

João Pacheco de Oliveira is professor of anthropology at the National Museum, Rio de Janeiro, Brazil.

François Ngolet is a graduate student at Old Dominion University in Norfolk, Virginia.

Alexander Pika works at the Laboratory of Ethnic Demography, Institute for Employment Studies, Russian Academy of Sciences.

Chris Peters works at the Seventh Generation Fund for Indian Development.

Glenn Petersen is a professor of anthropology at Baruch College and the Graduate Center at the City University of New York.

Nancy J. Pollock teaches in the Department of Anthropology at Victoria University in Wellington, New Zealand.

Irene Portis-Winner is a professor of anthropology at the Massachusetts College of Art.

John Prendergast works at the Center of Concern in Washington, DC.

Frank Proschan works at the Research Center for Language and Semiotic Studies, Indiana University.

Jennifer Rathaus is associate editor of *State of the Peoples* and a staff member of Cultural Survival.

Asesela Ravuvu directs the Institute of Pacific Studies at the University of the South Pacific, Fiji.

Antoinette Royo is a senior attorney with the Natural Resources and Legal Rights Center, Friends of the Earth, Philippines.

Richard Reed teaches in the Department of Sociology and Anthropology at Trinity University.

Robert Roy Reed teaches in the Department of Anthropology at Ohio State University.

Andy Rutherford is program coordinator at One World Action in London, England.

James R. Samson teaches in the Department of Geography and Anthropology at Louisiana State University.

Manik Sandrasagra directs the Cultural Survival Trust of Sri Lanka.

Louisa Schein teaches in the Department of Anthropology at Rutgers University, Douglass Campus.

Debra L. Schindler is an independent researcher in anthropology.

Carol Silverman is an associate professor of anthropology at the University of Oregon.

Caroline G. Sinavaiana directs the Pacific-Asia Institute for the Arts and Human Sciences, Pago Pago, American Samoa.

Aman Singh works for the Save Sariska Movement, India.

Matthew Spriggs teaches in the prehistory department at the Australian National University.

Richard Chase Smith is an anthropologist, currently on leave from his post directing OXFAM America's South America Program.

Thomas B. Stevenson teaches anthropology at Ohio University, Zanesville.

Daniel Stiles is a consultant for the United Nations Environment Program.

David Stoll teaches in the Anthropology Department at New York University.

Glenn Switkes works with the Rainforest Action Network.

Patricia V. Symonds is an anthropologist at Brown University.

James Taggart is the Lewis Audenreid Professor in the Department of Anthropology at Franklin and Marshall College.

Amin Tarzi teaches at New York University.

Mari Thekaekara is a leader for ACCORD in Nilgiris, India, and a free-lance journalist.

Robert and Myrna Tonkinson teach in the Department of Anthropology at the University of Western Australia.

Deborah Tooker is an assistant professor of anthropology at Le Moyne College.

Mililani Trask is the *Kai'ana* (elected head) of Ka Lahui Hawaii, a native Hawaiian sovereign nation.

Adolfo Triana is a lawyer and director of the Fundacíon Communidades Colombians.

Jacqueline Urla teaches in the Department of Anthropology at the University of Massachusetts, Amherst.

Diederik Vandewalle teaches in the Department of Government at Dartmouth College.

Sita Venkateswar is conducting research on the Andaman Islands with support from the National Science Foundation, Grant #BNS 9108383.

Toby Alice Volkman directs the Southeast Asia Program of the Social Science Research Council.

Janine R. Wedel is an anthropologist and adjunct associate professor at George Washington University.

Paul Williams is a lawyer in Toronto.

Geoffrey M. White directs the Program for Cultural Studies at the East-West Center, Honolulu.

Stanford Zent teaches in the Department of Anthropology at the Venezuelan Institute for Scientific Studies.

About Cultural Survival: Founded in 1972, Cultural Survival collaborates with indigenous peoples and ethnic minorities, helping them to secure economic and social justice. CS promotes their land and resource rights as the front line of defense for human rights. For more information, contact Cultural Survival, 215 First Street, Cambridge, MA 02142.